PORTFOLIO

ORBIT-SHIFTING INNOVATION

Devika Devaiah is a Director of Erehwon. She has led breakthrough research initiatives into challenger organizations, transworld partnerships and orbit-shifting innovation. Her cutting-edge insight into innovation also comes from her unique ability to transform business, organization and leadership paradigms across regions in global organizations like Unilever, Walt Disney, Intel, and Savola.

Rajiv Narang is the Founder of Erehwon, a twenty-year-old pioneering Innovation firm, where he has helmed the redefining and recasting of Innovation. Recognized as India's Innovation thought leader, Rajiv was part of the National Planning Commission Panel to recommend India's Innovation strategy. With his unparalleled insight into business, social and public service innovation, he has inspired leaders and organizations across cultures and across the world in adopting orbit-shifting innovation.

PRAISE FOR THE BOOK

'The insights contained in this book will enable organizations to break the bonds of gravity and the mental shackles that keep them from reaching the next orbit. Compulsory reading for businesses that aspire to be innovative'—Anand G. Mahindra, Chairman, Mahindra Group

'*Orbit-shifting Innovation* is a fantastic journey. It took us beyond the boundaries of the industry and turned into a gold mine of refreshing insights and pathbreaking ideas'—Michiel Leijnse, Global Brand Director, Water & Innovation, Personal Care Category, Unilever, UK

'Change is constant. Thus the ability to recognize paradigm changes and act on a leading basis is crucial to continued success. *Orbit-shifting Innovation* brings an exceptional thinking process that can facilitate organizations to reinvent themselves successfully. Strongly recommended based on personal experience'—Anuroop (Tony) Singh, former CEO, Vice Chairman, Max Group

'Inspiring and insightful, it will energize leaders to brave the odds and make the next orbit-shift happen'—Harsh C. Mariwala, CMD, Marico Innovation Foundation

'*Orbit-shifting Innovation* is a pioneering approach that can take diverse groups and introduce new thought paradigms to drive innovation. I have never worked with any other approach that could do this better. It builds the courage to target high-value/high-risk projects that can disrupt existing markets. I have no hesitation in recommending it for the toughest innovation projects'—Neal Matheson, Chief Technology Officer (CTO) for Consumer Products, Johnson & Johnson, US

'*Orbit-shifting Innovation* is a truly insightful and inspiring book. It will move organizations into rethinking and even reinventing innovation' —Dr R.A. Mashelkar, National Research Professor, Chancellor, AcSIR and President, Global Research Alliance CSIR-National Chemical Laboratory, Polymer Science & Engineering Building

'*Orbit-shifting Innovation* constantly impresses one, as I have never come across an approach that balances ideas and paradigms with such an ease, to successfully confront gravity and discover the orbit-shifting idea—Erehwon is leading the way'—Carsten Hallund Slot, Vice President Corporate Research & Innovation, Arla Foods, Denmark

'*Orbit-shifting Innovation* provokes us to step out of our prevailing industry and organizational paradigms, and re-visualize our markets, customers and businesses, for what they could be'—Pawan Goenka, Executive Director & President, Automotive & Farm Equipment Sectors, Mahindra & Mahindra Ltd

ORBIT SHIFTING INNOVATION

THE DYNAMICS OF IDEAS THAT CREATE HISTORY

RAJIV NARANG
DEVIKA DEVAIAH

PORTFOLIO
PENGUIN

An imprint of Penguin Random House

PORTFOLIO

USA | Canada | UK | Ireland | Australia
New Zealand | India | South Africa | China | Singapore

Portfolio is part of the Penguin Random House group of companies
whose addresses can be found at global.penguinrandomhouse.com

Published by Penguin Random House India Pvt. Ltd
4th Floor, Capital Tower 1, MG Road,
Gurugram 122 002, Haryana, India

Penguin Random House India

First published by Random House India 2013
Published in Portfolio by Penguin Random House India 2018

10 9 8 7 6 5 4 3 2

ISBN 9788184007244

For sale in the Indian Subcontinent only

Typeset in Garamond by R. Ajith Kumar

Printed at Repro India Limited

www.penguin.co.in

FSC www.fsc.org MIX Paper from responsible sources FSC® C047271

This is a legitimate digitally printed version of the book and therefore might not have certain extra finishing on the cover.

To our parents,
who encouraged us to step out and
foray into the unknown

Contents

Introduction

ORBIT-SHIFTING INNOVATION HAPPENS when an area that needs transformation meets an innovator with the will and desire to create, and not follow, history. At the heart of an orbit-shifting innovation is the breakthrough that creates a new orbit and achieves a transformative impact. Quality for Japan and technology for Israel have been transforming agents.

Making innovation the transforming agent for the organization and the nation: this is the mission that has inspired us, over the last twenty-two years, to take on over 250 orbit-shifting innovation challenges across industries, cultures, and countries.

Spearheading waves of innovation challenges, we repeatedly found ourselves faced with more questions and fewer answers. In spite of the existence of numerous theories of innovation, we were still confronted with a series of unanswered questions. *Orbit-shifting Innovation* is the result of a twenty-year quest to find answers for the unanswered questions of innovation.

This book offers a first-hand insight into the dynamics of making Orbit-Shifting Innovation happen. It is not theoretical; it is based on insights drawn from twenty-two years of work and research with organizations in making orbit-shifting innovation happen. It is not an academic, but a practitioner's point of view.

It draws from three powerful insight sources:

1. Cutting-edge insights drawn from over 250 breakthrough innovation missions that we have led and facilitated. These missions are spread across industries and sectors. The spectrum of industries includes telecom, information technology, FMCG, consumer durables, energy,

banking, media, pharma, and social enterprises and public services.
2. Deep insight into leadership mindsets that spur or limit innovation. This is a result of our Gravity Diagnostics and strategic transformational interventions with top leadership teams from across 150 organizations.
3. This book is also a result of first-hand research and insight into orbit-shifting innovation across sectors. Our focused and ongoing research has uncovered over 100 orbit-shifters and what differentiates them.

This book brings a rare insight into the oft-asked question: 'What are the real dynamics of executing an orbit-shifting innovation?' And it does so with focus on the dynamics of conceiving an innovation too.

The book's approach is not mechanistic; it brings alive the human endeavour that is intrinsic to innovation. It illustrates the excitement and the pains in making orbit-shifting innovation happen. It also defines a framework to navigate innovation, a framework that takes into account the premise that innovation is inherently about the unknown, and therefore cannot be managed, but has to be steered. It is a comprehensive counterpoint to the stage-gate process, which so far has only played the role of controlling innovation.

Surfing through these multiple uncertainties that confront innovation has unearthed many innovation myths that still need to be busted, which is what this book sets out to do.

At the outset, this book strives to democratize innovation. It puts the spotlight on innovators and innovation from across industries, countries, and cultures that can truly stand shoulder to shoulder with iconic innovators like Steve Jobs and Richard Branson. It deliberately expands the innovation canvas beyond business to encompass orbit-shifting innovations that have led to social and public service transformation.

The first innovation myth we have always found ourselves confronting is at the heart and soul of every innovation endeavour—the WHY of innovation. The world, we find, has gotten seduced with the romance of innovation. Most managers interested in innovation have become mesmerized with NEWNESS to such an obsessive extent that, 'What's new about this idea' is almost always the first evaluative question. This book starts by busting the newness myth and highlights that *orbit shifting is the real passion and the driving purpose* and *innovation is merely the means to make the orbit shift happen.*

In the course of our innovation journey, we have come across many organizations that start by saying, 'The problem is not ideas, we have over 3,000 ideas—the problem is execution'. Digging deeper, what we have almost always uncovered is that what appears to be a multitude of ideas is rooted in only a few and limited ways of thinking. The many ideas are often restricted to the conventional, *more of the same* track. This busts the myth that *innovation equals ideation.* In reality, we have found that *an orbit-shifting innovation emerges not with the search for ideas but by uncovering boundaries.* What this book will provide is the realization that creating breakthroughs needs us to move from *ideation to recognizing and then breaking through mental model boundaries.*

This book brings to the forefront our painful realization that *most big ideas don't get killed, they just get diluted.* It brings insights into overcoming execution obstacles. Most innovation journeys almost always end with the emergence of a powerful new idea. The strategists in organizations believe they are the thinkers and their role ends with the identification of the big idea. The execution is left to the implementers. This book ruthlessly busts the myth. *As much, if not more, innovative thinking is needed to execute a new idea as the one that was required to come up with it.*

Having assimilated the concept of orbit-shifting innovation, what does it take to activate it? This question has led us to bust another well-established myth *that breakthrough innovation starts with an out-of-the-box idea. Orbit-shifting innovation, by design, does not start with an out-of-the-box idea; it really starts with an out-of-the-box challenge.* An out-of-the-box challenge is what is needed to propel the thinking to go beyond the current box to generate an orbit-shifting idea. And in the process of busting this myth, we aim to provoke a positive restlessness in our readers, the restlessness needed to go beyond comfort zones and take on an orbit-shift challenge. In our work with organizations, this *orbit-shift trigger* has by now inspired over 1,000 orbit-shifting challenges.

One of the orbit-shifters in this book, Michael da Costa of *The Food Doctor*, has already been inspired to take on a massive orbit-shifting challenge. He demonstrates that taking on an orbit-shifting challenge is about *personal and not commercial risk.* A common myth is that it is the fear of commercial failures that prevent the taking on of the orbit-shifting challenge. In reality, it is the fear of personal failure and the loss of credibility that prevents leaders in organizations from burning the bridges or removing their escape buttons.

Yet another myth is that if you want innovation to flourish, then you have to hire new people with new capabilities. However, in reality, a new person can rapidly get sucked into the gravity of the organization, very quickly delivering *more of the same.* This myth is busted because we have seen a number of orbit-shifts that have happened when existing teams and leaders have broken through their gravity to lead the organization towards a transformative impact. Hence, it is not about 'who' leads innovation. Instead, it is the organization's capacity to confront gravity that uplifts the pursuit of innovation. Rather than old or new people, it is the resourcing for innovation that is a rubber-hit-the-road moment. Many leaders commit to innovation, and yet under resource during pursuit. *Spare people in spare time seldom make orbit-shifting innovation happen.* What organizations need is flexibility to guide a variety of innovations, based on their focus and context, rather than rigid structures of either full-time or part-time people chasing a challenge. Going beyond this rigidity, we provide a framework to define the extra-constitutional team and/or time focus needed to guide orbit-shifting innovation.

The belief that market research, market trend studies, and even direct consumer contacts will lead to a new market insight is another myth. Consumer insight is the new buzzword, and so most top managers meet consumers. However, meeting consumers does not guarantee insight. The Erehwon approach shows how an insight gap exists because the lenses with which we engage consumers are jaded. Hence, we first need to renew our lenses. Leading orbit-shifting innovation needs an *orbit-shifting insight approach that is a quest for questions, and not a search for answers.* Going further, the orbit-shifting innovation approach opens up an *Insight*

Spectrum—a spectrum of insight sources going much beyond consumers. Engaging with this wide insight spectrum will take innovators beyond consumers to engage with ecosystem entities, domain experts, and lateral experts. New insight sources are needed to open up new questions and join new dots. The greater the challenge, the wider the spectrum of the insight sources that need to be engaged with.

Another myth is that the top management can mandate innovation, or that innovation. Therefore, CEOs have begun to believe that if they bring in the right experts or create an innovation department, innovation will be delivered. The reality is that innovation cannot be mandated because ownership and excitement cannot be mandated: people have to take charge. Hence, innovation is as much a leadership journey as a structural journey. How do the people who lead innovation inspire others to also believe in the new idea, the new proposition, with as much commitment as they do? How can they get key stakeholders to be owners rather than just presiders or evaluators of the innovation journey? How do they get implementers to execute the new idea with the same passion that it was conceived with? It is about moving them from managing innovation to unleashing innovation.

The final myth, and in our experience the biggest source of dilution, is *that once the big idea has been developed into a working prototype, then taking it to market is a simple case of Test and Launch.* But a new idea entering the old pipeline may suffer its greatest dilution in the last mile. *Taking to market* is usually done with the conventional approach of piloting in one market and then simply cascading the formula to other markets. This book brings insight into taking the orbit-shifting idea to market with a *versioning mindset* instead, which is about *how to make it work* rather than the conventional piloting mindset, which is rooted in the *go or no go* mindset.

This book will bring alive *what it takes to make orbit-shifting innovation happen* in four sections.

The first section, **Orbit-shifts that Created History,** paints a vivid landscape of orbit-shifting innovation across countries and cultures, industries, governments, and social enterprises, delving into product, process, business model, and social innovation. It aims to inspire the orbit-shifter in all of us.

The second section, **Seeding Orbit-shifting Innovation,** focuses on what it takes to 'Conceive an orbit-shifting idea' by design. It brings insight into 'What it takes to uncover and confront the gravity restraining an orbit-shift. It provides triggers to identify and take on an orbit-shifting challenge and then highlights what is needed to burn the bridge so that the orbit-shift journey becomes irreversible. It goes further to explore how to break through mental model boundaries and discover orbit-shifting ideas. This section culminates in orbit-shifting insight, which reveals the Insight Quest—an exciting approach to overcome gravity-ridden lenses and to identify and engage with new insight sources for orbit-shifting insight.

The third section, **Combating Dilution in Execution,** highlights what it takes to execute an orbit-shifting innovation up to the point of arriving at an in-market success model. It brings insight into: What does it take to enrol stakeholders, implementers, and partners so that they execute the orbit-shift without dilution? How do Orbit Shifters navigate through the fog of obstacles that threatens to derail the orbit-shift in execution? And how do they evolve an orbit-shift through in-market versioning?

The final section, **Leading Orbit-shifting Innovation,** is for a leader interested in institutionalizing orbit-shifts. Spread across two chapters, it first focuses on mapping the thresholds of an orbit-shifting innovation journey, differentiated comprehensively against the stage-gate process. The final chapter then highlights the DNA of orbit-shifters. This DNA has been deliberately distilled across entrepreneurs, social innovators, leaders at the helm of their businesses, and innovators in organizations with multiple stakeholders. In doing so, this DNA holds true for those seeking to pursue orbit-shifts across all contexts.

Here, finally, is the compass to navigate the fog of innovation in all its messiness, uncertainties, complexities, paradoxes, and ambiguities, not just a sanitized formula, a tool, or a process for innovation. A compass that doesn't stop at conception but that navigates an orbit-shift end to end: from conception all the way to realization.

It will compel and empower businesses, social enterprises, and even governments to break through boundaries and pursue impossible challenges with orbit-shifting innovation.

SECTION 1

ORBIT-SHIFTS THAT CREATED HISTORY

Chapter 1

Orbit-shifts that Created History

1.1 – The original 12 Microsoft 1978 and 2008

THE ORIGINAL TWELVE. These are the twelve people who were there at the founding of Microsoft. They were specially brought together again thirty years later to photograph the anniversary of their start-up. A start-up that created history.[17]

Will your team be gathered for a photograph thirty years later? Yes! If you create history in your universe.

ORBIT-SHIFTING INNOVATION

Orbit-shifting innovation happens when an area that needs transformation meets an innovator with the will and the desire to create, not follow, history. At the heart of an orbit-shifting innovation, is the breakthrough that creates a new orbit and has a transformative impact.

Beginning with the Macintosh, what Apple succeeded in doing time and time again with Steve Jobs at the helm, was to break the boundaries of the current orbit and create orbit-shifting innovation that ignited the imagination of people across the world. Perhaps, fuelled by Steve's personal motto, *make a dent in the universe*, Apple has lived and breathed the life of an orbit-shifter.

The prime motivation, indeed the driving force behind all orbit-shifting innovation of the 'Mac kind', is the desire to create and not follow history. This fuels a positive restlessness with the current state, and unleashes an overwhelming desire to pursue the next orbit, as a result of which the transformation becomes a reality. Wealth and fame are, more often than not, a consequence rather than the purpose.

But then: Do you have to be in Silicon Valley to create history? Do you have to be a Steve Jobs to make a dent in the universe? Do you have to be an Apple to create breakthroughs, time and time again?

Apple may be the most iconic, the most well-known, and the most awe-inspiring orbit-shifter, but history has also been created across countries as diverse as India, Philippines, Mongolia, and Switzerland. Each of these orbit-shifting innovations has resulted in a breakthrough that, quite like Apple, transformed the lives of millions.

Transforming Lives: Eliminating Needless Blindness

In Madurai, a comparatively smaller city of south India, Dr Venkataswamy, or simply known as Dr V, created history when he set up the Aravind Eye Hospital to transform the cataract surgery process. Dr V was consumed with the idea of eliminating needless blindness. He was driven by the realization that when most people in rural and remote India start growing old and losing eyesight due to cataracts, they think it is due to the natural ageing process. They do not know cataracts are curable. And for a person at the edge of the poverty line, losing eyesight inevitably leads to losing life because he loses his earning capacity. This realization and his passion to make a difference led to challenging the conventional approach to cataract surgery. The redesigned process resulted in an Aravind surgeon becoming ten times more productive than the best in the world, without a compromise in quality. An Aravind surgeon performs 2,600 surgeries a year compared to 250 surgeries in the same period by compatriots in other hospitals, whether in India or in developed economies. Having transformed the productivity of a surgeon, Aravind is able to attend to a larger spread of patients across economic groups. Seventy percent of the patients are treated free of cost, with two million out-patients and over 3,50,000 cataract surgeries performed every year.[20, 26]

What is even more remarkable is that Dr V started the Aravind Eye Hospital at the age of 58, after retiring as a medical educator. Age, contrary to popular perception, is not a constraint when the passion to make a transformative difference is the driving force.

There are millions of dreamers, but very few dreams actually come to life. Big dreams are especially prevalent on graduation day. When you meet students and ask them: What do you want to do?— you will often hear a determined, 'I want to change the world.' You can literally see their smouldering passion and resolve, and feel the hope. But when you meet these same people ten to fifteen years later, it is a very different situation. *The world has changed them.* By now, they have practicality oozing out of every fibre of their being. They have become, to use that unfortunate phrase, 'older, wiser, and sadder'.

And then you have Dr V who exemplifies *dreams are never dead.* They are merely dormant. We have seen orbit-shifting innovators reclaim their dreams and change the course of their lives and those around them.

Transforming Lives: Purifying Water

1.2 – LifeStraw

The Swiss firm Vestergaard Frandsen has invented a product that is and will have a transformative impact in areas where there is a pernicious shortage of clean drinking water. It has created a straw through which water is purified as it is drunk from any water source, regardless of quality. With an ultra-filtration cartridge embedded into it, this straw filters 99.9 percent of the water-borne bacteria and parasites. A single straw costs under about USD 6.50 and filters about 1,000 litres of water, which is sufficient for one person for one year. This has brought potable water within the reach of millions of people for whom traditional water purifiers or bottled water are simply not affordable. Vestergaard is truly saving lives with this orbit-shifting straw, by safeguarding against water-borne diseases, which are among the most common sources of illness. No wonder then it has been named LifeStraw.[31]

Vestergaard was originally a clothing company, in the fabric industry. And yet fabric became the trigger, rather than the boundary, to create the LifeStraw—at the centre of the LifeStraw is a cloth-based filter membrane.

Orbit-shifting the Industry: The Prepaid Revolution

From Silicon Valley to Madurai to Switzerland, let us move the innovation landscape further east to the Philippines, where an industry orbit-shift in telecom originated.

Smart Communications in the Philippines introduced an electronic recharging service for the prepaid card. It was the first ever 'over-the-air' prepaid card recharging service. *Electronic recharging brought in flexibility in amounts that could be topped up, sometimes even lower than a dollar.* This immediately bridged a major need gap. A large multitude of the middle class and the poor could not afford to buy a postpaid mobile connection because of the unpredictability of the bill amount at the end of the month. For this vast populace, a prepaid mobile card that was cheap to buy and easy to recharge with small amounts of money when needed, became the liberating solution.[13, 25]

In Asia, the switch from postpaid to prepaid has brought about a revolution in the telecom industry; it exploded what was until then a niche market, to virtually include the entire population. It made communication accessible to millions who had limited or no access to a landline and who could not afford the classical postpaid mobile model that was the standard in developed countries. An interesting comparison shows the actual impact: the number of landlines in India grew from 1 million to 5.1 million in a period of twenty years (1971 to 1991),[24] while the number of mobile subscribers have grown from 3.58 million to an astonishing 908 million in the decade from 2001 to 2012, in effect covering more than half of India's population.[28, 29]

> **Orbit-shifting innovators like Smart Communications explode the market. They break through the barriers to make 'what is available to only a selected few', accessible to the masses, and in the process transform lives.**

Orbit-shifting the Industry Banking the Unbanked

Vodafone (Safaricom) in Kenya has gone even further. Less than 20 percent of the people in Africa (in 2011) had a bank account.[5] They usually transferred money from one location to another via a bus driver or other informal means that were usually slow, costly, and unsecured. Safaricom's M-PESA (M for mobile and PESA is the Swahili word for cash) was the orbit-shifting innovation that leapfrogged the banking system by helping Kenyans access *mobile cash*. They can now create and use a mobile account through which they make financial transactions. All they need is a personally registered SIM. Subscribers keep money in their mobile account and can use the money to pay for a purchase or transfer cash to another person with just one SMS (short message service).

M-PESA empowered Kenyans with a mobile finance highway. It had grown to 17 million subscribers by 2012, almost 80 percent of the adult population in Kenya.[1] With two million daily transactions in Kenya alone, Safaricom moves an equivalent of a massive USD 20.5 million every day.[27] This acceleration of the velocity of financial transactions has triggered a distinct improvement in the country's GDP.[12]

> **Rather than waiting for the traditional banking network to grow and bank the unbanked millions, M-PESA has liberated millions in Africa, where it has leapfrogged traditional banking**

and moved directly to mobile-led financial transactions. For millions in this part of the world their first bank account is likely to have been a mobile account. Orbit-shifting innovations like M-PESA go beyond impacting a market; they positively impact the development of a nation.

Microsoft, Apple, Vestergaard Frandsen, Smart Communications, and Vodafone are all business innovators that have created an orbit-shift. They all began by identifying a transformation need; *an area where following the existing route and mere incremental improvement was just not enough.* Once they had identified the potential of the orbit-shift, it created a restlessness that got them to challenge and break out of the current orbit. This restlessness lead to an orbit-shifting innovation: a breakthrough that has created a disproportionate impact.

Orbit-shifting Public Services: Community Policing

Orbit-shifts that create history have not happened in business alone, but in public services as well. It is fascinating to see how, in the most entrenched of situations with the most unfavourable circumstances, those with the desire to create history have still made an orbit-shifting innovation happen. Community policing is one such orbit-shifting innovation. It transformed the approach to policing from *combating crime* to *cooperating with the community* to prevent it.

J.K. Tripathy achieved the impossible when he adopted community policing and successfully transformed the police force in a most communally sensitive town, Tiruchirapalli (Trichy) in south India. As a result, the crime rate in a town with an almost equal distribution of Hindus, Muslims, and Christians and prone to communal violence, dropped by 40 percent.

The first breakthrough needed was to transform the role and image of the police. 'Most people in India see the policeman as a corrupt extortionist. How do I transform this into an "Anna", the neighbourhood friendly cop?'

is how J.K. Tripathy describes the challenge. From this was born the role of the neighbourhood policeman. Each hand-picked neighbourhood cop had to shift out of the comfort zone of the police station and take charge of a neighbourhood. Rather than wait for people to come to the police, the policeman now reached out to the community instead. He started to knock on the doors in the neighbourhood, introduce himself and build positive relationships with the people. In addition, he also began to engage with the community to identify and solve problems that could escalate into potential law and order problems. The local community also began to reciprocate as they volunteered and actually worked with neighbourhood cops on night shifts.

Over time, this ease of reach and increased trust also made people approach their community policeman to solve law and order problems rather than go to the police station. As a result, the length of queues at the police station reduced dramatically. The police had come to the people, the people did not need to go to the police. While India has become more communally sensitive over the last decade, Trichy has reversed this trend with zero incidents of communal violence since the Community Policing project.[18]

Orbit-shifting Public Services: Health Care

Let's move the landscape, to Mongolia, where an orbit-shift has led to the drastic reduction of patient visits to hospitals, by as much as 45 percent in some areas. The Mongolian government is handicapped in health care by the nature of the terrain. Mongolia is a huge country with a scattered population. Hence, the hospitals are widely scattered; sometimes the nearest hospital can be 40 to 60 km away. Rather than invest in the traditional approach of increasing access to health care by increasing the number of hospitals, doctors, and nurses, the Mongolian government has partnered with Japan's Nippon Foundation to create an orbit-shift.

Together, they first identified the most frequently occurring illness patterns. Then they developed *Do-it-Yourself kits* based on traditional Mongolian medicine, rather than modern medicine. The kit, much like first aid, helps a person self-diagnose and self-medicate, at a primary level. The patient goes to a doctor only if this doesn't work. Furthermore, as traditional medicines have a herbal base, they are risk-free.

Doctors were trained in traditional medicine and sent out to cover communities spread out over predefined areas. These doctors conducted a physical examination of families and placed a medical kit in each home. On the next visit, the doctor examined the medical kit and the family paid *only for what they had consumed. A thought-provoking model indeed; medicine as postpaid, rather than prepaid.* Not only did this lead to the reduction of patient visits by 45 percent in some areas, house calls by local doctors also reduced by 17 percent, freeing up the doctors' work load. In addition, more hospital budgets became available for areas where it was really needed.[21, 33]

Community policing and Mongolian medicine demonstrate the power of a transformative purpose. Both orbit-shifting innovations were initiated by a shift in the core purpose: In the case of community policing, the purpose of the police force was transformed from 'enforcing law and order' to 'cooperation with the community'. In Mongolia, the purpose shifted from 'increasing the supply of health care' to 'reducing the health-care demand'.

Orbit-shifting Public Services: Making the World's Highest Railway Line

The Qinghai plateau in Tibet has remained one of the most impenetrable and inhospitable locations in the world. With an altitude that averages 4,300 metres (that's half the height of Mount Everest), the air has 30 to 40 percent less oxygen than at sea level.The temperatures here are as low as -40^{0}C, it is sometimes referred to as the third pole. The only way to travel across this remote and forbidding region was a perilous journey by road often leading to death. For over fifty years, China dreamed of building a railway, one that connected the outer regions of the plateau, Golmud, to the Tibetan city Lhasa at the heart of the plateau. To fulfil this dream, they were confronted with a challenge that had been deemed impossible by the rest of the world. A large part of the plateau is permafrost; unstable land that turns to mush and sinks in the summer, and freezes, hardens, and rises in winter. Previous efforts in building railways on permafrost had failed and had been abandoned. But the Chinese team took on the impossible challenge and they have successfully built the world's highest railway track on the roof of the world. At 1,100 km, it is not the longest, but it certainly is the most difficult railway project with breakthrough engineering solutions, to counter the challenge of permafrost, in an earthquake-sensitive region and with a minimal ecological impact. This 21st-century wonder of the world was completed in five years in 2006,[16] one year ahead of schedule.

China's Qinghai Tibet Railway was a public service orbit-shift of an altogether different order. It took on the challenge of doing what the world said was impossible and could never be done; achieved it was through extraordinary engineering solutions.

Orbit-shifting Public Services: Transforming a City

An orbit-shift of yet another kind occurred when S.R. Rao transformed Surat from a plague-ridden city in the early 1990s, into India's second-cleanest city in twenty months. Malaria cases came down from 22,000 in 1994 to 496 in 1997, and doctors' bills reduced by 66 percent. What's more, the change has sustained more than ten years after S.R. Rao was transferred out of Surat.

Surat was no small town. In 1995, it was actually India's twelfth-largest city, one of the country's eleven metropolitan cities, and had a population of nearly 3 million. Its population density in some areas was an astounding 54,000 people per square km. Over 40 percent of its population lived in slums, most with no drainage (before 1995) whatsoever. Dirty water flowed and stagnated around houses, particularly in the monsoon, with low-lying areas getting inundated. The city had always been noted for epidemics of water-related diseases like malaria, gastroenteritis, cholera, dengue, and hepatitis. The plague was no accident. It was a logical next step in the disease hierarchy of Surat. To make matters worse, the Surat municipality, among the oldest in the country, was infested with a corrupt, cynical bureaucracy.

S.R. Rao's orbit-shift was in the way he got an inertia-ridden bureaucracy to take charge of the transformation.

Surat was divided into six zones. Functional departments were disbanded. Shift engineers were made commissioners in particular areas, combining both administrative and financial powers. Each zone was made a profit centre. *While empowerment was an essential first step, it wasn't enough. The bigger challenge was to transform how this organization solved persistent problems.* They overcame city hygiene problems, tax collection problems, and even the problem of dealing with political pressure. When problems arose, the team dealt with them in a fundamentally different way and new solutions were found. A series of solutions *implemented together* snowballed into an orbit-shift for the city.[19]

Orbit-shifting Public Services: Access to Electricity in Rural Brazil

Let's now turn the lens to a country on the other side of the globe, Brazil,where Fabio Rosa lead the way in transforming the *access to electricity* in rural areas, with not one but multiple innovations. According to Brazil's National Household Sample Survey (PNAD), the electrification of Brazil has increased from 74.9 percent in 1981 to 88.8 percent in 1992, and from 92.9 percent in 1996, to 98.9 percent in 2008.[10]

Fabio Rosa was appointed Secretary of Agriculture of Palmares do Sul (a rural municipality in southern Brazil) at the age of 22. He realized that lack of access to electricity was the primary cause for poor farm productivity, which was, in turn, one of the reasons why an increasing number of people migrated to cities.

This triggered Rosa's first innovation, 'a mono-phase power system'—mono, because it uses one wire instead of three—called the 025 norm, which reduced the cost of accessing electricity from USD 7,000 to USD 450 per household. This was inspired by Ennio Amaral, a professor at the

Federal Technical School of Pelotas who had developed an inexpensive rural electrification system. Some farms increased their income by 400 percent in a year, by irrigating their crops with groundwater now made accessible by electricity. He extended this system to more than 27,000 people during the late 1980s and early 1990s. He worked with state electrical companies to take the mono-phase power system (the 025 norm) to hundreds of low-income-group people across rural Brazil.

But then, he was struck with an unexpected challenge. Electric utilities were privatized in Brazil. The companies were now not interested in pursuing low-cost electrification. It simply wasn't as profitable as serving cities. As a result, rural electrification slowed down to a trickle while at the same time, the number of squatters and the landless in urban Brazil continued to rise. But this didn't deter Fabio Rosa. He recognized that his work was important to the many people who still lacked electricity. So, Rosa influenced the Brazilian government to change public policies and declare 'electricity as a fundamental right'.

He then went on to create yet another orbit-shifting innovation. Through a market study, he realized that more than 70 percent of low income families spent at least USD 11 per month on non-renewable energy sources such as kerosene, candles, batteries, and liquid petroleum gas. He recognized that this USD 11 is about the same amount of money they need to spend each month to rent a basic photovoltaic solar home system equipped with lights and outlets with the necessary wiring, plus the boxes and locks.

This has led Rosa to work out at innovative business model that brings affordable solar electricity, at USD10 per month with micro-leasing, in a project aptly named The Sun Shines for All (TSSFA), through his non-profit organization called IDEAAS.[3, 4]

Both S.R. Rao and Fabio Rosa's experiences bring alive 'what it takes to innovate and orbit-shift an ecosystem'. What emerges is that one big idea alone is not enough. It takes a series of innovative solutions to the entrenched problems to

transform an ecosystem. S.R. Rao transformed the ecosystem of a city and Fabio Rosa has influenced a transformation of the rural electrification ecosystem of Brazil. What both cases domonstrate is that an ecosystem innovation often needs technology innovation, people transformation, policy change, and innovation in organization design.

What also stands out is that government officers like S.R. Rao and Fabio Rosa, who are usually restricted in scope and action, can also make the seemingly impossible happen.

Orbit-shifting Innovation for Inclusive Growth

Can we bring together the best of business and the best of social innovation?

Is this just a dream, or is it possible?

Orbit-shifting innovation did happen when the two came together in the form of the Grameen Bank in Bangladesh.

Muhammad Yunus was driven by the urge to help people at the bottom of the pyramid break the vicious poverty cycle. They clearly needed credit lines to start micro enterprises but banks were not willing to lend money without collateral. *Banks give you money only when you have money, they won't lend you any money if you have none.* People at the bottom of the pyramid have no collateral to offer. This was the transformation need that Muhammad Yunus addressed. With the orbit-shifting idea of using 'community as collateral, rather than assets as collateral', Muhammad Yunus developed the microfinance model that has played a revolutionary part in transforming the lives of millions at the bottom of the pyramid. This was inclusive innovation at its best. A true win-win that has created history.[9]

Orbit-shifting innovation peaks when a breakthrough transforms both business and society. Muhammad Yunus and Grameen Bank have demonstrated that innovation is not just

about business growth, but about inclusive growth. When you begin a business by putting economic and social growth at the centre, then not only does the community grow, but so does the business.

VisionSpring has also shown how an inclusive innovation can contribute to the growth of the entire community and also be a sustainable business. Started by a pair of entrepreneurs in New York City, the idea behind VisionSpring was that presbyopia can be simply corrected by reading glasses. *The reason why many people in developing countries go blind is the lack of access to inexpensive reading glasses.* VisionSpring has created a business model that is startlingly simple in hindsight, but elegant in the way it works. A complete vision kit is provided in a bag to Vision Entrepreneurs (locals from the community). Vision Entrepreneurs set up camps, test eyes, and sell high-quality reading glasses at a very affordable USD 4 a pair, on the spot. Making appropriate glasses accessible on the spot at a price that is much cheaper makes a huge difference to the customers. It also creates a business benefit for everyone in the value chain, with a dollar each going to VisionSpring and the Vision Entrepreneur and USD 2 to the manufacturer in China. With 9,000 vision entrepreneurs who have sold one million reading glasses so far, VisionSpring has impacted people in seven countries in three continents—South Africa, South America, and South Asia.[7, 32]

Orbit-shifting Innovation for Inclusive Growth: Transform the Impact on the Environment

On the west coast of India, in Malara, Gujarat, Tata Chemicals was faced with a problem like many other soda ash factories across the world. Solid waste from its soda ash factory had led to the creation of a dumpsite of 30 acres over thirty years. It was a barren wasteland with fine dust pollution rising and settling on homes that had cropped up in its vicinity, years later. In fact, world over, no new factory has been commissioned in the last fifteen years, as a result of the environmental impact of solid waste. The time had now

1.3 – Malara, before and after

come to relocate the 30-acre dump or to find an orbit-shifting innovation. Instead of relocating, Tata Chemicals chose to innovate, by attempting to green the soda ash wasteland. Located on the western coast, Malara is one of India's most fresh-water-scarce regions. It is also among the hottest areas in the country, where temperatures in the summer can rise to 45^{0}C. Tata Chemicals partnered with The Energy Resource Institute (TERI) to reclaim the wasteland. With a breakthrough bio-engineering solution, Tata Chemicals and TERI succeeded in greening 22.5 acres with saline-resistant local plants, special microorganisms to help extract nutrients from the soda ash, and using only sea water for irrigation, once the plants had taken root. Today, it is a living ecosystem, with more than 20,000 plants of six varieties, with vegetables like tomato, beetroot, and cucumber being grown during favourable seasons. It is also populated by insects, frogs, butterflies, ants, rats, snakes, and birds, and there is zero fine dust pollution to disturb the surroundings.[11]

What the TERI and Tata Chemicals team had understood was that while the soda ash substratum per se was full of nutrients, the issue was that these nutrients were present in an inert form. If the nutrients could be converted from inert to an active form, they could easily be absorbed by plant roots. This began their innovation, fuelled by TERI's philosophy: 'If there is a problem in nature, then somewhere it has also been solved by nature'. They knew that perhaps somewhere there would be a microorganism co-existing symbiotically with plant roots that works in saline conditions to convert inert nutrients into active forms for easy absorption by the plant. Driven by this philosophy, they set about identifying and exploring microorganisms in other saline plantations. Sure enough, they managed to identify the microorganisms that could act on nutrients in soda ash, using only saline water. The orbit-shifting solution born from Malara is now being taken to other countries where there is great shortage of fresh water and a need for reclamation.

Orbit-shifts like Grameen Bank and the one at Malara lift inclusive innovation to another level altogether. Inclusive innovation is transformative not just for the people but also for the environment. It finds solutions that are both people and planet positive.

Countries and organizations are talking about pursuing inclusive growth. But for inclusive growth to happen, it will need inclusive innovation.

REDEFINE AND RECAST INNOVATION

This vast landscape of orbit-shifting innovation provokes us, indeed forces us to re-examine and recast innovation as a concept.

The first myth to be shattered is the deep belief in the romance of innovation. Today, the world is seduced with the act of coming up with 'novel, first-to-the-world ideas'. For orbit-shifters, however, the spotlight shifts from innovation in itself to actually making the orbit-shift happen. For them, *orbit-shifting is the purpose and the passion, and innovation is merely the means.* Orbit-shifters are not obsessed with the romance of creating the Big New Idea. They didn't set out to create a novelty for its own sake. Their innovation was a response to a transformative need. Orbit-shifters first set out to create a transformative impact. What followed later was the innovation.

Further, the type and the kind of innovations needed to make the orbit-shift happen shatter even more myths. The next myth to be shattered is that 'innovation equals technology and product innovation'. Having originated from invention, most traditional models of innovation are still preoccupied with R&D, technology, and product innovation. In fact, the dominant criterion used to rank countries on the innovation index is often the R&D spend. The orbit-shifting innovation landscape painted earlier in this chapter breaks this myth of technology and product innovation, comprehensively and absolutely.

What stands out is that equally powerful orbit-shifts have come through with service, process, and business-model innovation.

What also stands out equally strongly is that the canvas of orbit-shifting innovation doesn't furnish only new products, business processes, and business models. It goes further with innovating the *people-engagement model*, and even further to include *ecosystem innovation.*

THE CANVAS OF ORBIT-SHIFTING INNOVATION

Not just Technology, but Service and Process Innovation

Singapore Airlines triggered an orbit-shift in the 1970s when it went beyond technology and identified *in-cabin experience* rather than modernity of aircraft as its prime differentiator. This orbit-shift, almost forty years ago, re-calibrated the customer-flying experience. Even today, Singapore Airlines remains far ahead of its competitors and is etched in its customers' minds as an unparalleled in-cabin experience provider.[2]

Aravind Eye Care has made their surgeons ten times more productive than the global best and this did not involve a new technology. It was led by a *process innovation* that brought in an assembly-line approach to the cataract surgery process.

Managerial-Process Innovation

Orbit-shifting innovation is not just about innovating the technical or operational process, it is as much about innovating the managerial process. Some of the biggest public-service innovations have come from managerial process innovations that created a large-scale impact.

Uganda has demonstrated how an innovation in the managerial process can create an orbit-shifting impact on a national scale.

Uganda has just 131 hospitals for a population of 36 million people. Children are dying needlessly of treatable diseases such as malaria, not because there is no medicine available, but because the distribution of medicine is hampered by bureaucracy and corruption. How do the decision makers get the right information in real time to identify and treat diseases? The traditional form of reporting is usually historical, with reports reaching the centre too late. Uganda has leveraged the power of the mobile phone instead, with a three-pronged solution called mTrac. In the first prong, health workers simply message details of drug supplies and disease outbreaks. This is collated in real time into a dashboard for public health officials' decision making. There is a chance that health workers could under report or hide information. The second prong therefore, is an anonymous SMS hotline, where anyone can leave information on any problem they face in medical assistance. And the third prong is a Facebook kind-of-solution but on SMS, through a community called U-report, facilitated by UNICEF. A hundred and forty thousand people communicate by text to send and receive information on health issues. All three prongs are integrated in mTrac to ensure transparency and accuracy in information at the top, speedy resolution of health issues at the outset rather than after the event, and a mechanism to raise and resolve these issues if at any stage they are subverted by the system.15

This amazingly simple (in hindsight) managerial-process innovation that substituted managerial reports with an SMS-driven online dashboard, has played a big part in bridging the gap between health care demand and supply.

Orbit-shifting with Business Model Innovation

While the prepaid card was a product innovation that led to increased accessibility and deeper market penetration, it was Bharti Airtel's business model innovation that actually made the prepaid model economically viable. The market reality of the prepaid card is that the Average Return Per User (ARPU) drops significantly. In 2003, the ARPU from a postpaid user was INR 1,182, while for a prepaid user, it was a mere INR 313.[30] This market reality led to the business question: how to make the prepaid model economically viable, when the returns are as little as one-third of the postpaid business model. This was especially critical as the infrastructure had been set up with cost assumptions of the postpaid market. Bharti's orbit-shifting innovation dramatically cut the cost of operations. It was driven with a breakthrough construct: Convert Capital Expenditure (CAPEX) to Operating Expenditure (OPEX). This construct opened the door to a genuine partnering model: where vendors were converted to partners. Bharti outsourced the network equipment to Nokia, Siemens, and Ericsson. IBM was chosen to build and manage the network. Bharti didn't stop here, but went a step further to collaborate with competitors by sharing mobile towers and their cost, thus reducing the final cost even further. This pioneering business model has led Bharti Airtel to become the lowest-cost producer of minutes in the world, and made the prepaid model economically viable.

In another pioneering initiative lead by Victoria Hale called OneWorld Health, an orbit-shifting business model has found a way to create affordable medicine for the neglected diseases in the developing world, by leveraging the shelved molecules of the large pharma companies. *This business model innovation has addressed a market gap that, though known, had remained visibly and even embarrassingly unfulfilled for many years.* OneWorld Health is the first non-profit pharmaceutical company in the U.S.[22]

ORBIT-SHIFTING BY INNOVATING ON THE PEOPLE-ENGAGEMENT MODEL

Innovation is usually linked to hard outcomes: like a visible product, a service, or a business model, and yet some of the biggest transformations have happened by innovating upon an entrenched model of people engagement.

Getting people to engage with the fight for independence through non-violence rather than war and bloodshed has easily been one of the most amazing orbit-shifting innovations of our times.

As Mahatma Gandhi said, 'I am not a visionary, I claim to be a practical idealist. Non-violence is the law of our species as violence is the law of the brute. The spirit lies dormant in the brute and he knows no law but that of physical might. The dignity of man requires obedience to a higher law—to the strength of the spirit. I have therefore ventured to place before India the ancient law of self-sacrifice. For Satyagraha and its offshoots, non-cooperation and civil resistance, are nothing but the new names for the laws of suffering.

Non-violence in its dynamic condition means conscious suffering. It does not mean meek submission to the will of the evil doer, but it means the pitting of one's whole soul against the will of the tyrant. Working under this law of our being, it is possible for a single individual to defy the whole might of an unjust empire to save his honour, his religion, his soul, and lay the foundation for that empire's fall or its regeneration.[23]

Pioneered by Mahatma Gandhi, non-violence created history by liberating India. It also inspired Martin Luther King to challenge and overcome segregation in the United States, and Nelson Mandela to liberate his people in South Africa.

Community Policing as a concept has innovated on the people-engagement model of the police, moving it from *combat to cooperation*—thus reducing crime rates significantly, as was demonstrated by J.K. Tripathy in Tiruchirapalli.

Orbit-shifting with Ecosystem Innovation

The microfinance industry pioneered by Muhammad Yunus with Grameen Bank was not merely a business model innovation. It was, in reality, an ecosystem innovation. To bring alive the orbit-shifting idea, 'using community rather than assets as collateral', it was not enough to put only elements of a business model in place, the entire ecosystem had to be transformed.

This pioneering ecosystem, built at a village level, was anchored in three entities, the self-help groups (SHG), the microfinance organization, and the banks. At the centre are the self-help groups—it involves forming women into *neighbourhood self-help groups*. The microfinance institution plays the role of a catalyst, facilitating group formation, training in financial understanding, and how to work together as a group. Then starts the cycle of giving micro loans and payback that is self-regulated by the self-help groups. The third critical entity is the money lender—a bank.

While intense, this ecosystem has proved to be immensely scalable, and has rapidly moved from Bangladesh to other parts of the world. According to India's National Bank of Agriculture and Rural Development's report on microfinance, as on March 2012, there were about 7.96 million SHGs in India, with an estimated membership of 97 million. They have savings accounts in the banks with an aggregate bank balance of about INR 65.5 billion.[6]

Transforming health care in Mongolia with traditional Mongolian medicine was also an ecosystem innovation. It needed the creation of the self-help kits for each house, for which suppliers of traditional Mongolian medicine had to be cultivated (this form of medicine had been overridden by western medicine during the years of Russian rule). It also needed the rebuilding of a pool of traditional medicine doctors to regularly cover pre-defined areas. These doctors were also responsible for the commercial management of the postpaid medical kits (checking the usage and collecting the payment).

Kudumbashree has gone further and led the next orbit-shift to the ecosystem pioneered by Grameen Bank.

In Kerala, south India, a team of fifty people *seconded from public service* have created history with an ecosystem innovation that uplifted 3.75 million at the bottom of the pyramid in a five-year period, from 1998 to 2002. Kudumbashree succeeded where many other poverty-alleviation programmes have failed. Most of these kinds of programmes traditionally fail because first, they don't reach the people who need it the most, and second, they are built on unsustainable models of governmental subsidy or public charity.

Kudumbashree's orbit-shift began with a set of orbit-shifting questions: 'Who needs poverty alleviation the most? Why have so many poverty-alleviation initiatives failed? Why do real people with real needs never get the poverty-alleviation help they need?' These challenging questions led to a total redefining of poverty. Rather than using *income deprivation* as the key parameter to identify a needy family, the team shifted to looking at '*family risk*'. They adopted a nine-point index to identify and ensure that their programme focused on the neediest of families. The nine factors included: living in a sub-standard house or hut, no access to sanitary latrines, no access to safe drinking water (150 metres), getting only two meals a day or less, having children below five years of age, having one or no earning member, belonging to socially disadvantaged groups, having an illiterate adult member, having alcoholics or drug addicts.

A family with at least four of these factors was to be classified as a *family at risk* or *poor family*. Total risk was profiled to identify high-risk families rather than only a lack of income.

Their real orbit-shifting innovation was to break away from giving *charity and subsidy* by creating *a people-transformation process that focused on infusing self-reliance.* With learning from the microfinance movement, this process centred around first forming families into Neighbourhood Help Groups (NHG). A NHG brought together twenty to forty women. Once formed, the primary focus was to build openness within the group, to acknowledge and accept problems. In fact, when one woman in the group shared a problem and the others acknowledged that they had a similar issue, the immediate feeling was one of *solidarity; 'I am not alone'*. Once this solidarity was established, the group was encouraged to *taking charge.* They started with thrift saving small amounts every week, even INR 2 per head, and also taking the initiative to *solve their own problems* rather than wait for the government. Collective savings were deposited in banks and the banks started giving out micro loans to group members. A total of 0.24 million NHGs were formed covering 3.75 million families. These groups collected a total thrift amount of approximately USD 304.5 million and the bank loans to them were around USD 1.28 billion.

Kudumbashree created an innovative ecosystem that focused on rallying women belonging to high-risk families into self-help groups. Rather than avoid or sidestep political agendas, the team directly involved the local political representatives in setting off the movement. They further integrated banks and even educational institutions to fuel the growth of micro enterprises. This ecosystem innovation, bringing together high-risk families, local politicians, bankers, and educational institutions has not just transformed the lives of 3.75 million families, but also led to the creation of over 30,000 micro enterprises in various sectors—mainly handicrafts, processed foods, garments and accessories, and health and hygiene.

Beyond loans, Kudumbashree initiated programmes to address other basic necessities like capability building for employment, community health, housing, and education. So well has Kudumbashree's mission flourished, that it has had many positive ripple effects, the most powerful of them being the political empowerment of women: In 2010, 11,773 women contested in local village elections (panchayat) and 5,485 won.[8,14]

DEMOCRATIZING ORBIT-SHIFTING INNOVATION

Singapore Airlines, LifeStraw, and Bharti Airtel bring alive the width of the orbit-shifting innovation canvas. All these are industry orbit-shifts spanning across process, product, and business model innovation. The microfinance model led by Grameen Bank and the Mongolian health care model expand this innovation canvas even under with ecosystem innovation.

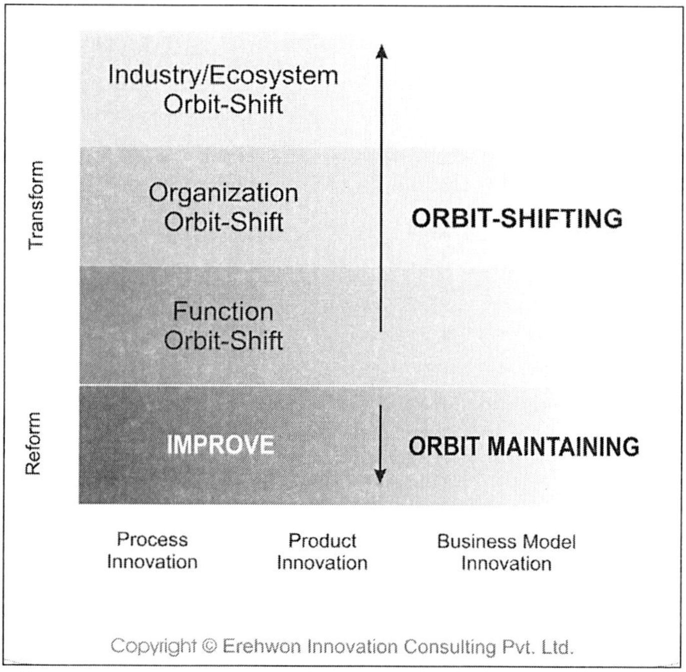

1.4 – The Orbit-Shifting Innovation Canvas

All these industry and ecosystem orbit-shifts are dramatically visible, and amazingly impactful. However, the orbit-shifting innovation canvas is not limited to them.

The reality is that people pursuing an industry or ecosystem orbit-shift are usually among the top leadership in the organization, industry, or domain.

Does this mean that aspiring for and making an orbit-shifting innovation happen is limited to the organization/ industry leadership? No!

Orbit-shifting innovation is not the fiefdom of a select few. It goes much further and wider, and is within the reach of every citizen. Orbit-shifts in an organization can be pursued across functions and across all levels.

By pursuing orbit-shifting innovation at three distinct levels, (industry, organization, and function) an organization can *democratize innovation.*

While industry and ecosystem orbit-shifts change the game, an organization orbit-shift transforms the impact in the current game. For example, the business model transformation at IBM where the business model moved from product to services.

Pursuing orbit-shifts at the industry plus organization levels will not only ensure current and future competitiveness, it will also go beyond the top leadership to engage and unleash key thought leaders at the next levels. As organizations have realized, making an orbit-shifting innovation happen doesn't merely transform results. It transforms people. It is the seeding ground of future leaders.

At the third level, function orbit-shifts can be pursued across the organization, across functions, and bottom up. A manufacturing plant has achieved 'twice the output from the same infrastructure'. A new career proposition for the next generation has been an orbit-shifting product innovation for the talent market from an HR (Human Resources) team. An orbit-shifting marketing strategy to reach twice the number of customers without using any of the existing advertising or promotion mediums is an orbit-shifting process innovation from a marketing team. Transforming the productivity of the sales force has been an equally impacting orbit-shifting innovation, taken on by a sales team.

Orbit-shifting innovation can, and is, being made to happen at the ground level too, by front liners. On the shop floor of a manufacturing plant, teams have created function orbit-shifts, like 'enhancing the life of a tool by a factor of 50, and doubling the throughput of an assembly line.' Both of these are not improvements in the current orbit. They are orbit-shifts, because they have gone beyond the industry best practice and created the next practice.

Orbit-shifters can and do create transformational impact at the industry, organization, and function level. Spanning across functions and levels, this orbit-shifting portfolio truly democratizes innovation. Any person who dreams big and has the desire to pursue this dream also has the space to make orbit-shifting innovation happen.

LEAPFROGGING THE DEVELOPMENT CURVE OF A NATION

Countries in south Asia, the Middle East, South America, and Africa are faced with the biggest developmental challenges. If the response to each challenge was merely *follow the development curve* of the western nations, it would take decades to catch up. Western nations are also facing their own developmental challenges of stagnating growth and economic models that seem to be trapped in the previous century; they are seeking fresh and revolutionary approaches too. *When developmental initiatives hit the wall of diminishing returns, the time is right for an orbit-shifting innovation.* On the other hand, the next generation is coming in with much bigger dreams and aspirations and a huge urgency to get things done faster and better. They do not want to wait for the world to change. If we are to create new futures for them, we need radically new approaches. *We need orbit-shifting innovation to meet the out-of-the-box ambitions of the next generation.*

The mobile revolution has already demonstrated how countries like China, the Philippines, and India can leapfrog the developmental curve rather than merely follow it. M-PESA also showed how people in Kenya leapfrogged traditional banking by directly going to mobile banking. Community Policing shows how maintaining law and order can be leapfrogged, no matter how entrenched the scenario is. This is orbit-shifting innovation in action—where great impacts are made, in a telescoped time period, by challenging all known beliefs of the current orbit. This is why it becomes imperative for organizations, industries, and nations to create orbit-shifting innovations and to find new solutions. Solutions not just for persistent problems, but also for future-led opportunities.

The time, more than ever, is now ripe for orbit-shifting innovation. It cannot be accidental, or incidental, waiting for the right person to come along and then hoping that by some miracle or divine intervention, this person is struck with an orbit-shifting idea or aspiration. We can't wait for another Steve Jobs. We have to make it happen by design. And we have to make it happen now!

SECTION 2

SEEDING ORBIT-SHIFTING INNOVATION

Chapter 2

Confronting Gravity

2.1 – Dinosaur Mindsets

ORBIT-SHIFTING INNOVATION STORIES ARE VERY ROMANTIC IN HINDSIGHT. They inspire, they encourage, and they even provoke dreamers into positive restlessness and action.

However, what is usually not visible behind these stories are the extreme odds that orbit-shifters had to overcome to make their dreams a reality. It is here that most people give in and give up. Most orbit-shifters recognize and realize that when the rubber hits the road they are all alone. It is easy to dream up orbit-shifts but it is far more difficult to pursue them, and so many give up in that pursuit.

So, what drags down and even decimates orbit-shifting dreams and ideas? *As the innovation wave gathers momentum, all business, public and social enterprises are pre-occupied with this question. They all need to innovate, want to innovate, but rarely do orbit-shifting intentions come alive as orbit-shifting innovation.* Many surveys have identified factors that help and hinder innovation. A few years ago, BCG and Business Week asked the top twenty innovative organizations across the world—including Apple and Google: What are the enemies of innovation? The key enemies identified were: lengthy development times, lack of coordination, risk-averse culture, limited customer insight, poor idea selection, inadequate measurement tools, dearth of ideas, and marketing or communication failure.[3]

Do these enemies sound very familiar? Most managers will almost immediately connect and identify with a number of them. We have all experienced them at some point in our careers and some of us will even candidly confess to having played the villain by employing one of these enemies to knock down an innovation.

But are these indeed the real enemies of innovation? Will a conscious attempt to overcome these hurdles truly accelerate orbit-shifting innovation?

Going deeper to study these so-called enemies, we have found that they are merely symptoms, and not the real enemies of innovation. Any attempts to deal with these symptoms will only end up being sub-optimal. A quick fix to accelerate organization innovation by putting structures and practices in place often ends up in failure, for *it is a superficial response to a symptomatic issue.*

These enemies are manifestations of a far deeper driver-entrenched mindsets. Most people are not stuck because they want to be stuck, or because structures limit them, or because there's no reward mechanism. Most people are stuck because their mindsets block them. They have come to perceive 'reality' in a certain way and this, more than anything else, limits them from innovating.

We have spoken to and worked with a number of leaders who have made orbit-shifting innovations happen. At no point in time did any of them consider structures and practices as blocks to innovation. Rarely was someone motivated by an external promise of a reward to innovate. In most cases, it was a transformative purpose, a personal trigger, or a breakthrough insight that had led to an orbit-shifting innovation. And from this, the rewards and recognition flowed.

THE REAL ENEMY IS MINDSET GRAVITY

The real enemy is Mindset Gravity. Just like gravity is an all-pervading force that cannot be seen or even felt, day on day, but prevents us from breaking the bonds of earth, so is mindset gravity a pervading force that traps people, without conscious realization, into their current orbits.

At a personal level, the breaking of New Year resolutions reveals *mindset gravity in action.* We make promises—from losing weight to watching our temper to learning a new hobby—and toil towards them with great commitment. However, a week or two down the line, gravity creeps in and we are back to our old ways. The old is usually more powerful and stronger than the new. Similarly, in a bid to stimulate innovation, organizations make conscious attempts to expose their people to inspiring and insightful speakers. Their impact lasts a few days, with a bandying about of new vocabulary and new ideas learnt, and then people return to business as usual, almost with a sense of relief.

A visionary CEO of a mid-size consumer goods company wanted to leverage innovation as a way to accelerate growth. He had single-handedly grown the business through tough times. It was a journey that had made him a good business leader, but not necessarily a risk-taker. He championed innovation in every conference and in every presentation he made to his organization or investors. Yet, when anyone came to him with a new idea, his previous experience came unconsciously to the fore and his first question usually was, 'Has anyone else tried it anywhere else in the world? I do not want to be the guinea pig for a new idea'. So while he talked innovation, he actually displayed a *safekeeping/avoid-uncertainty mindset*. And unless he confronts and deals with this mindset gravity, it is unlikely that his organization will be able to break free of the current orbit of predictability and efficiency. This organization will, at best, be an efficient follower, following the leadership of other organizations in the industry.

Layers of Gravity

2.2 – Layers of Gravity

Gravity accumulates over time and pulls down the new. Not one, but four layers of mindset gravity stall orbit-shifting innovation. *Organization gravity conditions most people within the organization to think alike, then there is deep-rooted industry gravity, which ensures that all players across the industry start to think and act the same. Deeper still, country and cultural gravities choke people across industries and even across generations into conforming, rather than innovating.*

Mindset gravity creates gravity tunnels that condition and trap communities, organizations, and even countries and civilizations. It consciously and unconsciously blocks attempts to conceive, pursue, and sometimes even attempt orbit-shifting innovation.

Organization Gravity

Organizations accumulate gravity with frightening ease. Past successes become best practices. Best practices become templates. And templates become the unquestionable sacred truths.

A revealing illustration of this is the superficial attempts a number of organizations make to stimulate innovation by increasing the cultural diversity of their workforce. *They hire new people from different backgrounds and then proceed to induct them very well!* So well that the new employees get seamlessly inducted into the same old gravity-infested mindsets. While a person is still fresh at an organization, he is often bubbling with ideas. However, if he happens to share one of his bright ideas with a senior manager, the most likely response is: 'So, how long have you been here? Did you say one month! I'll ask you after you have been here for one full year.' After a year, he is likely to cease raising *stupid* questions, for he now knows what questions are not to be asked. He has become an integral part of the organization gravity. He has become one of them.

Organization Gravity: Entering a New Market with the Old mindset

An organization entering a new market with the old mindset is a disaster waiting to happen.

In the early 1990s, Titan had become the most admired and successful watch company in India, with multiple marketing awards to its credit. Driven by success and the aspiration to grow, Titan created a strategy to enter the jewellery market, with the launch of Tanishq. In doing so, the organization succumbed to gravity. Riding on their successful watch strategy, the Titan team, without conscious realization, replicated more of the same in the jewellery market. *International design and great retail stores was the formula that had made Titan watches a resounding success in the market.* This was directly transferred into the jewellery strategy, but it failed miserably. This failing strategy was relentlessly pursued for *five years,* and Tanishq remained in the red. So severe was the situation, that the J (jewellery) word became unmentionable in the Tata boardroom. It had become an embarrassment.

At this point, Jacob Kurian became the COO of Tanishq. His most significant realization was: 'In moulding the jewellery strategy in accordance with the watch strategy, Tanishq had lost sight of what women really wanted. Tanishq had ended up selling jewellery to women just like Titan sold watches to men.'

The turnaround for Tanishq began only when it went back to zero and revisited basic assumptions, throwing out all the baggage created by Titan. Finally, Tanishq began to see the Indian woman for who she really was and how she shopped for jewellery in a uniquely Indian way. This was not a happy realization or an easy turnaround, but a painful one that took all of two years to rework and set Tanishq on a new trajectory, independent of the Titan legacy.

In hindsight, the questions are intriguing: What made such a successful Titan team create such a big initial failure in Tanishq? Why didn't they recognize the fundamental flaw in their approach and why did it take so long to turn around: not in the first, or the second year, but only after years of failing again and again? This is how powerful and paralysing organization gravity can be. It can trap a team of brilliant, well-intentioned people into a shared belief that the strategy was right, it was the execution that fell short. However, once the mindset gravity was confronted and broken through, the turnaround began and now Tanishq is a glorious success.

This is not a singular story of Titan. It has happened again and again where organizations have gotten trapped in and entered a new market with the old mindset. A multinational entered the *power backup* industry in south

Asia with the *UPS mindset*. It came with the belief that home Uninterrupted Power Supply (UPS) was primarily for the computer and hence tried to penetrate the market through electronic stores. This belief was based on its previous success in developed markets. It failed to recognize that the context of electricity and power supply in south Asia was entirely different, for not only are there frequent power cuts; the voltage fluctuation is also high. Hence, there was a latent and bigger need for a UPS: to serve as a temporary backup for homes, when there were power cuts. They overlooked this larger—in fact, huge—opportunity. It took an Indian entrepreneur, unfettered by the gravity of the UPS industry, to leverage the real opportunity. Sukam Power Systems opened up an entire new industry with the business of *home inverters and UPS* for power backup.

As one of the business heads of this multinational that missed the opportunity reflected, 'Earlier, our measurement criteria for the market used to be based on PC (Personal Computer) penetration (it had worked for the UPS markets). As the PC penetration in south Asia is only 4 percent, that came to be the size of our market. It is only after local companies like Sukam, Microtek, etc., came out with their inverter products that we realized that the market of power backup is much larger.'

Organization Gravity: Fitting a New Opportunity into an Existing Category

Organization gravity not only stifles a new market-entry strategy, it also prevents the emergence of new opportunities. Managers and organizations excel in slicing and dicing the market into neat categories—customer categories, usage categories, and socio-cultural categories. Categorization simplifies but it also becomes the mindset gravity that prevents the emergence of the new. The category mindset gravity settles into an even deeper groove when an organization designs and institutionalizes the organization strucutre to match market categories. As an example, in one organization, cooking oils, hair care, and baby care were three market categories, and hence they were also structured into the three matching business units. In such a category-focused business, even *if a new category-creating idea does dare to emerge, it is often immediately pulled back to fit into the existing category.*

A large consumer goods multinational organization identified health care as a potential opportunity. It zeroed in on *lifestyle and preventive health care* as the next big idea that would be category creating. The action started with great fidelity to the big idea, but began settling into their existing category in no time. Soon enough, rather than be driven by the uniqueness of the new category, they ended up launching their first product—a shampoo—in that most familiar of territories: hair care. As a hair care brand manager said, 'because we are strong in hair care.'

In fact, even their health care research had unconsciously been dominated by the *old category* lens. The key research finding was that the proportion of consumers starting with a herbal brand is higher in personal care, in comparison with health care. This led to an anti-dandruff shampoo and a skin cream being the first products launched. Again, formats in their comfort zone of an existing category.

Within a few years what had started out as a preventive health care opportunity was reduced to a series of reactive and curative products, dramatically contrary to their initial vision.

The big orbit-shifting opportunity had been successfully reduced to an incremental has-been by category gravity. As some team members later reflected:

- 'We started looking for health care variants in existing categories.'
- 'Our traditional thinking is too trapped into creating variants and line extensions, riding on existing consumer knowledge.'
- 'Most of us do not see category creation; the focus is on how I can use it for immediate category interest.'

One person summed it up, with a sigh, 'We went into health care with a powerful vision but we are essentially a soap-and-shampoo company. So we immediately converted the health care opportunity into "shampoos and soaps".'

Organization Gravity: An Orbit-shifting Idea or a Marketing Gimmick?

Novo Nordisk had been driven dominantly by the mindset of new drug discovery. Drug delivery devices had seldom been at the heart of their strategy. So much so, that when the NovoPen® was first launched, the marketing team in Novo Nordisk saw it as a gimmick to increase sales, rather than as a vehicle to transform the diabetes industry. The device was not even patented. It is only when the device took off successfully in the market and started transforming the lives of diabetics, did the marketing team and the rest of the organization sit up and take notice of NovoPen®. It went from being treated as a marketing gimmick to becoming the future of diabetic care. As of 2004, the NovoPen®, NovoLet®, and its successors like the FlexPen had 25 percent of the global market share in the total volume of insulin sold.

As a CEO, think about this:

Where have you and your organization fallen into the trap of pursuing a next-orbit idea with the 'old-orbit' mindset?
What are you doing to consciously confront this gravity and prevent these self-created disasters from happening?
What are you doing to ensure that even the process of opportunity identification is not being unconsciously limited by the mindsets of the current orbit?

Industry Gravity

From Pigs to Snow White

One of Walt Disney's iconic films was *Three Little Pigs.* It became a huge success. Walt Disney gathered his team and posed the question: 'What film should we do next?' The answer, as you would expect, conformed to the beaten track with the most usual response when a film succeeds—*extend the genre with more of the same.* The Disney team's instinctive reaction was: 'Pigs work, pigs sell! Let's make another film on pigs.'

Rather than jump in with agreement, Walt Disney paused and reflected on this approach, and an insight struck him. He gathered his team and said, 'You cannot top pigs with pigs'. Walt Disney had realized that doing more of the same would not be enough, they needed to do something different. This insight led to the making of *Snow White and the Seven Dwarfs*. *Snow White* became a landmark in the film industry, launching a new film category of full-length animation feature films. It went on to become the most successful motion picture of 1938, with earnings of over USD 8,000,000 on its initial release. In 2012, these release earnings would be the equivalent of USD 127,600,000. Today, it is the only animated film to make it to the American Film Institute's list of all-time great American films. Disney was right, 'You cannot top pigs with pigs.' *It took a Snow White to beat the pigs.*[10, 17]

Industry Gravity: Leaders from Day One

How long does it take for a new newspaper to gain leadership in a city? Most experts with a view into the newspaper industry would say: 'Give it seven to ten years'. This seven-to-ten-years conclusion for market leadership in a new city is driven by the conventional wisdom of industry experts: Newspaper reading is a habit and habits are very difficult to change. People get used to the feel of the paper, the font, the layout, and once comfortable do not change easily.This belief has led to most newspapers adopting the same pig strategy. First, *free sampling to build familiarity and only then the formal launch and hopefully leadership after continuous grunt work for many years.* The breakthrough that this is *not industry wisdom, but industry gravity,* has been vividly brought to the fore by a revolutionary newspaper—*Dainik Bhaskar.*

Dainik Bhaskar broke through this industry gravity. It created an orbit-shifting strategy to become the *Leader from Day One*, in a new city launch. Rather than adopting the usual pig strategy, *Dainik Bhaskar* created a Snow

White, by co-creating the newspaper with the entire market. In Ahmedabad, the paper was literally co-created with 1.2 million households and achieved a first-day launch volume of 4,52,000 newspapers, setting a new record. The market leader's circulation was 3,50,000. And in less than eight years, *Bhaskar* has achieved circulation figures that many others in the global newspaper business have taken decades to achieve.[11]

As a CEO, think about this:

Most industries inevitably reach a point where everybody is busy making pigs. A stage arrives where everything looks the same. Products look the same, processes look the same, and even business models look the same. A stage is reached where most people are also changing jobs within the same industry, so even people begin to look the same. The whole industry becomes an extended pig factory, where players have lost sight of significant differentiation and are trapped in benchmarking instead. The best innovation they can come up with is usually an incrementally better pig: 'Mine is a bigger or smaller pig or it is a thinner pig or it is a blue pig'. But it is a pig nevertheless! This is not innovation, it is rationalization. Conditioned minds excel at developing such self-serving definitions of innovation.

Look at your innovation agenda.

Is it an extension of the industry pig factory?

Is there a Snow White on the agenda? If not, why not?

What is the gravity that is preventing a Snow White from even appearing on the agenda, let alone making it happen?

Industry Gravity: Creates a Smaller Box Within the Given Box

Organizations in highly regulated industries like pharma and finance often fall into the trap of attributing the reason for not innovating to the imposed regulations. The question is: 'Are regulations and regulators the real hindrance or is it something deeper?'

While regulations are necessary and mandatory, what begins to happen over time is that gravity makes organizations follow the regulations to the letter, rather than to their original intent and purpose. Coupled with this is the possibility that time has obscured the original reason for a regulation and no one even attempts to unearth the source and figure out its meaning. Everybody settles on adhering to what they assume it means. *Over time, gravity sinks in and more and more assumptions get treated as facts.*

A pharma firm in Europe found itself at the constant receiving end of the competition's innovation. Tired of being continuously outwitted and blindsided, the company's leadership team members paused to reflect and understand the reasons. They found that the greatest gravity was their subservient attitude towards the regulator. What is fascinating is that most of this subservience was driven by internal myths, rather than any real experience with the regulator. As some leadership team members said on reflection:

- 'We are proactively compliant to minimize risks.'
- 'We engage in assumptive nos and shoot down innovative methodologies. Because we thought the regulator would not accept it, we would not risk it. Tried and tested is the best way.'
- 'We invest so much time in self-protection. As a result we are in a world of self-inflicted constraints and a smaller boundary.'
- 'We have become over compliant, more than is necessary. As a result we are not even trying out in areas where we have flexibility.'

As a result, organization leadership habitually self-censored new ideas in the early stages saying: 'It won't go through with the regulator.' A number of ideas had been shot down over the years based on assumptive nos. They hadn't even bothered to check the real regulations. They had created a self-restricting playing field; this creation of *an even smaller box within the given box* provided by the regulator had become a prime contributor to their falling behind the competition. It is like a 'self-goal' in football; it was like playing for the other side! *The more people work in a regulated environment, the more they end up working in a regulated manner—their mindset gets equally regulated and conditioned. This is at the heart of industry regulation gravity.*

Industry Gravity: The Regulator Breaks Boundaries

Regulators, contrary to what gravity-infested organizations think, sometimes even help companies break boundaries and grow their business. In 2001, Bristol Myers, the USD 20 billion pharma company, had a fairly successful over-the-counter general purpose headache medicine called Excedrin. Bristol Myers discovered, from observing patient behaviour, that Excedrin was being used to effectively treat migraine conditions as well. While Bristol Myers identified this patient behaviour, it didn't necessarily convert it into a business opportunity.

Since migraine is a serious medical condition with distinct symptoms, the regulator, Food and Drug Administration (FDA), mandated that the product would need to have separate labelling since it was being used for the treatment of both headaches and migraines. This led to the same product/ formulation now being available in two variants, namely Excedrin and Excedrin Migraine, with each having distinct packaging and labelling to avoid confusion on retail shelves. Excedrin Migraine went on to become a USD 80 million-plus brand in the overall USD 200 million-plus Excedrin business. This is a unique case of a brand extension launched in effect due to a push by the regulatory authorities.

Bristol Myers had treated the Excedrin migraine effect as an aberration, and let the drug remain as is, without identifying the bigger opportunity. The regulator in this case actually helped Bristol Myers create a new opportunity that worked to the company's advantage. It shows that regulators are not always trying to choke and limit organizations, they work to serve the greater common good. And yet, most organizations feel imprisoned by what they perceive as regulator gravity.

Orbit-shifting innovators, on the other hand, are not gravity bound by regulations. They see regulations as serving a purpose and work out ways of achieving the orbit-shift without compromising on the regulatory purpose, rather than allowing themselves to be trapped into following the regulation to the letter.

As a CEO, think about this:

Newton's laws were taught like 'laws'—laws that were absolute truths in the field of physics and therefore could not be questioned. Perhaps, that's why it took over 200 years for an Einstein to come along. What if they had been taught like Newton's assumptions rather than laws? Is it possible that an Einstein could have emerged much earlier?

Where have you let your industry, domain and market assumptions become facts and even laws for your organization? What if you treated them like assumptions instead?

Domain and Sector Gravity

Ecosystem Nexus

Deeper and more insidious than market gravity is domain and sectoral gravity, where an entire domain or sector believes in a norm and accepts it as sacred and untouchable. This norm is so deep-rooted that the entire industry/sector accepts its boundaries and limitations.

The nexus between business, politics, and media often means that scandals and corruption are either brushed under the carpet or too little is revealed too late. Mediapart, a small and young media organization operating in France, has broken out of the mould. In what can only be delicious irony, Mediapart put the unrelenting spotlight on the President of France, François Hollande's former tax enforcement minister, Jérôme Cahuzac, for tax evasion. After a spate of denials and a brazen statement where, according to *Time* magazine, Cahuzac 'also told the French Parliament he had "not now, not ever" hidden funds abroad', he was forced to resign when Mediapart released tapes where he discussed his secret Swiss account.

Underlying Mediapart's success is the gravity of the French news industry. The big traditional newspapers dismissed and even undermined Mediapart's brave attempts and refreshed business model. *In breaking the sector gravity, Mediapart*, set up in 2008 by Laurent Mauduit and Edwy Plenel, *abandoned the traditional advertising model as a way to generate revenues, in favour of a subscription model.*

Quoting from *Time* magazine, 'The small, feisty site has beaten the odds by breaking some of the biggest scandals of the decade in France, on a shoestring budget and against widespread scepticism from the much richer French newspapers. This week's revelations have not only stung politicians but also the traditional French media. As Mediapart hammered away at the Cahuzac story for months, news outlets questioned whether the information was true, and on occasion dismissed it as trivial'.

Further on in the magazine, Plenel describes their business model, 'At the time, their business model seemed unworkable. "Five years ago nobody believed in our project," Plenel, who's also Mediapart president, said on Friday. Plenel said when he left *Le Monde* in 2008, he was determined to show that people would be prepared to pay for high-value information—particularly since it offered French citizens revelations that the old-style newspapers shied away from. "They all said it could not work."

'To the surprise of many, subscriptions steadily increased as readers sought out investigative probes that were missing from France's established newspapers—they now have some 62,000 subscribers. Last year Mediapart, which employs about 30 journalists, made a profit of about USD 780,000, according to the founders'.

Mediapart has broken the settled approach in journalism, by bringing back investigative reporting that puts the citzens of France at the centre, rather than its advertisers or other interested parties.[19]

Domain and Sectory Gravity: Development Norms

The developmental world has long believed that poverty leads to illiteracy. Such beliefs become the basis on which aid and developmental work is carried out. However, while well intentioned, they can often become the gravity that locks people across borders into only one way of approaching a developmental challenge.

This norm, *poverty leads to illiteracy* therefore prioritizes poverty eradication before child education. *If you want to get children into schools focus on reducing the family poverty first, because poor families find it necessary to send their children to work for food, rather than to school for education.* This perspective remained unquestioned for decades.

Until Shanta Sinha and MV Foundation in India challenged this norm and reversed the equation. She threw open a whole new opportunity when she flipped around what was until then the gospel truth in the world of development: *poverty leads to illiteracy.* Shanta Sinha asked herself, *what if it is illiteracy that leads to poverty instead.* In a powerful experiment in a school district, she swept all children otherwise occupied in labour into school. Their freed-up jobs were taken by adults. Adults were paid more than children and hence family incomes went up, while the children were now being educated. Thus, Shanta Sinha found a model that was not sequential; it alleviated both poverty and illiteracy. An independent research revealed that in the villages where the interventions were made, wage rates increased by 131 percent for female adult workers and 105 percent for male adult workers from 2005 to 2009, compared to 51 percent and 56 percent respectively in other villages.[5] As of 2012, one million children had been enrolled in schools and over 1,500 villages were child-labour free.[6] *And actually, it is the first educated child in the family who fundamentally breaks the family poverty cycle.*

It all started by breaking through the mindset gravity created by the sector norm, *first poverty eradication, followed by education.*

Domain and Sectory Gravity: The Race for the Bottom-of-the-Pyramid

One big business growth idea that captured the imagination of many organizations was C.K. Prahlad's 'Fortune at the Bottom of the Pyramid (BoP)', where he uncovered a huge, largely unserved market for corporations. It was estimated in 2004 that the BoP was more than four billion people who had an annual per capita income of USD 1,500.[14]

This concept triggered a Wild West-like scenario, where everyone was racing towards an undiscovered, unexplored gold mine. It opened up a whole new world for corporations to exploit; if only they could figure out how to reach and unlock the wealth that existed at the bottom of the pyramid.

As a CEO, think about this:

Powerful new ideas are often interpreted and pursued with an old mindset. This gravity reduces the big potential of the new to the lowest common denominator. In this case, corporations approached the BoP opportunity with the extraction mindset, where the overriding focus was to 'get a bigger share of the BoP wallet!' Everyone wanted to do it, but no one seemed to have figured out how. As a result, this extraction mindset reduced the BoP opportunity to a massive untapped treasure chest.

Where else have you and your organization been seduced by a big growth idea like the fortune at the BoP, but pursued it with the old orbit mindset?

Sivakumar of ITC-IBD, on the other hand, recognized the real transformation need at the BoP. He empathized with the need of farmers, who made the least returns in the food value chain. This empathy fuelled his creation of e-Choupal with the belief, *'First, fortune for and only then at the bottom of the pyramid. First increase the size of the wallet and then take your share.'* Until e-Choupal, a serious handicap faced by an Indian farmer was that he had to transport his produce over great distances to a market and only then discover the price that the buyers were offering on arrival. Having already made an enormous effort to reach the produce to the market, he was more often than not left with no option but to compromise and sell. This pressure to sell was even higher because he had little access to storage facilities. A pressured sell greatly reduced returns, creating despair for farmers at the bottom of the pyramid. e-Choupal pioneered a new business model that involved placement of e-kiosks in villages that empowered farmers by providing online, real-time market price information. Now the farmer knew the price options in various markets before starting out and so he could now choose when to sell and where to sell. e-Choupal also offered to buy his produce at a market-equivalent price for ITC, and a majority of farmers preferred to sell directly to ITC.[12]

As a CEO, think about this:

e-Choupal first increased the size of the wallet and then also gained a bigger share of it. This belief is the heart of inclusive growth. It breaks through the gravity of Fortune at the BoP with 'First Fortune "for" and then "at" the BoP'.

Where could an inclusive innovation be the lever to tap into a big untapped market or to create a new market?

Country Gravity: The World's Finest Airline

Most constructs around disruptive innovation explore and discuss barriers in making innovation happen, but only up to the industry level. However, any game changer at the industry level is strongly influenced by the undercurrents of the country and culture mindset gravities. If these mindsets are not surfaced and resolved, this deep, unquestioned gravity can become the silent killer to a disruptive innovation attempt.

So powerful is country and cultural gravity that it sweeps across sectors and traps entire nations of people into self-limiting beliefs that are invisible, endemic, and even paralysing. It often prevents leaders and organizations from even attempting an orbit-shift.

From its very first days, Singapore International Airlines (SIA) had crafted a bold aspiration—*to become the best airline brand in the aviation industry*. A team set about identifying their core differentiator. It was immediately confronted with the popular industry wisdom of airlines in Asia. Led by Thai Airways, the accepted and favoured winning formula at that time had become *modern aircraft and Western pilots*. The SIA team realized that all airlines would soon become homogenized and though reliability and modernity were important to customers, they would soon become qualifiers (an expected given) and not a competitive advantage. Breaking through this industry gravity, they identified their big differentiator as *what goes on during the flight: the in-cabin experience.*

However, what appeared like a breakthrough was soon confronted with country gravity. The senior management reminded them again and again, that Singapore in 1972, was primarily seen as a third-world state and *they cannot have an airline whose brand image is bigger than the image of the country. This country gravity sharply defined the belief that a third-world country cannot aspire to create the world's finest airline. It seemed much more professional and acceptable to build the airline's brand around modern fleet, extensive network, and experienced people. A safe and defensive strategy, surely, but still only a better pig.*

Fortunately, the team did not give in, and broke through this country gravity. SIA was launched in October 1972 with in-flight experience as its core differentiator. Over the years, SIA has pioneered a whole host of in-flight services and continues to remain far ahead of the competition with exceptional in-flight experience even today. In fact, it was SIA that helped lead the change of the brand image of Singapore.[1]

Cultural Gravity Cultivates Subservience

Cultural gravity embeds itself even deeper than country gravity and can breed the extremes of arrogance and subservience—instinctive arrogance in developed markets and deep rooted subservience in the developing markets.

Cultural Gravity: Have the Swiss Done it?

Cultural subservience became a visible boundary when Xerxes Desai of Titan exhorted his team to create the world's thinnest, water-resistant watch. The teams instinctive reaction was, 'How can we, when even the Swiss haven't been able to do it.' The Swiss were considered to be the gods of precision engineering. Hence, the dominant and self-limiting belief in Titan was that *if they cannot, then no one else can.*

Xerxes inspired the team to push through this self-limitation by refusing to take no for an answer. The Titan team came through in 1994 with a 3.5-mm water-resistant watch, a watch with the thickness of a floppy disk. Originally, Xerxes' orbit-shifting aspiration had been faced with incredulity within Titan, for they had to solve many extreme engineering challenges. It meant reducing the existing watch movement by about 40 percent. It meant making it water resistant and no other watch in the world with *this level of thinness* was water resistant. Then, they had to radically miniaturize all the parts, specifically the battery and the step motor, to make them fit into the available space. Each problem came with a further set of challenges; the battery had to have a long life as it could not be removed frequently, but longer life required larger size. How would they solve this either-or challenge? And then, they had to find a casing supplier who could make the casing slim enough, with break- and water-resistant glass, a slim crown, and rear casing.

The team went to the Basel watch fair in Switzerland to find a supplier. But all the suppliers were incredulous. In sheer disbelief they asked, 'Have you really created a movemet this small?' They couldn't believe an Indian firm with a pedigree of just two years had made it happen. And they all declined to make the prototype because it needed breakthroughs in many components, which was beyond their capability! *Beyond the capability of the Swiss. Imagine that!* The team was taken aback. *The Swiss had not done it and they believed it couldn't be done.* They came back demoralized, believing that the product had hit a roadblock. But fortunately, they didn't give up.They found a new resolve, 'If the Swiss haven't done it, we will!' They returned to the drawing board and started building prototypes. There were no reference points on how to do it and at each stage they faced insurmountable challenges, but the catchphrase of *'we will do what the Swiss cannot'* kept them going and finally, the Edge—the world's slimmest water-resistant watch—was born. It went on to become the reference point for all other slim watches to come. *This making of Titan Edge was as much a remaking of the Indian mind as it was an engineering breakthrough; to build belief that indeed they could outdo the Swiss* in making an exceptional watch.[13]

This cultural subservience in developing countries is all-pervading: most people are not aware of how deeply it runs in their veins and how much it drives how they think and operate with respect to the developed world. Nelson Mandela made this vivid when he observed that *'the problem is not that they consider themselves to be superior, the problem is us, we think ourselves to be inferior'*.

As a CEO, think about this:

This cultural subservience that the Titan team overcame is most often the invisible enemy. It leads to self-doubt in the minds of innovators. We have often been part of innovation dialogues where a team comes up with a first-to-the-world orbit-shifting idea and immediately starts doubting it with statements like: 'How could we have been the first ones to have thought of it'; 'I am sure the organizations in Silicon Valley have already considered it, in fact they must have dismissed it, that is why it hasn't happened!' This self-doubt becomes the invisible box that prevents organizations and leaders from even attempting an orbit-shift.

Where has a similar self-doubt surfaced and blocked your 'first-to-the-world' idea? How would this Titan team have dealt with the self-doubt?

Cultural Gravity: Samsung—The Challenger

In the mid 1990s, Samsung was the poor man's Sony.[18] However, Samsung's desire was to be the challenger rather than the follower of Sony, and hence it set out to create breakthrough products. Design, they decided, was to be the key differentiator and they identified the capability for breakthrough design as a key skill gap in the design team. So Samsung decided to equip the design team with the most cutting-edge design tools with experts from the best design institutes in the US. While the capability building was successful, yet breakthroughs were absent. In getting to the heart of the issue, Samsung discovered that the real barrier was not the skill; it was the mindset gravity.

When challenged to create a breakthrough design for the world, what the Korean designers were unconsciously doing was *taking the latest from the US, combining it with the latest from Japan and the latest from Italy—these elements were then being put together and presented as a breakthrough design for the world!* There was nothing Korean in the design, all inspiration sources lay outside, in the developed markets.

The real breakthrough came when the designers challenged this cultural mindset gravity by realizing they couldn't beat the Italians at their game. Instead, they needed to create their own game. This eventual breaking through of mindset gravity led to product breakthroughs. The first big success was the clam-shaped Samsung phone, which went on to become a bestseller in the US in 2002. *The clam-shaped Samsung was a small phone for smaller hands, appropriate for the Koreans who are small-bodied people.* The designers had leveraged their cultural uniqueness.[9, 15]

Cultural Gravity: Reverse Engineering

Organizations and employees in underdeveloped countries often live in awe of those in the developed countries. As a result, they focus on seeking trends in developed markets and then adopt them or at best adapt them locally. In fact, a whole lot of savvy organizations have built *reverse engineering* into a core competency, with the success formula being—*pick up a successful product, process, model from the developed world, unscramble it, and put it together at a much lower cost and then take it to the market at a lower price point.*

Teaching breakthrough innovation skills to an organization with a *reverse engineering* mindset is unlikely to produce a Snow White. The new innovation skills will be deployed to reverse engineer even faster, at best leading to a cheaper and sometimes a better pig. A first-to-the-world, orbit-shifting innovation is only likely when the cultural gravity underlying *reverse engineering* is broken through, like Titan and Samsung did.

As a CEO, think about this:

No amount of skills and capability building helps when confronted with cultural mindset gravity. Tools and skills are ultimately subsumed by mindsets. The deeper the mindset, the deeper the need to acknowledge and break through it. What appears to be a skill gap could actually be the symptom of a deep-rooted mindset that has become gravity. Building new skills without confronting and overcoming the mindset gravity rarely ever works, since people deploy the new skills with the old mindset.

Where is your organization trying to build a new innovation capability?

What mindsets will act as gravity?

How can you break through these mindsets to leverage, rather than diminish, new capability?

Cultural Gravity: Fear of the Giant

The fact that building innovation capability is not enough came through equally strongly when Marico faced an extreme threat from Unilever. In the year 2000, Hindustan Unilever launched Nihar, to compete with Marico's leading brand Parachute (coconut oil). Hindustan Unilever's aggressiveness was visible in its extensive advertising campaign, outspending Marico at every step, its deafening voice drowning Marico out in the media. This was followed by worrying news from the field, where Marico sales personnel reported 'walls of green in retail stores'. Nihar's brand colour was green, while Parachute was blue. Visions of green walls became a nightmare for the Mariconians. The reality was that Parachute was the largest contributor in Marico's portfolio. If the blue walls of Parachute collapsed, it would certainly take Marico down with it; it was, in effect, a life-or-death situation. And Marico was, at that point of time, considered *a prime takeover target in industry circles.*

Rattled by this onslaught, Marico put together a high-level team to devise a creative-response strategy. This team *had previously been trained extensively in creativity with lateral thinking skills, so they should have been able to come up with creative strategies.* The team members came together for a two-day workshop and generated a host of ideas, none of which pointed to a breakthrough. They were hitting the wall of diminishing returns, by the end of two days. There was by now a growing sense of despair: 'What can we do, Hindustan Unilever is a giant; they have far greater resources than we do'.

Towards the evening of the second day when the leadership had also joined in, a deeper dialogue was triggered by this statement, made by Shreekant Gupte, the division head: 'Let's face it. We are all scared. The fact that we are sitting in this room, late in the evening, looking like this! We are afraid of what this might do to us.' From this emerged the mindset gravity; *the team members were struck with the realization that in their minds, they had already lost.* They were thinking like defenders!

Cultural gravity had reduced them to being defensive. They doubted their own ability to take on and win against a multinational giant.

No wonder most of the ideas that had been generated over the last two days were driven by *defensive but invisible questions: 'How can we prevent encroachment, how can we minimize loss?'* Finally, that evening they confronted and broke through their mindset gravity. *They made the shift from Defender to Attacker.* After all, they reckoned that while the MNC may be the muscled player in the FMCG market, in coconut oil, however, it was Marico that was the bigger and stronger player. So their focus shifted from 'rather than lose, we will increase our market share'. *And the new mantra they committed to was 'we cannot beat them with resources, we will beat them with ideas'.*

This shift led to a wave of new thought, orbit-shift possibilities opened up and the resulting new strategies were passionately pursued in the market. Instead of losing, Parachute actually gained its highest market share ever. Nihar was beaten back. Four years later, the cycle was completed when Hindustan Unilever sold Nihar to Marico.

The last decade has seen the emergence of entrepreneurial organizations that have lost the fear of giants. Earlier, the thought that the big guys were entering a territory left the smaller organizations in awe and fear because they felt they would be thoroughly beaten in the market. But as the world order changes, many are defying this gravity, as Marico did, and are stepping up to take on and beat back the giants. They have realized that 'you can't beat them with resources but you can beat them with ideas'.

Cultural Gravity breeds Arrogance

French Wines

While cultural subservience breeds self-doubt, cultural arrogance builds a blinding self-confidence that can become an equally strong force of gravity.

French wines are a living role model and a painful reminder of what cultural gravity in the form of cultural arrogance can do. For as long as the wine industry has existed, French wines have been the dominant market leaders. Spanning a history of 2,600 years, the image of France as the foremost creator of the finest wines was well-established. World over, wine was almost synonymous with French wine. However, in the late 20th and early 21st centuries, the predominance of French wines was challenged. Just like most industries, this market leader was confronted with a wave of challengers like the Californian, Australian, South African, and Chilean wines. These challengers saw an opportunity in targetting consumers outside of France, those who were just beginning to develop wine drinking as a habit. They began to make wines for the new adopters and to expand the wine market in other countries.

The French or old-world wines were traditionally more *terroir** and structure driven where the wine's personality is dependent on the location it is grown in. The important elements were the soil, weather, etc., which lead to wines being named after the place of origin, such as Burgundy, Bordeaux, Chablis, Alsace, Champagne etc. The challengers brought in the concept of industrial wines. They placed less sanctity on the location or *terroir*, and more on preservation of the fruit character. They believed that the harnessing of appropriate scientific and technological best practices in the vineyards and wineries could iron out any *terroir* imperfections. Hence, they were freed from the limitations of location and could source the grapes from across the land, as they were not locked into a particular vineyard. This industrialized model of winemaking made the new-world wines actually more consistent in quality than the single-vineyard wines from France. The new emerging consumers were also eager to try new wines.

The early warnings were visible to the French, but cultural arrogance became the gravity that blocked a creative response. The Paris Blind Test in 1976, or the Judgment Day as it is called, was the first explicit warning. French wine experts carried out a blind test comparing French wines with Californian wines. A Californian wine was rated best in each category. This was an earth-shattering event, but the French were in denial. *Le Figaro* (a French daily) published an article that virtually dismissed the result, terming it laughable. Six months later, *Le Monde* continued the denial in another dismissive article. Not only did the French refuse to accept the reality of the taste test, the French wines continued to be overpriced and under communicative.[16]

The Bordeaux vineyards were guilty of taking prices further upward in the 1980s and 1990s, to the extent that most wines became out of reach of the educated middle class, the broadest and most loyal market. These prolific spenders looked elsewhere and discovered the new-world wines where they found both 'quality and value'.

---

* A *terroir* is a group of vineyards (or even vines) from the same region, belonging to a specific appellation and sharing the same type of soil, weather conditions, grapes, and winemaking savoir-faire, which contribute to give its specific personality to the wine. Source: http://www.terroir-france.com/theclub/meaning.htm

Further, the French wine industry refused to acknowledge the barrier that the French language imposed on the non-European buyers or even non-French European buyers, for that matter. The French wine bottles were always labelled in French. *It doesn't matter if you cannot understand it, if it is French it must be good!* The new-world wines, on the other hand, were providing information about the fruit, the flavour, and even the food combination best suited for the wine. '*This is myopic marketing*,' said Jean-Claude Mas, a winemaker in the southern region of Languedoc, France. 'Our over arrogance caused us to ignore how serious the competition from the new world was.'

This cultural gravity caused the downfall of French wine; and their market share dropped to 17 percent.[8] Amazingly, a second blind test conducted thirty years after the Paris Judgment Day, comparing Californian and French wines, came through with the same result![7]

Only in the recent past have the French begun to adopt new world wine models to win back the market.

Cultural Gravity: Leads to Extinction

Mindset gravity doesn't merely drag down or annihilate orbit-shifting aspirations, it can have more disastrous consequences. Deep rooted, unquestioned, and unchallenged mindset gravity has not just led to the demise of organizations, it has led to the extinction of civilizations. As Jared Diamond so clearly brings alive in his book *Collapse*, the Norse in Greenland paid the ultimate price for not being able to confront deep-rooted cultural gravity.

Like most colonizers, the Norse entered Greenland with the intent of expanding their civilization. Rather than adapting to and finding new solutions for the challenges posed by Greenland, they tried to replicate their Norwegian way of life.

The Norse were essentially dairy farmers. They built their livelihood around breeding cows, goats, and sheep. When they reached Greenland, in 985 AD, the weather was mild, perfectly conducive to breeding livestock. Their livelihood became centred on dairy products in the winter and the meat of wild animals in the summer. In the month of May, the transition month between winter and summer, they were hugely dependent on migratory seals, because by now, the winter stock of dairy products was exhausted and summer hadn't fully set in.

By 1400-1420, the climate got colder. The Little Ice Age had set in. The seal migration reduced and this became the Norse's undoing. What makes this even more tragic is that a solution to this problem was actually literally around the corner. The Inuit, the local nomads of the region, had mastered the craft of hunting for whales in water and ice. Why didn't the Norse learn to cope with the Little Ice Age's cold weather by learning from the Inuit?

The reality is that the Norse had not only transported dairy farming to Greenland, but had also brought along their religious beliefs with Church bishops from Norway. Like most colonizers they had brought with them their deep-seated country and cultural beliefs. The Christian Norse therefore treated the Inuit as pagans. They didn't believe they could learn from them.[4]

As a CEO, think about this:

As Arnold Toynbee observed in his book, *The Study of World History*, 'Civilizations that have survived and thrived were those who found a new, creative response to the adversity that faced them'. The Norse failed to find a creative response and paid the heaviest price for it.

Orbit-shifters confront gravity while traditionalists accept it and accommodate it. Over time, they rationalize it and even joke about it. 'We are like this only'. However, behind that joke is a deep denial of gravity.

Where are you denying gravity?

What opportunities to renew and orbit-shift your organization will emerge if you acknowledge and challenge gravity?

CONFRONTING GRAVITY

What all these examples demonstrate is that in order to generate the escape velocity to puruse an orbit-shifting innovation, an organization needs to uncover, confront, and then consciously break through gravity: organizational, industry, country, and cultural gravity. The innovators who do this, create Snow Whites; while those who are trapped in gravity, replicate pigs.

Since the dawn of humankind, man has always gazed toward the sky, aspiring for, dreaming of, ways to break the bonds of earth. Nothing captures our imagination, our excitement as much as the human quest for space travel, because that's where we believe the greatest adventures now lie. First the moon, then Mars, then the outer reaches of the solar system, and beyond. James Cameron, however, turned 180 degrees in the opposite direction by going to the very depths of the Marina trench, a place so deep that it is a mile greater than the height of the Everest.[2] Fewer men have plumbed these depths than the numbers who have gone to space. This is an apt metaphor for organizations seeking to innovate. It is not the adventure outside, but the challenge inside that can make or break orbit-shifting innovation. It is not breaking the bonds of earth but breaking the gravity of the human mind—the mindset gravity—that is the greatest endeavour of them all.

Chapter 3

Take on an Orbit-shifting Challenge and Burn the Bridge

ALL EXCITEMENT AROUND INNOVATION IS CENTRED ON GETTING THE *BIG IDEA*. Thinking out of the box is talked about with obsession. The world of innovation is full of stories of how a leader got to an out-of-the-box idea that created a *transformative impact*.

Nearly all of these stories are really about incidental and accidental innovation. The core question is: *How do we make orbit-shifting innovation happen by design?*

The reality for most organizations is that layers and layers of gravity can make it very difficult to come up with an out-of-the-box idea. Come to think of it, out of which box is the real question. For there is the organizational gravity box, the industry gravity box, the country gravity box, and the cultural gravity box. The deeper you go, the more invisible the box becomes.

Most orbit-shifting innovations did not start with an out-of-the-box idea, but with an out-of-the-box challenge, an orbit-shifting challenge.

It takes an orbit-shifting challenge to create the escape velocity needed to break through gravity. An out-of-the-box idea is a consequence. An orbit-shifting challenge leads to an orbit-shifting idea and not the other way round.

THE ANSARI X PRIZE

One orbit-shifting challenge that truly created escape velocity was the Ansari

X Prize announced in 1996. The Ansari X Prize was a USD 10 million cash award to the first team that:

- privately finances, builds, and launches a spaceship capable of carrying three people to 100 km;
- returns safely to Earth; and
- repeats the launch with the same ship within two weeks.

The orbit-shifting element in the Ansari X Prize challenge was that each spaceship's development and launch had to be funded privately. Until this point, all Space ventures across the world had been government funded.[10] Further, it had to have the demonstrated capability to carry three people and to repeat the journey within two weeks, seeding the potential of Space tourism. This orbit-shifting challenge created the escape velocity for twenty-six teams to sign up and compete globally. Collectively, teams spent more than USD 100 million to find the solution. Eight years and countless prototypes later, a winner emerged. *Spaceship One* successfully completed two flights in the period September to October 2004.[9, 39]

The winning of the Ansari X Prize democratized space travel and launched an orbit-shifting idea—space tourism. Just the right trigger was created, where ideas met technology met funding met action and today, Space flight is in our grasp. The first tourists are set to go to space in our lifetime.

What the Ansari X prize demonstrates very clearly is that an out-of-the-box challenge, or what we call an orbit-shifting challenge, ignites otherwise dormant minds for a different order of ideas to emerge. Not ideas steeped in incrementalism, but ideas that make the impossible, possible.

FROM A QUIZ SHOW TO THE BIGGEST SHOW

In early 2000, Star TV was number three, behind Zee TV and Sony, in the TV entertainment channel space in India. Every year in the annual planning exercise, the leadership team would share with Rupert Murdoch the ten programmes that would take them to number one in the year. But until then none of those promises had materialized. The India team had just picked up *Who Wants to Be a Millionaire*, the most successful game show from the United States—for replication in India and it was one of their big bets for the coming year.

Rupert Murdoch asked an out-of-the-box question: 'What is the biggest draw on Indian TV?' The answer was: an India-Pakistan cricket match. And then the next question: 'What can be bigger than an India-Pakistan cricket match?' The answer: 'Only another India-Pakistan cricket match on a Sunday!' From this came the orbit-shifting challenge posed by Peter Mukerjea (former CEO, Star India) and Rupert Murdoch: 'Create a game show that will be as big as an India-Pakistan cricket match on a Sunday'. The first reaction of the team was one of disbelief, 'Impossible!' Only another India-Pakistan cricket match can do it and nothing else!

But, the *out-of-the-box challenge* led to an *out-of-the-box question*: Who is the one person who can bring the country to a halt for an hour? The answer: Amitabh Bachchan, India's mega movie star. This led to an out-of-the-box idea of making him—rather than a conventional quizmaster—the host. The jackpot prize was also increased from INR 1 million to INR 10 million (1 crore).

This led to *Kaun Banega Crorepati (KBC)*. Launched on July 3, 2000, the show was a runaway success. It created a world record in viewership. In only four weeks after the launch, nine out of every ten Indian cable and satellite viewers were exposed to *KBC*. Star TV's channel share went up from 2 percent to 25 percent. The one-hour show on Sunday froze all other channels. They were at a loss over how to respond.[33]

So powerful was the impact of *KBC* that it even became the subject matter of a book that was adapted into Oscar-winning movie *Slumdog Millionaire*. Without the orbit-shifting challenge, this would have been, at best, a better game show, and not the game changer that it became. A few years later, Peter Mukerjea said, 'Forty-six of top fifty programmes are Star. My only question is what are the other four?'

MONETIZE THE NON-MONETIZED

Korea's SK Telecom, on the other hand, posed an orbit-shifting challenge: *How do we monetize the non-monetized part of the network?* The pursuit of this orbit-shifting challenge stimulated one of their partner firms, SK WiderThan, to discover the blind spot: caller-to-receiver dialling. When the caller dialed a number, he/she waited for the phone to ring; this was downtime for the telecom company, where the network was being accessed but not charged for. SK Telecom introduced Ring Back Tones (RBT branded COLORing)—a service that comprehensively leveraged this non-productive call time. It played a ring-back melody, rather than the conventional ringtone, when a caller dialled the subscriber's number. This was advanced further with features like missed call alerts. In October 2002, just seven months after the launch, revenue from Ring Back Tones (COLORing) exceeded revenue from the ringtone download service.[37]

THE ORBIT-SHIFTING CHALLENGE VS PERFORMANCE GOALS

All three, Space Tourism, *KBC*, and Ring Back Tones, are orbit-shifting ideas that were triggered by an orbit-shifting challenge.

An orbit-shifting challenge provokes a new direction. It aims for transformative impact and deliberately decimates the current orbit. *It is never current-orbit forward because it cannot be achieved by doing more of the same.* What qualifies as an orbit-shifting challenge is one that is considered impossible when seen from the *current-orbit* lens.

Taking on and pursuing an orbit-shifting challenge triggers an orbit-shifting innovation by design. On the other hand, most well-managed organizations pursue a well-oiled goal-setting process—Management by Objectives (MBO). Here, an ideal goal is defined as challenging, while being realistic.

Realistic! What is the reference point of realistic? It is the current orbit. Making objectives realistic ends up accommodating the gravity embedded in the current orbit, rather than breaking through it.

As a CEO, think about this:

Management by Objectives is by now a norm in most organizations. However, it only serves orbit-maintaining innovation, resulting in most leaders taking on improvement goals.

To unleash orbit-shifting innovation, the organization needs to go beyond improvement and take on orbit-shifting challenges that are transformative, and by definition, impossible, given the reference point of the current orbit.

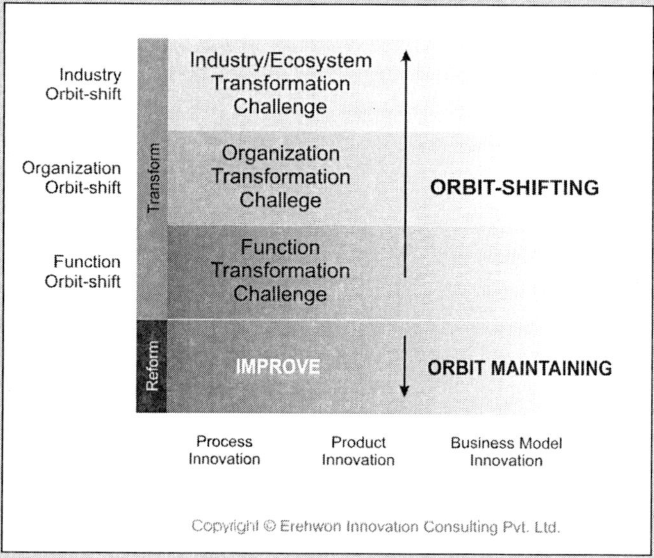

3.1 – Orbit-shifting Challenge Portfolio

Orbit-shifting challenges need to span across the orbit-shifting portfolio.

An Industry/ecosystem transformation challenge is aimed at creating an orbit-shift at the industry or ecosystem level.

For Vodafone M-PESA, using the mobile phone to create

financial access for the unbankable millions was an industry-transformation challenge. The business model innovation that followed created a new market for mobile operators.

The NovoPen® from Novo Nordisk was the outcome of product-led industry-transformation challenge. This drug delivery device has been a game changer in the diabetes care industry.[35]

Dainik Bhaskar adopted a process-led industry-transformation challenge. The newspaper took on an orbit-shifting challenge of achieving leadership from day one of a new city launch. It was truly an industry-transformation challenge, because leadership from day one of a new city launch was unthinkable in the conventional wisdom of the newspaper industry. They actually grew the market, as a large majority of households started buying two newspapers, rather than one.[26]

An industry-transformation challenge fuels a game changer while an organization-transformation challenge is aimed at transforming the organization's impact in the current game. An organization-transformation challenge taken on by a global firm in cold drinks was to 'double the market penetration in one country'. They found that cold drinks were being sold in less than 50 percent of the outlets that sold daily household products because their cold drink had to be made available cold at 4°C. To do this, the outlet needed a cooler, which most of them didn't have. The orbit-shifting challenge became to 'create a cooler that can make the cold drink available at the smallest outlet leading to doubling market penetration'. Another organization-transformation challenge taken on by the International Flavours and Fragrances (IFF) team was to 'double the strike rate of new client briefs'. Pursuing this challenge didn't merely lead to an improvement, it led to a transformation in the way they engaged with a new client brief. This transformation more than doubled the strike rate and fuelled quantum growth.

Pursuing industry- and organization-transformation challenges is powerful but it will only engage a few key people in a large organization. On the other hand, functional-transformation challenges are orbit-shifts that can be pursued right across the organization—both top down and bottom up.

Titan industries has championed and instituted orbit-shifting innovation on the shop floor.

Challenges like:

1) A breakthrough process, which increases the yield in gold casting from the global norm of 30 percent to 60 percent
2) To develop an XRF machine at 15 percent of the current procurement cost.
3) Reduce the lead time of the gold-quality checking process from the global average of two hours to two minutes.

Each of these challenges is not just an improvement. Instead, each one beats, rather than just meeting, global benchmarks.

As a CEO, think about this:

What does your current orbit-shifting challenge portfolio look like? What are the blindspots?

Are you pursuing orbit-shifting challenges with the same ferocity with which you pursue orbit-maintaining goals/performance goals? If not, why not? What is stopping you?

Redefine Goal Setting

To trigger orbit-shifting innovation by design, organizations need to start by going beyond performance goals. They need to redefine goal setting into a twin-track exercise: orbit-maintaining PLUS orbit-shifting goals. A powerful principle is: for every three orbit-maintaining (performance) goals, a leader needs to take on at least one orbit-shifting challenge.

Adopting and institutionalizing the 3+1 twin-track goal-setting construct will unleash orbit-shifting innovation by design.

Going further, by ensuring orbit-shifting challenges are not skewed, but straddle across process, product, and business models and at all orbit-shift levels, a leader will ensure a powerful orbit-shifting portfolio: to not just build competitive advantage but sustain and grow future advantage. Twin-track goal setting is a powerful way to embed strategic flexibility into the organization's DNA.

TRIGGERING THE ORBIT-SHIFTING CHALLENGE

How does a leader or an organization go about uncovering and identifying orbit-shifting challenges? What are the new reference points? What triggers the identification of an orbit-shifting challenge as against a traditional performance goal?

Most traditional goal-setting exercises get consciously or unconsciously rooted into the reference points of the current orbit. Last year's achievements and industry projections become the first reference point for next year's goals.

Orbit-shifters, unlike followers, don't reference last year and create stretch goals. They trigger orbit-shifting challenges with a series of nine triggers.

1st Trigger: Discovering a Positive Inflection Point

While followers look at market trends, orbit-shifters sense a positive inflection point in the market—*an ecosystem need gap that when bridged, can unleash a huge wave of demand.*

The Healthy Inbetween

In the last decade, increasing awareness about the impact of food and the environment on health has been a trend relentlessly on the rise. From fast food to pollutants in ingredients to healthier ways of cooking, whole nations are beginning to realize that unless they control how and what they eat, and where they source it from, the long-term impact of both obesity and disease is high. This is the positive inflection point that Food Doctor, a nutritional practice in the UK, identified early on, when the company began in 1999.

Michael da Costa, who heads Food Doctor, remembers, 'It was the early days of health and nutrition seeping into public awareness and we realized there was a gap; the food in between meals was unhealthy, tasty, and guilt inducing. We felt Food Doctor had the unique opportunity to convert *in-between food to healthy food.*' This became their orbit-shifting challenge. What Michael had done was to identify a market inflection point: consumers had increasing access to and could create healthy meals; but there was no such thing as a *healthy in-between* and here is where consumers were now seeking *taste good and do good*, rather than only the *taste good* snacks.[42]

A Call at the Cost of a Postcard

Dhirubhai Ambani of Reliance Industries sensed a positive inflection point in the telecom market in India. On a trip to Gujarat, what hit him was that while millions of Indians are illiterate and can't read or write, they can talk. A telephone call at the cost of a postcard could transform the lives of millions who could not afford to make a call and who could not write a letter or a postcard.[40]

He converted this into an orbit-shift challenge for his newly formed telecom team—*a call at the cost of a postcard*! This orbit-shifting challenge, when announced in the papers, shook the telecom industry in India. The industry players viewed the Reliance challenge seriously because Reliance is known for executing mega projects in record time.

With this orbit-shifting challenge, Dhirubhai had successfully moved not just his team, but the entire industry to think out of the box.

Bharti Airtel was also propelled to think out of the box, and it set up a crack team to find and launch a solution to meet this challenge and do it in ninety days, even earlier than Reliance. This Airtel crack team literally scoured the world for solutions. It was in this search that the team came across the prepaid card in the Philippines. It actually took not three, but four months to bring the prepaid solution to market (Easy Charge!), but Airtel did become the first to launch the prepaid solution in India and then went on to develop a breakthrough business model to make the prepaid solution economically viable.

As a CEO, think about this:

A positive inflection point can be an ecosystem need gap that when solved for can become a mass movement. 'A call at the cost of postcard' was one such positive inflection point, that when solved, became a mass movement that has created over 900-million mobile technology adopters in India.

Where do you sense a positive inflection point in your market?

Sensing a positive inflection point and converting it into an ambitious orbit-shifting challenge could create history in your world.

2nd Trigger: Design for Extreme Conditions

Space Food

Extreme conditions present extreme challenges. There are many instances when orbit-shifting innovation has emerged when a society or an organization has been thrust into extreme conditions. Coming up with solutions for an army that is based in extreme terrain and for astronauts in space have led to an array of new ideas. While most of these orbit-shifting innovations have been reactive, Arla Foods took on an extreme conditions challenge proactively.

The extreme conditions challenge began in 2001 for Arla, a Denmark/Sweden-based company, when Michael Stevns, their innovation director, was pondering on how to find a radical challenge that would stretch Arla's products and capabilities to a new level. Without a radical challenge, he felt that all innovation would, at best, be incremental.

Then one day on a flight, inspiration struck at 9,144 metres (30,000 feet). He met a co-passenger who was telling him how NASA had approached his company for collaboration and he'd turned them down. A bulb went on in Michael's head. *He'd been looking for an extreme challenge that would force Arla to really push the envelope and he had just found it: they would create milk-based foods/dairy products for Space.* He brought in Carsten Hallund Slot, a leader with extreme drive and a history of closing challenging projects, to head up the project.

Michael and Carsten decided to call the project Lacmos—lac for milk and mos for cosmos. They identified the potential spin-offs for both NASA and Arla from Project Lacmos. NASA was interested in nutrition for astronauts. In Space, and under zero gravity, there are a number of debilitating physiological changes that astronauts go through, one of which is loss of bone density. Astronauts lose as much as 1 percent of bone density every month. Some other issues are muscle atrophy, loss of blood volume, etc. Carsten and Michael thought that if they could address some of these problems through milk-based products, NASA would be even more interested.

But what about Arla? What would be the spin-offs and potential benefits for Arla Foods? For without spin-offs for Arla, it was unlikely that the top management would bankroll the project. Interestingly, bone density loss is a common result of ageing and geriatrics and also for bed-rest patients. Each of us loses bone density at the rate of 10 percent over ten years between the ages of 50 to 60. If Arla could find a way to prevent or slow down loss of bone density in conditions as challenging and as extreme as Space, a market would definitely exist back on Earth. Also, developing these products would force them to go beyond usual Earth-based formats. For example, they would need to create chewy milk bites, as neither liquid nor powder would do in a zero gravity environment. Yoghurt would need to last at least two years without refrigeration, as refrigeration took up too much power and could not be used on the space station. Out of this thinking, Project Lacmos, an orbit-shifting challenge, was born.

As a CEO, think about this:

Designing for the normal, average-use conditions is likely to produce more of the same. Designing for extreme conditions will move the thinking out of the box, new dots will need to be joined.

Where is your work interfacing with an extreme condition? Don't ignore it.

How can you convert it into an orbit-shifting challenge instead?

What could be the most extreme-use conditions for your product/process?

How can solving this extreme challenge unlock a different or an even bigger market opportunity?

3rd Trigger: Turning Around a Threat

Innovate the Conventional

When faced with a threat, gravity-infested followers play safe and even withdraw into a shell. Orbit-shifters turn a threat into an orbit-shifting challenge.

Mico Bosch demonstrated how a *threat to survival* can trigger an orbit-shifting challenge that leads to a path-breaking idea. The emergence of a new technology was an imminent threat to the existing, older technology. Mico Bosch India was the centre of excellence (for Bosch, Germany) for single-cylinder pumps, called PF pumps, for diesel engines. But as the world moved to higher and tougher emission norms, a new technology called the Common Rail (CR) system had been developed. To go beyond the Euro 3 emission norms to Euro 4, 5, and 6 would need the high-pressure pump of the CR system; the older technology of PF pumps could only meet Euro 2 norms.

Moving to Euro 4 and higher norms also called for the older diesel engine manufacturers to shift to CR systems. This meant making extensive modifications to the design of the diesel engine, which could cost anywhere from 3 to 20 million Euros. Even within Bosch India, there was the feeling that *CR is the present and PF is the past*. The CR team looked at the PF team as relics who would be phased out in time. The parent organization's focus was also towards CR, as the torchbearer of the future. Questions about the contribution of the PF product-development team were beginning to be raised internally. After all, they were just modifying and tweaking Bosch Germany's products.[21]

Out of this threat was born an orbit-shifting challenge: *innovate the conventional PF pump to meet Euro 4 norms*. The PF team took on this impossible challenge and found a reason to make themselves relevant again.

Camel Racing

Camel racing is a traditional bedouin sport in the Middle East. Over the years, it has become more commercial and competitive with huge prize monies. It is a multimillion-dollar industry today, with its own camel-breeding programmes, retinue of specialists and trainers, and even an exclusive TV channel dedicated to the racing season.

However, hidden within it was a dirty secret. Racing speed is dictated by the size of the jockey, and therefore, it is more likely that an animal is faster with a lighter and smaller jockey. Beginning in the early 1970s, the competition to be faster and speedier than others escalated, and smaller, younger children were sought to jockey—children as young as 4 to 8 years. These children were imported from countries as far as Pakistan and Bangladesh, from poor families who traded their children in for a few hundred dollars or for the fame of camel jockeying, unaware or uncaring of its dangers.

Child jockeys face great risks during the races; with camels speeding at 50 km an hour, a child jockey can be trapped underfoot, maimed, or killed. Training conditions are harsh, and the children were, no doubt, exploited. Worse still, they had become a lost generation of strangers to their parents and cultures.

In the early part of the century, increasing international and national pressure put the spotlight on what UNICEF called the 'worst form of child labour'. Sheikh Hamdan Bin Zayed Al Nahyan of the UAE announced a ban on all child jockeys on July 29, 2002.[21] (Children under 16 and weighing less than 45 kg.) Qatar followed, when Sheikh Hamad Bin Khalifa Al-Thani declared a complete ban on child jockeys *and ordered that by 2007, all races would be conducted with, unbelievable as it sounds, robotic jockeys.*[2]

In the face of international scorn and with national honour at stake, both UAE and Qatar first banned child jockeys and then threw an orbit-shifting challenge: *create robotic jockeys that will mimic child jockeys*. And so, while a traditional approach could have led to the races dying out or a refusal to adapt to the threat of changing demands, the visionary approach adopted by the leaders of the two nations leveraged technology, to create a whole new era of camel racing—robot jockeys are a reality today. The industry has revived and revitalized itself. Camels ridden by robot jockeys are in turn guided by handlers racing in vehicles, parallel to the track, with remote controls in hand.[19]

It's not just all about the business of racing. A second, very human challenge, emerged with how to repatriate the child jockeys. A simple way could have been to just send them back to their homes and parents. However, the UAE government was committed to fully reintegrating each child back into his original habitat. 'We didn't want to just collect all the children and send them back home with nothing. We wanted to address this in a humanitarian way and solve the problem at the source,' said Colonel Najim A. Alhosani, director of the community policing pepartment, Ministry of Interior, Abu Dhabi.

And therefore, the UAE government, UNICEF, the International Organization for Migration, and representatives from government and non-governmental organizations of the countries of origin of the child jockeys, like Bangladesh, Pakistan, Sudan, and Mauritania, met in May 2005 to pledge to an end-to-end action plan and repatriate close to 3,000 underage jockeys in UAE. The UAE government and UNICEF agreed to provide USD 2.7 million, and the countries of origin agreed to build initiatives to not just repatriate the children, but also reintegrate them meaningfully into their families and society.[41]

The Film: 300

In the early years of the new century, the big studio, Warner Brothers, had had its fingers burnt with two successive big budget movie duds in the genre known as 'swords and sandals' films, which were based on Greek mythology. Both *Troy* (helmed by Brad Pitt, Orlando Bloom, and many other A-list stars, and directed by Wolfgang Petersen) and *Alexander* (directed by Oliver Stone, with Colin Farrell and Angelina Jolie) underperformed against the expected box office earnings. *Troy* at USD 175 million,[6] was one of the most expensive films made in the modern era.

Zack Snyder entered this context with the dream of making yet another 'swords and sandals' film—*300*, based on Frank Miller's iconic 1998 graphic novel.[7] The studio, in spite of the threat of the previous failures, bought into his vision and gave him the green signal. However, in translating *300* to the screen, Snyder's mandate from the studio, according to producer Bernie

Goldmann, was 'to create a world that you hadn't seen before, to reinvent the epic movie and do it much less expensively'. At about a third of the cost of *Troy* and *Alexander*, that meant no big marquee names.

Snyder took on the challenge and made one of the most successful films of 2007, with a then little-known actor, Gerard Butler in the lead role. *300* pulled in USD 70 million in its opening weekend, and grossed a business of USD 450-plus million worldwide[23] (including USD 210 million from North America).[8]

As James Cameron says of the film: 'There are filmmakers that come along that are quite iconoclastic. And that I'm in awe of, frankly. Zack Snyder's *300*. I think that was a really revolutionary film...'[45]

So the context in which Snyder had to make *300* was certainly an orbit-shifting challenge—*two big failures, half the budget, and no stars.* Snyder could have played it safe and more conventional. Instead, he went the other way. With the extensive use of CGI (Computer Generated Imagery), a graphic-novel feel and texture, and with a big launch at Comic-Con targetting the right audience—young adult males—the film went on to create movie history.[24]

As a CEO, think about this:

What are the market or technology threats facing you?
What could be the orbit-shifting challenge that could turn around and transform the threat into an opportunity?

4th Trigger: Making an Exception the New Reference Point

Some followers look at the average and create stretch goals, others benchmark with the industry best practices and create catch-up goals. Orbit-shifters go beyond the average, go beyond best practices. They search for the exception, across industries and domains, and make the exception the reference point for an orbit-shifting challenge.

From Sake Brewery to SK-II

SK-II, a skin care brand (from P&G, Proctor and Gamble), as P&G announced in an article in *pgscience.com*, 'has become one of two P&G brands to recently achieve billion-dollar status'. *What is fascinating is that the successful brand of today originated due to the spotting of an exception, almost forty years ago,* which then triggered an orbit-shifting challenge.

To quote from an article in *pgscience.com*: 'The achievement has been more than 40 years in the making, dating back to the 1970s, when scientists were developing a skincare line called "Secret Key." Their mission: To find the "secret key" to crystal clear skin a naturally derived ingredient that made skin more beautiful.

"During a chance observation of workers at a sake brewery in Japan, scientists noticed the elderly workers had wrinkled faces, but something was causing their hands to stay smooth, clear and younger looking," said Dr Colin D'Silva, Associate Director of External Relations for SK-II. "Their hands were in constant contact with the yeast fermentation process."

'Researchers discovered that the sake fermentation process created a natural by-product: a clear, nutrient-rich liquid that could nourish and care for skin. Research into the yeast fermentation process began, and after years of study involving more than 350 different strains of yeast, scientists were able to isolate a naturally occurring yeast that could produce a nutrient-rich ferment filtrate. They called it Pitera™.

'A blend of vitamins, amino acids, minerals and organic acids that work together to allow the skin's natural surface rejuvenation process to function at its prime, Pitera™ is similar in composition to the skin's natural moisturizers and makes skin crystal clear. The ingredient was added to the "Secret Key" skin care line. The brand was renamed SK-II and was launched in December 1980.'

This orbit-shifting innovation that started with a chance observation in a sake brewery is today a billion-dollar brand. As the article in *pgscience.com* states: 'SK-II has touched and improved the lives of millions of women around the world. As a leading skin care brand in Asia, it is sold in

13 markets, including Japan, Korea, China, Taiwan, Hong Kong, Malaysia, Singapore, Thailand, Indonesia, Australia, USA, UK, and Spain.'[34]

The Most-Watched Show

The *KBC* orbit-shifting challenge came to life when Rupert Murdoch and Peter Mukerjea asked 'what is the most-watched TV programme in India' and 'not what is most-watched game show in India'. *They made the exception across all TV formats as the reference point,* and this went on to trigger the orbit-shifting challenge—make the Indian version of *Who Wants to be a Millionaire* as big as an India-Pakistan cricket match on a Sunday.

The F1 Pit Stop

A low-cost airline was constantly on the lookout for ways to cut and even eliminate cost. A prime focus was the turnaround time of an aircraft, from landing to take off. How could they reduce turnaround time? Rather than going the usual way, which would have led to a target like, 'reduce the turnaround time by 10 to15 percent', they asked themselves a new question. What is the most exceptional turnaround time that they had ever seen? The answer bubbled up quickly—the F1 pit stop. The pit-stop turnaround is in seconds, at most a minute!

The F1 pit stop became the new reference point; it inspired the leader and the team to make this exception their orbit-shifting challenge—aircraft turnaround like a pit stop.

This orbit-shifting challenge provoked out-of-the-box ideas leading to the turnaround time coming down to a dramatic 20 minutes.

As a CEO, think about this:

Traditionalists focus on the average; they treat exceptional events/occurrences as abnormalities to be ignored. For orbit-shifters, what is an exception today could be the norm tomorrow.

Acting like an orbit-shifter, look for: the absolute exceptions in your industry. What is an exception across industries? For each reference point defining the current orbit, look for an abnormality, look for an exception—within the industry and across industries.

Make the exception the new reference point of the next orbit-shifting challenge.

5th Trigger: Rediscovering Lost Pride

Sometimes, it is not an intellectual but an emotional trigger that leads to an orbit-shifting challenge.

The positive provocation to reclaim lost pride can lead to an orbit-shifting challenge with the highest escape velocity. Nothing fires up people more than reclaiming dented pride. They are willing to go to extraordinary lengths to reclaim it.

Mahatma Gandhi lived a good barrister's life under the flag of the British government, until his moment-of-truth incident occurred, where he was humiliated and discriminated against when he had done no wrong. Who doesn't remember the brilliantly wrought moment in the Oscar-winning film *Gandhi*, which brought alive in full emotion, the pain and impact of Gandhi being thrown out of a train, in spite of being in possession of a legitimate ticket? That fall on the platform encapsulates his provocation, the defining moment when he came to the painful realization that following the English law to the letter wasn't necessarily going to produce equality. And it was this trigger that initiated the orbit-shifting campaign of non-violence. Atal Bihari Vajpayee (former Prime Minister of India) said, on visiting the location where Gandhi was thrown out of the train in South Africa, 'This catalysed Gandhi's transformation from a barrister to the Mahatma'.[4]

This is precisely what a provocation does. It shakes up some very settled beliefs that have gone unquestioned, and provokes the aspiration of a new reality. Such a powerful provocation can fuel even very settled minds into an orbit-shifting challenge.

National Pride was Hurt

Varaprasad Reddy was similarly provoked. As an ex-government employee between jobs, who was twiddling his thumbs in his cousin's house in the United States, he chanced upon a cheap airline ticket and so accompanied his cousin to an International Health conference in Europe. At the conference, he came across hepatitis B for the first time and discovered it to be a far bigger threat to Indian lives than AIDS. In fact, the hepatitis B virus is carried by about 4.75 percent of the Indian population, *that's 42 million walking atom bombs*[44] *and kills 3,40,000 people every year. Yet, as it is not as sexy a disease as AIDS, it receives very little funding.* The vaccine cost was INR 2,250 for three doses in 1991. Hence, south Asia had no option but to beg its western counterparts for cheaper drugs. He experienced first-hand the derogatory remarks westerners made about south Asians and it cut him to the quick: 'Here come these Indians with their begging bowls again'. Varaprasad Reddy was shocked. He asked the other Indians, 'Aren't you offended by this demeaning and disrespectful treatment?' The others, by now settled in the ways of the world, replied nonchalantly that there was nothing to be offended about, when the truth is, south Asians do indeed beg for cheaper vaccines. It was this treatment, which others considered normal, that insulted Varaprasad deeply. In fact he was so personally offended that he *took the out-of-the-box challenge upon himself to create India's first indigenous recombinant DNA hepatitis B vaccine—an INR 50 vaccine per dose, 94 percent cheaper.* It took seven years of trials and tribulations before it actually happened. But, Varaprasad Reddy never forgot this provocation: *Indians are beggars.* This provoked his pride and led to the successful Shanvac vaccine that finally sold at INR 150 for three doses, transforming the accessibility to safe vaccines for hepatitis B across India.[28]

When you speak to Varaprasad Reddy, he says very simply, 'I was provoked, my national pride was hurt.' Positive provocation can trigger orbit-shifting challenges that lead to a positive life-changing impact.

The Street Fighter

But it's not only individuals who get provoked and rediscover pride, sometimes an entire team, or division, or organization can get provoked, so that it becomes positively restless and even angry with the current status quo.

The hygiene division of Unilever in Indonesia was part of a well-performing organization. Unilever Indonesia was outstripping performance, constantly paying out maximum bonuses; a star in the Unilever Asia sky. It was winning awards as the best company in Asia, beating out Toyota, Singapore Airlines, Lenovo, etc. Hygiene in Unilever Indonesia was the biggest of all divisions, responsible for about 40 percent of the turnover, but had been performing poorly for five years, especially in the laundry category. It was in this scenario that Laercio Cardoso, a Brazilian, arrived to lead the hygiene division. As he says, 'When I arrived in Jakarta, I found the hygiene division in disarray. The laundry category was de-growing and its market share was fast plummeting behind the local upstart, Wings.'

However, what really caught his attention and became a major cause for concern was the team morale. 'But worse than the market performance was the hygiene team morale, the team energy was at its nadir, the relationships adversarial, and the environment detractive.'

The team had begun to believe it could not win in the market. Even worse, it was fast losing credibility inside Unilever Indonesia and was seen as a pariah that could not perform. Within the organization, people did not want to be associated with hygiene. Laercio says, 'The hygiene team was very frustrated. At quarterly company meetings when the results of each division were presented, the hygiene team only showed excuses for its poor performance. Embarrassed, walking around the conference room with their heads down, avoiding their peers, and feeling shame and guilt for staining the company's amazing track record, the hygiene team was isolated. They did not live the Unilever Indonesia winning pride and spirit.'

Laercio Cardoso inspired and provoked his team to reclaim this lost pride, both internally and in the market. They put their hearts and minds together and came through with an inspiring orbit-shifting challenge—Street Fighter: Move out of comfort zones and win the market street by street, fight for credibility and margin, fight for redemption and volume.

And nine months from this point, the hygiene division had undergone an amazing turnaround. They had beaten back Wings in the market, outstripped the growth aspiration that Laercio had started with, and reclaimed their pride in Unilever Indonesia.

Man on the Moon

Not just a division or an organization, a country can get provoked too. In April 1961, during the Cold War, the United States was provoked when the Russians shocked them by putting a man, Yuri Gagarin, into orbit. On May 25 that year, the then US president, John F. Kennedy, made the speech to a special joint session of Congress announcing his dramatic promise to the nation: that America would put a man on the moon before the end of the decade. It was vision driven as much by pressure and embarrassment as by aspiration. The Americans had been beaten not once, but twice by the Russians—in 1957 by launching the world's first manmade satellite into Space, *Sputnik 1*, and now again, by Yuri Gagarin's orbit of Earth. JFK could take no more. He had been provoked to make a public promise that would capture the imagination of the world and reclaim American pride as the first nation of the world by beating the Russians in the Space race.[17] The rest, as we know, is history.

As a CEO, think about this:

Where has your team lost pride?
Where have you been taken for granted?
Where will you never be good enough?
What will it take for you to be provoked, for you to rediscover your lost pride?
How can this be at the heart of your next orbit-shifting challenge?

6th Trigger: Refusing to Accept a Sub-optimal Equilibrium

Gravity creates comfort zones and comfort zones lead to the acceptance and even rationalization of sub-optimal equilibriums. A sub-optimal equilibrium occurs when a community or society has learnt to live with an inequality or a gap that causes great dissatisfaction as an inherent part of life.

Orbit-shifting challenges get triggered when an orbit-shifter spots and chooses to eliminate a sub-optimal equilibrium rather than live with it.

Fabio Rosa recognized a sub-optimal equilibrium in Brazil. He realized that lack of electricity was making farming significantly less productive and causing people to flock to cities in pursuit of a better life. It was this realization of a sub-optimal equilibrium that triggered him to take on the orbit-shifting challenge of transforming access to electricity in rural Brazil.[5]

Dr Venkataswamy saw a sub-optimal equilibrium in eye care that 'millions of Indians in rural India lose eyesight because they just don't know that they are suffering from cataracts and that cataracts are curable'. He took on an orbit-shifting challenge to eliminate needless blindness. This out-of-the-box challenge provided the escape velocity that led to the breakthrough in the cataract surgery process.[29]

A team at Arla Foods hit upon a sub-optimal equilibrium in the milk-and-dairy ecosystem. The team realized that the power of choice is centralized in the hands of a retailer. It was the retailer who decided both the type (in terms of fat content) and the variety of dairy products, and the quantity to be put out on the shelves. It was really the retailer who was dictating the needs of the consumer and directing how the industry should be shaped. As the team reflected and dialogued around the industry power equation and its interplay, the direction for a powerful orbit-shifting challenge began to emerge. Their orbit-shifting challenge became: *democratize milk to shift the power of choice from the retailer to the consumer.*

The Person Who Clears Dead Bodies

Anshu Gupta, a young student aspiring to become a journalist, had a life-changing experience on the streets of Delhi. One winter morning, Anshu found himself with his camera in Old Delhi looking for an interesting story. He caught sight of an unusual placard behind a cycle rickshaw driven by a very old man with his wife. The sign read: Dilli Pulis ka Laash Dhonewala (the person who clears dead bodies for the Delhi police). Habib and his blind wife Amana Begum had a strange occupation. They were responsible for picking up and disposing of unclaimed bodies on the streets of Delhi, bodies where no foul play was suspected. He was given INR 20 and three yards of cloth for each body and had to cart them away to the nearest crematorium. Anshu, intrigued by this story, spent some time following Habib and his wife and learnt that the body count went up drastically in winters. Naturally, the reason was insufficient protection from the cold. Try as he might, Anshu could not shake off his anger at the apathy that was causing these deaths on the streets of Delhi. And so while most people accept the cold streets of Delhi as a given from the warmth of their house, Anshu was haunted by the dead bodies in the cold and decided to do something.

Anshu had been confronted with a sub-optimal equilibrium—he could not accept the extreme apathy that this situation demonstrated, that the body count went up drastically in winter purely due to lack of protective clothing! Clothing, he realized, was not even on the national or global developmental agenda.

From here emerged Anshu's orbit-shifting challenge. There are many people and organizations that tackle poverty, hunger, and education, but very few actually tackle clothing. 'I want to put clothing at the centre of the global development agenda,' said Anshu. And thus Anshu's NGO, GOONJ—Voices That Won't Be Silenced—was born. He set about finding ways to address the dignity and survival of individuals by having their bodies covered and protected.[3]

As a CEO, think about this:

Refuse to accept a sub-optimal equilibrium.

The indicators of sub-optimal equilibrium are clearly the points where a market or a community has become used to, and learnt to live with, a high degree of dissatisfaction. This state of first getting used to and then starting to live with some kind of a dissatisfaction is a sub-optimal equilibrium waiting to become an orbit-shifting challenge.

What are the sub-optimals in your industry? Where have you accepted and learnt to live with the sub-optimal? What is stopping you from taking on an 'eliminate the sub-optimal' orbit-shifting challenge?

This is one potential orbit-shifting challenge that just can't wait.

7th Trigger: Pursuing a Cause Adjacency

What do we do when we reach a point where growing a business is not enough to motivate us; where business as usual has reduced itself to a series of meaningless chores without inspiration or drive? Most people give up or get out. However, orbit-shifters can literally reinvent the path forward by finding a cause adjacency to the business: Where a cause becomes the anchor around which the next business is built or pursued.

Vodafone and Millennium Development Goals (MDGs)

Vodafone put a cause at the centre and found a completely new business, one that it wouldn't have discovered in the normal trajectory of business development—M-PESA, or mobile cash delivered through the mobile network. As Nick Hughes, who led the creation of M-PESA for Vodafone writes, 'Why and how does a telecom company like Vodafone start a banking project like this? It's not part of Vodafone's core business; it was not developed in a core market (Kenya is a relatively small market in Vodafone's terms); and it has little to do with the voice or data products that drive Vodafone's revenue streams. Telecom companies are young and fast moving; banks are old, traditional, conservative, and slow moving'.

How did Vodafone come up with M-PESA? Because it was looking for a cause to support, and found it in the Millennium Development Goals (MDGs). In fact, Nick was brought in with the mandate to understand how Vodafone could contribute to the MDGs. One of the eight MDGs is the commitment to reduce poverty by 50 percent by 2015. It is here that Nick found a possible fit for Vodafone—creating financial access through the mobile.

An unorganized market economy has trouble in cash transactions. Without a bank account or the assistance of any technology, people in remote villages and towns across the world have struggled to pay and send money. And yet, as Nick says, 'The ability to move it from A to B—the so-called "velocity of money"—has been a fundamental cornerstone of economic activity.' And from here emerged the orbit-shifting challenge that wed Vodafone to the cause. 'Enter telecom network operators, who can adapt mobile technology to deliver financial services in a fast, secure and low cost way, especially in the developing parts of the world where microfinance institutions have begun to spread and begun to build infrastructure'. M-PESA was the result of this orbit-shifting challenge.[18]

Cloth is the Business; Saving Lives is the Cause

Vestergaard Frandsen began life as a uniform-making company. How did it transmute into *preventing water-communicable diseases* with the LifeStraw? On the surface, it seems to be a completely different business, but when we go to the heart of the matter, the real trigger emerges. Torben Frandsen took over the company from his father Kaj in 1970. In 1990, he bought one million yards of Swedish army surplus fabric, which was made into blankets for aid organizations, the company's first foray into aid. When his son Mikkel joined the company with a background of having worked in Africa, *he transformed his passion for the continent into a viable business proposition of saving lives with textiles.* In doing so, Mikkel found a cause adjacency. *While most people look for business or market adjacencies, what Mikkel had done was to find a cause adjacent to his business.* Could he save lives by leveraging textiles and merge his passion with his profession?

Indeed he could and he did. At the centre of LifeStraw is the cloth-based filter membrane.

Today, Vestergaard Frandsen is twice the size than when Mikkel joined and has several disease-control textile-based products including LifeStraw, PermaNet—a mosquito net impregnated with a long-lasting insecticide—and ZeroFly—durable plastic sheeting coated with insecticide.[43,44]

As a CEO, think about this:

What both Nick Hughes of Vodafone and Mikkel Frandsen of Vestergaard Frandsen did effectively was find the cause that resonated with business and make it an orbit-shifting challenge. Solving for these challenges has created a transformative impact.

Look beyond market adjacencies; look for a cause adjacency.

What is the cause your business can serve?

What is the biggest cause adjacent to your business?

Taking on a cause can become the next orbit-shifting challenge to transform your business.

8th Trigger: Not Targetting the Best Possible, but the Theoretical Best

AT&C Losses

'*What is practical*' and '*What is possible?*' are the two core questions rooted in the current orbit. They incessantly become the gravity that reduces a challenge to the point of being immediately doable.

In 2002, Tata Power-DDL (previously known as New Delhi Power Ltd) had set about trying to reduce aggregate, technical, and commercial (AT&C) losses. AT&C losses can be as high as 70 percent. The team quickly managed to bring down AT&C losses from 53 percent to 19 percent. This was, as the team leader said, 'Low-hanging fruit, just effective administration was enough.' But the real challenge was in reducing the loss below 19 percent. Now every next percent was tough.

An innovation team was formed and they were asked to define their challenge. The first challenge definition read: 'Reduce AT&C losses from 19 percent to 15 percent', because this was the best that had been achieved in India. When provoked further, with reference to the global standards, they took on the challenge to bring it down to 13 percent.

Then they were asked an orbit-shift question: 'What is the theoretical best? Don't look at existing benchmarks, just define the theoretical best.' The theoretical best, according to them, was 9 percent. The final orbit-shifting challenge surfaced from shifting the reference point from the best in India to the best in the world to the theoretical best. This was taken on in 2008.

Chasing the theoretical best forced the team to suspend judgement and look for fundamental breakthroughs and not just solutions as good as the best in the world. The breakthroughs that followed brought down the AT&C losses to 10 percent by 2012.

As a CEO, think about this:

Where are you ignoring theoretical bests because you believe they can only be achieved on paper, not in real life?

How can taking on the theoretical best fuel your next orbit-shifting challenge?

9th Trigger: Transforming the Input-Output Equation

Orbit-shifters transform the input-output equation. They do this by taking on orbit-shifting challenges that upend the established input-output equation. They take on development and growth challenges that are deliberately non-linear.

The Ansari X Prize was a non-linear orbit-shifting challenge. It questioned the input-output equation of the domain of space travel by demanding a privately funded spaceship that can carry at least three people to space. The dependence of space travel on government funding (the input) had been virtually taken for granted till that point.

Challenging the Input-Output Equation in Drug Development

Scott Johnson, a business consultant and entrepreneur, was afflicted with multiple sclerosis (a disease that affects the protective myelin tissue of the brain and spinal cord) at the age of 20 (in 1976).

Twenty-six years later, he decided to do something about it, rather than keep waiting in hope for some treatment. Why does it take so long to bring a workable drug to market? According to Johnson, USD 139 billion is invested in medical research every year, of which there are 8,00,000 research papers published by academia, and 21 drugs are finally approved by the FDA. There is something hugely wrong in the input-output ratio; where so much money is being pumped in for so little output.[16, 32]

This triggered the creation of the Myelin Repair Foundation (MRF) in 2002, with the orbit-shifting challenge to shorten the time to market for myelin repair treatment for multiple sclerosis and in doing so, revolutionize the process of all medical treatment.

Why is there this huge gap between investment in research and the number of new drugs that get introduced to the market? The issue is that academia is driven to publish, this is their end goal, and pharma is driven by shareholder value. As a result, a *valley of death* is created; a black box where research accumulates for it and proves early possibilities, but not enough for a pharma company to put up millions of dollars to convert a possibility into a working solution. This is where MRF comes in. With a dedicated science team, it collaborates across labs to pick up early possible indicative research and convert it, through its translational medical platform and clinical trials, into drugs attractive enough for pharma companies to invest in. It forms the bridge across the valley of death.[32]

'When Johnson started his foundation (in 2002), he was told myelin repair treatments were at least thirty years away. Today, researchers at the Cleveland Clinic are recruiting patients for a clinical trial of one potential treatment that grew out of studies Johnson's centre helped fund.'

NASA has also consulted the Myelin Repair Foundation for ways to improve its own research. 'In our world, we're trying to flatten the same process,' says Dr Jeffrey Davis, director of NASA's human health and performance division, who, several years ago, invited Johnson to speak to his staff.[36, 43]

Challenging an Embedded Problem-solving Equation

Over a period of time, all industries and domains develop and settle into established ways of solving a problem. Orbit-shifters challenge the input-output equation embedded in how a problem is being solved.

Dengue is a disease transmitted through the *Aedes Aegypti* mosquito, one for which there is still no cure, and inflicts misery on populations across tropical regions. Over fifty million people are infected by dengue fever every year. Scott O'Neill and his team based in Monash University in Australia have taken on the challenge of eliminating dengue.

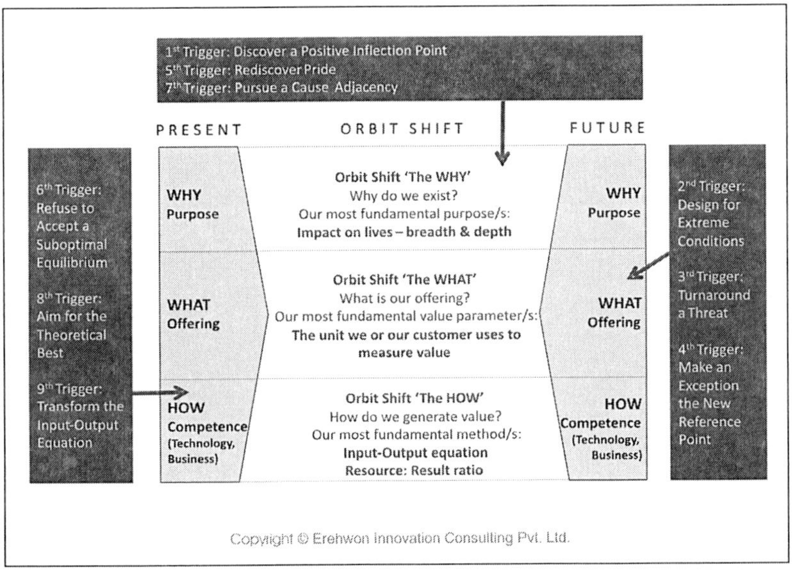

3.2 – Trigger an Orbit-Shifting Challenge

Conventional ways of solving the problem, reducing dengue infection (the output), had focused on protecting the body with mosquito repellents, or eradicating the mosquito by identifying and eliminating mosquito breeding sites (the input). But Scott and his team upended this by taking on an orbit-shifting challenge of *using Wolbachia to block the ability of the mosquito to transmit dengue.*

The naturally occurring Wolbachia bacteria neutralizes the dengue virus. And this triggered their orbit-shifting challenge to infect the mosquito carrying the dengue virus with Wolbachia, resulting in their inability to transmit dengue. These would now be called Angel mosquitoes, which when released into natural environments, could mate with wild mosquitoes carrying dengue and neutralize their impact.

As a video on their website shares: 'Scientists have been working on the biology of Wolbachia for a long time. In the 1990s, Seymour Benzer's lab in the US found a strain of Wolbachia in fruit flies that roughly halved the adult lifespan of the fly. Mosquitoes live to around the same age as fruit flies. Around 30 days, but what's really interesting about dengue is that it takes eight to ten days after a mosquito has bitten a person with dengue before it can pass on the virus to another person and what that means is the mosquitoes that transmit dengue are all old. So we had an idea and that was, what if we take the bacteria that shortens the lifespan of a fruit fly and transfer it to the mosquito that transmits dengue and maybe it would shorten the lifespan and who knows possibly reduce its ability to transmit dengue'.[11, 25]

As a CEO, think about this:

Where is your organization taking an existing set of industry and ecosystem input-output equations as a given?

How can you, like Scott O'Neill and Scott Johnson, challenge these ratios to trigger an orbit-shifting challenge?

THE CAPABILITY TRAP

It is not as if orbit-shifting challenges do not get conceived. They do, but then very few get adopted. For a number of leadership teams, this is a moment of déjà-vu. As we have heard from many leaders over time saying repeatedly, 'We do think of these kind of challenges in our annual strategy meets and then business as usual takes over'. After the event, once the dust has settled, these challenges get assessed, evaluated, and eventually made to fit the organizations' comfort zones—the current capability.

A traditionalist's typical reaction to an orbit-shifting challenge is to question if they can do it. Do they have the proven capability to do it? Gravity-infested leadership teams go further to ask: 'Has anyone else in the industry done it?'

Faced with a clear capability gap, a traditionalist leader's first instinct is to start watering down the challenge. 'I don't like curtailing our ambitions but let's be practical…' 'These are all great challenges but what we can attempt now is…' Another conservative but smart leader would inevitably say: 'Sounds great and challenging, but let's attempt this in Horizon 2, let's attempt what is more within our control in Horizon 1.' It's an altogether different matter that Horizon 2 is a constantly shifting timeline that never seems to arrive.

More often than not, gravity takes over and starts dragging down the ambitiousness of the orbit-shifting challenge. And soon what started out as an orbit-shifting challenge can get watered down to an incremental improvement initiative in the form of an orbit-maintaining goal. As some managers confess:

- 'Our mindsets are around doability and experience. We believe first comes experience and then the project. A man-on-the-moon kind of mission or even Microsoft's X-Box kind of project would never be taken up by this team.'
- 'For big projects, we need experience. But to get experience we need to do big projects.'
- As another CEO shared, 'We want step change. But within my leadership team there are some people who are preoccupied with execution. Their first reaction to a step-change goal is, "Let's focus and let's not get ahead

of ourselves". This attitude leads to a trade-off and the focus shifts to the pragmatic here and now.'

The first reactions of the Titan team that eventually produced the Edge were very similar: 'We don't have the capability. The Swiss couldn't do it, how can we?' 'We can't do it. We don't have those kind of skills.'[30]

Orbit-shifters Don't Work Capability Forward, They Work Challenge Back

Here are two teams that took on orbit-shifting challenges, without the established capability—challenges that had never been done before. One is a physical engineering challenge, by the Chinese, who made a fifty-year-old aspiration come true. Despite being constantly told that it could never be done, China built the highest railway line in the world, against extreme physical and climatic conditions. The other is a software solution—Wipro built the Global Command Centre as a solution for offshore infrastructure maintenance. No known solutions existed. It was inconceivable. And yet, both the Chinese and Wipro made it possible.

The Extreme Engineering Challenge

Challenge back and not capability forward is how the Chinese approached the challenge of creating the world's highest rail line.

They were faced with a number of unsolved problems. This did not deter them. They moved forward, as orbit-shifters do, with the belief that *once they had taken on the orbit-shifting challenge, they would find ways to solve the unsolved problems. They didn't have the answers, but they were confident of their capability to find the answers.*

The First Impossible Challenge for the Chinese: Permafrost

How to make a stable rail line on unstable ground? Half the distance of 550 km of the track had to pass over permafrost. The overarching principle was, keep the ground systematically cool, especially during summer where rising temperatures boosted by work on the railway line could hasten the soil conversion to mush.

The Chinese engineers came up with a slew of solutions, ranging from the simple (in hindsight) to the more high tech:

- In many stretches the track is laid on embankments, with beds of crushed stone. The spaces between the crushed stone allow cold air to circulate over the ground in summer, keeping it cool.
- In more volatile permafrost, the Chinese deployed another low-cost solution that they learnt by observing the practices of the local inhabitants, who built their houses on top of empty drainage pipes that they took care to keep clear of any blockages. The empty pipes insulate the ground from the house above, keeping the ground at a lower temperature.
- For even more fragile zones, a more high-tech solution was found—filling liquid ammonia in heat pipes lined with numerous fins. The pipes are partly embedded in and partly rising out of the embankment. As the ground heats up in summer, liquid ammonia absorbs heat, turns to gas, and rises up. As it comes in contact with cooler air at the top of the heat pipe, it transfers heat to the air, liquefies again, and flows back to the ground.
- But for the toughest stretches, where the ground is too watery to take the weight of a railway embankment, the engineers resorted to building kilometre after kilometre of tracks on pillars. Even the way these pillars were embedded into the ground was an engineering feat in itself, because a solution had to be found to ensure that no overheating of the ground took place in embedding the pillars. The longest such land bridge is about 12 km in length!

The Second Challenge: Earthquakes

The Qinghai Tibet plateau lies at the edge of the Indian and Eurasian tectonic plate, thus leaving the region vulnerable to earthquakes. As one of the engineers says in a film made by Discovery, 'We are standing on a seismic fracture zone. There are more than 140 seismic fracture zones along the Qinghai Tibet railway...'

In November 2001, an 8.1 Richter-scale earthquake shattered the region. A crack in one of the tunnels halted progress for repairs. The team understood that constant repairs would not be practicable once the project was done and so they decided to go around the seismic zones rather than go through them. However, wherever this was not doable, they created simpler structures that could be easily repaired rather than what the design required. So a bridge (that would face greater destruction and be more difficult to repair) was substituted with an embankment, which would be easier to repair.

And finally, all of this had to be constructed through a fragile ecosystem that was on the radar of environmentalists around the world, who watch the Qinghai Tibet plateau for the impact of climate change and global warming. So in addition to coping with permafrost and earthquakes, the team also had to ensure minimum impact on the environment.

Grass was removed, stored, and replanted on the railway bed once the lines were built. The line was diverted around breeding grounds of rare birds, and special bridges and underpasses were built to facilitate the migration of the red antelope without interruption.

But most importantly, the engineers also ensured that the three giant rivers of which the plateau is the source—the Yellow, the Yangtze, and the Mekong—were protected from water pollution. Any polluted water was put through not one, but two settling ponds, tested for safety by environmental scientists and only then released into the Yangtze river. What started as an impossible mission and took fourteen years of planning, came to reality in five short years, one year ahead of schedule.[22]

The Radical Business Challenge

Wipro's Global Command Centre (GCC) is another powerful example of how an orbit-shift challenge drove a business from USD 4 million with 0 percent offshore work in 1999, to USD 146 million with 70 percent offshore work in 2006, in just seven years. All this with zero capability when they started out.

GCC manages and maintains infrastructure offshore. As a senior manager shared, 'Managing IT (Information Technology) services offshore is an easy enough job, it is about software maintenance.' However, even the thought of maintaining hardware at great distances boggles the mind. How does one maintain a computer or a server long distance, with opposing timezones (day at client site, night in India)? Hardware maintenance had, therefore, always been an on-site assignment.

It started with an orbit-shifting aspiration. G.K. Prasanna, who was heading GCC and led this initiative, says, 'In 1999, if we wanted to triple, quadruple our operation, a big limitation was availability of visas. With the old model of sending people to the United States/United Kingdom, we could grow only so much. Therefore, a paradigm shift was needed to manage work offshore, in order to achieve the aspiration. A second driver was operating margins—they are much higher offshore, even with considerable discounts for customers. Once the team decided to manage the work offshore, they asked, "What do we need to do to make this possible?"'

Rather than fitting the aspiration into the current capability, Prasanna's team started challenge back. As Prasanna says, 'We sat down and wrote the ideal service definition saying that our Global Command Centre will do the following things. Then we figured out technically a way to go do them.'

He vividly brings alive how orbit-shifters work challenge back and not capability forward when he says, 'If something is not possible it only means a tool doesn't yet exist. Create the tool and the impossible becomes possible. Once we understood this, nothing could stop us. "What will stop the customer from giving work out here?" The tool doesn't exist, to take control of a server from 10,000 miles away. We needed to create the tool.'

Prasanna continues, 'How do I know a server is down (in Europe or America) while sitting in India? Therefore, a monitoring and administering tool was needed. Another gap was that links were not there. Therefore, we invested proactively in a link to the United States. Other problems existed that may look trivial now, but back then were non-trivial. For example, the technology for a pager to go off when a system crashed existed. But that was only within the United States. We said let's bring this here. But that was a big deal. Pager companies couldn't do it in a guaranteed period of time. The team needed the pagers to go off in 5 minutes, but their SLA (Service Level Agreements) was that they would respond within fifteen minutes. That technology didn't exist. So the team sat down with the pager companies, discussed the technology issues and solved their problem. Now everybody uses this, even the competition in India.'

Working back from their orbit-shifting challenge and solving problems that had never been attempted before, GCC succeeded. They created a viable business model that spawned an entire new business in the IT industry—remote maintenance of hardware.

Orbit-shifting teams like GCC all have a similar starting point. They all know that they don't have the capability. The capability may or may not exist globally, but it doesn't exist with them. What differentiates these teams from others is their belief that in the process of working on the orbit-shifting challenge, they will acquire any new capability needed.

As a CEO, think about this:

The entire global car industry told the Nano team that nobody in the world had the capability to produce a USD 2,000 car. As Shankkar Aiyar writes in *India Today*, January 11, 2008, 'All along, the competition, including Japanese and Korean giants, ostensibly masters of efficient design and innovative pricing, scoffed at the very proposition of a car that cost a lakh of rupees. Can't be done, they said. Osama Suzuki, president, Suzuki Motors, jokingly speculated that it would be a three-wheeler or a stepney'.[1]

When faced with an orbit-shifting challenge, most orbit-maintainers first evaluate and reject the challenge when confronted with the capability question. And even when they do accept it, they often pare it down to fit the current capability.

In contrast, orbit-shifters realize that the orbit-shifting challenge will invigorate and excite the team. They create an aspirational marker which will then open up doors to new capabilities. Some capabilities come alive only on being forced to surface as a result of the challenge.

What are you and your organization doing to inspire and enable people to deliberately go beyond the current capability and take on orbit-shifting challenges?

Orbit-shifters don't start capability forward, they work challenge back. In fact, capability is the one box that they go out of. They take on an orbit-shifting challenge that is not just beyond the organization's but beyond the industry's capability.

BURN THE BRIDGE: NOT A COMMERCIAL, BUT PERSONAL RISK

3.3 – Burn the bridge

An orbit-shifting challenge gathers escape velocity only when the leader, the team, and the organization adopt it, commit to it, and burn the bridge. *Once the bridge is burnt, there are no second thoughts, there is only one way and that is forward.* The question now is not 'should or shouldn't we', it is only 'how to get it done?'

What makes leaders back off or attempt to pare down an orbit-shifting challenge? What will it take to reach the point where the orbit-shifting challenge has reached the point of irreversibility?

When J.F. Kennedy announced in the early 1960s that the United States of America would put a man on the moon before the end of the decade, NASA believed it was an impossible-to-reach challenge. They had to fundamentally rework both their goals and strategy to achieve it. But JFK had made an international commitment, that too in the era of the Cold War. The bridge had been burnt. The orbit-shifting challenge had been taken. It was irreversible. With national pride at stake, there was no going back.

The Tata Nano has been a global game changer. The USD 2,000 car orbit-shift challenge started dramatically. Ratan Tata, the then chairman of the group, declared in the media that: Tata would be making INR 1 lakh car—USD 2,000 car.

In a conversation with the team that championed the project, we asked them, 'When did you first hear about this project?' The team leader smiled and said, 'The first time we heard of it, when it was in the papers.' Surprised to hear this, our next question was, 'Really? You mean, there was no project plan when it was announced?' They nodded in affirmation. 'So what did you do?' 'What was your reaction to the announcement?' The team members looked at each other and then one of them said, 'Honestly, we did nothing, we thought this must be a PR exercise, hopefully he will forget about it. And then, a few months later, it was in the papers again. It was then that it struck us—"Oh My God! This is serious! Looks like we'll have to do something about it".' And that is how the team set about the orbit-shifting challenge to make the Nano a reality.

What had Ratan Tata done by going to the media? Quite like JFK, he too had burnt the bridge. He had put his personal credibility on the line. There was no going back. The INR 1 lakh car had become a publically committed orbit-shifting challenge. By going public, Tata had broken through both his and the organization's gravity and the challenge reached the point of irreversibility.

It did not take a change of teams to make this orbit-shift happen. *The same team did it.* There were many unanswered questions that they answered and many unsolved problems that they solved. They didn't start with the know-how. They started with the confidence in their ability to solve unsolved problems.

The biggest fear of orbit-shifting innovation is not the fear of commercial risk; it is the fear of personal risk. An orbit-shifting challenge acquires escape velocity only when an organization leader and the innovation team adopt it and then burn the bridge.

For most organizations, conceiving an orbit-shifting challenge is still the easier part. Getting a leader and a team to burn the bridge, in the media like Ratan Tata did, or even publically within the organization, can be very difficult and amazingly painful.

Taking on an orbit-shifting challenge involves stepping out of the personal comfort zone and going into the unknown. It evokes the dreaded fear of failure, this fear only magnifies with every year of successes added to our resumes. *The biggest personal fear is not the fear of monetary risk or even one of losing a job. The bigger fear is the fear of losing reputation, of losing personal credibility among peers.* This is personal risk. 'It has taken years to build this position, this job, this reputation—what if I lose it, wouldn't I become a laughing stock among my peers'. It is this fear of personal risk that holds the dreamer back. *Dreaming up an orbit-shifting challenge is a good start but it is the next step, burning the bridge—putting one's personal credibility on the line, committing to go after it—that is difficult.* This is the rubber-hit-the-road moment. This is where most dreamers develop cold feet.

As a CEO, think about this:

Who are the people who are considered heroes in your organization?

Most organizations cultivate a culture where heroes are managers who excel in under-promising and overachieving! By now learning how to promise just less than what you believe you can achieve has become a well-developed art form.

This under-promise-and-overachieve culture becomes the mindset gravity that actively discourages personal risk and reinforces orbit maintaining.

Today no CEO dare be caught not talking innovation, but very few succeed in doing it. Numerous CEOs who talk innovation, end up promoting an under promise and overachieve culture. Are you consciously or unconsciously doing the same?

Going Beyond the Under-Promise-and-Overachieve Way—Remove Escape Buttons

Stepping into the unknown to take on an orbit-shifting challenge in an organization culture that is built on under promise and overachieve is not just tough, it can appear to border on craziness.

However, going against the grain of a risk-averse culture and taking on an orbit-shifting challenge is exactly what was at the core of the big growth drive at Cholamandalam Vehicle Finance.

Cholamandalam Vehicle Finance, part of the Chennai-based conglomerate, The Murugappa Group of Companies, was headed by a taciturn P. Vasudevan, at the turn of the century. The vehicle finance industry was in a flux. The floodgates to car and vehicle ownership had recently opened up and the government was now beginning to closely regulate it, as a result of which the industry was consolidating. Plenty of small players were falling by the wayside, whereas the bigger fish were stabilizing, learning, and growing.

Chola was one of the smaller players on the tightrope with an opportunity to grow or sink. At one of the Murugappa Group leadership off-site meetings, the leadership group was focusing on their low growth and trying to identify its root cause. The conversation soon converged to 'our risk-averse culture'. Everyone accepted the fact that 'we are risk averse'. By the way, in a discussion like this, where everyone is discussing 'We' nobody actually means 'Me'. Everyone in the room usually thinks—'I am not risk averse, these people are. If only some of them were different!' While the others discussed risk aversion, the penny dropped for Vasu. He went back thinking, 'It's not we who are risk averse; *I am* risk averse.'

This crucial shift from 'We' to 'I' went on to transform Vasu and Cholamandalam Vehicle Finance from being a settler to a pioneer. No more, in his own eyes, could Vasu hide behind the comfort of the 'We'. He had to do something or else he would lose credibility with himself. Vasu went on to devise an entirely new strategy for growth, which was based not on the usual *shoving numbers down a sales team* route, but rather through an inspirational route called *Dream Meetings*. He visited each of his twenty branches and asked them to dream up their targets for the year, which if they accomplished, would give them a sense of achievement and fulfilment. Vasu was surprised to discover that most of the branches dreamed up far larger targets (monster targets as he called them) than he would have handed out to them. His people told him, 'Since you gave us the freedom to come up with the target, it is ours, so we dream big'. But what he did after was the key to success. In one final meeting with his team, when they were putting together their business goals for the next year, one team member raised a doubt, 'What do we commit to the board? Are you sure we should be taking on such monster targets, won't we look foolish if we don't achieve them?' 'In any case, we won't make our incentives,' another member added. Soon the conversation got loaded with gravity. Suddenly one member put up his hand and said, 'I have an idea'. Between you and me, between us, we will aim for INR 3 billion but let's promise INR 1.7 billion to the board.

Does this sound familiar? Have you been a part of a similar conversation? Where buffers meant to ease pressure on the goal become the actual goal instead? Where would this team have

finished if they had aimed for INR 3 billion but promised INR 1.7 billion to the board? INR 1.7 billion, in all likelihood, would have become the escape button!

For Vasu, this was the rubber-hit-the-road moment. He realized that promising less to the board was an escape button that would bring down both the energy and the aspiration that had just been unleashed. He chose to remove the escape button. He went to the board and announced his orbit-shifting challenge. He took on the personal risk and he burnt the bridge. As Vasu says, 'It is easy to lose money, it is difficult to lose credibility and so we put our credibility out there, in front.'

This capacity to convert a challenge from an intellectual stimulation to a living reality happens when the bridge is burnt. Otherwise, the tendency, indeed the temptation, to retreat into the comfort zone, to go back, almost with a sigh of relief, to the previous way of doing things, can be overpowering. Recognizing this, orbit-shifters burn the bridge; they remove escape buttons.

Cholamandalam Vehicle Finance surprised everybody but themselves when they actually hit their INR 3 billion target. However, the story is not that they did it once, but they did it year on year on year, by burning bridges and removing escape buttons with monster targets, to go on and grow from INR 3 to 6 to 9 to 12 billion in four years. *The team's mindset had shifted—they were working challenge back and not last-year forward.*[31]

The Indian arm of an American multinational had shifted from the periphery to the centrestage of global leadership attention when they achieved their challenge of outgrowing China, which was, until then, twice as big and the biggest contributor from Asia. To honour the moment, the global corporate office instituted the Indian bell, as an award for the team that grew the most every year. This was presented in New York during the annual conference. Now they needed to take on an even bigger challenge to retain the bell. They got into a co-creation dialogue. It was not enough to just grow, as the Indian market was growing anyway. They wanted to be seen as leaders, but that would happen only if they grew unimaginably big, and hence, they set up a mammoth challenge: to grow 2.5 times more than anyone else in the region! Even as the team had just finished discussing this, the leader disappeared for a while, and when he came back, he said, 'I have just dashed off an email to the head office confirming that we will be growing at 2.5 times and retaining the Indian bell!' He had deliberately burnt the bridge, removed the escape buttons. Now there was no going back!

The Buffer Comes Back

Contrast this with another multinational, where they had the same burning desire as this American corporation to grow phenomenally. However, in this case, the leader did not make a public commitment. What he said instead was: 'In private, between us it will be the big target, but I will go to the regional board with our conventional target. Because I don't want to create pressure on us by committing to a number they'll hold us to that we may not achieve.' Sure enough, at the end of the year, he achieved only what was promised—the conventional target. But he also achieved an unpredicted but natural fallout—a disillusioned team, whose hopes had been raised by the big aspiration and dashed to the ground when the leader settled at the lowest common denominator.

These two leaders, one who decided to burn the bridge and the one who didn't, bring alive the deepest, the most fundamental barrier to taking on an orbit-shifting challenge—the fear of personal risk. This is the fear that makes organizations and managers cling to the current orbit.

Success Equals Not Failing

Success means not failing is the dominant mindset of an under-promise-and-overachieve culture.

The key reason why most leaders hesitate to take on an orbit-shifting challenge is the lens through which they view failure. In a performance-oriented culture, failure is not an option. In fact, in very merit-driven cultures, performance gets equated with not failing. **People will go to greater**

lengths to not fail than they will to succeed. So once the *not failing* paradigm is set, they become too afraid to take risks. In this environment, moderation becomes the key, where leaders build the art of under promising and over delivering.

How does one take on an orbit-shifting challenge that is rooted in the unknown in a culture where success equals not failing?

Consider the low-cost airline that had taken on the orbit-shifting challenge of making the turnaround time of an aircraft like an F1 pit stop. An F1 pit stop turnaround is just a few seconds. The airline team finally reached a turnaround time of 20 minutes. *Did they fail?*

By performance goal standards, they had failed. Twenty minutes is much more than a pit stop turnaround, which is in seconds. So should this be considered a failure? It is not a failure if you look at the progress. This initiative brought down their aircraft turnaround time by 50 percent. The progress against the current orbit was remarkable. As a result, they were able to add an extra flight per aircraft per day, in comparison to others in the industry, which gave them additional revenues.

The Orbit-shifting Challenge: A Transformation Vehicle and not a Performance Goal

How does an organization overcome this strongly entrenched culture of under promising and overachieving? What can an organization do to inspire people to take on an orbit-shifting challenge?

An organization can take the giant step of redefining goal setting and make it a twin-track exercise with the 3+1 goal setting: 3 orbit-maintaining goals plus 1 orbit-shifting goal. This is the easy part. *What is tougher is inspiring people to actually take on and pursue the +1, the orbit-shifting challenge.*

What truly inspires people to take on an orbit-shifting challenge *is the realization that it is a transformation vehicle and not a performance goal, or even a stretch target.* This means institutionalizing a culture where the orbit-shifting challenge is seen as a transformation vehicle through which people can achieve a big impact.

An orbit-shifting challenge as a transformation vehicle is exciting because it fuels the aspiration to go after the impossible; it liberates people to boldly go where no one has gone before. *And in steering a transformation vehicle, what matters is the movement. The reference point of success is the progress made, the leap against the current status, rather than measuring the shortfall against the promised target, as is the case in assessing a performance goal.*

For the Star TV team, the orbit-shifting challenge of creating a quiz show that would be as big as an Indo-Pak cricket match on a Sunday was a transformation vehicle; it propelled them to rethink every aspect, the content, the format, and the marketing of the show.

They fell short of the stated goal. The TRP rating of *Kaun Banega Crorepati?* did not achieve that of an Indo–Pak cricket match, but they succeeded in creating a transformative impact. The show ratings leapfrogged what any quiz show or any live show had ever achieved in India. They did create history; the show became a new reference point for the industry.

This is the power of an orbit-shifting challenge that is designed as a transformation vehicle; it pushes the organization to break the industry boundary, it sets a new reference point where success means a leap against the existing status rather than becoming yet another 'achieve-the-number' exercise.

The Ansari X Prize was also a powerful transformation vehicle.

Twenty-six teams pursued the Ansari X Prize, only one team won, but as Peter Diamandis, head of the X Prize Foundation, said just before the second flight that would make *Spaceship One* the final winner, 'If the Ansari X Prize is won (today), I think you'll see the first Canadian, the first Russian, the first British, the first Romanian...all the X Prize teams outside the United States will continue their work to become the first of their nation to carry out a first private flight into Space'. [38]

The award was merely a trigger; it is the technological leap made in the pursuit of civil aerospace travel that is the real progress achieved from this orbit-shifting challenge. It has actually democratized access to Space.

The space-food venture in Arla came to a grinding halt with the recession of 2009. And yet, Carsten says, 'It was not a failure. We learnt so much. In fact, many new product concepts came out of this venture. We now understand both technology and usability for extreme conditions really well. As a direct consequence of Lacmos, we learnt a whole new way of getting close to markets, and it has become a way of working; for example, we are at the beginning of a new market opportunity having linked dairy habits of Europe with India.'

This illustrates the power of a transformation vehicle. Where a far out, out-of-the-box challenge birthed new skills, capabilities, and revenue-based products for the organization, even as the original project faced a sudden and quick demise.

The Street Fighter becomes the Transformation Vehicle

Reeling under poor performance, the hygiene division at Unilever Indonesia was demoralized and demotivated. What most organizations would do when they are losing badly in the market is focus more and more on numbers: Create hard and focused targets, monitor people closely, continuously, and minutely to achieve these targets. Laercio had committed to the challenge of tripling the hygiene business in three years with his regional heads.

But when he discussed the possibility of taking on this challenge with his team, they collectively realized that to truly uplift the organization they didn't need another performance goal, they needed a transformation drive that would ignite and galvanize the team. From here, the orbit-shifting challenge, Street Fighter, was born. This was truly a transformation vehicle because it spurred every team member into action on a daily basis.

Once the Street Fighter spark was ignited, there was no stopping the hygiene division. In nine months they were back on top of the market, and were a key pillar in Unilever Indonesia again. The striking part of the Street Fighter is the fact that they actually achieved the target of tripling the business in three years, in just nine months. The Street Fighter as a transformation vehicle had transformed their formidable business goal into an insignificant target. It became just a milestone in their journey as they went on to achieve more and more with the Street Fighter spirit.

As a CEO, think about this:

The Street Fighter did not have any hard outcome, like business numbers, to be achieved. It was all about winning—winning the market, winning credibility, and winning respect. Yet it went on to outperform business goals, not incrementally, but significantly. Where can you create a transformation vehicle like the Street Fighter to galvanize your team to create history, rather than just achieve business numbers?

The Gates Foundation: Grand Challenges as Transformation Vehicles

In a pioneering initiative to transform health, the Bill and Melinda Gates Foundation funds developmental initiatives that respond to grand challenges like:

- Develop needle-free delivery systems for vaccines
- Develop a chemical strategy to deplete or incapacitate a disease-transmitting insect population
- Create therapy that can cure latent infections, etc.

Each of these challenges is designed to be a powerful transformation vehicle.[15]

As Dr Harold Varmus, the Nobel laureate who led the scientific thought leadership team that crystallized the fourteen grand challenges in global health in 2003, said, *'These are all very significant and difficult scientific problems. If we could solve any one of these grand challenges the impact on health in the developing world could be dramatic, and we hope to solve several in the course of this new initiative.'*

'These grand challenges capture the tremendous potential for bright, creative scientists to make a difference in the lives of billions of people around the globe,' said health and human services secretary, Tommy G. Thompson. 'By focusing resources and research on developing practical solutions to these challenges, we are creating a real opportunity to dramatically improve the health and well-being of people throughout the developing world.'

What both Dr Varmus and Secretary Thompson are implying is that the focus on these challenges will bring about transformative solutions in areas that have long been festering without solutions.

To facilitate the pursuit of these fourteen challenges, forty-five grants were finally awarded, with a total of USD 458 million, involving scientists across thirty-three countries. Scott O'Neill's *Eliminating Dengue* was one of these projects.[14]

Not a Flop, Just a Wasted Opportunity

The spirit of the orbit-shifter stands out when three years later, the Nano has not lived up to the starting hype and the humungous sales expectations. However, Ratan Tata is still at the forefront, promising to revive and turn around its fortunes. It is not a project that will go quietly or that can be killed without notice. Tata continues to pull out all stops to make it happen. The creation of the car is just a first step in a long journey—the destination is yet to come, and they will pursue the direction relentlessly. As he said in January 2012 at the India Auto Expo, 'I don't consider it to be a flop. I consider that we have wasted an early opportunity'. He reasons that the advertising had not been adequate and that the dealership network had not been well addressed.

He said, 'I believe we will see a resurrection of this product as we move forward'. The journey continues.[20]

As a CEO, think about this:

Tata, in the most public way possible, is demonstrating how an orbit-shifting challenge like the Nano is a 'transformation vehicle and not a performance goal'. In spite of very public failures, he remains steadfast in pursuing the original dream with which the Nano was built, to help millions of Indians who travel on dangerous roads on overloaded two wheelers.

An organization culture that promotes 'success equals not failing' reduces the willingness to take on and pursue an orbit-shifting challenge.

What orbit-shifting challenges in your organization have stalled because they are treated as performance goals?

How can you revitalize and revive the orbit-shifting challenges in your organization by treating them like a transformation vehicle and not a performance goal, focusing on progress rather than shortfall?

Who Will Pursue the Orbit-shifting Challenge?

The Same People Did It

Arla's Space Food Mission, the Tata Nano, and Wipro GCC have one strong commonality. In each case, it did not take a change of teams to make the orbit-shift happen. They did not start with the capability; they acquired the capability in the pursuit of the challenge.

This shatters the myth that, 'to create breakthrough the organization needs to build diversity and that means bringing in new talent it from outside'.

What these orbit-shifting innovations illustrate powerfully is that once mindset gravity is broken through, the *same team can make an orbit-shift happen*. And what is also very visible through our experiences across organizations is that deep-rooted mindset gravity can condition and decimate new people quite like it decimates new ideas. It doesn't matter how diverse the people are, the battle for survival usually does them in.

Bringing in a diverse team is not a magic formula for innovation.

What is your conscious effort to break through mindset gravity and unleash the same teams to make an orbit-shift happen?

Spare People in Spare Time don't Create History

Annual strategy meets, which are usually done off-site, do manage to shake off gravity. Management teams begin to think beyond, allowing new opportunities to emerge. These opportunities generate excitement and anticipation till another rubber-hit-the-road question is posed: Who will pursue this opportunity? Who will take it on as a goal? We need a cross-functional team, with members from across the organization, who will it be?

Now the gravity takes hold. The functional heads look at each other and their usual reaction initially is 'who can we spare?' It becomes a bartering exercise. 'Who can you spare and whom can I spare?' And within the next few minutes they have settled on a four- or five-member team, all working part-time.

As a CEO, think about this:

Resourcing an orbit-shifting opportunity is the real rubber-hits-the-road moment. Across companies, we find this is a crucial point where the gravity of the current orbit reduces an orbit-shifting opportunity.

The same managers, who have been very excited about the new opportunity so far, now start to pull back. They are not prepared to nominate their best people to work full-time on the orbit-shifting mission. Their best people are busy protecting the current orbit and can't be spared. So they end up looking for people who are less essential in the current orbit, and then agree to let them work part-time.

This is the managers' self-protect mode in action. Dedicating a full-time team of even two to three is like burning the bridge—the one thing traditional managers don't do.

But, spare people working in spare time don't create history! An orbit-shifting challenge being pursued by spare people in spare time will create a disaster by design.

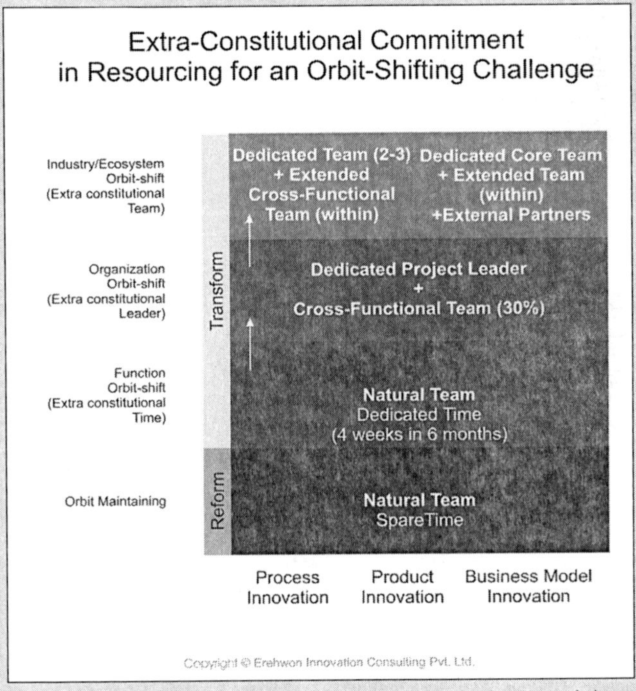

3.4 – Matching the innovation team with the degree of the innovation challenge

Orbit-shifting Challenges Need Extra-Constitutional Commitment

Improvement projects are pursued by cross-functional teams, where getting together and working once or twice a week is enough. Squeezing out bits of spare time is reasonable in order to pursue orbit-maintaining innovation.

Succeeding with an orbit-shifting challenge will, however, require extra-constitutional focus and commitment.

Orbit-shifters don't create part-time, cross-functional teams and hope for the best. They match the extra-constitutional commitment of the team to the size of the orbit-shifting challenge.

An industry transformation challenge needs the extra-constitutional commitment of an entrepreneurial start-up. It is designed to be an industry game changer and it will need a dedicated team of two to three key leaders. An ecosystem transformation will even need dedicated external partners. Not spare people, but the best the organization can put forward.

And like an entrepreneurial start-up, the team needs to be charged with not just coming up with ideas, but with the responsibility of taking the challenge all the way from the conception to in-market success.

An organization transformation challenge, needs a 100 percent dedicated team leader plus an extended team of cross-functional experts who are structured to invest at least 30 percent of their time. Carsten of Arla foods was a 100 percent dedicated team leader of Project Lacmos with a cross-functional team.

A function transformation challenge may not need a dedicated team or even a dedicated team leader but it does need dedicated bursts of time. Function transformation challenges will need a cross-functional team to extra constitutionally commit a minimum of four dedicated weeks across four to six months. This time is needed to propel the transformation challenge to a point where 'business as usual working' can sustain it.

The greater the orbit-shifting challenge, the greater is the need for extra-constitutional commitment. What is needed is an extra-constitutional team and time commitment plus an extra-constitutional budget and an extra-constitutional reporting channel that connects the team directly to the decision stakeholder, cutting out the bureaucracy.

As a CEO, think about this:

What is the extra-constitutional commitment with which your organization is pursuing orbit-shifting challenges?

An orbit-shifting challenge which is pursued in a 'maintain-the-constitution' manner is a disaster waiting to happen.

Making an irreversible extra-constitutional commitment to pursue the orbit-shifting challenge is the real 'burning the bridge' that launches a mission to create and not follow history.

Chapter 4

Breaking through Mental Model Boundaries

There is no such thing as a saturated market, only saturated mental models.

AN ORBIT-SHIFTING CHALLENGE NEEDS ORBIT-SHIFTING IDEAS TO BRING IT TO REALITY. To discover orbit-shifting ideas, mere ideation is not enough. *What is needed is the ability to first recognize and then break through mental model boundaries.*

A number of organizations with ambitious CEOs come up with orbit-shifting aspirations, like three in three—*grow the current business three times in the next three years* or *create a new business equal to the size of the current business*. The core reason why most of these organizations' dreams don't even take off, let alone succeed, is that when managers finally get down to identifying opportunities and developing strategies, they remain stuck in the old orbit. Orbit-shifting aspirations pursued with mental models that are trapped in the current orbit fail to take off.

LOCKED-IN MENTAL MODELS

When confronted with this map, most people recoil with confusion and flip it around immediately so that it is *right side up!* They instinctively react to the inverted map: when in fact, the map, shown the way it is, is not inverted

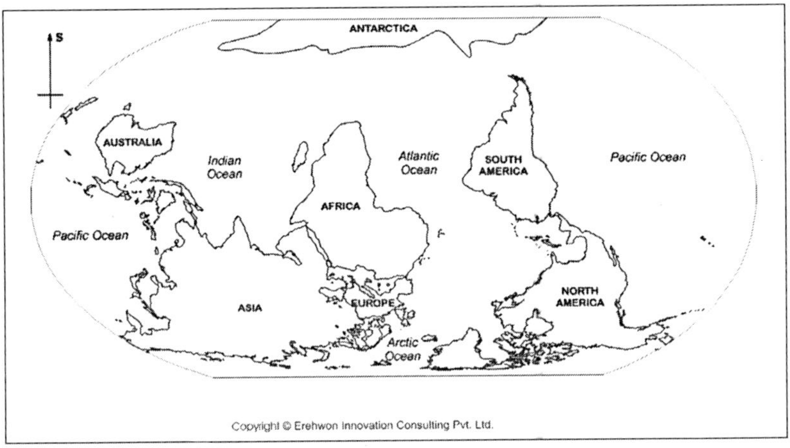

4.1 – Map of the World

at all. It is another valid perspective of the world. A teacher in Argentina shared the map with us along with an interesting story. One day, she asked her students to draw a map of the world, with Argentina on it. Now, we all know that Argentina is at the bottom left of a conventional map. However, one student drew Argentina at the centre of the world. The teacher corrected the student, by showing her where Argentina *ought* to be. The child replied with something so profound that it led the teacher into extensive research on the narrow perspectives of cartographers in map making. She said, 'For me, Argentina is at the centre of the world'.

World maps are actually designed only to provide locational information and can be presented in any number of ways. Yet, amost all maps are presented in only one way, with the North Pole at the top. *Seeing the same thing in the same way for many years transforms it from being mere information into becoming a mental model,* one that we are unaware of. It becomes the only way of looking at the world. The mental model is by now well and truly locked in. Present us with a perfectly accurate map with the south at the top and we immediately turn it around, because it just doesn't fit into our conditioned mental model.

Aliens in movies are almost inevitably presented as deformed human beings. Their symptomatic characteristics may vary—height, colour of body, number of digits, size of organs, etc., but they seem to follow the fundamental design of physical form and intellect similar to human beings. In fact, loosely paraphrasing a quote in an issue of *Reader's Digest*: *Why is it that we always imagine aliens to be more intelligent but less good looking than us?* It is a reflection of the extension of the human mental model of aliens. We are unable to go beyond our mental model boundaries and imagine an alien that is radically different in every other way. We cannot even begin to fathom any other form of life different from ours. And even if someone did conceive of an alien 'completely unlike us' for a movie, it might not strike a chord with the masses. People connect with the unfamiliar through an extension of the familiar—total unfamiliarity might result in estranging the average audience.

Most organizations and teams have a tendency to settle into an orbit that works, that is reasonably successful, that is fairly predictable, and one that minimizes uncertainties. The more settled an orbit, the greater the desire to cling to it, the greater is the accumulation of mental model inertia.

As a CEO, think about this:

Mental models are the most fundamental beliefs, the assumed givens that are usually not questioned, and become the boundaries within which we think.

Quite like the world map, our mental model maps of our industry are equally locked in.

What is your current mental model map of your industry? The map that defines your markets, customers, channels, and business models? Is that the only way of mapping it? What are the mental model boundaries, which if inverted or breached, can unlock completely new orbit-shifting opportunities?

Mental model boundaries can box even the most brilliant teams and organizations. These become layers of invisible constructs and beliefs that unknowingly limit the thought spectrum, reduce the exploration space, and stifle new possibilities.

Traditional methods of stimulating innovation, like introducing new ways of ideation or building diversity usually fail to uncover and break through mental model boundaries. This leads to more and more innovation initiatives hitting the wall of diminishing returns.

To move the innovation and growth drive into the next orbit, an organization needs to break through mental model boundaries. It needs to:

- Recognize and confront the invisible limits of the existing orbit
- Uncover the strategic blind spots embedded in the current orbit

Have you been part of an intense brainstorming session only to feel that nothing new has really emerged or that most of these ideas have come up in the past? This is a sure indication that the group is hitting an invisible wall of diminishing returns. This invisible wall is the mental model boundary. Idea saturation is not an indication that there are no more ideas to be had in this field. It is only an indication of a stuck mental model. *Recognizing and then breaking through this mental model boundary will unleash a fresh wave of new perspectives and possibilities. Real breakthroughs emerge only when fundamental mental models are recognized and challenged.*

Inventively, George Lucas broke a movie-making mental model by starting with the fourth film in the *Star Wars* series. Who dares start a phenomenally ambitious franchise in the middle of the story, especially a story being told for the first time? This is so unlike a famous book or a well-known character, where the audiences are already familiar with the storyline. Who then returns, by design, to make the prequels sixteen years later?[18,19] George Lucas triggered a new wave of prequels when he broke that boundary.

However, the making of *Star Wars* also brings alive a locked-in mental model. When the first *Star Wars* film was made in the 1970s, mechanical engineering was at the forefront of technological development. Lucas imagined a future many, many centuries ahead, a much-advanced civilization with the knowledge of space flight, existence on different planets with different life forms, and futuristic military technology, where light sabers ruled. *Yet, the spaceship navigation portrayed was through mechanical levers.* Chances are, if the movie was made today, the navigation would be portrayed as digital. This is how strongly and *unconsciously mental models guide our thinking.*

Orbit-shifting innovators succeed in uncovering these deep-rooted, unquestioned mental models and breaking through their boundaries.

The 5.5-minute Song

One of the most famous songs of all time, 'Bohemian Rhapsody' by Queen, almost never got into the public domain. Written by Freddie Mercury for their album *A Night at the Opera*, the song in itself was genre defying by combining a ballad, an operatic section, and a rock ending. Putting these three forms together in a popular song broke through a mental model boundary. When the band wanted to release the song in 1975, record producers prevented them from doing so, believing that at 5 min and 55 seconds, it was too long to ever be a hit. It went firmly against their mental model of what a popular rock song should be like. Quoting from a *Sound on Sound* article (October 1995) on the making of 'Bohemian Rhapsody', the producer of this song, Roy Baker, brings this alive:

> 'It was, after all, breaking all the rules', says Baker. 'So we rang EMI and told them we had a single, inviting them down to have a listen. We told them how long the track was (5 min, 55 seconds) and before they had even heard it, the comment was, "Oh, I don't know. I don't think we'll be able to get any radio play with a song that long". We said, "But you haven't heard it yet". They said, "Well, just going by what the current formula is, if it's longer than three and a half minutes, they won't play it."'

An orbit-shifting idea was confronted with the formula of the old mental model. But Queen and Baker decided to do something different. They went directly to a radio jockey Kenny Everett with the song. He loved it, but they gave it to him only on the condition that he promised them 'not' to play it!

> 'He said, "I love this song. It's so good, they'll have to invent a new chart position. Instead of it being Number One, it'll be Number Half!" It

> was the oddest thing I'd ever heard! We had a reel-to-reel copy but we told him he could only have it if he promised not to play it. "I won't play it", he said, winking.
>
> 'On his radio show the following morning he played the beginning of it, saying, "Oh, I can't play anymore, 'cause I promised". Then he played a bit more later. Eventually, he played the track 14 times over the course of the weekend. By Monday, there were hordes of fans going to the record stores to buy "Bohemian Rhapsody", only to be told it wasn't out yet. There was a huge backlash at our end from EMI's promotion department, who told us we were undermining them by giving Capital Radio a copy. But we said that we had no option, because they told us that nobody would want to play it. During the same weekend that Ev (Kenny Everret) was playing the song, there was a guy called Paul Drew, who ran the RKO stations in the States. He happened to be in London and heard it on the radio. He managed to get a copy of the tape and started to play it in the States, which forced the hand of Queen's USA label, Elektra. It was a strange situation where radio on both sides of the Atlantic was breaking a record that the record companies said would never get airplay!'[8]

'Bohemian Rhapsody' has gone on to become one of the most iconic rock songs of all time. The British Phonographic Industry called it the 'best British Single' of the period 1952–77.[16] The Guinness Book of Records identified it as the Top British Single of all time, in 2002.[9] In 2004, *Rolling Stone* magazine placed it at number 166, on its list of The 500 Greatest Songs of All Time.[39] The song is also listed in the Rock and Roll Hall of Fame's 500 Songs that shaped Rock 'n' Roll.[38]

IDEAS, FRAMES, AND MENTAL MODELS

Ideas emerge from frames. Frames are like windows to the mind. Opening a window reveals an idea track. Going along the track will uncover a string of ideas. But looking and working harder along the same track will not yield

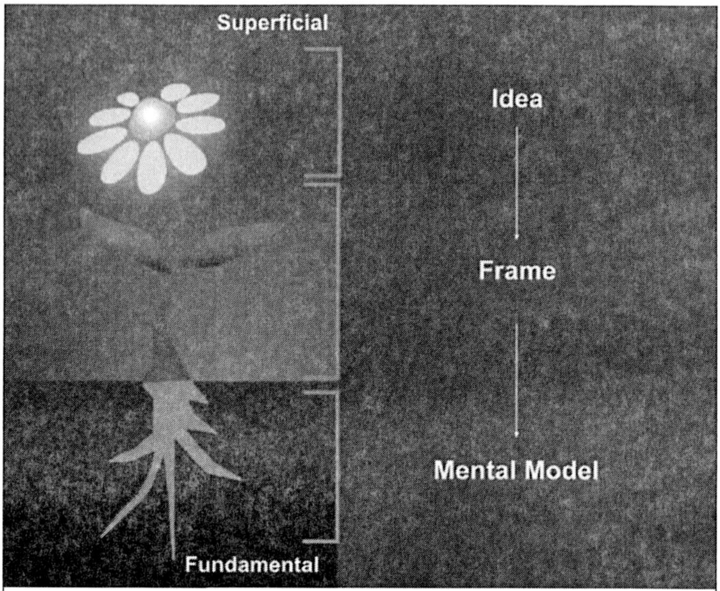

4.2 – Idea-Frame-Mental Model

anything new. Getting a completely new perspective needs us to *shut the old window* and open a new one. It calls for a frame shift.

From Sunset to Sunrise

In the early 1990s, a team from a paging company sat down to brainstorm as they were ridden with anxiety because the paging industry was under threat from mobiles. The team began the brainstorming session with the question 'What can we do next that will revive this paging industry?' However, rounds and rounds of ideation didn't yield much.

On further contemplation, they started mapping the evolution of the paging industry by uncovering and mapping the frame shifts that had fuelled industry growth. The first frame shift they traced was how paging had gotten redefined from paging as messaging to paging as information sharing. They recognized that so far, the industry had seen *paging only as messaging*. This frame shift had opened up a new business stream of *paging as information sharing*, while a message was sent only by a person known to the receiver, information could be sent by a third party. This led to a new revenue stream, where people subscribe to and receive stock information, news updates, game scores, etc. The next frame shift they spotted was from one-way to two-way messaging, where a person could receive as well as send messages. However, all these frame shifts had been reduced to nothing because the mobile could easily address all these needs and do much more. Paging, it appeared, was a sunset industry.

Having mapped the frame shifts, the team was provoked to look deeper. Is there a common underpinning to all these frame shifts? Is there a deeper mental model boundary that has remained undetected through all these evolutions? This deeper reflection uncovered the mental model boundary. All these frame shifts had a fundamental commonality—they were all focused on getting/giving information from one person to another; all exchanges were person to person. This led the team to challenge the mental model boundary from *paging as person to person* and exploring *paging from person to object*. Breaking through this mental model boundary uncovered a dramatic possibility: *Paging objects—anything intelligent could be paged. People could talk to machines via paging or machines could talk to machines! And amazingly, the size of this market was, if anything, much bigger that their existing one.* The number of objects in the world is many more than the number of people. Uncovering and breaking through this mental model boundary had yielded a radical possibility.

If frames are like windows, mental models are the lens through which we see the world. No matter how many windows are opened, if the lens is the same, nothing new will emerge.

As an experiment, ask people to count the number of clocks at home. The usual answer is about four to five. *Most people count the wall clocks and wrist watches at home, while a few restrict themselves to only the wall clocks.* This is the obvious count of watches. Get them to now examine the underlying frame: what is the meaning each of us attaches to a clock? The thinking now reaches the frame level: a clock is a time-keeping device. Now that the frame has become obvious, it will expand perspective immediately and explode ideas: what are the other time-keeping devices in the house? Suddenly, the number goes up significantly. *Mobile phones, computers, televisions.* Now shift the frame further—how about devices that keep time for a job, rather than time of the day? Now the washing machine and the microwave become time-keeping devices as well. The count reaches to fourteen to fifteen devices. And yet underlying all of these frames is a limiting mental model of *time keeping: that it has to be kept by a device. What else keeps time that is not a device?* With this mental model breakthrough, still more options emerge: the human body clock keeping time, the pattern/ angle of the sun's rays on the house every day tells time, the time at which the newspaper lands at your doorstep is usually the same every day. Another way of marking time! *Our view of the number of clocks we have at home is limited to or expanded by our mental model of time keeping.*

At a large tea plantation in south India, rats kept attacking the water pipes that transported water along the large acreage of the plantation. For years managers had tried to solve the problem with little success. From rat traps to rat poison, to changing the material of the pipes and also burying pipes underground where possible, many measures were taken, but to no avail. The rats got through anyway. So the ideas were plenty, but perhaps they were all trapped in a single frame. The common frame underlying all the solutions was: 'How do we keep the rats away from the pipe? How do we get rid of the rats?' Then one of the managers asked, 'Is it possible the rats are attacking not to damage the pipes, but only to drink water? How else can we provide them with water?' A very simple solution arose, because the frame of reference had now been shifted from keeping the rats away to providing them drinking water. They experimented by putting coconut shells with water at regular intervals along the water lines. The rats now had easy access to drinking water and the damage to the water pipes stopped immediately.

Generating an orbit-shifting idea like 'Bohemian Rhapsody' by design requires a fundamentally different capability. It needs the ability to recognize and break through the mental-model boundaries embedded in the current orbit.

Mere brainstorming is not enough. What is called brainstorming usually ends up as just an idea storm, where the focus is inevitably on quantity: 'We've come up with a thousand ideas today!' What matters is not the number of ideas that came through, but the mental-model boundaries that were breached. One or two orbit-shifting ideas are all we need, not a thousand incremental variants.

A Locked-in Mental Model Leads to a National Disaster

Attempting an orbit-shifting challenge with an orbit-maintaining mental model does not merely minimize the orbit-shift, it can have a life-threatening impact.

In an excellent article which appeared in *Nature*, April 2011, Robert Geller, a professor of seismology, describes how an entire nation was lulled into a false sense of security based on faulty theories for years on end.

Geologists began to accept plate tectonics as a theory of movement of the earth's crust in the middle of the last century. Many academics were excited with this theory for it now paved the way to *link plate tectonics with seismic activity* and if the link could be comprehensively shown, earthquakes could actually be predicted along deep and moving fault lines where plates collided. The hypothesis that emerged was quite logical on paper. It postulated that *areas along plates where there had been no earthquakes for a reasonable amount of time could be dubbed as seismic gaps, with a greater likelihood of future earthquakes.* The seismic gap theory failed to withstand rigorous study and was finally shelved because scientists found that over time, it was difficult to predict the catch up of earthquakes against gaps, as it does not happen regularly or predictably.

However, in the mid-1970s, when it was still a fairly accepted theory, Japanese seismologists identified a plate around the south of Japan in an area called Tokai with its neighbouring regions of Tonankai and Nankai and labelled it as a likely location for an 8-plus magnitude earthquake in the near future. It was a perfect seismic gap candidate as there had been no major earthquake in the recent past along its plate. The Japanese government even passed a law to ensure constant monitoring of the Tokai tectonic plate along with an escalation mechanism, such that it was seared in the nation's psyche as the location where the next big earthquake was likely to hit. Now, here is the tragic fallout: in the interim, from 1979 onwards, ten earthquakes with fatalities greater than ten people happened in the so-called low-risk areas (identified as low-risk by the government) and yet Japanese scientists and successive governments continued to focus obsessively on Tokai. The catastrophic consequences came to a head in 2011, when the brutal Tohuku earthquake struck *outside the seismic gap* in the east of Japan, killing 16,000 people and causing billions of dollars of damage, including nuclear meltdowns. The ten earthquakes had been merely a prelude, but a clear warning, nevertheless. However, the Japanese were so locked in to the theory that had been discarded thirty years ago by the rest of the world, and to a law that had been created in the 1970s that they could not see the new data that stared them in the face. They were completely blindsided by the Tohuku earthquake! This, harrowingly, shows how strong mental model lock-ins can be.[14]

As a CEO, think about this:

The Tohuku earthquake is an extreme example of not being able to recognize the mental model boundary. The signals, however few, were there, but they were ignored as they did not fit into the established mental model.

Similarly, most organizations do get early signals of a locked-in/saturated/ ineffective mental model. However, these signals are usually dismissed as abnormalities.

What are the current signals that could be product, organization, or brand threatening? Where have you, in the recent past, come across such signals that could be indicative of your mental model boundary? Are you making a conscious attempt to recognize the mental model boundary or are you just dismissing the signals? What could be the consequences if you ignored these signals?

BEGIN BY UNCOVERING MENTAL MODEL BOUNDARIES AND NOT WITH IDEATION

Faced with an orbit-shifting challenge, traditionalists directly launch themselves into 'idea-generation' sessions. Orbit-shifters, on the other hand, don't do this. They hold back their natural instinct to rush into ideation and instead start by deliberately mapping and identifying the boundaries of their thinking. This means they uncover the underlying thinking: the patterns underlying the current ways in which the challenge is being pursued across the industry. They probe and push the boundaries of their thinking by exploring questions like, *What is currently hitting the wall of diminishing returns? Where are we saying no to the customer? What do we consider impossible? What are the sub-optimal equilibriums that we have gotten used to? What parts of our industry do we consider saturated?* They use a series of such triggers to first uncover and identify the mental model boundaries.

Orbit-shifters have experienced the power of recognizing a mental model boundary. It is amazing how often the mere recognition of a mental model boundary is enough to reveal a blind spot that points towards an orbit-shifting idea.

The team charged with the challenge of reviving paging had tried multiple rounds of ideation earlier, but most ideas had remained incremental.

The breakthrough idea came through only when they recognized their mental model boundary that all their ideation so far had been limited to considering paging to be from person to person. This almost immediately revealed a blind spot and an orbit-shifting idea emerged: from paging as *person to person* to paging as *person to object.*

Like many others, Fabio Rosa had identified solar power as the way to ensure 100 percent of rural electrification in Brazil. But his breakthrough idea emerged when he recognized the mental model boundary underlying the approach to solar power. 'What does it mean to buy solar panels?' asks Rosa. 'It means to buy energy for the next 25 years. Who buys food for the next 25 years? You buy food for the next week or month. It should be the same with electricity'.[6] This recognition of the mental model boundary has lead to the orbit-shifting idea of *micro-leasing solar power* with a monthly bill.

What an orbit-shifting challenge needs—which orbit-shifters have—is the capacity to recognize and break through the mental model boundaries embedded in the current orbit.

Among all the mental model boundaries orbit-shifters have broken through, here are the nine that were breached to create a transformative impact across industries.

Transforming Access

Ambitious organizations, impassioned NGOs, and driven governments have one common goal—they all want to create an impact on the masses. Across all sectors in the world, the greatest divides are between the haves and have nots.

Some of the biggest orbit-shifting ideas have bridged the divide. They have made products and services that were earlier restricted to the few become accessible to the masses.

Transforming access to a product or service and creating a mass market requires the breaking through of a combination of four Access boundaries—Physical Access, Economic Access, Intellectual Access, and Emotional Access.

Transforming Access: Breaking through the Physical and Economic Access Boundaries—Smart Load

At the core of the mobile revolution is the breaking through of the physical and economic access mental model boundaries. The key question facing Smart Communications in Philippines was—what could they do to dramatically increase market penetration and get the masses to adopt the mobile? *The challenge, they realized, was economic access.* On digging deeper, the mental model boundary emerged—the postpaid business model. The traditional postpaid model made the average citizen nervous. People weren't sure of their bill amount at the end of the month. Breaking through this mental model boundary, Smart Communications adopted the orbit-shifting idea—the *prepaid* mobile card.

The second challenge was *physical access*—how could they make it convenient to physically access and top-up the prepaid card? The response to this was Smart Communications' orbit-shifting idea of electronic recharging. In 2004, Smart Communications was awarded Best Mobile Application or Service by the GSM association for Smart Load, the first over-the-air prepaid card reloading service. The service replaced prepaid scratch cards by allowing store owners to download airtime directly from Smart and resell the airtime as top-ups to their customers, again through a download, by sending a text message to Smart to make the accounting transfer.[23,44] This unleashed the orbit-shift. As of 2012, 96 percent of subscribers in India are prepaid, which is an incredible 870 million prepaid subscribers in total.[1] This is the significance of this history creating idea.

Transforming Access: Breaking through the Intellectual and Emotional Access Boundaries—Revising Culture

Intellectual boundaries are created not only by the lack of access to education, but also by traditional languages becoming extinct, or obsolete. As a language loses popularity and fewer and fewer people speak it, it takes with it its myths, stories, and culture.

One of the biggest concerns for most societies is the erosion of culture.

What worries people is that the modern generation is disconnected with our traditions; kids today are not rooted in our culture.

One of the most powerful vehicles for building culture is folklore, usually mythological stories that bring alive the values and establish the culture of a community.

In the late 1960s, Anant Pai was watching a school quiz show on TV in India. He was perturbed that the students were fluent in Greek and Roman mythology, but could not answer the question: Who is Rama's mother? He then asked his nephews and nieces to write a story. It was a good story, but about a child in England. And this, by a group of children who had never travelled beyond the shores of India! It reinforced his belief that children in India did not know their own mythology due to lack of exposure. After all, all library books were in English.

This realization provoked Anant Pai to recognize and break through a mental model boundary. The basic barrier was that the mythology was buried in an ancient language, Sanskrit, that very few people understood. Rather than go the usual way and propose translating all books from Sanskrit to English, and evangelize the teaching of Indian mythology in schools, he probed deeper. He searched for a breakthrough method to bring alive Indian mythology for the next generation.

He realized that the folklore had to not just be communicated in English; it also had to be in a format that would appeal to a young generation. His orbit-shifting idea became *Amar Chitra Katha* (ACK), which literally means 'immortal picture story', bringing out mythology in the most popular format—comic books. This broke through not just the intellectual access barrier but also the emotional access barrier—kids love to read comics.

It resulted in almost every child of the 1970s and 1980s growing up with an ACK in his/her bag or desk. The fortunate generation grew up with an intimate knowledge of Indian mythology, unlike their predecessors. Today, parents, whether living in India or outside of it, continue the tradition of ACK with their kids. It has now become a fundamental building block of contemporary Indian culture.[2,43]

Breaking through the *intellectual access boundary brought alive a fading culture and embedded it into the rhythms of the next generation.*

As a CEO, think about this:

A lot of organizations talk about educating the consumer. This is, at one level, an imperialistic statement but at another level, it is a symptom of an intellectual access boundary. It may not be about what the consumer can't do, it may be more about what you are not doing! You may need to simplify the message and engage him/her differently.

Where can you do the *Amar Chitra Katha* to your product?

Rather than educate consumers, give them an engaging way to discover and learn for themselves.

While the prepaid mobile card *broke through physical and economic access boundaries* to make communication accessible to the masses, *Amar Chitra Katha* broke through *intellectual and emotional access boundaries to make folklore accessible to the next generation.* GE's orbit-shifting idea, the Mac 400, the portable ECG, has broken through three access boundaries: physical, economic, and intellectual.

Transforming Access: Breaking through Physical, Economic and Intellectual Access Boundaries—The Portable ECG

GE is renowned for its world-class ECG machines. In India, however, it was faced with a unique market challenge.

Heart disease is the number one killer globally, and 60 percent of the cases are from India.[3] ECG testing is the first step to early detection. Eighty percent of India's health care practices are in urban centres while 75 percent of India's population is in rural areas.[12] For many Indians living in the rural areas, accessing an ECG was an arduous task. It meant getting to the nearest town, and so losing at least two days of work time and income.

GE saw the uniqueness in this challenge; it forced the company to question its existing mental model of ECG design, development, and take to market. As a senior manager said, 'We realized that the biggest impediment was that we were selling what we were making, rather than what the customers here needed.'

Confronted with a radically different market and empathizing with unique customer needs provoked GE to recognize and break through their mental model boundaries. They challenged their *conventional mental model of making bigger, better, and more sophisticated ECG machines.* The conventional way of handling the India market would have been to cut the price, and reduce the eight-to-ten-week waiting period. Rather than merely 'adapting to India', GE set about 're-designing for India'. Rather than create a new and improved ECG, they created the Mac 400—the portable ECG.

The first boundary they broke through was physical access—the Mac 400 is portable, in that the ECG machine comes to the patient. The patient doesn't have to go to it. By reducing the cost of the machine by 80 percent, they broke through the economic access boundary too. For a consumer, the cost of an ECG test came down from INR 150 to INR 50. The Mac 400's interactive User Interface (UI) and one-touch operation broke the intellectual access boundary. A trained paramedic, without the knowledge of English, can easily operate it, removing the need for a highly qualified technician. GE didn't create a poor man's version of the ECG machine; rather it created a version unique to the conditions of the Indian rural market. In fact, GE incorporates an analysis programme and a built-in software device that interprets the ECG in English, like any pathology test; features that were available only in GE's high-end ECG machines.

To deal with power outages it had to be battery operated. Some parts of rural India get only six hours of power per day. With a recharge time of three hours and hundred continuous readings from a single recharge, the Mac 400 needs to be charged just once a day during use.[13,40]

The Mac 400 has revolutionized the ECG machine by breaking through the physical, economic and intellectual access boundaries. This easy-to-use, portable ECG machine will help save many lives.

Transforming Access: Breaking through the Physical, Economic, Intellectual Plus Emotional Access Boundaries—Sprinkles

Sprinkles is an orbit-shifting idea that transformed access to health care by breaking through four access boundaries—physical, economic, intellectual, and emotional.

Dr Stanley Zlotkin took on the orbit-shifting challenge to eliminate malnutrition. In the mid-1990s, UNICEF contacted Dr Zlotkin to know if anything else could be done to overcome anaemia deficiency in children in developing countries, since what they had been doing so far was not working.

For Dr Zlotkin, the challenge was immense. Vitamin and mineral deficiencies affect more than two billion people in the world. Infants and children are the most vulnerable to micronutrient malnutrition, given their need for a high vitamin and mineral intake, and their rapid growth relative to the amount of food they consume.

Dr Zlotkin started by identifying the mental model boundaries that needed to be challenged.

In developed countries, children did not have the same deficiencies because they had access to fortified food that is mostly prepared in factories and reinforced with all the necessary minerals and vitamins. But in most developing countries, food is prepared at home, especially among the poorer population. This threw up two challenges.

- Putting factories in and around these neighbourhoods was not financially viable.
- Changing eating habits of people that had been built over centuries was not practical.

Further, he observed that the supplemental route of syrups, tablets, and injections, tried by UNICEF and others, had its own challenges:

- They tasted unpleasant (compliance was low because mothers did not want to give nasty-tasting supplements to their children).
- Administering the right dosage was difficult (illiteracy was one cause of this).

- There was difficulty in transportation, especially liquids.

Dr Zlotkin broke through these mental model boundaries and arrived at the ideal solution that would be:

- Something that could be added to the food that they already cooked on a daily basis without changing the taste or colour, breaking through the emotional access boundary.
- It should be feasible to pre-measure a dosage and easy to transport—breaking through the physical and intellectual access boundaries.[27,41]

He set out to conceive a solution that would do both. *The result was an orbit-shifting idea, micronutrient powder in sachets. It had all the advantages: controlled dosage, easy to transport, fortifying food without changing its taste or colour.* Sprinkles are sachets containing a blend of micronutrients in powder form, which are easily sprinkled on food prepared at home. Any homemade food can be instantly fortified by adding Sprinkles. A coating of iron prevents changes to the taste or texture of the food in which Sprinkles is added.

Tests showed that this home fortification reduced anaemia by 31 percent and iron deficiency by 51 percent in infants and young children.[33] They had positively impacted four million children by 2009.[42]

Breaking away from the factories-in-the-neighbourhood model and the liquid format model to the sachet made the solution physically and economically accessible. The single serving of a controlled dosage made intellectual access also easy for the consumer, and finally, since it was sprinkled ON the food, it didn't interfere with the cultural habits of the consumer, or with the taste buds of the child, making it emotionally accessible.

As a CEO, think about this:

What are the physical, economic, intellectual, and emotional access mental model boundaries that are implicitly embedded into the configuration of your industry?

What are the boundaries that are limiting the reach and impact of your products and your industry?

What orbit-shifting ideas could be unleashed by deliberately challenging and breaking through these mental-model boundaries?

What could be your equivalent of the prepaid mobile card, the Mac 400, or the Sprinkles solution?

Rediscover the Market Need

Organizations get easily locked into a mental model that categorizes and then freezes a market need. Some of the biggest business differentiations and growth stories have come from the breaking through of this mental model boundary, with the rediscovery of a market need.

Orbit-shifters usually have the greatest opportunities to rediscover market needs in markets that are considered mature and settled. For one, breakthroughs have occurred when the frame of reference of looking at customer needs shifted from functional needs to the emotional needs of the customer. Second, rather than just focus on obvious functional needs, orbit-shifters have discovered co-temporals: the points of time in the lives of customers when two or more functional needs coexist and how they can leverage the coexistence of these needs. Going further, they have also uncovered and leveraged co-spatials: the spaces that customers live through where two or more functional needs coexist. Third, in sectors that have settled into a polarized view of the market, orbit-shifters find ways to reframe the market spectrum in itself—uncovering a new, third space that had been completely missed earlier. And fourth, while settled players in the market get stuck in the cycle of creating value adds, orbit-shifters question and redefine the core purpose.

Rediscover the Market Need: From Functional to Emotional

NovoPen®

Novo Nordisk broke through a mental model boundary by making the shift from a functional to an emotional (social) need. It led to the creation of the NovoPen®, an orbit-shifting drug delivery device for diabetics.

In January 1981, Sonnich Fryland, the marketing director of Novo Nordisk called Jorn Rex, the head of packaging, and Dr Ivan Jensen into his room. Fryland removed his fountain pen from his pocket, and as Jorn Rex says, 'He asked us if it would be possible to produce a device that looked like a fountain pen, was easy to use, which could hold a week's supply of insulin and administer two units of insulin at the touch of a button. The pen had to be simple and discreet, and preferably look like, well, an actual fountain pen.'

The idea of the NovoPen® came as a result of breaking through a mental model boundary defining the market need. The unearthing of a market need that had been previously unleveraged happened as Novo Nordisk recognized that most people were uncomfortable using syringes. Considering a diabetic needs to inject himself three to four times a day, the usage of a syringe is a very daunting prospect. Further, there was a social stigma attached to the idea of using a syringe and vial in public.

Pursuing this orbit-shifting challenge, the team at Novo Nordisk came up with the NovoPen®, a compact fountain-pen-like object whose cartridge had the capacity to hold insulin for one week. NovoPen® had solved a major problem faced by all diabetic patients, the problem of having to carry a separate syringe and vial to administer their daily dose.

After the launch of the NovoPen®, Novo Nordisk, which had been battling the threat of losing market share in its core product—insulin—now became the leader in Europe and Japan with more than 60 percent and 80 percent market share respectively.[5] The difference in price between NovoPen® and the traditional syringe and vial was not a deterrent in its popularity. Diabetic patients were much happier to use it as it answered their most immediate concerns about using syringes. For one, it was easily portable, as it was shaped like a pen. It was also compact and easy to carry, and saved the user from social stigma. In addition, NovoPen® had a mechanism to meter doses hence improving the accuracy of usage. The process of using it was less painful and easier to understand so it appealed to young patients and the elderly as well.[37] It made the drug delivery mechanism much more user friendly and it liberated diabetics to live a normal life, 'Now I control diabetes rather than diabetes controlling me'. Novo Nordisk had identified patients' deepest emotional needs and produced a device to address them, breaking through its own mental model that had so far focused more on drug development rather than on drug delivery.

Rediscover the Market Need: From Functional to Co-Temporal

M-PESA

The NovoPen® has demonstrated how redefining the market need from functional to emotional has created an orbit-shift in growth and impact. But when functionality itself is redefined, yet another mental model boundary is broken.

When the one-product-one-core functionality mental model is broken, co-temporal needs emerge. While most settled players focus on the single need that their industry was originally built on and focus on delivering extremely well on that single need, *orbit-shifters ask a fundamentally different question: at what points of time do two needs coexist?* By combining the two needs into one product or service, an orbit-shift is created.

Vodafone (Safaricom in Kenya) identified a parallel need. A need that is as large as the need to communicate is the need to make financial transactions. In doing so, they had broken through an industry mental model boundary of having just one core functionality of communication, as defined by the telecom services industry. In bringing the two together, the need for communication and the need for financial transactions, Safaricom created M-PESA. This breakthrough has lead to mobile phones becoming the new 24x7 tellers. A mobile phone enables interpersonal communication at all times in a day; now it could also enable financial transactions between people, throughout the day.

At most points in time, while the mobile is in the hand, the wallet is in the pocket. The need to communicate and the need for financial transactions coexist. They are co-temporal. From here emerged M-PESA—the mobile wallet where money can be transacted from one person to another with an SMS. ***Calling plus financial transaction became a winning co-temporal combination.*** With fifteen million transactions per month, M-PESA powers the financial needs of those who need it the most—the unbanked millions.[24]

Medical Tourism

Historically, people travelled to developed nations for good medical care, especially for highly complex or advanced diseases. Globalization has brought increased medical sophistication in developing countries, in some areas almost on par with the developed countries. Cosmetic procedures in South America, gender reassignment in Thailand, cardiac and orthopaedic replacement, and pediatric care in India are some examples. As costs and waiting time of medical procedures in the West soared and with an increase in the lifespan of the baby-boomer generation, an entirely new industry has spawned, that of medical tourism, where people from the West (primarily the United States and United Kingdom) now travel to developing nations for surgery. Included in the package is a medical intervention coupled with a tourism agenda—whether it is sightseeing or some well-needed relaxation and rejuvenation at a spa or a resort. This co-temporal package often costs 15 to 20 percent or less than the cost of the medical intervention in the home country. As hotels, hospitals, and airlines of host nations come together to offer attractive packages, medical tourism has become an industry leveraging globalization. With a market size of about USD 20 to 35 billion in the year 2012, and approximately 7 million patients worldwide, medical tourism is here to stay.[33]

As a CEO, think about this:

When is the last time you consciously focussed on rediscovering the market need? Looking at customers through the functional, emotional, co-temporal and co-spatial lens can potentially lead to a rediscovery of the market need. What could be the Novopen or the MPESA in your industry?

Redefine the Core

Redefine Airlines

Over a period of time, the best of industries get caught in the trap of value adding. In the zest to add value, they forget to question and re-examine the core. Every bit of value added seems good when seen independently but if the core remains the same, the additions can soon become peripheral. Unknowingly and inevitably, the product or service gets over engineered.

The airline industry became the epitome of an industry that focused on adding value with vision and zest. Reward miles, gourmet meals, and increasing freebies were among the never-ending list of value adds that they hoped could build the franchise and ensure loyalty.

This mental model was broken with the emergence of low-cost airlines. *They redefined the core. At the heart of it, the core need is to get from one point to another, on time, and at the lowest cost. The rest is peripheral, desirable but not essential.* A service that promised comfortable seats, on-time arrival, at a low, in fact unbeatable cost, became the success model of budget airlines.

Redefine Cricket

A radical redefinition of the core has brought about an orbit-shifting format in the most traditional of sports—cricket.

The Board of Cricket of England was really concerned as the game was losing mass appeal. More and more spectators and media viewership were turning towards football and there were fewer and fewer takers for cricket. The classical format of cricket was a five-day test match between teams from two countries. The first innovation had been the introduction of the one-day cricket format. Even this was no longer drawing crowds.

As James Sutherland, the head of Cricket Australia explained, 'A core group meeting was called to discuss and come up with options to win back mass interest. Nothing new came up for a long time till somebody asked a question that "challenged the core!"'

'Think of a cricket format that the purists would hate!'[45]

This trigger led to an orbit-shifting idea, T20 cricket, where a match could be played in three hours. This format increased the pace of cricket and made watching a match even on a week-day evening more easily possible.

This breakthrough has brought back the interest in cricket in not just England but in most other cricket-playing nations.

What orbit-shifters do is upend the market by asking what is the core of the proposition, how far has the industry moved away from the core, and how do we re-innovate the core to create new opportunities.

As a CEO, think about this:

What is the core purpose that drives your industry?

Step back to re-examine and redefine the core.

How would the originator of Budget Airlines have redefined the core of your industry?

Ask yourself, as the Cricket Board did. 'What would the purists in our industry hate?'

Reframe the Market Spectrum

Rediscovering and redefining a market need leads to an innovation that grows the market. Going further, reframing the market spectrum of a market can uncover a blind spot by identifying a third space that leads to the creation of a new market.

Two fundamental development challenges faced by developing nations—increasing literacy and correcting presbyopia (shortsightedness)—have found elegant solutions when the market spectrum was reframed.

VisionSpring—Reframe Vision Correction

In 2001, Jordan Kassalow, an optometry student, volunteered in Mexico as a part of a programme called Voluntary Optometry Services for Humanity (VOSH). A young mother brought her blind son to see if his eyesight could be restored. When Jordan examined the boy, he discovered something he wasn't prepared for. He rummaged through the inventory of glasses and eye drops and placed one of the glasses on the boy's face. To everyone's surprise, the boy who had been told that he was blind could see almost perfectly.

What that little boy had was a profound case of nearsightedness—presbyopia—something that can be corrected with simple reading glasses. But due to the complete lack of eye care facilities in many developing countries like Mexico, children like him continue to live 'blind'.

Presbyopia usually occurs from natural ageing of the eyes, and affects both the eyes in the same manner. The biggest fallout of presbyopia is that it is difficult to see things up close, and having this means a productivity loss for a large number of people. In the urban areas, where literacy levels are high, it affects people's ability to read, though in urban areas this problem is treated easily due to easy access to optometrists. In rural areas, it affects people whose occupation requires close-vision capabilities the most, like tailors, weavers, crafts producers, etc. Another important category of people affected by this is housewives who do various chores that require close vision, like mending, threading a needle, etc.

The realization of this market gap led to the creation of VisionSpring, a social enterprise that broke through a mental model boundary and made an orbit-shift happen.

In eye care, it was assumed that even the simplest ailments require a consultation with a doctor. But making doctors available to cover large populations, across all developing countries, is a very tough proposition and it will also take a long time.

Rather than approach the problem conventionally, by trying to plug the doctor availability gap, VisionSpring challenged the mental model boundary and reframed the market spectrum. The first mental model boundary breached was an intellectual boundary that *only an ophthalmologist can identify an eye problem*; this in turn, uncovered a deeper premise: that *of treating all eye problems the same way without differentiating presbyopia* from the more serious vision problems that require medical intervention. Presbyopia can be easily remedied by reading glasses and requires no medical intervention. A widely prevalent condition, it is simple to diagnose.

From here emerged the Vision Entrepreneurs business model—equipping local community entrepreneurs to diagnose and solve presbyopia, through what is now called Business in a Bag. VisionSpring had separated complex eye problems that require a doctor's presence from a simpler one, like that of presbyopia, which simply needs vision prescription glasses. In unscrambling this need spectrum, they identified a completely new way of treating presbyopia.

VisionSpring focused on simplifying the eye-testing and vision-prescription process to one that a local entrepreneur would be able to implement easily without the need for extensive learning and coaching. The Business in a Bag was the ultra-simple solution that enabled the entrepreneur to conduct eye tests and deliver glasses on the spot.

For example, how does the Vision Entrepreneur (VE) ensure that the distance between the patient and the eye chart is just right, while doing an eye test at every patient's location? A pre-measured piece of rope is enclosed. This extends from the point the chart is hung to the point where the patient has to be seated. Many patients are illiterate, so how will they read the alphabet? Replace the alphabet with the letter E in the four cardinal directions—they don't want to test the person's reading capability, they just need to know if s/he can see clearly, and that can be determined by whether the person is able to see the direction of the letter as the line decreases in size![50] Along with the screening equipment, the bag contains a set of 36 glasses. The up-front investment for a new VE is USD 10 for the bag. Customers pay a relatively low USD 4 for high-quality reading glasses that they get on the spot.

By reframing the market spectrum, VisionSpring uncovered a blind spot that led to the identification of a third space: people whose need could be solved without going to an eye specialist. With this breakthrough, VisionSpring has provided not just eyesight but productivity and a chance to work and earn to millions of people suffering from presbyopia in a world where at least 1.6 billion people are afflicted with it.[51]

SLS: Reframe the Literacy Spectrum

Same Language Subtitling (SLS) is an orbit-shifting idea that promises to make the entire planet read. It came about after Brij Kothari challenged the mental model boundary of the way the world identified literacy needs and tried to solve them.

There is no shortage of literacy solutions across the world, and for decades, organizations with both the vision and the funds have been attempting to raise literacy rates. In fact, UNESCO says, 'Literacy is a human right, a tool of personal empowerment and a means for social and human development. Educational opportunities depend on literacy'.[48]

Embedded even into UNESCO's mental model of literacy is a belief that it has to be a long-term solution: improving the basic and continuing educational system. However, this is also labour and infrastructure intensive, and often goes against the grain of the communities' way of life, especially where adult literacy is concerned. Investing in teachers, hiring or building learning spaces, providing learning tools like books and flash cards is only one part of the problem. Why would an adult learner in a developing country give up lucrative earning time or work time to attend a learning programme? In fact, many literacy programmes fail due to poor learner motivation.

Brij Kothari realized that while we look at the world as only literates and illiterates, in reality there is a third and large segment of people who are early or neo-literates. This realization came from a survey. As Brij shares, 'We commissioned an independent five-state study by Nielsen's ORG–Centre for Social Research, to measure literacy in two ways: i) using the census method of simply asking the head of the household; and ii) requiring every household member to actually read a simple paragraph at Grade-3 level. The data was collected by Nielsen's ORG-CSR and analysed by the SLS team. The literacy rate of our relatively large sample of over 23,000 individuals from five states (aged 7 and above) turned out to be 68 percent, using the census method. Yet, by the paragraph-reading method, the literacy rate was, at best, 55 percent. At best, because only 17 percent of these were fully literate and the other 38 percent were "early-literate"—people with rudimentary alphabetic knowledge who were unable to read the simple paragraph. These key findings redefined the India literacy spectrum as 17 percent literates, 38 percent early literates and 45 percent illiterates. Thus, India can be estimated to have 146 million fully literate, 327 million early-literate, and 387 million non-literate people.'

The discovery that India had 327 million people who were early or neo-literates—people who can string alphabets together but can't read fluently—seeded the orbit-shifting idea.

Rather than invest in a long-drawn process of building literacy infrastructure, Brij broke through a mental model boundary and developed SLS for/of a popular TV programme as the fastest way to get the 327 million neo-literates to become literates. He hit upon the idea of using the most popular Bollywood music programme called *Chitrahaar* (or *Chitrageet* in regional languages) for SLS. While watching their favourite film songs, the people were now also seeing and instinctively reading the words in the subtitles, in the same language. What a powerful, simple idea! It turned out to be phenomenally successful.

Since SLS drives learning through popular Bollywood music, learner motivation moves from *should do* or *must do* to *want to do*.[35] As Bill Clinton says about SLS, 'A small thing that has a staggering impact on people's lives'.[36] And due to the sheer ease of the solution and its great reach, it becomes a low-cost, high-impact initiative. What Brij has so effectively done is reframed the market spectrum and uncovered a third space—the neo-literates—and then solved for them. SLS also creates physical and emotional access to literacy that ties in with learner motivation: there is no physical effort required as it is beamed into their houses through TV and people don't even realize they are learning as they sing along, so the 'effort' of educating is gone.

As a CEO, think about this:

Where in your market/industry is the market need being defined in a rather binary manner (literates and illiterates) or where is the market clubbing a variety of needs into one approach? (ALL eye problems need a specialist).

Rather than looking for ways to bore further into the market, look for ways to reframe the market spectrum instead. This could uncover a third space and create a new market opportunity.

Breaking through the Sacred Sequences

Industries build processes; processes are institutionalized and standardized, they get reinforced by best practices, and these best practices go on to become the benchmarks. After a while, these processes become sacrosanct: they are inviolable. It's like a religious ritual that can never be challenged. Orbit-shifters are able to see the sacred sequences for what they are: just one way of doing things, not the *only* way of doing things. They break through the underlying mental model boundary of sacred sequences to create an orbit-shift.

LifeStraw: Purify as You Drink

The entire water purification and supply industry works on the belief that you need to *first purify, then drink.* So, bottled water is purified at the source, or in factories, and then supplied through retail to consumers. Home water purifiers either have pre-purified water dispensers or purify the water, which is filled into containers (jugs and bottles) and then dispensed. LifeStraw broke this sequence by making it simultaneous: *purify as you drink.* The real shift that LifeStraw made was not in miniaturizing the system. Deploying technology to make it smaller, sleeker, and speedier is a given in the natural progression of development and growth. It is the delivery mechanism in the format of the straw that changed the game comprehensively. By putting a miniaturized system into a straw, LifeStraw broke the mental model boundary from *purifying and then drinking* to *purify as you drink.*[49]

e-Choupal: Bringing Market Information to Farmers

Traditionally, commodity selling and buying in India was advantageous to two out of three involved parties: the trader—middleman—and big business, usually at the expense of the third, the poor farmer.

Until *e-Choupal broke through a sacred sequence—it decoupled the single step of find out the price and sell* into three distinct steps. *First learn the price, then decide, and finally sell.* e-Choupal gave farmers access to global commodity markets within their villages, via the Internet. Earlier they discovered the market price only upon reaching the market with their produce and this forced them to sell at the given price. Now farmers were able to ascertain global and local market prices by the hour at home, observe trading trends, and decide exactly when the best day to go to the market was and what price to sell at. The power of decision making had now shifted from the trader to the farmer.[29]

As a CEO, think about this:

What are the sequences that have become sacred in your organization/industry or domain/sector?

Where is there a lock-in into a defined series of steps? What new opportunities emerge when you break, reorganize, morph an industry sacred sequence?

Breaking through the Boundary of Progression

One of the most established mental models is that *new answers must come from new technology. New solutions can only come from new scientific and technological advances.* This mental model fuels the ever-growing need to invent, patent, and uncover new technology trends. In fact, many R&D organizations have the number of patents as a goal in itself.

While there is no denying the fact that new knowledge opens up new possibilities, orbit-shifters have also challenged this mental model, going back in time and mining the wells of traditional knowledge to solve new problems. Some of the most powerful orbit-shifting innovations have come from harvesting traditional knowledge in a new format.

Mongolia—Solving for Health Care

The challenge for the Mongolian government was to provide health care to thousands of families who live in the scattered hinterland, where the nearest hospital can be 30 to 40 km away.

The usual mental model would have suggested an increase in the number of doctors and hospitals. But instead they partnered with Nippon Foundation in Japan to provide a traditional Japanese health care solution, breaking a mental model boundary in the process. They placed medical kits in each home and empowered the families with the knowledge to diagnose their basic symptoms and self-medicate from the kit. The kit contained traditional Mongolian remedies, and not modern medicine. [31]

The Mongolian government broke through the normal progression mental model and went back to a traditional medicine solution, packaged in a modern format.

This dramatically reduced the number of people coming to hospitals.

Ekal Vidyalaya: The Traditional Gurukul

Ekal Vidyalaya has similarly turned to traditional wisdom to create, literally, 'one school' (ekal means solo, vidyalaya means school).

Rather than wait for the government to set up school infrastructure in remote tribal areas and then send trained teachers, *Ekal learnt from the traditional gurukul model* (an ancient form of teaching and learning).They simplified the school model: pick a teacher from the community, who was then trained (by Ekal) to deliver education to the local children at suitable times (so if the children worked in the fields in the morning, then school was held in the afternoon), with the minimum possible resources; if a classroom or a shed isn't available, the group learns under a tree. Ekal Vidyalaya is a school that leverages local community resources and is customized to community needs. Today, Ekal Vidyalaya is one of India's largest grassroots education movements operating in around 47,000 villages and educating over 13,35,000 students. By going back to the traditional gurukul model and focusing on the minimum required to teach and learn—one teacher and one tree—Ekal Vidyalaya has ensured that education doesn't cease for lack of infrastructure or funds.[11]

So going back in time and in solution seeking is not necessarily regressive and old fashioned. Sometimes the best way to move forward is by going back.

As an Innovation Leader, think about this:

Re-examine your current offering through the lens of traditional wisdom. How could leveraging wisdom unlock a new value proposition?

Breaking through the Boundary of Resourcing—From Scarcity to Abundance

Resource scarcity is one of the most oft-cited reasons why something is not possible or doable.

Orbit-shifters have demonstrated how resource scarcity is often not a fact but, in reality, a mental model blind spot. Challenging and breaking the resourcing mental model boundary has made orbit-shifting innovations happen in multiple industries and development sectors.

Resourcing Tutors

TutorVista has created a new orbit-shifting business model where, rather than having the talent come to them, they have gone to where the talent is. In India, they have built a business model converting housewives with graduate degrees into remote tutors. It is not as if remote tutoring services had not existed in India before TutorVista, it is just that they followed the conventional Business Process Outsourcing (BPO) model, where local tutors travel to a physical location and tutor children over the Internet. Almost immediately, the gap becomes visible, for a business is handicapped by the location and the number of tutors available.

TutorVista, through its unique software, made remote tutoring location agnostic, infrastructure agnostic, and time agnostic. Now, anyone could tutor from anywhere at any time, provided they had the software installed in their home computers. This blasted open a huge resource pool that was so far under leveraged: the average Indian housewife with a good education and with time on her hands, when her kids are away at school and her husband is away at work. She could choose to tutor at her convenience in her downtime.

As of 2009, when TutorVista won the Innovation for India award, it had 2,000 tutors in 98 cities teaching 20,000 students across 48 countries.[28] TutorVista is truly impacting the globe. And this teach-from-home model has also brought down costs for the customer significantly. Whereas the traditional tutoring model costs anywhere between USD 30 to USD 150 per hour, TutorVista charges USD 100 per month for unlimited tutoring hours.

Resourcing Finance

A number of micro entrepreneurs struggle to raise micro loans since large banks, financial institutions, and venture capitalists are not interested in amounts that are simply too small. Kiva broke through this resourcing mental model boundary with a key insight—while on one side there are hundreds of micro entrepreneurs whose micro capital needs are not being met, there are, on the other hand, thousands of potential micro lenders who would love to support the passion of entrepreneurs with micro loans. The capital that is scarce at the location of a micro entrepreneur is actually abundantly available across the world.

Microfinance has changed the lives of millions in the developing world. However, microfinance brought alive only one part of the equation—the borrower. By working in self-help groups, communities of women were able to borrow money and succeed with micro enterprises. The lending side of the equation was unchanged; it still came from big funding houses—banks and microfinance institutions.

Jessica Jackley and Matt Flannery transformed the lender equation with Kiva. When visiting Kenya, they discovered many entrepreneurs with a lack of access to funds. On the other side of the pond, they realized there were many individuals (not corporations) who want to feel connected to doing good in the developing world, by giving funds. *There was just no bridge to move the money from individuals to entrepreneurs across the world, until the creation of Kiva.* Kiva is an online platform providing opportunities for people to connect with and invest in small-to-medium enterprises in the developing world through soft loans. It broke the mental model that only a large faceless corporation flush with cash could be a financier. With loans as little as USD 25, an individual could invest in an entrepreneur on the other side of the world and expect investment returns! Kiva puts up individual stories of the entrepreneurs. And these stories and their passion is what connects with the lender. Hence Kiva becomes a personalized way to reach out and help, rather than just an investment. Kiva has innovated on the lender side of the equation, by opening up who could lend. It has created a financial resource lending pool of close to USD 420 million as of April 2013.[21, 22]

Resourcing Molecules

Resourcing tutors and resourcing money is understandable, but an even more profound breakthrough has come in the form of resourcing molecules.

It is well-known that large pharma companies do not invest in R&D

that is focused on illnesses unique to the developing world. The real issue that prevents them from doing so is that the R&D cost of new product development 'cannot be managed for a product aimed at emerging markets, it is just not profitable'. The only new product R&D they focus on is 'what is needed by the developed markets'.

This gap, of companies not investing in the molecules needed to cure developing world diseases, struck Victoria Hale forcefully when at a conference in Belgium, she heard Dr Shyam Sunder speak of the tragic effects of black fever (kala azar) when left untreated. Dr Sunder said, 'The tragedy, maybe even the crime, is that we have known this drug (paromomycin) is an effective treatment for kala azar since the 1960s, we could do something, but we are choosing not to.'

Victoria Hale broke through this resourcing mental model boundary when she explored the *matching of orphaned/neglected diseases with the shelved molecules from pharma companies, shelved because though there is high potential, there is a low prospect of making a profit.* From this initiative was born OneWorld Health, the United States' first non-profit pharma company.

One World Health describes this breakthrough clearly on its website:

> 'We challenge the assumption that pharmaceutical research and development is too expensive to create the new medicines that the developing world desperately needs. By partnering and collaborating with industry and researchers, by securing donated intellectual property and finding new uses for orphan drugs, and harnessing the scientific and manufacturing capacity of both developed and developing countries, we can deliver safe, effective, and affordable new medicines where they are needed most.'[32]

As an Innovation Leader, think about this:

What TutorVista, Kiva, and OneWorld Health reveal is that a resource that appears scarce when seen from one frame of reference may actually be abundant when viewed from another frame. The challenge is to break through the mental model boundary by exploring where this resource is abundant and how can the unleveraged be leveraged.

Where has your orbit-shift challenge stalled due to resource scarcity? How could you do a TutorVista or a OneWorld Health to move it from scarcity to abundance?

Breaking through the Mental Model Boundary Underlying an Either/Or

Most domains and almost all industries have their favourite either/ors .The existence of an either/or becomes embellished in industry wisdom: 'You can *either* have quantity *or* quality, you can't have both', 'You can *either* have mass *or* customization, you can't have both'. For orbit-shifters, an entrenched either/or is really a symptom of an underlying mental model boundary. Uncovering and breaching that boundary is what is needed to move the outcome *from either/or to a powerful AND.*

Human and Wildlife Conflict

Human-wildlife conflict has been one of the major issues faced by conservationists across the world. Nepal, which has around 29 percent forest area including wildlife parks, reserves, and community forests, has also been facing difficulties in handling this friction. Every year, wildlife that ventures out of forests causes havoc across the country, damaging property and killing people.[46]

This human-wildlife conflict has always posed a fundamental either/or dilemma. Either protect the human settlements with fences (an expensive solution which also blocks animal corridors), or unleash the lethal option—to kill the animals that venture out.

Local people near the Shiv community forest in Bardiya district have discovered an AND—a non-lethal method to keep rhinos away from farms and prevent crop destruction, and therefore also avoid the resultant human-wildlife conflict.

In 2002, they discovered that mint and chamomile are plants repulsive to mega herbivores like rhinos, as they are driven away with just the smell. They cultivated these fragrant plants between the borders of their farmlands and the jungles, as a natural fence. The farmers then didn't have to sit in bamboo towers to keep a lookout for wild animals.

The brilliance of this AND solution is that these two plants are not only an eco-friendly defense mechanism against wild animals, they are also highly valued cash crops. In 2003, with technological support from the World Wildlife Fund (WWF), Nepal, the Shiv Community Forest Users Group (CFUG) set up a distillation plant to extract oil from the mint and chamomile harvest. Now they have twelve such distillation plants processing essential oils, which are a great source of income. More than 60 percent of the families of the CFUG were below the poverty line. Now, the users' group earns an average of USD 13,500 per year.[15] As of 2012, 995 farmers cultivated these medicinal and aromatic plants in over 100 hectares of land and extracted nearly 2,800 kg of the essential oils menthol and chamomile, which sold at INR 1,200 per kg and INR 2,300 per kg respectively.[47]

Internet Copyright Conflict

The prevailing belief is that if a copyright holder wants content to go viral on the social networks, then it can't be protected. A copyright holder can either protect content or let it gain mass engagement by making it available and giving up copyright. *It is an either/or choice; both can't co-exist.*

This conflict came to the fore when Viacom sued Google, the parent company of YouTube, in 2007, for USD 1 billion citing copyright infringement on videos uploaded on YouTube. Traditionally, copyright holders want to be in complete control of their material and prevent any other party from using it. Both Google and Viacom have spent millions of dollars in the courts fighting this legal battle. As YouTube proliferates to 72 hours of video being uploaded every hour, chances of such copyright infringement only increases.[52]

This is a classic either/or case—either the copyright holder wins or the distribution platform does. But what lies beneath is hours of litigation and wasted time and money for both parties.

Around the same time in 2007, Google broke through the copyright either/or mental model. It launched Content ID, an audio fingerprinting technology, which searches through uploaded content to identify, much like unique fingerprints, the unique identity of a video. With Content ID, copyright owners can trace videos of their content uploaded by other users, and block it. However, two new options have also emerged. Instead of blocking violators, content owners can choose to track the usage and can even monetize the usage.[10]

Now, an AND has emerged that has transformed the approach to copyright. Content ID has broken the only option of the either-win-or-lose kind of litigation battles between copyright holders and content platforms like YouTube. It has opened up a plethora of choices to the copyright holder. Interestingly, it is to the advantage of not just big copyright holders like Viacom and Disney, it is now also changing the game for small players who did not have the wherewithal to deal with copyright infringement in the old world.

'Harlem Shake', an Internet meme that went viral in February 2013, is a typical example of how Content ID can be leveraged. The song, a high-energy repetitive music track by Baauer, was released by the label Mad Decent Records in March 2012, with minimal impact. However, in early February 2013 it took off with great and unexpected speed, like most Internet crazes do. The song played out in a thirty-second video format where one person in a crowd dances while the others remain still, and then they all join the first person in rocking to the beat. This easily replicable format went viral and became a global phenomenon, with people enthusiastically uploading their versions of the 'Harlem Shake'. By February 10, 4,000 videos on the 'Harlem Shake' were being posted per day on YouTube.

INDMUSIC is a company that helps independent musicians and labels track and make more money on CPM (cost per thousand user rate) on sites like YouTube. Using Content ID, INDMUSIC tracked and claimed at least 4,000 videos, with over 30 million views. Now Mad Decent had a choice:

block these videos or monetize them. They chose to monetize the videos.

Quoting from a *Billboard* article, 'This is where the financial upswing comes in for Baauer and other beneficiaries of future music memes: Of those 103 million video views, YouTube is able to charge an estimated average of $2 for every thousand viewers—that translates to $206,000.'

Once this money is shared between all partners, like INDMUSIC, YouTube, and Mad Decent, 'Harlem Shake's' label still makes roughly $83,500, and this is in one week! And this on videos uploaded by others! Now, a content creator has a lot more to gain by going viral, than to lose by losing copyright.[4, 17, 26]

And so the mental model has shifted from control and restrict to share and monetize. So rather than block the videos, it is working to Baauer's advantage, for the more users upload videos, the more money Baauer ends up making. 'We've, from the beginning, been very much a proponent of allowing everybody to do whatever they want with our stuff, as long we're able to monetize it', says Jasper Goggins, the manager of the label. 'It's a great way to help spread the music.'

As E. Michael Harrington, a music business professor and member of the Future of Music Coalition Advisory Board, says, 'The idea of trying to control everything seems futile because it's like whack-a-mole. It's going to get out, it's going to get shared, so you may as well try to profit off of it.'[25]

As a CEO, think about this:

What are your industry's favourite either/ors?
Which of these either/or boundaries, when bridged with an AND, will open up a new orbit-shift opportunity?

Transforming the Mental Model of Engagement

Breaking mental model boundaries and transforming the way people and societies engage has transformed war into peace, suspicion into trust, and combat into cooperation.

Non-Violence

That the struggle for India's independence could be won by non-violence was not just considered impossible, it was even incomprehensible. In fact, legend has it that when Mahatma Gandhi first shared this orbit-shifting idea with a group of professors, they reacted with scorn and asked him to reread his history. *Did he not know*, he was asked, *that not a single country has gained independence without war and bloodshed? Mahatma Gandhi reacted by saying the he was not talking about following history, he was talking about creating it.*

With the philosophy of non-violence, Gandhi broke through the mental model boundary that preached *an eye for an eye* and believed that only war can lead to independence. The mental model of *war to correct a wrong* inevitably creates two adversaries fighting to win at any cost. The casualties are very often the very people it was meant to 'liberate'. The politically correct word for this is now collateral damage.

Non-violence called for a dramatically different mental model, that of galvanizing people and staging non-violent protests. It called for even more courage and conviction than the much romanticized courage at the war front.

Mahatma Gandhi's movement of non-violence held up the most powerful empire in the world and forced it to give up the jewel in its crown.

Guatemala: Combat to Collaboration

Adam Kahane, a facilitator with Generon, has worked with governments on national reconciliation. He shared a moving account of his experience in Guatemala, a country scarred by one of the longest running and most violent civil wars in Latin America, from 1962 to 1996. In his book *Solving Tough Problems*, he brings alive how a generative dialogue between entrenched adversaries *broke through the mental model of engagement, thus moving them from combat to collaboration.*[20]

Backed by the United Nations, Vision Guatemala was set up to conceive and promote a new vision for the country. The project team was diverse; it included academics, business and community leaders, even former guerilla and military leaders, and government officials.

When the team gathered together for the first meeting, the divides were clearly visible. As Adam writes, 'The indigenous people were sitting together, the military people, the human rights group were all sitting together.'

At first there was little dialogue, and it was at best superficial. Most people argued from their entrenched perspectives. The schism was strong because everyone was frozen in his or her current mental model of engagement.

The first shift was triggered when a young man stood up and questioned the pessimism of the group. He called them 'old pessimists'. To its credit the group gave space to such voices, took in this provocation, and reflected on it. This moved the conversation to a deeper level, but they still avoided the deep and unspoken divides across the room.

The dam that blocked engagement was finally broken in one moment-of-truth experience that opened the floodgates to a generative dialogue. Ronalth Ochaeta, a human rights activist, told the story of a time he had gone to a Mayan village to witness the exhumation of a mass grave (one of many) from a massacre. When the earth had been removed, he noticed a number of small bones and he asked the forensics team if people had had their bones broken during the massacre. They replied that no, the grave contained the corpses of pregnant women, and the small bones were of their foetuses.

Ochaeta's narration evoked complete silence. This one story brought alive the profound human dimension of the brutality the country had been through. It was not a statistic anymore; everyone could actually feel it. It was the story of this experience that joined them as human beings.

That moment shifted the engagement from 'holding on to and promoting their individual perspectives' to 'connecting with a shared new reality that they were all committed to, and to preventing it from happening again'. *Their purpose now became to work together to help ensure that Guatemala's terrible history did not repeat itself.*[7]

This dialogue broke through the deep silos and suspicions that were dividing the group and built a new reality with a shared purpose.

What created the breakthrough was that the mental model of engagement had shifted from a convince-and-defend debate to a generative dialogue.

Later on, the Vision Guatemala team discovered that the greater value of their work for the people of Guatamala was not so much the output of the team's vision for the country, but how they had engaged in arriving at it. The real breakthrough was in the way they had engaged generatively to go beyond the defend-and-attack boundary to bring people together.

Community Policing—Combat to Pre-empt

The traditional and dominant model of policing is to *combat crime.* This mental model is so dominant that the word *policing has become equivalent to micro inspecting.* When a police force is asked to think of ways to reduce crime, the usual response is *to ask for more people, better transport, faster communication.* All these ideas are rooted in the mental model of *combating crime—enhanced ways to spot a crime and catch the criminal.* This has led to the fast emerging 'big brother is watching' technologies and methodologies that are focused on finding ways to keep watch over and track the entire population at every move.

Adopting Community Policing has been a challenge to this deep-rooted and even highly romanticized (in movies) mental model. J.K. Tripathy's move to Community Policing was triggered by a recognition of a mental model boundary that *the vast majority of people are law abiding, in fact just 3 percent are criminals or* have a criminal mindset. But the mental model of combat crime makes us treat the majority with suspicion, and we end up alienating the majority. In fact, the people in a community are usually aware of unusual and suspicious events in their neighbourhood. But in such a situation, they don't inform the police; they prefer to remain silent. His challenge in Tiruchirapalli became: *How do I win over the cooperation and the confidence of the honest majority to prevent crime and apprehend criminals?*

Community Policing moved policing from being reactive to being proactive; it involved building proactive relationships with the community members. Each constable reached out to community families to overcome anonymity, establish proactive contact, and build trust. Neighbourhoods began to feel an affinity with their beat constables and soon they were being called upon for any number of issues from resolving disputes, solemnizing marriages, and the like. The combat crime mental model is essentially reactive. It comes into action only once a crime has been committed and reported. Conversely, Community Policing focuses on preventing crime by recognizing that a crime is a consequence and not a cause. So if the public street lighting was poor, the community police worked toward better lighting with the electricity board. Better lighting in the neighbourhood deterred crime.

This shift in the policing mental model from combat crime to pre-empt crime has led J.K. Tripathy into another orbit-shifting idea—to *prevent the process of criminalization.*

Recognizing that urban slums are fast becoming the breeding grounds for criminals, Tripathy diagnosed the real issue. He says, 'Men are usually the sole earning members of an urban slum family. They often take to alcohol, become near alcoholics, and end up spending most of their income on alcohol. This creates income pressure on the family, leading to women taking to prostitution and pushing children into child labour. These children are being bred into criminalization.' To prevent and turn around this vicious cycle, J.K. Tripathy has started the Police Boys Clubs. Urban slum children are made members of the Club, where they are provided with effective education and training on crime prevention and social values. The pride of being affiliated with the police goes towards building a lasting impact against crime.

Pre-empting crime and building community cooperation are the cornerstones of community policing—*a breakthrough that has transformed the way a police force engages with the people to not just ensure compliance, but to enhance citizen security.* It moved the role of the police from *law enforcers* to *community protectors.* In Tiruchirapalli, the community policemen became 'anna'—the local term of respect meaning elder brother. The crime rate dropped by 40 percent, far beyond what the conventional methods achieved. It has sustained even after J.K. Tripathy was transferred.[30]

As a CEO, think about this:

Some of the biggest conflicts have been resolved by breaking through the mental model of engagement. Indeed, some of the biggest societal divides have been bridged by transforming the mode of engagement.

What are the biggest conflicts that you and your organization are facing in the industry/ecosystem? Where is the biggest divide? What is your current mental model of engagement, which, if challenged and transformed, could fuel an orbit-shift?

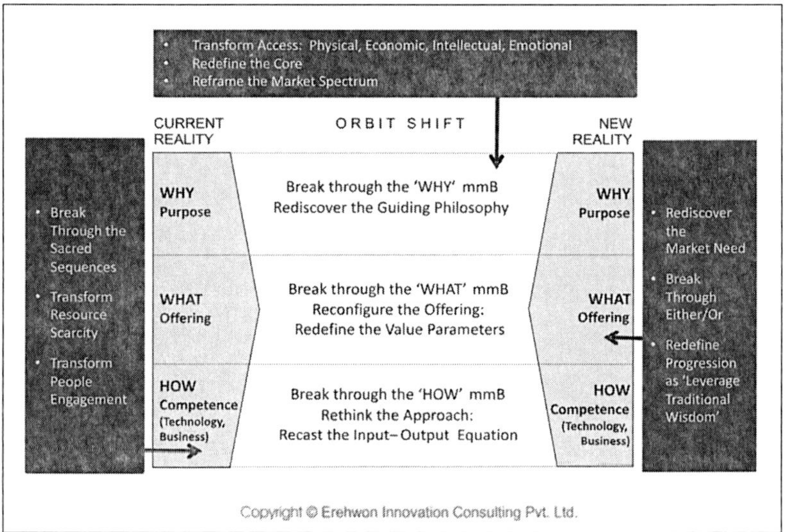

4.3 – Breaking through Mental-Model Boundaries (mmB)

An orbit-shifting challenge is a transformation vehicle—to transform the current reality into the new reality.

This chapter has brought alive how orbit-shifters start generating breakthrough ideas. They start by breaking through the mental model boundaries underlying The WHY, The WHAT and The HOW of the current reality:

Breakthrough The WHY mental model boundaries:

Challenge the guiding philosophy and the key construction that anchor the current reality by:

- Transforming Access: Challenge the Physical, Economic, Intellectual and Emotional Access boundaries.
- Redefining the Core: Challenge the core purpose that the industry is locked into.
- Reframe the Market Spectrum: challenge the core construct defining the current market spectrum.

Breakthrough The WHAT mental model boundaries:

Reconfigure the value parameters defining the current offering by:

- Rediscovering the Market Need: From funtional to emotional, Co-temporal and Co-Spatial.
- Redefining Progression: Leverage traditional wisdom.
- Transforming an either/or into an AND.

Breakthrough The HOW mental model boundaries:

Challenge the dominant input-output equation by:

- Challenging sacred sequences.
- Transforming resource scarcity.
- Transforming people engagement.

These are the nine mental model boundaries underlying The WHY, The WHAT and The HOW of the current reality, which when broken through have created orbit-shifts.

This chapter has described the nine mental model boundaries, which, when broken through, have created orbit-shifts. *But, are these nine the only mental model boundaries? Are there no more?* Not at all, these nine are just a good starting point. They are not all, or enough. An orbit-shifter needs to dig deeper and get into the flow of uncovering and breaking mental model boundaries. These nine are great springboards to start looking for a breakthrough.

ZEROING IN ON THE ORBIT-SHIFT KEYSTONES

The *exploratory* process of breaking through mental model boundaries ends with the identification of orbit-shift keystones.

Orbit-shifters converge and synthesize their thinking to identify orbit-shift keystones: the three to four key boundaries, which, when breached, have the greatest potential to yield orbit-shifting ideas.

For Muhammed Yunus, *asset as collateral* was the orbit-shift keystone: the key mental model boundary that needed to be breached in order to create access to loans for people at the bottom of the pyramid. Exploring the market through the lens of this keystone led to the orbit shifting idea, *community as collateral*, which seeded the revolutionary microfinance model.

Different Orbit-shift Keystones Lead to Distinct Orbit-shifting Ideas

VisionSpring and Aravind Eye Hospital demonstrate how the pursuit of the same orbit-shifting challenge, *eliminate needless blindness*, can lead to two very different orbit-shifting ideas. This is because the pivotal mental models VisionSpring and Aravind had chosen to break were very different, resulting in two very different orbit-shift keystones.

VisionSpring chose to eliminate needless blindness by reducing presbyopia (nearsightedness). The first mental model boundary they identified was 'all vision problems have to be treated in the same way'. And the second boundary they identified was, 'highly trained medical specialists are needed to deal with all vision problems'. VisionSpring broke through both these boundaries to create a new business model for eye care in presbyobia. Semi literates from within rural communities, called Vision Entrepreneurs, were trained to check and remedy presbyobia, with *Business in a Bag.*

Aravind, on the other hand, chose to eliminate needless blindness by making affordable cataract surgery accessible to the masses. The key mental model boundary they identified was the sacred process of cataract surgery, which had remained unchanged and unchallenged through the years. Dr V broke through this boundary with a process innovation to transform efficiencies and crash costs, resulting in a surgeon who is ten times more productive than his counterparts elsewhere.

How the challenge shapes up into an actual orbit-shifting idea is dependent on which mental model boundary or set of boundaries the orbit-shifter chooses to break through. As Aravind and VisionSpring show, dependent on the boundaries chosen, very different outcomes are possible—the surgery process mental model boundary became the keystone around which Aravind developed its orbit-shift, whereas reframing the market spectrum became the orbit-shift keystones around which VisionSpring developed its orbit-shifting business model.

By breaking through mental model boundaries (one or a set), orbit-shifters arrive at keystones based on which they build the orbit-shifting idea. There is no dearth of opportunities in any industry or ecosystem—the possibilities of orbit-shifts are limitless. To minimize the possibility of a blind spot, orbit-shifters identify not one, but the three four most powerful mental model boundaries, which they then crystallize into three to four orbit-shift keystones.

Orbit-shifting innovation really starts to gather momentum when mental model boundaries are challenged and broken through: organization, industry, ecosystem, and engagement mental model boundaries. A mental model boundary can limit or liberate a person, a team, and an organization.

Chapter 5

Orbit-shifting Insight

AN ORGANIZATION HAS TAKEN ON AN ORBIT-SHIFTING CHALLENGE AND BURNT ITS BRIDGES. It now needs to break through mental model boundaries and discover an orbit-shifting idea.

What does it take to actually uncover and break through the mental model boundaries of an organization or an industry, especially when the people attempting to do it are usually as much a part of the established mental model?

What is needed is an orbit-shifting insight that will break through mental model boundaries, join new dots, and make the orbit-shifting idea visible.

ORBIT-SHIFTING INSIGHT: BEYOND TECHNOLOGY ROAD MAPS

Two big mental-model-boundary breakthroughs in two very different worlds, gaming—Nintendo Wii (originating in Japan)—and microfinance with Grameen Bank (originating in Bangladesh), were both triggered by orbit-shifting insights.

The gaming industry had long been locked into the mental model of following technology road maps. As Genyo Takeda, who was part of the Nintendo design team, says, 'We started developing Wii right after Nintendo launched the GameCube. You know, as soon as we complete one system, we start thinking about the next one. Needless to say, we don't design new components or technologies from scratch. Rather, we have to base our designs on existing technologies. In the world of technology, there are so-called road maps (overviews of proposed technologies/products) that are used by each industry in order to make general forecasts about where semi-conductor technology is heading, as well as the evolution of disc and wireless technologies. Engineers and developers normally refer to these road maps while developing hardware that they plan to release in the future. Looking again at the completed Wii, I feel that it has turned out to be something completely different from what was predicted in the mainstream technology road maps.'

Rather than playing within the mental model boundaries as was the norm in the industry for decades, this team paused and asked a breakthrough question: 'Technology road maps for whose benefit?' And immediately, the mental model boundary became obvious.

Genyo Takeda adds, 'If we had followed the existing road maps, we would have aimed to make it "faster and flashier". In other words, we would have tried to improve the speed at which it displays stunning graphics. But we could not help but ask ourselves, "How big an impact would that direction really have on our customers?" During development, we came to realize the sheer inefficiency of this path when we compared the hardships and costs of development, against any new experiences that might be had by our customers.'[6]

This question breached the mental model boundary and led to the orbit-shifting insight—*to move gaming from a singular game played solo by teenage boys in their rooms into a family game played in the living room.* Rather than meeting the engagement and entertainment needs of teenagers, Wii tuned into the social needs of the family as a whole.

Nintendo announced that its new console would be called Wii. Nintendo said that the name was in accordance with its philosophy of creating a gaming world without boundaries, attracting new gamers and making a fun product for everyone. Nintendo's press release explained: 'Wii sounds like *We*, which emphasizes that this console is for everyone. People around the world can easily remember Wii—no matter what language they speak. No confusion. No need to abbreviate. Just Wii'. The unique spelling was also expected to be easy to search on the Internet as well as to serve as a trademark.[7,8]

Even though its graphics and visual realism were lesser than the competitors', its emotional involvement by drawing the player in through physical movement was far greater. Usually, new editions of gaming devices are restricted to the gaming world. However, the Wii created a worldwide impact when it was launched. It was sold out and was unavailable in several countries even as it hit the market. It went on to explode in the market by becoming the highest-selling console of its generation. On a cumulative basis, Wii had sold 95 million devices, far outstripping Xbox 360 with its 66 million devices (2012).[1]

By breaking the sacrosanct mental model of the industry—that technology road maps determine the next game—Wii broke new ground. It also had another competitive advantage—with the traditional model of high quality graphics and high power came high cost and for years, the industry had operated on a 'sell hardware at a loss and make your money on the software' business model. However, Wii, with lesser technology and power needs than conventional consoles, costed less and hence sold at a better margin.

Sony Missed the Insight

While Nintendo succeeded in recognizing and converting an orbit-shifting insight, Sony failed. As reported in *The New York Times*, Sony's outgoing president of Worldwide Game Studios, Phil Harrison, spoke of his failed attempts in trying to convince his Sony bosses on the value of social gaming.

> 'Mr Harrison blatantly stole the show by baldly admitting that his own bosses at Sony's brain trust in Japan completely misgauged the direction of the entertainment industry. In designing its latest console, PlayStation 3, Sony focused on delivering high-tech single-player experiences, while Nintendo has dominated the market with the Wii by delivering casual, social games. Mr Harrison had tried to emphasize casual play with products like Buzz, the EyeToy and SingStar, but he said he was not supported by the corporate mother ship.'

As Phil Harrison said, 'It's a very interesting and frustrating thing for me to experience because I have been banging the drum about social gaming for a long time. And our Japanese colleagues said that there is no such thing as social gaming in Japan: "People do not play games on the same sofa together in each other's homes. It will never happen." And then out comes the Wii.'[10]

> The leadership of Sony had allowed itself to get trapped in self-projection. They were seeing the market through their own lenses—their own mental models. Unknowingly and unwittingly, self-projection came in the way of first recognizing and then accepting a path-breaking insight.

ORBIT-SHIFTING INSIGHT: THE ORIGIN OF MICROFINANCE

The microfinance model that broke through the mental model of traditional banking began when Muhammad Yunus got an orbit-shifting insight. Muhammad Yunus spent long hours with the people at the bottom of the pyramid trying to understand their context and needs. What stood out for him was that these people lay completely outside the mental model of traditional banks that needed assets as collateral in order to sanction a loan. It was a vicious cycle: they had no asset for collateral but they did need loans to move out of the poverty cycle. His determined and empathetic drive led to a social insight—for people in this part of the world, losing face in their community was far worse than losing money. This further led to the breakthrough business insight: *use community, rather than assets, as collateral.* It was then developed into a business model of *small loans to women with community as collateral.* This started the microfinance revolution.

Banks Missed the Microfinance Insight

The microfinance insight did not come from a bank! What made it genuinely difficult for even a very progressive bank to get a microfinance-like insight?

This is a reflective question we have posed to many groups of managers across industries (including banking) and cultures.

Most groups inevitably conclude that 'self-projection is the real barrier that prevents very successful organizations from even getting and acknowledging a radically different insight'—the same barrier that blocked Sony from recognizing the social gaming insight. *Self-projection traps us into seeing the world through our lens. A first world organization sees the third world through its first world lens.* When multinational organizations enter developing markets, they hire local people but they usually end up with *people like themselves* who fit into the organization's developed market mindset. *Managers in the metros of India and Bangladesh are as far removed from the realities of the rural market as their counterparts in New York are. Looking at the third world through a first world lens blocks an orbit-shifting insight and the organization remains stuck in the existing mental model.*

As a CEO, think about this:

When an MNC's replication strategy in an emerging market doesn't work, the usual response is that the market is not ready yet! The reality is that markets are always ready; we aren't ready for the market. This market does not want a poor man's CitiBank, the people want a Grameen Bank.

Where or when have you and your organization been the ones saying, 'This market is not ready yet?'

Is this a reflection of the market or your mental model? Could it be blocking a microfinance-like orbit-shifting insight?

SELF PROJECTION

Self Projection Blocks the Next Insight: For 10 Years

Self-projection, built over years of experience in the industry, has a lingering impact that can keep businesses dangerously locked in to their mental models for years to come. Oticon, the hearing-aid manufacturing company in Denmark, is a classic example of this. By the mid-1970s, Oticon was one of the world's top ten manufacturing companies of hearing aids.

As Lars Kolind, the CEO of Oticon from 1988-1990, says in his book, *The Second Cycle*:

'Oticon was the master that took the lead in moving hearing aids from the pocket to behind the ear—a great achievement, marketing-wise and technologically. The behind-the-ear mental model of the 1970s was indeed a winning formula for Oticon.

But customers wanted to move to the next stage: they wanted hearing aids to move into the ear and the ear canal, a distance of less than an inch. However, this move was difficult from two points of view: space in the ear was much smaller than behind the ear and worse, the shape of ear canals differed tremendously from person to person. That required the behind-the-ear mass-produced product to become a customized one. The market moved from mass production to mass customization.'

Customers' needs changed significantly; they were demanding *in-the-ear products* and the market responded to them. However, Oticon, as a successful market leader, dismissed this demand, genuinely believing it was just a passing trend. It actually went further to create even more technologically advanced *behind-the-ear products,* even as it started to lose business. The organization leadership was classically self-projecting its own beliefs on how the market *should* and would shape up and how the customers *should* respond. They ended up denying the reality staring them in the face and reacted with a business strategy that resonated with their self-projection rather than with the real needs of the market. When sales teams returned with market feedback, the leadership pushed the sales people to go and sell *more of the same* rather than return with examples of how the competitors were winning the market. *Their self-projection made them blind to the writing on the wall. And self-projection can be so strong that it can blind an organization, for not one or two, but ten long years.*

As Kolind says, 'Oticon continued to defend and improve its irrelevant mental model for almost ten years. And when the headwind became too strong, Oticon's entrance into in-the-ear hearing aids was only half-hearted.

'Even at the time when custom-built in-the-ear products had captured half of the world market, Oticon maintained that the market was wrong and the whole thing would blow over.

'It didn't.

'Finally, Oticon's response was to develop a mass-produced, standard, in-the-ear product that needed no customization—that is, a behind-the-ear product to be clicked directly on to the ear mold. Sound was fine, but it looked nothing but terrible and the market completely rejected it and bought the customized products instead.'[4]

And so, even when Oticon reluctantly did enter the in-the-ear market, its approach continued to be driven by self-projection! No wonder then, the market completely rejected its products. The company leadership realized the need for drastic change only when it had lost more than half its market equity.

Self-projection almost killed Oticon and it took them ten painful years to recognize it. The company had to be brought down to its knees and shocked into transformation. And yet we'd call Oticon fortunate; for it did break out of the self-projection and craft a new path to success; others are not so fortunate. Continued self-projection simply suffocates businesses to death.

Self-projection Arises From Bureaucratized Market Insight

Organizations have long since recognized the need for new market insight and most mature organizations have, by now, very mature insight processes. In order to be objective and to overcome bias, they even outsource market insight to research organizations.

However, in most organizations this process has matured to the point of becoming bureaucratized. A senior marketing manager decides, 'we need to understand the mass affluent segment better, there could be new opportunities'. He then calls in a market research agency that goes on to do a thorough qualitative and quantitative research. What usually comes through from this exhaustive process is loads of data, some useful information if you are lucky, but almost never an orbit-shifting insight. *In all our work*

5.1 – Bureaucratized Insights

with organizations, we have virtually never come across an orbit-shifting insight that emerged from a conventional market research study.

Yet, most managers continue to seek insights from market research almost as a business given, even when they realize its inadequacies to the extent that it has become the unquestioned and only way to explore markets.

As some managers openly expressed:

- 'We're focused on market studies and surveys but innovation doesn't happen because surveys are usually biased towards what exists, rather than what doesn't.'
- 'We're so afraid of ambiguity that we grasp at any straws that promise to predict the future and put all our faith in them.'

And herein lies the rub. For if thinking is outsourced to market research and most market research merely gathers information *of what has already occurred*, then in reality, most managers are preoccupied in catching up with *the past*.

As one manager said, 'Most third-party analysis and inputs tend to bias us towards the incremental rather than the orbit-shifting. They can be useful for business as usual but not for orbit-shifts.'

As an Innovation Leader, think about this:

A market research is inevitably focused on seeking answers to questions. The search for an orbit-shifting insight is, in contrast, not about seeking answers; it is more a search for new questions.

A market research study cannot, by definition, bring answers to questions we never asked. And our questions and our hypotheses are usually rooted in the current mental model.

No wonder a market research, more often than not, ends up being an extension of the current orbit.

You can't create the next orbit with an orbit-maintaining tool.

Reexamine your previous market research hypotheses and questions—what are the dominant mental models underlying these hypotheses and questions? This in itself could throw up blind spots, uncover new questions, and breach a mental model boundary.

Seeking Answers from Market Trends

Recognizing the limitations of market research, some managers actively seek market trends and projections. As one person said, 'Our marketing head doesn't move a step unless he has market trend reports from at least five different think tanks before him.' In a world seeking the perennial crystal ball, market studies highlighting market trends present a great way to reduce anxiety about the future. But that's often all they do—reduce the anxiety temporarily.

When India's largest telecom company, Airtel, first explored the possibility of launching cellular phones in India beginning in New Delhi, they too initially turned towards the crystal ball. But then soon changed track. As an Airtel spokesperson said, 'The first market study of mobiles in Delhi showed a market size of only 15,000. People said, "Why do I need a phone during travelling?" They had a phone at home and a phone at office. Why would they need another one? If we had followed the market research and believed the trends it threw up, we'd never have launched Bharti Cellular (now Airtel).' The Airtel team did not treat this market trend as a definitive answer; they treated it as a mental model boundary. And for this reason, it triggered a new question—'What will it take to penetrate the bigger market?' This led to their market success. In 2011, the size of the New Delhi mobile market was 2.27 million subscribers.[2]

Orbit-shifters don't go about seeking predictions for the future; they actively go about creating it.

As a CEO, think about this:

Orbit-shifters create trends, consultants publish them, and followers adopt them.

Is your innovation agenda directed by published market trends? If your answer is yes, then in all probability, you are a good follower.

What if you were to start by questioning the market trend, like the Airtel team did? A new orbit-shifting insight may burst through.

ORBIT-SHIFTING INSIGHT: NOT OUTSOURCED, BUT FIRST-HAND

Orbit-shifters seek that one insight that will unleash a new trend. They realize that depending on market research or on published trends is not just limited because it is a *search for answers*; it is tantamount to outsourcing thinking. This will not yield a breakthrough. They go about discovering new questions that point to the one orbit-shifting insight and seek it directly and personally.

Orbit-shifters believe that the one thing that cannot be delegated or outsourced is market insight. They demonstrate the will and the focus to immerse in the market and get first-hand insights. They believe only first-hand market experiences have the power to uncover new questions and new insights. Jacob Kurian of Tanishq said it the best. He said, 'There is an altogether different energy, a different calling when you hear a woman tell you, the personnel in your stores suck, they are standoffish and snobbish, than when you hear the same thing via a sanitized PowerPoint presentation in a boardroom—33 percent of your customers dislike the store personnel. The call to action is very different. The former hits you in your gut.' The first-hand experience provokes a new question with a force that is unavoidable.

The Trust-building Insight

In fact, Tanishq's turnaround came from Jacob's capacity to engage deeply with his customers. When Jacob became its COO, Tanishq was a minnow in the jewellery industry in India. Corporatization of the unorganized, unregulated jewellery industry had begun with Tanishq. It was struggling to establish this new paradigm primarily because it hadn't managed to break the *trust* between a woman and her family jeweller. In India, a woman bought jewellery almost in a ritualistic fashion—going to the jeweller her mother went to, who in turn, had patronized only the jeweller her mother had been to.

On the other hand, the jewellery businesses had also been hereditarily passed on from father to son, so they had long and deep bonds with their customers. How was a professional jeweller like Tanishq to break this bond of trust built over generations?

At about the same time, Tanishq developed a machine called the Karat Meter, in which jewellery could be measured in order to access its caratage accurately. Tanishq knew that many of the so-called family jewellers who had built a great degree of trust with their clients actually skimmed off a percentage of gold, so women could never be entirely sure of the caratage of their jewellery. Jacob now felt he had a way of breaking the trust—he could invite women to measure their jewellery and demonstrate to them that their jeweller was untrustworthy. He felt confident that this demonstration would break the bond between the woman and her traditional jeweller and help her build a relationship with Tanishq, with its guaranteed purity.

However, when he floated this idea with women, they pooh-poohed him. As one woman said, 'Why would I want to discover if the jewellery my mother gave me is of lower caratage? What will I do apart from feel miserable?' So it seemed that the Karat Meter idea was doomed to fail.

Most settlers who seek answers from consumer panels would have given up at this point because it was apparent that the customers had soundly rejected the idea. However, an orbit-shifter like Jacob recognized that somewhere there was a deeper, unarticulated need in the customer—the Karat Meter was merely the means to the solution. He felt there was a missing link still waiting to be uncovered. He reflected and delved deeper to find the new question that would point to the differentiating insight.

What Jacob uncovered was the question that broke through his mental model boundary. 'Am I focusing on how to make the woman feel good so as to build trust or is my focus on making her feel unworthy, by proving her wrong?' It struck him that women were not interested in being proven wrong and were equally uninterested in Tanishq being proved trustworthy at the cost of their jeweller being proven a cheat. He realized that so far, the Karat Meter idea had centred around a mental model of *proving the jewellers untrustworthy.* It had been entirely focused on the jeweller rather than the customer; the customer gained nothing but a feeling of having been cheated. Jacob now saw a way of leveraging the Karat Meter to create a solution that centred on the woman. The *new question* had provoked a *new insight.*

It led to Tanishq's now-legendary campaign, asking all women to come to a Tanishq store with their traditional jewellery and to have the purity measured in a Karat Meter and then exchange the jewellery regardless of caratage for the same weight of authentic Tanishq jewellery, if such a need arose. *Now women had a solution to the problem of low caratage.* Droves of women of all economic backgrounds came in to have their jewellery tested and exchanged. Some, shocked to find that the caratage was as low as 19 carats as compared to the Indian standard of 22 carats, walked out awestruck when no questions were asked and Tanishq exchanged it for 22-carat jewellery.

Jacob says, 'Women had tears in their eyes as they discovered the family heirloom or the piece given by their mother on their wedding day was worth far less than they thought it was, but finally they had a solution at hand.' Tanishq had become the hero who helped her reclaim her loss, generations of loss due to the so-called trustworthy family jeweller. And from that day on, Tanishq became the jeweller of choice for many Indian women. The bond with the family jeweller had been broken.

Jaocb's experience highlights that even engaging in first-hand dialogues with customers is not enough. In their first level of dialogues, Jacob and his team were merely seeking to validate their Karat Meter idea—they were seeking answers, and were taken aback with the negative response. Then, they moved from *validation to discovery (seeking new questions).* Rather than using the negative response as a judgment, they started to uncover and discover what the woman was really seeking, what she was not saying, her deep-rooted, unarticulated need: *not to know that the family jeweller is untrustworthy, but to come back feeling good about her treasured jewellery with which she had tremendous emotional attachment.*

The Validation Lens

Most companies have realized the need for direct contact with customers. Many of them have even mandated customers visits and meetings. However, while Jacob and his team managed to move from validation to discovery, most managers in most companies remain stuck in the validation mode.

When we go in with a validation lens, we go in to confirm a hypothesis (to seek answers). But insight is not about validating a hypothesis; it is about discovering a hypothesis. And this really means going in with an empty cup and searching for new questions. For instance, as someone told us, many so-called 'consumer insights' are nothing but hypotheses conceived by the bosses, and the rest of the team is supposed to validate the bosses' hypotheses, on consumer visits.

A Self-fulfilling Prophecy

In one instance, two teams, one with a services background and another with a products background, were both asked to explore the customer's world of wellness. Both teams came back very excited with the confidence that they had gotten great insights. The services team was keen on launching a neighbourhood health service, whereas the products team was keen to launch healthy food supplements. Two teams, same target audience, two completely different business propositions. But interestingly enough, each business proposition was an extension of their current business model.

On digging a little deeper, some interesting facts emerged. The services team had gone out and asked the question: 'If we provide you a neighbourhood service, which improves your wellness and makes you feel good, will you buy the service?' The customers said yes!

The products team had asked: 'If we provide you products that complement your diet in a tasteful way while simultaneously providing nutrition, will you buy the product?' And again, the customers said yes!

This is an amazing example of getting answers to the questions we ask. The teams were meant to be on an explorative journey to figure out the customers' unarticulated needs. Instead, they went out on a validation journey and came back with a confirmation of their own thinking. They were, in reality, self-projecting their own beliefs on to the customers. So when someone says they got it 'straight from the horse's mouth', it's quite likely they put the words in there in the first place.

And this is the heart of why people don't get insights; they are validating a hypothesis that stems from self-projection. Self-projection creates the boundaries within which the questions are asked and answered. This self-fulfilling loop goes on only to validate what we already believe in and what we already know— perpetuating more of the same.

The Validation Lens Leads to Market Categorization

In a bid to better understand and respond to markets, companies catergorize the market into sections and segments. As time passes, the segment becomes the end in itself. Organizations start viewing the market through these segments and often lose sight of the real and emerging needs of customers. The segments become self-fulfilling prophecies.

This categorization came across equally vividly in a conversation between a team from a consumer durables company and a customer. This team was visiting a customer, who had just moved into a new house. All her products had come from a rival company. The team immediately told her the rival products were not as good as theirs and that they had recently brought out a fabulous high-end washing machine that she should have purchased as it was very appropriate for *an urban homemaker and a working woman's needs.* She asked them a strange question, one they didn't quite comprehend: *Did they have an absolutely low-end machine with just a stop-and-start button?* The team was puzzled, and said, yes, they did, but they sold these washing machines only in rural India, where there were 'starter customers' and that for her, being a high-end customer, the high-end machine was more appropriate. She went on to explain to the team that as a working woman who travelled, the machine had to be operated by her maid, who didn't read instructional English and hence couldn't operate a high-end machine. But a low-end one with a start-and-stop button would be easy for her to handle. It is only then that it dawned on the team that they had segregated machines as 'high-end machines for high-end customers and low-end machines for low-end customers' rather than on the usage realities of the Indian market.

An Insight Breaks through Market Categorization

The under one-tonne load carrier market in India was dominated by three-wheelers. Most of the players were trapped in defining the market as *the three-wheeler category that is very price sensitive.* The industry was obsessed with providing functionality at the lowest cost. When Tata Motors entered this category, its challenge was not just to compete, but to redefine the market.

Girish Wagh, the project leader, had a conversation with a farmer in Andhra Pradesh that helped break through the categorization. This farmer said, 'Honestly I am embarrassed to be driving a three-wheeler. I never take it to my in-laws' place. In fact, whenever I go to my in-laws' place, I park it a couple of streets away and walk. If I had a car, I would park it right in front.' For this customer, the vehicle was not just a small goods carrier. It represented his social status, it affected his self-esteem. Another person said, 'My vehicle has no doors, but if it had one, I could slam the door hard. The noise would announce my arrival. People would stop and notice.' And another said, 'I wish I could drive with one hand and sling the elbow of my other arm on the door like other car drivers do.'

Once they joined the dots across these dialogues, it made Girish pause and wonder. 'Why are we so consumed with the three-wheeler category? So far we have only been improving efficiencies and reducing costs because we think that the customer wants a cheaper three-wheeler. But doesn't he really want a car with the functionality of a three-wheeler?'

This redefining of the category led the Tata Ace team to develop *a four-wheeler, with the functionality of a three-wheeler*, where all the functional needs from a three-wheeler, like overload capacity, fuel efficiency, hyper speed, etc., would be met. Once the frame had shifted from a three-wheeler to a four wheeler, the team began to explore the driving experience. They discovered more need gaps like *the gear-change experience in a three-wheeler is really painful.* They ensured that the pleasure of driving was not compromised, a factor not even considered in the three-wheeler industry. *The idea was to create a product that didn't merely look like a four wheeler but provided the feel of a car in terms of driving experience, free of noise and vibration.*

The Tata Ace disrupted the category, and the same customers who had been called price sensitive were now willing to pay 44 percent more than the sub-one tonne carriers that dominated the market.

As a CEO, think about this:

What is a three-wheeler category? The customer doesn't buy a three-wheeler, he buys a small load carrier. An expert opinion like, 'This is a price sensitive, commoditized segment,' is very often a self-projection.

Where in your organization do you come across similar expert opinions? They could very likely be self-projections.

When engaging with customers, are you fitting them into the segments you create, or are you shaping and reshaping segments to reflect the changing and emerging market needs?

Are your market research questions aimed at evolving the segment perspective or simply to reinforce it?

Are you exploring intersections at all the points where your category is engaging with other parts of the customers' world?

A search for new questions, aimed at uncovering how your category is connecting with other categories and other parts of the customers' world, is likely to uncover new insights.

Overcoming the Validation Lens: Sparks a New Insight

A team from Kuoni, a leading tour operator, had come together to find ways to increase their holiday travel business. They started mapping the boundaries of the holiday industry and soon recognized that their mental model boundary was *planning, planning, planning.* Their deep belief was that *good holidays are well planned*, and deeper still, *the best holidays are the best-planned—detailed itinerary, travel papers, budgets, etc.* Challenging this boundary led to an orbit-shifting insight—*an unplanned holiday: where no planning can mean a great holiday.*

For this team, overcoming their intrinsic bias, that good planning leads to good holidays, was proving to be difficult even while conducting insight dialogues. In a conversation with a customer, an office executive, their first questions were the usual, 'Which has been your best holiday?' and they got the usual response: 'The best holiday I have had was in a coastal area, where everything went like clockwork—the backwater tour, the food, the spa session.' *But then they managed to overcome their planning bias and asked a new question:* 'What was one of your most memorable experiences that just happened, that maybe you wouldn't even call a holiday?' One executive then went on to narrate a fond memory of when his family was driving from home to another town and they happened to stop midway for a refreshment break. With a growing smile, he shared how they had gone to a resort for the stopover, and the kids loved the layout and wanted to stay longer. They discovered something unusual was happening in the evening that made them stay the night. A series of pleasant surprises followed, to make it a memorable event. This wasn't what either the team or even this customer called a holiday because somehow the mental model of a holiday had meant a *planned holiday*.

A string of new questions further explored *the many moments* when people wanted to go on a holiday that had not been planned. These insight dialogues led to a breakthrough idea: *holiday in-a-box* for those who want a holiday at the spur of the moment; a holiday they haven't planned for. The breakthrough market proposition became *a holiday that can be purchased like a box in a store.* This *holiday in-a-box* would be buyable off a retail shelf. It could be an impulse purchase like any other. Buy the chosen holiday in a box, call the phone number on the pack, and your holiday can start within twenty-four hours.

Orbit-shifters recognize their biases that cause self-projection. This awareness and sensitivity to self-projection enables them to go beyond it and ask new questions to arrive at an orbit-shifting insight.

As an Innovation Leader, think about this:

Orbit-shifters recognize that this tendency to seek answers comes from a self-projection/validation mindset. Their purpose of stepping out into the market is to seek new questions by reviewing, recognizing, and challenging their most fundamental assumptions.

They recognize that simply going out and asking questions and going by the first answers is too superficial to reveal a genuine insight. As some managers shared, 'We have realized that when we ask customers what they want and give it to them…they don't want it!'

Insight is the capability to go beyond what they want, to uncover new questions into why they live the way they do or don't.

Why are you going to your customers—to validate your thinking or to challenge your thinking and find new insight?

Outsight to Insight

Self-projection also shows up in how we engage to get customer insights. Often, managers tend to approach the customer and his world with an analytical lens, as if the world outside has to be studied as independent and apart from oneself. In doing so, a list of questions or areas to explore is prepared and the recipients are then peppered for answers in a typical interview format. They come back satisfied that all questions have been answered. However, this process also results only in an *outsight*—a view of the outside shell of the customer they have gone to study rather than any earth-shattering orbit-shifting insight.

Here are two contrasting dialogues, both from conservative cultures—India and the Middle East:

Two men found the danger of this method quite by accident. They were in the heartland of rural India, and wanted to understand the cosmetic-usage habits of women. They were talking to a housewife in a village about what and how she buys and uses her cosmetics. She told them of her weekly trips to the local store and how she chose her products. As they were wrapping up the conversation, her husband came home and was flabbergasted to see his wife talking to two strange men. He flew off the handle and started yelling at the men, then turned to berate his wife in the filthiest language, threatening to break her face. In fear, the pair fled from the place, but the incident left them troubled. They were worried that the husband would indeed carry out his threats and so returned the next day to explain why they had been talking to his wife. By then, the husband had calmed down and the men tentatively explained their purpose, that they meant no harm; they were merely trying to understand her buying behaviour, and they restated all that they had heard from her. The man broke out into a sarcastic laugh when he heard what she had told them. He said, 'Are you stupid? She never steps out of the house, I do all the shopping, even whatever she wants.' It was only then that it dawned on the pair that what the woman had been sharing was her aspiration, not the reality. In their pursuit of running through the list of interview questions, they had only explored the surface. They hadn't dug deeper to uncover and understand the reality of her world and how vastly different it was from their own.

Similarly, a marketing team had set out to understand women and their hair in Saudi Arabia and across the Middle East region. Their discoveries broke their mental model of women and haircare in a fundamental way. Wherever they talked to women, they heard, 'My beauty is for my husband's eyes... My husband likes my long hair, I want it short, but he will not like it... My mother doesn't encourage me to cut my hair, she always comments on it...when matchmakers ask about a girl, her hair plays an important factor...'

When the team sat down to gain insight from their dialogues, these conversations crept up again and again. The team kept thinking about the meaning, the implications, and the purport of these statements. The first conclusion was that *everyone in the family has an opinion on the woman's hair in the Middle East.* But this was not quite it. While it was a fair conclusion to make, the team realized it was still superficial; underlying it was a deeper insight. They felt they hadn't got to *it* yet; they were close, but not quite there. And as they kept mulling over it, playing it over with each other, looking at it through various perspectives, the orbit-shifting insight emerged. Whereas in most parts of the world, a woman is the sole decision-maker on her hair—she decides the cut, colour, length, style, etc.—is it possible that in Saudi Arabia and the Middle East, the woman's hair is a *shared property* of the family? She has no decision-making rights on it. Until she gets married, her mother decides what she should do with her hair, and after marriage, it falls on her mother-in-law and husband to take decisions on her hair; and once her children grow up, they get the first decision-making rights. *The orbit-shifting insight came from the comparison with the rest of the world: hair, as individual property with sole-decision rights versus hair as 'shared property' and 'family-decision' rights before her own.*

As an Innovation Leader, think about this:

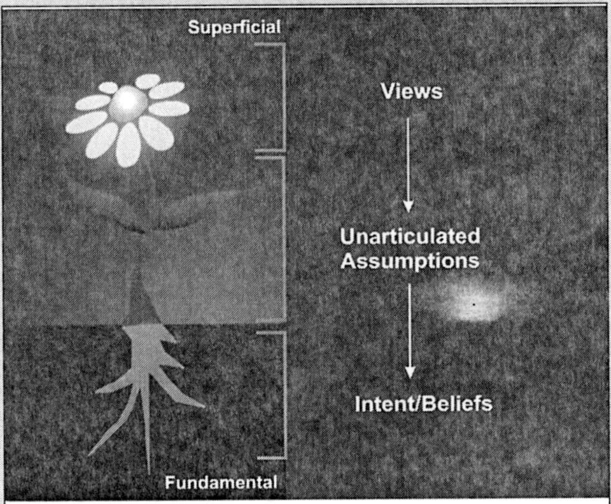

5.2 – Not a Question & Answer but an Insight Dialogue

What this team had uncovered was a deep-rooted insight, embedded in the cultural norms of the region. It was not easy to talk about or surface, and it was not reflected in the women's stated views or opinions. It was an unarticulated expression of the way their world is. This required deep dialogue; it needed active de-layering to go beyond the stated answers to allow women to explore their most vulnerable selves and that too, in the dialogue with a stranger.

'My husband will not like it; the matchmaker said my hair was too thin to find a good husband...'

How do we get women (customers) to engage so deeply?

How do we shift from just asking questions to engaging deeply and finding an orbit-shifting insight?

And how do we come away with not just a list of answers to questions we seek, but rather a deeper understanding and appreciation of their world and the way it operates, for this is where an orbit-shifting insight originates.

Mere observation or superficial conversations are unlikely to lead to insights.

Outsight to Insight: Redefining Care Giving

A pharmaceutical firm in Europe was seeking to improve the support for family care givers providing care to last-stage renal disease patients. This was critical given that family care givers who provide care for thirty-six hours or more a week are more likely than non-care givers to experience symptoms of depression or anxiety. For spouses, the rate is six times higher; for those caring for a parent, the rate is twice as high. Rather than conduct a traditional market survey, the innovation team conducted deep insight dialogues with patients, care givers, and with players across the entire care-giving ecosystem.

In talking to patients across Europe, they began to realize just how much of one's own self the patient lost; both in terms of self-respect as well as in terms of self-care. For example, there was an architect who said, 'I was a competent architect, but now I am a kidney patient. My life has changed altogether. I came home from hospital and had to reconfigure my whole house. I now have to have a wheelchair to go outside the house.'

The feelings of helplessness and loss of self-worth can be devastating. In many cases, patients are unable to reconcile their new situation with their former fully functioning selves. However, rather than give up, the architect went on to start an Internet portal for new patients to act as a facilitator to guide them through the difficulties of dealing with renal disease. This made her feel more valuable, and new patients gained confidence from her journey.

She felt she was making a positive contribution to society. As she said, 'A new phase in my life has begun. Looking back, it is much better than the earlier phase.' This was the orbit-shifting moment; this exchange with the architect made the innovation team pause. They realized that so far they had only approached the patient as just a patient, a helpless individual, completely dependent on his/her care giver, whereas the point of turnaround for this architect was the shift from being helpless to 'making a positive difference in life'. They asked themselves, 'Why is it that we have been treating patients only as helpless bodies that need looking after?' This led to the realization that 'there is a possibility of inducting patients into a new life, which is even better than the previous one'. This could now become the new purpose for care giving, and patients themselves could be the deliverers of this care-giving model. This realization breached a very deep-rooted mental model: the belief that the patient is only a passive value consumer. *This orbit-shifting insight broke through their mental model of seeing the patient as a passive value consumer. It revealed the possibility of the patient as a value generator instead.* This would also reduce the pressure on the conventional care givers, the spouses, family, and nurses.

Outsight to Insight: As a Supplier

The fragrance division at International Flavours and Fragrances (IFF) took on the challenge to 10X their growth (a ten-time increase), in 1995. The orbit-shift challenge was simple—increase the strike rate with client briefs. This was essentially a business-to-business (B2B) organization that supplied fragrances to product manufacturers for shampoos, soaps, etc. Every time any company wants to insert or even change a fragrance, it sends out a brief to fragrance suppliers and asks for a bid. Increasing the success rate of winning these briefs was critical to growth.

At that point in time, the fragrance division was losing more briefs than it won. And yet, when they collected annual customer feedback, there seemed to be nothing to be concerned about as all customers said they were satisfied with the relationship. In addition, many of them were long-term customers, which, as some team members said, they wouldn't have been if they weren't happy with the relationship. But the division head, Jayan Pillai, realized that they had to do something fundamentally different to make a quantum jump in winning briefs. And they had to begin by understanding the customer through deep-discovery dialogues rather than through their annual feedback questionnaire. This team undertook a first-hand Insight Quest, with one-on-one explorative dialogues rather than 'an interview format with the usual set of stock questions that sought the usual answers'. As they said, 'Our clients were suspicious in the beginning when we requested an hour for an open feedback session. They were impatient and said, "Look, we have already filled out your annual questionnaire." We persisted, asking for a minimum amount of time, even twenty minutes. But once they began talking they wouldn't stop and we ended up talking sometimes for two hours at a stretch. One of our oldest customers had some very cutting feedback for us and we were taken aback. We asked him, "Why didn't you ever tell us this?" There was silence and then he said, "Because you never asked!" We discovered more in that one Insight Quest than we did in all the years of collecting feedback.'

And out of this Insight Quest emerged an orbit-shifting insight that broke through their mental model boundary. They realized that they had settled into a mental model of *client subservience and just responding to client briefs.* This was the classic mental model of an unquestioning supplier. *The orbit-shifting insight revealed the client's real decision-making driver—the fragrance that won was the one that would be most attractive to the end consumer.* This insight led to an orbit-shifting idea. Take the client's brief but come back to him with not one but two submissions: *the first submission* to meet the client's brief and *the second submission* to meet the client's consumers' need. To achieve the second submission, the IFF team initiated a process of getting first-hand market insights and designing a fragrance to meet end-consumer needs—their second submission was now rooted in first-hand consumer insight.

This shift, when executed, led to more than doubling the client strike rate and fuelled an exponential growth in the next six years that went beyond their 10X aspiration.

The conscious shift from a traditional customer feedback process, which was largely about outsight to a proactive insight dialogue led to this orbit-shifting insight that fuelled exponential growth.

ORBIT-SHIFT INSIGHT NEEDS A MUTUALLY REFLECTIVE DIALOGUE

One day, the top leadership of a leading telecom company in Asia decided to do first-hand insight dialogues with the youth, as that segment was particularly weak in their offerings.

They were to have a conversation with a young man, who was on the cusp of adulthood; and in that first flush of confidence, he had no reservations. Utterly candid, he opened up completely about his life and how he lived it. He painted a fascinating picture of how his real life started only after his folks went to bed—once the bedroom door was locked, between 12 to 2 am, was when he surfed the Internet and kept in touch with his friends simultaneously on the computer and phone. The leadership team was riveted by the ways in which he connected with people. As the conversation wound down, he shared one last secret. He had been in touch with a young girl for the last eight months, primarily through SMS. They messaged each other at least eight to nine times a day and he was finally going to meet her the following week. He closed the conversation with a wink and said, 'Perhaps I will get lucky'.

When he left, there was absolute silence in the room and one of them said dismissively, 'He is too edgy, not like most teens.' On this note, they broke for lunch. After lunch, just as the group was to move on to other things, one of them intervened. 'We missed the point this morning,' he said. His trigger made the group pause and reflect on the dialogue with the teen. The tone of the conversation around the room changed to a reflective one. The leaders candidly admitted they had indeed missed the point, because they had avoided wanting to see who this boy really represented. What if he was a representation of their sons? Or even worse if the girl he was meeting next week was one of their daughters? The thought was so scary that it was preferable to deny rather than acknowledge it. For acknowledgment would mean having to come to terms with the fact that indeed the teen they had just spoken to was not an exception or edgy but a real representation of most teens, including theirs. It struck them that they were bound by their own fears and expectations of how they saw teens and hence had instinctively refused to acknowledge the insight.

And here lies the crux of the issue. The leadership team was unconsciously self-projecting its deepest fears onto the young man. And it was only on deeper reflection of about what blocked them that they were able to surface and challenge their self-projection. *Insight is not just about insight into the world outside, it is as much of an insight into our world as well.* Often, the orbit-shift comes from a discovery of our own self-projection. It is the capability to first recognize and then overcome self-projection that leads to an orbit-shifting insight.

An orbit-shifting insight occurs when the team doesn't merely talk at, or talk to, or even interview a customer. It occurs when the members explore their own beliefs, assumptions, and mindsets in a dialogue along with the customer's world. An insight dialogue is a *mutual* exploration, it is a mutual deep dive between the team and the market they want to impact, as had happened with this leadership team.

As a CEO, think about this:

Self-projection begins to happen when the lens with which we view the world is dominated by *what we think the world ought to be* rather than *by what the world is telling us that it is*. An orbit-shifting insight happens when a powerful experience breaks through a strongly held mental model boundary. For this telecom leadership team, this dialogue with an edgy consumer broke through their 'generational mental model boundary'. They came to terms with how the needs of the new generation were different.

What kind of insight dialogues are you engaging in?

Are you engaging in such edgy dialogues?

Or only in customer visits and interviews that confirm your mental model?

Do you find yourself commenting on customers or reflecting on your own mental model boundaries?

> Orbit-shifters follow through market insight experiences with a reflective dialogue to identify and breach mental model boundaries.

GOING BEYOND THE USUAL: THE ORBIT-SHIFTING INSIGHT SPECTRUM

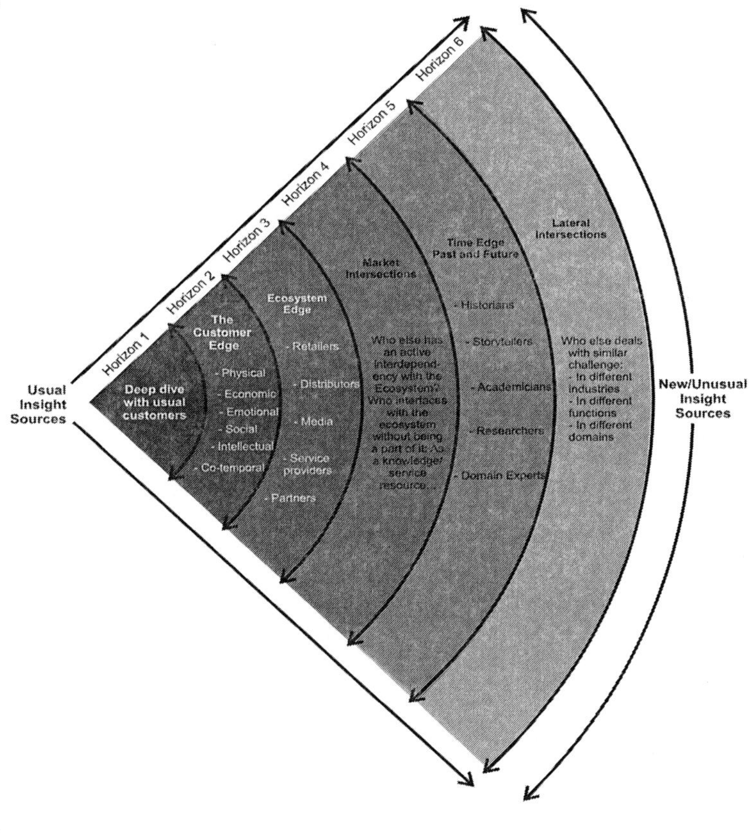

5.3 – The Orbit-shifting Insight Spectrum: The Six Horizons

Going to the same insight sources with the same questions can hit a wall of diminishing returns rather quickly. *Discovery of orbit-shifting insights needs insight dialogues with new insight sources.*

Orbit-shifters open up a wide spectrum of insight sources, across six horizons, to uncover a radically new opportunity or discover a new way of solving an unsolved problem. They first start with the usual customers, who they engage with deeply in discovery dialogues, rather than validation dialogues.

Moving on, orbit-shifters expand the spectrum to explore the customer edge—they identify and engage with edgy customers to uncover blind spots in the physical, economic, and emotional needs, and even further, the social, intellectual, and co-temporal needs. Then they go on to expand the insight spectrum to engage with all the entities across the ecosystem.

Horizon 2: The Customer Edge (Figure 5.3)

Orbit-shifters realize that *when the challenge is to uncover new questions and discover an orbit-shifting insight, it won't happen by talking to the same, average customers. They need to do insight dialogues with customers who break through their mental model boundaries. They need to find and meet customers who are at the edge of all that they believe a customer stands for.*

Sonnich Fryland of Novo Nordisk was struck by an article in *Lancet* magazine of a young girl from England stricken with diabetes. She filled up a disposable syringe each morning with enough insulin for the day, but found it unwieldy and difficult to administer a dose of insulin. She had commissioned an English company to develop a dosing tool that would deliver metred doses of two units each. This story actually prompted Fryland to think of a pen-like device that could accurately measure and administer the required dose of insulin. This triggered the idea of the NovoPen®. Most managers would have read the article and put it aside as an interesting read about one young girl and moved on. However, Fryland saw an opportunity in that one girl, whose need was not even part of the organization's current R&D focus. Their focus was on drug discovery and not delivery devices. And yet, he was able to pick up the insight that breached the current boundary of

Novo Nordisk and became the catalyst in converting it into a very successful product: the NovoPen.®[9] Connecting and empathizing with an edgy customer led to the orbit-shifting insight.

A company that has made an electric car wanted to crack an orbit-shifting marketing strategy that would enrol the masses. They set up an orbit-shifting Insight Quest that first focused on insight dialogues with edgy customers—those who are highly or minimally invested. They challenged even the concept of edgy and came up with four frames of customers.

What defines an edgy customer with reference to:

> *Mobility*: Highly invested—the over-provisioned customer who has much more mobility capacity than his/her functional needs (more per capita car capacity; high frequency of replacement) and the minimally invested customer.
>
> *Access*: Highly invested—the customer who wants to own everything to get access; minimally invested—the customer who is open to other low-investment access formats like shared ownership or renting.
>
> *Attitude towards technology*: Highly invested—the technophiles; minimally invested—the technophobes.
>
> *Sense of propriety*: Highly invested—the customer who has an exaggerated sense of what's right and what's wrong; minimally invested—the customer who is almost indifferent to causes other than his own material pursuits.

As an Innovation Leader, think about this:

Doing an insight dialogue with these four kinds of edgy customers is more likely to yield an orbit-shifting insight than by just observing the same average set of customers. Exploring these edges in a discovery state of mind is more likely to uncover blind spots and yield an orbit-shifting insight.

What are the three to four customer edges in your market that when explored, could yield an orbit-shifting insight?

Horizons 3 and 4: The Ecosystem Edge and Market Intersections (Figure 5.3)

A team that set out to create a game changer in the laundry industry engaged in insight dialogues with not just customers, but all the players in the laundry ecosystem—retailers, media, city water boards, laundromats, and traditional washermen.

They first met edgy customers who were healthy and lived in water-abundant areas, and on the other extreme, they met customers who lived in water-scarce areas, with low immunity and skin problems. They then engaged with all the other players in the ecosystem in both contexts—water abundance and water scarcity. *Exploring laundry with an 'ecosystem lens' in two extreme contexts of abundance and scarcity provoked new market insight.*

In an insight dialogue with the head of the water board of a water-deficient city, an insight struck them. The head said with a sense of anguish, 'We invest so much money and energy to supply drinking water to the city, but what is very difficult to live with is that only 5 percent of the water we supply is used to drink; the rest goes in other uses like bathing, laundry, and house cleaning'.

This insight provoked them to redesign the laundry process into one that would minimize the usage of fresh water or that would recycle the water.

As a CEO, think about this:

When is the last time your team went beyond customers and engaged in insight dialogues with the entities across your ecosystem?

What is the last big opportunity that emerged from an Ecosystem Insight Dialogue?

What are the opportunities that you may be missing because you are not engaging with the ecosystem?

In searching for insights into care giving, the pharma team met and explored perspectives from across the care-giving ecosystem. Post the insight dialogues, the entire ecosystem was mapped and put up on the wall for the team to examine and identify the leveraged and underleveraged areas. One of the team members looked at the chart and said, 'In this chart, something is not quite right, the whole ecosystem is not configured around the patient, it is configured around doctors. Why are the patients not at the centre of the ecosystem?'

There was silence, and then the realization that the entire system was built to the convenience of the doctor rather than the patient. Every activity in the care-giving system focused on making it easier for the doctor, even if it was at the cost of the patient and the care giver. This insight gave the team space to now craft patient- and care-giver-centred solutions. It came because the team was looking at the ecosystem and its linkages as a whole, rather than focusing on just the key players in the ecosystem, one player at a time.

As a CEO, think about this:

What this team had uncovered was an orbit-shifting insight that could redefine the epicentre of the care-giving ecosystem.

What are you doing to uncover and redefine the epicentre of your ecosystem?

Market Intersections

A quest for ecosystem insights goes beyond engaging with players within the ecosystem. It also includes insight dialogues with players at the market intersections those who engage with the ecosystem but are not directly a part of it. These are players who provide products and services into the ecosystem. As an example, for a team exploring health care, marriage counsellors were an ecosystem entity that engaged actively with the health care ecosystem, but was not directly a part of it.

A mother-and-baby-care chain of retail stores also went on a quest for ecosystem insights, to explore the ecosystem of a young mother/ pregnant woman's life. They met a diverse group of insight sources at market intersections such as fitness clubs, birth doulas, nursery schools, paediatricians, dermatologists, reception centres (for naming ceremonies), office environments of pregnant women, etc.

A couple of team members went to a fitness club where new mothers exercised after child birth and uncovered an interesting insight. As the fitness club manager said, 'A new niche is emerging in fitness, with special classes only for pregnant women, or mothers with newborn children. They sign up in pairs or groups; of may be fifteen women and often they exchange a lot of notes on baby care and health during their classes.' The retail team was struck by the fact that entire groups of mothers were meeting together to exercise. Here were women who were actively seeking access to better mother and child care. A new business opportunity of partnering with fitness clubs opened up for the retail organization. As one of the team members later said, 'It's not as if we didn't know that women want to lose weight immediately after having the baby. We knew that, but we'd never quite connected the dots. By actually talking to fitness club owners we've discovered a "whole new engagement space" for new mothers. The fitness zone is a hang-out zone for them, and it's a win-win partnership for us and fitness clubs, if we can find a meaningful way to engage with mothers in this zone.'

Interactions with a dermatologist on the other hand, raised a completely new need. They were taken aback to discover that the concept of beauty kicks in far earlier than they had thought, with mothers bringing in children from as young as six months to two years with beauty-related skin issues (can an ugly wart/mole be removed, will it cause issues later on, can skin be whitened, etc.). It opened up a new need area of beauty for kids.

The paediatrician threw similar light on intelligence needs, where she said, 'In this competitive environment, parents want their children to earn an MBA in the womb. There are actually audio cassettes that supposedly increase intelligence, which a pregnant woman is meant to listen to, and parents are constantly asking what diet and stimulation the child needs to raise his IQ. These are real worries of parents today and they are willing to do anything to achieve it.' It also opened up a need of intellectual stimulation for children. Only by reaching across the ecosystem of their customer was the team able to get not just a 360-degree view, but also discover genuinely new opportunities.

As an Innovation Leader, think about this:

As a result of the ecosystem Insight Quest, this retail team discussed new opportunity insights that could not have been uncovered by engaging only with customers. Some of them were interesting opportunities, like co-partnering with fitness clubs. Others were more disturbing. Many team members found the early beauty and intellectual needs clashing with their own values as parents and their beliefs on how a child has to be brought up. There were heated arguments around the table: 'Is this good? But we, as parents, are not like this (self-projection)? Should we leverage this? Is this a choice we want to make? Is this who we want to stand for as a corporation?'

The team could never have understood the size and the scope of the need for beauty and intellectual competitiveness at an early stage by meeting individual customers. It took a meeting with a dermatologist and a paediatrician—who see hundreds of their customers but at a different market intersection point—to give the team the sheer magnitude of parents' hunger for beauty and intellect. It jolted them. It penetrated their settled beliefs and gave them a new discontinuous insight. This discomfort is a sign that the team's mental model had been breached.

> Does your opportunity search stir up emotional and intellectual discomfort and dilemmas?
>
> If not, chances are you have not yet breached a mental model. How can you make your insight search edgy enough to create discomfort and breach your mental models? Every discomfort, every dilemma, every paradox is a potential opportunity.

Horizon 5: The Time Edge (Figure 5.3)

Engaging with edgy customers and the players at the edges of the ecosystem is indeed a powerful way to trigger an orbit-shifting insight, but it may not be enough. Orbit-shifters merely start here, they don't stop here.

Orbit-shifters look for new insight sources beyond the current ecosystem—insight sources that can take them beyond their mental model boundaries. They recognize that the customer and ecosystem edge is only one edge. They ask, 'Where are the other potential edges of the current orbit?'

Time is one such powerful edge. Orbit-shifters realize that the ecosystem they are engaging with is still rooted in the present. If mental models are embedded in the present scenario, then it is tough to imagine a scenario beyond the present. Orbit-shifters go about *exploring the orbit-shifting challenge with the 'past' and 'future' lens.*

An Indo-China team set out to explore the space of health and well-being. The top management felt that health and well-being was a big market provided they could uncover a disruptive opportunity. The team went into a quest for insights aimed at mapping the health and wellness market.

They met consumers and industry experts but were unable to reach any real breakthrough. They found that *while all consumers wanted to focus on well-being, they really got into the act only when illness struck them.* More and more conversations brought them to the same old conclusion. *People want wellness but they don't want to invest in it, the only way to get them to engage in wellness is to scare them into it.* But this so-called insight was leading them to the *more of the same opportunities.*

The breakthrough came in one dialogue with a doctor of traditional Chinese medicine. In speaking with him they realized that the wisdom in traditional medicine had been lost by modern medicine. In now joining the dots between traditionalism and modernity, the team discovered that they had been exploring the health market with a bipolar lens. Their minds had frozen into a mental model that saw only health on one side and illness on the other. It struck them that they were further limited by the World Health Organization's (WHO) definition of normal health, which is, the absence of illness.

This insight dialogue opened the third space in the health spectrum—sub-health. What struck them was the realization that *invariably, over 60 percent of the population in any society is in a state of sub-health at any point in time. A state between health and disease when all necessary physical and chemical indices test negative and things seem normal, but the person 'feels' unwell.*

This was an orbit-shifting insight that breached their mental model boundary and remapped the health spectrum. It pointed to a huge opportunity of *reframing wellness* as *recognizing and overcoming sub-health*. It was also a solution pointer to the question of urgency, that people are usually reactive and not proactive when it comes to health. It identified a space where most people were already willing to act, in fact, wanted to act, but were unable to do so as it was outside the realm of modern medicine. It opened a floodgate of business opportunities aimed at empowering consumers to identify and overcome sub-health.

An insight dialogue with an authority on traditional medicine had broken through their mental model boundaries of the health market. Going into the past, this team had discovered business opportunities for the future.

On the other hand, a team from Microsoft went into an imaginary future and uncovered an orbit-shifting insight from a science fiction story. A Microsoft team had actually devised the electronic reader (e-reader) in the late nineties. It was inspired by the 1979 book *The Hitchhiker's Guide to the Galaxy*, which envisions a single book that contains everything in the world. This inspiration led to a touch-screen e-reader, which, if Microsoft had leveraged, could have resulted in becoming the world's first e-reader.[3]

Exploring the time edges—looking at the present through the lens of the past and through the imagined future lens—can unlock orbit-shifting insights.

One TV channel took on an orbit-shifting challenge of conceiving dramatically new television formats. To trigger new insight, the team engaged with edgy customers and then explored the time edge.

Approaching the challenge through the past lens, they identified the insight question: *What are those engagement and entertainment formats that have endured over a long time? Revolutions (political, economic, technological) have come and gone but what are the entertainment and engagement formats that have endured through them*? They explored this insight question with a number of lateral experts like writers, storytellers, psychologists, and historians. This led to powerful insights around one question—what makes the enduring format so enduring?

The engagement and entertainment formats of the emerging future were another insight source. Here, the team conducted insight dialogues with social media experts, and IT and telecom experts who had designed new engagement platforms. This led to insights around *what makes the compelling so compelling?* Still another insight need was to explore areas where a *process of engagement* had developed into a *mass movement*. The team's source was a viral campaign expert; someone who had created a successful campaign for a political leader.

Joining dots across these edges has led to powerful insights and into breakthrough television formats.

Horizon 6: Lateral Intersections (Figure 5.3)

Sometimes even genuine insight dialogues with customers and ecosystem players don't yield a breakthrough. This usually happens when the team is steeped in an industry where the mental models are deeply stuck and saturated. What is needed now is a lateral insight trigger.

To breach mental model boundaries orbit shifters deliberately engage laterally, across industries. They explore intersections with other markets and with other domains, to do *insight dialogues* with insight sources at these lateral intersections.

The laundry team tasked with finding a game changer in the industry went beyond its ecosystem and into *lateral insighting.* One key challenge area that the laundry team had identified was a solution to minimize water consumption. They decided to connect with a lateral insight source, *where the consumption scenario was extreme and stringent.* They met representatives from Space research who design close-loop systems. This dialogue made them explore the extreme water consumption edge. They further explored the time edge by engaging with an anthropologist who provided insight into the relationship of human society with water, and from here emerged the insight of *water hierarchy* in communities.

Finally, they went even further to engage with *lateral experts* across domains. The fundamental mental model of laundry is about removal. What needs to be removed is not just the physically unwanted but also the biologically unwanted—microbes. To get insight into removal of microbes they met a dermatologist to explore *removal of bacteria.* But then he shook their mental models with a question: 'Why are you talking only about removing bacteria, when not all bacteria are bad?' Then he went on to share the story of barnacles and how bacteria on the skin surface protect them and also take in nourishment from the environment and passes it on to the barnacle. The orbit-shift insight this triggered was—*why is everything we put into the laundry solutions just for clothes—making them clean, soft, fragrant, etc.? What if we could put ingredients in the laundry solutions that at the end of the day, were for our body, not for the clothes?*

This orbit-shifting insight, which could have a transformative impact, came from joining dots across domains. These lateral conversations broke through mental model boundaries and led to orbit-shifting propositions that were given a go-ahead by the organization's leadership.

As a CEO, think about this:

Discovering game-changing opportunities in saturated and stuck categories will require a radical stimulus. This requires radical insight sources who bring alive the time edge-past experience and the future imagination, plus insight sources at lateral intersections across industries and domains.

For a team exploring a new opportunity in skin and hair, a breakthrough came from an insight dialogue with a medical devices (drug delivery) expert. Another powerful insight came from Nancy Etcoff, author of the book, *Survival of the Prettiest*.

Examine your insight sources for the most mature and saturated markets. Are you doing insight dialogues with experts to bring the time edge (past and future) as well as with lateral experts across industries and domains?

Lateral Insighting to Solve Unsolved Problems

Lateral insighting is powerfully deployed to not just uncover new opportunities but also to solve unsolved problems.

In building the Qinghai Tibet Railway, Chinese engineers came up against the challenges of nature, none of which had ready-made engineering solutions. Lateral insighting became their source for breakthrough solutions to build a stable railway line on the unstable, changing permafrost. As described in Chapter 3, they learnt from local inhabitants who built their houses on empty drainpipes. Wherever the drainpipes were empty, the construction was sound and the house stood steady. But the walls had begun to crack where the drainpipes were clogged with soil and debris. The engineers *cross fertilized* this idea and built sections of the railway on empty drainpipes, and made sure they were kept empty.

Also in Chapter 3, the engineers embedded heat pipes with fins filled with liquid ammonia, in the embankments for cooling. The use of heat pipes is an idea cross-fertilized from the air-conditioning/refrigeration industry, where the same principle is used to keep food in the fridge cool. The refrigerant in liquid form removes the heat from the refrigerator, and turns into a gaseous form, which is then sent out to the cooling fins. The heated gas now cools down and turns back into liquid form. The cycle then repeats, taking away more heat from the refrigerator every time.[5]

As an Innovation Leader, think about this:

Most people, when faced with an impossible challenge with no known solutions, give up saying, 'This has never been done in our industry; it can't be done'. The Chinese engineers recognized that it may not have been done in their field of railways and searched for someone in another knowledge domain who had solved the same problem, in principle, for example, keeping a house steady (similar to how the railway line had to be kept steady) or refrigeration solutions (similar to the need to keep the ground insulated and cool).

Their purpose in each case was different, but the problem they solved was the same in principle. And hence what was completely unknown or unsolvable in the permafrost context was familiar and had been solved in non-permafrost contexts. Lateral insighting helped them find it.

What are your unsolved challenges? How can insights from intersections help you find solutions to these long unsolved problems?

Teams at the Titan factory have leveraged lateral insighting to make orbit-shifts in the manufacturing process, not by accident, but by design.

One team took an orbit-shifting challenge of *enhancing the tool life of the hook-embossing tool from 5,000 watches to 7,500 watches*, to contribute to the organization's vision of *doubling* watch production from the *same* infrastructure.

The rear cover of a watch must fit into the watch case. Hooks, on the rear cover, help in fitting it into the case. These hooks are created using a hook-embossing (HE) tool.

The design of the HE tool had not been challenged for fifteen years. The breakthrough insight came from a lateral-insight source outside the industry. The manufacturing process used in making ball-pen refills intrigued the team. A video showed the balls of the ball-pen refills being polished simultaneously, in multiple grooves, carved at the micron level. It gave rise to the idea of having multiple profiles for embossing on the HE tool, and led to an increase in the number of profiles from eight to forty on a single tool. This increased the tool life from 5,000 watches to 3,00,000 watches (far beyond the original aspiration of 7,500).

THE ORBIT-SHIFTING INSIGHT SPECTRUM IN ACTION: ACROSS THE SIX HORIZONS

An ambitious team had taken on the orbit-shifting challenge of developing *convergent security solutions* that brought together two very different forms of security ecosystems—physical and logical. They undertook an orbit-shift Insight Quest to look for new insights. Their first step was to conduct insight dialogues with players within the ecosystem. They engaged with insight sources from all three categories of entities in the ecosystem—the security 'suppliers' (products, services companies), the security 'consumers', and the security 'breachers' (the team met entities like hackers and convicts; they also met people who know these entities well—police, intelligence agencies etc.).

They then engaged with edgy customers whose 'security stakes' were the highest (and were therefore highly invested in security). This led them to engage with celebrity bodyguards, schools, and airports, especially those who were responsible for the security of sensitive national assets and spaces (government buildings, etc.). These conversations led them to further connect with academicians and thought leaders.

Still further, they engaged with lateral insight sources—experts from radically different domains who were also dealing with security, but from a completely different lens. They met an entomologist who brought alive how ants and bees build security and also met with a doctor who gave them insights into security systems of the human body.

One such insight dialogue with a kindergarten school principal joined new dots and created an orbit-shifting insight, challenging all known notions of what security in systems traditionally means. Imagine a bunch of software engineers finding inspiration in a kindergarten school! They discussed how the children were protected with the principal. She shared an interesting story: A father came to pick up a child one day and the child was sent off with him, but it was discovered later that the parents were estranged and the child had been, in effect, kidnapped. As an initial response to this, the school devised an elaborate method of registering all possible individuals who were authorized to pick up a child. However, while they were putting this process into place, what struck them was that the best security indicator was to watch the child's body language, ask her, and check for signs of discomfort in going with the person. There would be NO handover if the child displayed any unusual sign. This insight solved an unwieldy problem for the school. Children are wired to self-protect; they know who they are supposed to go with and who they aren't supposed to go with. Multiple authorizations treated the child as helpless, when in reality, he/she had a way to self-protect. This insight also struck the security team. They realized, that much like schools, they also treated all devices as helpless. This helped them identify that the mental model boundary around security in the industry—is like a fortress, where machines/devices and software are helpless and need to be protected from the outside, physical security solutions secure the hardware and logical security solutions secure the software. Essentially the hardware and software are treated as helpless. The team picked up the powerful insight of self-protect and asked themselves—what if the key assets had an in-built ability to self-protect?

Whereas settlers play with a very limited spectrum for insight, orbit-shifters expand the insight spectrum across the six horizons constantly—the customer edge, the time edge, the ecosystem edge, market intersections and on to lateral intersections. This joining of new dots across six horizons fuels orbit-shifting insights.

As a CEO, think about this:

Most of our Current Insight Sources are:

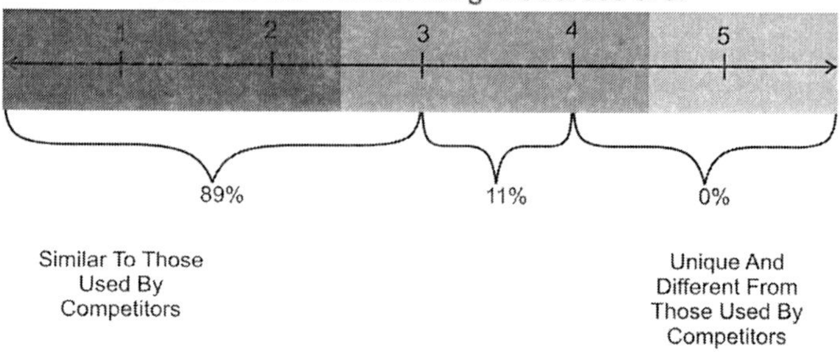

Close to 90% of managers across industries state that Insight sources used by their organisation are similar to those used by others in the industry.
(**Source:** Erehwon's Gravity Diagnostics)

During our innovation diagnostics, what emerges is that in organizations across an industry, almost 90 percent of the managers recognize and admit that the insight sources that they use are more or less the same as the rest of the industry. Rarely have we come across an organization that uses insight sources unique and different from the other players in the industry. No wonder then, after a period of time, products, processes, and even business models across an industry begin to look like more of the same.

How similar are your insight sources to all other players in your industry?

Usual methods of engagement with the usual sources can only bring more of the same.

What is stopping you from opening up the insight spectrum to go beyond the usual and explore other horizons?

What is stopping you from uncovering blind spots, discovering new market opportunities and solving unsolved problems?

How can you transform the orbit-shifting insight capability of your organization by opening up all the six horizons of the insight spectrum?

SECTION 3

COMBATING DILUTION IN EXECUTION

Chapter 6

Overcoming Walls of Doubt: Excite and Enrol Stakeholders

'We need to hire mavericks, only people with this kind of a rebellious attitude can come up with innovative ideas and see them through to the end.'

THIS NOTION OF A MAVERICK ACTING LIKE A LONE RANGER TO CONCEIVE OF AND SUCCEED WITH A RADICAL IDEA CAN AND DOES WORK FOR ENTREPRENEURS. However, in large organizations, if mavericks become lone rangers, they still can—and do—conceive bright new ideas, but rarely are they able to make them happen.

Many organizations have also romanticized the Skunkworks approach, originating in Lockheed Martin in the 1950s. They create a small team, separate it from the main organization, and give it the autonomy—*'ring fence it'*— to develop innovation. Again, a Skunkworks team often does succeed in coming up with 'big ideas', but seldom does this translate into innovation success, especially in large organizations.[5]

WALLS OF DOUBT

A passionate team in an organization breaks through mental model boundaries and succeeds in coming up with an orbit-shifting idea! It's been a great voyage of discovery so far and they are now ready to share it with, and showcase it to, the rest of the organization. They also now need the expertise of other functions, others who have not been involved in the journey so far to *develop the idea into a working solution*. The team believes the *others will be equally excited and will come forward to contribute actively in growing the big idea into an In-Market Success.*

Now, the first hard reality hits the innovators. What is an exciting, irresistible, and an even obviously great idea for them is confronted by walls of doubt. The idea can begin to crumble when it comes up against sceptical gatekeepers and indifferent peers.

In the late 1990s, a group at Microsoft had almost presciently come up with an e-Book—an electronic reader that would allow customers to download digital versions of books, magazines, newspapers, etc. By 1998, a prototype of this orbit-shifting idea was ready.

As Kurt Eichenwald documents in an article in the *Vanity Fair* magazine: 'In sheer excitement the technology group sent the prototype to Bill Gates. But he promptly turned it down. "The e-Book wasn't right for Microsoft", he declared'.

The working group was disbanded and restructured to focus on Office, the big money-spinner for Microsoft. From dreaming up new ideas, they were now driven towards business as usual. They had, in effect, been moved away from orbit-shifting to orbit-maintaining. Microsoft lost the opportunity of the decade. This innovation team with an orbit-shifting idea had been confronted by and was unable to deal with a Sceptical Gatekeeper.

Faced with Gatekeepers Seeking Certainty

Most gatekeepers, like Bill Gates in this case, seek certainty. An orbit-shifting idea is out of the box, but the gatekeepers, in their search for certainty, try to 'fit the new idea into the existing box' by referencing it against an existing success template. And if it doesn't fit into 'how they see the world', then their conclusion is 'it doesn't work: the answer is a no go'. *'Bill Gates didn't like the user interface, because it didn't look like windows', one team member said.*[4]

Some gatekeepers are willing to explore and even consider an orbit-shifting idea, but demand the certainty of success before giving it the go-ahead. As an innovation team in an automobile firm said of their experience, 'Every time we go with a new application or a killer idea, they ask for how well we think it will do in the market, they want to map the current sales trajectory against the new idea, as a predictor of the future—but if we knew that, it wouldn't be new. How can you design the future with the current?'

To overcome his doubt and feel secure with an orbit-shifting idea, the gatekeeper feels the need to connect it to a pattern of success that he has experienced in the past. And if the idea is so new that it doesn't anchor to any known success pattern, he seeks a strong business case before proceeding. And this is but natural given that the stakes of investment, both hard and soft, are high. So, a bulletproof case is needed to overcome the intrinsic doubt with the new. As a CEO said, 'In the absence of any other metric, ROI (Return on Investment) becomes the key metric.' This seeking of a bulletproof business case for something that is completely new has halted many innovation champions. As they say about their experiences:

- 'We keep asking for manpower and resources to innovate, but we never get them. It's a chicken-and-egg question. They say show business and we'll invest, but without manpower, we can't.'
- 'Risk-taking is based on proper "conviction", lots of "justification". For example, in one project, three to four months have already been spent on interminable studies: market study, potential study, supplier study, raw material supplier details, and so on. And, at least another four to five months will be required before we get to the next round of decision-making.'

Beyond Gatekeepers: Confronted with the Silo Battlefield

The Microsoft team's orbit-shift may have been halted at the first *wall of doubt—the gatekeeper*, but there is no guarantee that even if the go-ahead does come from the key stakeholder, the innovation is likely to succeed. There are still more sceptics in the system to contend with.

To develop a new idea into a working solution, the innovation team has to now involve individuals, teams, and departments that have not engaged with it so far. It is almost always a shock for innovation teams to discover at this stage that 'what appears as an exciting opportunity for them is more like a headache, and at best merely another task to the other functions'. The innovation team is up against a hardened silo battlefield. Executing an orbit-shifting idea disturbs the comfort zones of existing functions and this creates resistance.

Unlike the Microsoft team, the Titan team that was in charge of creating the slimmest water-resistant watch in the world had not only been given the go-ahead, but also had the active championship of their managing director. But they were confronted with the next *wall of doubt—their peers.*

During the manufacture of the Edge at Titan, there was considerable tussle between departments. As a team member says, 'We used to have big fights and arguments when people would come up and say, "I want to increase the clearance by 50 microns or so. Assembly used to say: I cannot assemble. Manufacturing used to say: I cannot manufacture". Each time somebody or the other would say they were not able to work with these tolerances and ask us to increase them. We had to go and convince people, constantly reminding them that this is the Edge watch, it's not like any other watch.'

To execute a breakthrough, most departments will need to go beyond their comfort zones and solve new and unsolved problems. Sticking to comfort zones makes each department take the path of least resistance. Unfortunately, many functions believe, *'Yes, we need a breakthrough. Only, I don't need to contribute to it.'* As a result, an orbit-shifting idea gets diluted almost at every stage as it passes through various departments.

The Titan R&D and design team finally did overcome the first series of technical silos and they did end up producing the slimmest water-resistant watch in the world! The watch was developed in a remarkable feat of engineering that challenged almost every paradigm of watch making. They had delivered to the challenge thrown at them by Xerxes Desai, the managing director of Titan.

But then came the final *wall of doubt—marketing*. The Edge was parked internally for nearly two years because marketing refused to touch it. Their market research told them that the trend was towards chunky watches; slim was out. Viewing the Edge from the marketing lens, they told R&D *that market trends were leaning towards chunky and so marketing was interested only if R&D produced a chunky watch, and not a slim one*. The Edge lost two years because it didn't fit the marketing lens of *'what will succeed in the market'*.[7]

Fit In Becomes the Default Setting

At the heart of these silo battles are the Functional Default Settings. Most functional experts, when confronted with a new, out-of-the-box, orbit-shifting idea, react with *what they know and therefore what they can do or can't do, rather than 'what is really needed'*.

As a metaphor, imagine a functional expert like *a very experienced triangle manager*. He has dealt with all kinds of triangles over many years and developed a deep expertise in them. Give him a bigger, smaller, different triangle, and he knows what to do with it. But what the innovation team is now bringing to him is a circle. What is his first instinct, when confronted with a circle? *His dominant instinct, inevitably, is to fit the circle into the triangle, rather than adapt and change to deal with the circle. The triangle is his default setting.*

In the mental model of a siloed functional expert, anything that lies outside the comfort zone is not doable. All parts of the orbit-shifting innovation that lie outside the *current know-how, are either termed impractical or will take a long time, probably many years*. They approach a new challenge with the lens of their current capability. This *capability-forward* approach leads them to immediately start debating and asking the innovators to *adjust the innovation to suit their current capability*. And this adjustment will inevitably mean compromising some features of the innovation. *Faced with a scenario of 'either adjust to our current capability or wait a long time', inevitably forces the innovator to make compromises. He settles for less.*

An orbit-shifting idea very often needs a breakthrough at each level, but is often forced to *settle at the lowest common denominator because functional experts lack the internal motivation needed to overcome obstacles, to solve unsolved problems.* Most functional experts end up trying to *fit the unknown to their current capability frame*, rather than *expanding their capability to solve the unsolved problems.*

What's important in the *fit in syndrome* is that objections or limitations are seldom raised through ill will or malice. People do not object because of mal intent, it's just that they are seduced by the rules of the present. *They tend to get blinded by the status quo and believe in it.* The marketing department at Titan, for instance, didn't mean ill towards the watch. They genuinely believed, by examining trends that 'chunky is in and slim is out'. And if you base your decision on current trends, then their conclusion and strategy was right. But it's the right conclusion and the right strategy only if the mindset is one of *fitting in.* If the mindset is one of *rethink the existing*, then it's the wrong strategy and conclusion. *The Edge was about rethink, not fit in.*

Compromise, Compromise

When we asked people across organizations what comes first within a cross-functional innovation project team: loyalty to the function or loyalty to the purpose, *a whopping 86 percent said 'loyalty to the function'.* Each function approaches the innovation with its own needs at the forefront, and assumes that others won't dilute. A 'tragedy of the commons' plays out where each does the minimum needed rather than the maximum possible.

Engaging with these hardened silos can fatigue even the most persistent innovation champions. After repeated battles, the innovation champion reaches the point of the first compromise: he/she accepts a 10 percent compromise saying, '*Never mind, at least 90 percent of the idea will happen*'. But this is just the start of the series of compromises that inexorably take place and finally *what reaches the market is a mere 30 to 40 percent of the original idea. And when this idea fails, most will dismiss it saying, 'The idea didn't work', without recognizing that what they had taken to market was not the original idea at all, just a pale shadow of its original self.*

THE JOURNEY FROM DOUBT TO CONFIDENCE: LEVELS OF ENGAGEMENT

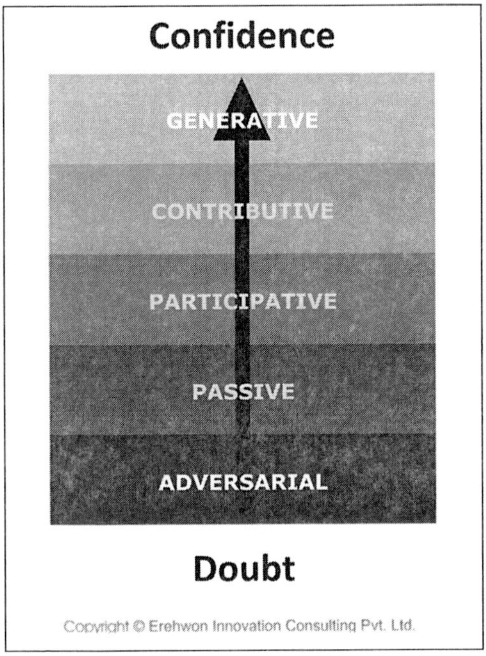

6.1 – Enrolling Stakeholders: From Doubt to Confidence

What does it take to excite and enrol stakeholders? What does it take to uplift stakeholder engagement from negative to positive? What does it take to move stakeholders from doubt to confidence and conviction?

The journey from doubt to conviction is traversed when the key stakeholders' engagement with the orbit-shifting idea moves from adversarial and passive to being generative across this continuum.

The most visible manifestation of doubt is scepticism; often the starting viewpoint of stakeholders is directly evaluative and critical. A number of stakeholders start by poking holes in the orbit-shifting idea and take on the devil's advocate role with reasons *why this can't be done.* This is the stakeholders' doubt expressing itself in a negative and combative manner.

It is *adversarial.* While difficult to deal with, adversarial responses are at least visible, so the orbit-shifter knows where and why the doubts arise. What can be equally, if not more daunting, is a *passive* stakeholder, who displays complete indifference to the idea. Passive stakeholders' doubts are revealed in their silence, for it is this indifference that makes them silent at key decision points. It becomes worse when this passivity takes the shape of *public agreement and private disagreement*, where the stakeholder agrees in formal meetings with the idea, but airs dissatisfactions at 'water-cooler' gatherings. The innovator never really knows what he is up against; the doubt and the source of it are invisible, as they never surface openly and directly. When the rubber hits the road, a passive stakeholder, ignored or left as is, is more likely to become adversarial.

In contrast, a *participative* stakeholder's doubt is expressed in a very matter-of-fact *will do as required* attitude. A participative stakeholder goes through the motions faithfully, but does *'not a penny more and not a penny less'*. This mental model boundary makes them faithfully execute *what they can, within their current know-how, and refuse to go beyond.* A participative stakeholder's doubt stems from past precedence and is visible in the unwillingness to step out of the comfort zone.

An orbit-shifting innovation needs *contributive* stakeholders, who openly express their doubts and then collaborate with the team to overcome them. *Their doubts become positive contributions. They are raised as: 'Here is a concern I have, let's look at how to overcome it'.* The clear intent of a contributive stakeholder is to be supportive and air doubts so that they are resolved, and do not stall the orbit-shift.

However, what an orbit-shifting innovation really needs are *generative* stakeholders, who not only help solve unsolved problems, but are also proactive in uncovering and leveraging opportunities to maximize the innovation.

What does it take for innovation champions to positively engage both decision and implementation stakeholders, gatekeepers, and peers? To move them from adversarial and passive towards being generative? What will he need to do differently to move participative stakeholders out of their comfort zones to become proactive and generative?

Enrolling Stakeholders: Co-build with Stakeholders

At Unilever, Massimo Pozzetti had led a laundry team in conceiving a portfolio of orbit-shifting ideas and now he was faced with the challenge of enrolling his gatekeepers. As he reflects, 'When confronted with a new and an unfamiliar idea, most stakeholders start with doubt rather than confidence.' *Confidence comes from familiarity, from experiences in the past.* When faced with an unfamiliar idea, the gatekeeper is usually left thinking: *How can I give feedback without knowing the outcome?* This doubt in the gatekeeper's mind can lead to an outright rejection or some random feedback.

'We enrolled stakeholders by giving them a broader perspective and connecting the new to their domain expertise,' Massimo says. In a bid to enrol gatekeepers, Massimo went door to door, to connect with and engage and enrol all gatekeepers before a decisive board meeting. 'When I met with the CFO, I shared the orbit-shifting idea with a business model perspective, with him. The CFO got engaged, he, in fact, started co-building with me and said, "You are the only marketing person who has involved me at the early idea stage".'

Moving stakeholder engagement from *evaluating to co-building* is what an Innovation Champion needs to be able to do. *The biggest realization for an orbit-shifter at this stage is that he has to move from thinking of the orbit-shifting idea as 'my dream', towards building it into a 'shared dream'.* This move can be emotionally and intellectually tough, as the innovation champion is, by now, in love with his idea, and as he enrolls stakeholders, chances are that the idea could grow and be shaped differently from the creator's original thought. In addition, the innovator most naturally wants acceptance and even admiration. He does want it to be known as *his idea.*

But an orbit-shifter also realizes that to get the stakeholders to go the extra mile, to solve problems beyond their current know-how, will take extraordinary motivation. And this can only happen if the stakeholder's ownership of the idea is as big as his. Rather than convince and push stakeholders to merely accept and implement, the orbit-shifter focuses on enrolling them till it becomes a shared dream.

Co-evolve, Co-own

Sivakumar co-evolved the orbit-shifting e-Choupal idea with the top management till it reached a very high level of co-ownership.

In March 2000, all business divisions of ITC had to present their business plans to the board of directors for their consideration and approval. The business plan of each division was typically about a hundred pages, which was then summarized into four pages by the chairman's executive assistant, for circulation among the directors prior to the meeting of the board. The four-page document was further abridged into a one-page document on the day of the board meeting. During the meeting, the head of each business unit was given thirty minutes to present his business plan to the board of directors. Sivakumar's organization, IBD (International Business Division), had been given a similar time slot for its presentation.

Sivakumar was apprehensive that the directors would never be able to appreciate the potential of his orbit-shifting idea if they read a *four-page abridged version of it. This process was all right for a business-as-usual plan but not for a radical, out-of-the-box idea.* He was afraid that in the executive summary the nuances that *differentiated the idea and made it a big one* would be lost. He also felt that the directors would not be able to recognize the uniqueness and the potential opportunity that this idea presented. They might react passively or participatively to his orbit-shifting idea. So, rather than conform to the process, Sivakumar chose the more informal process of enrolling each board member through one-on-one meetings prior to the board meeting after sending them, not the abridged, but the entire proposal on e-Choupal. At a party prior to the board meeting, Sivakumar finally cornered YCD (YC Deveshwar, the chairman) and asked him if he had read the full text of the IBD business plan. YCD candidly confessed he hadn't. Sivakumar insisted that he read the full text before the presentation. In Sivakumar's words, 'I cornered him and kept repeating my request so he finally gave in. The party got over at midnight and at two o'clock in the morning, YCD was so involved in our strategy that he called the head of IT to read the full text too. "There is a fantastic possibility here, do you know about it," YCD asked the IT head. The next day they changed the order of presentation, brought

IBD up front and continued with it for the rest of the day.' ITC decided to back the e-Choupal idea to the hilt. The board's passion and aggression was now even higher, they wanted the first Choupal to be up and running within three months. They had become generative. Sivakumar accepted on one condition—that YCD would be there personally to inaugurate it. YCD agreed.

Sivakumar now had to ensure that his team lived up to the promise. He says, 'We didn't know how we were going to do it, but the fact that YCD was going to be there at the inauguration gave wing to our spirits and we made it happen.' Three months later, Sivakumar contacted YCD to inaugurate the first e-Choupal in a little village in MP (Madhya Pradesh in central India). As they drove down to the remote location, Sivakumar had ten exclusive hours with the chairman to talk of the potential of e-Choupal and how ITC would do well to own it end to end, rather than partner with another organization.

YCD's measured response was that ITC would remain the brain behind e-Choupal but they would need to partner with a large IT firm to scale it up. On reaching the location and seeing the 2,000 farmers excitedly gathered to inaugurate the Choupal, the magnitude of e-Choupal's potential came alive to YCD like no presentation or argument could ever have done and he voluntarily announced that ITC would go alone on the project. As Sivakumar says, 'On the way back, YCD was giving me all the reasons why e-Choupal was the future of ITC and why we needed to go on this alone!'[6]

DON'T MANAGE PERCEPTION; ENROL STAKEHOLDERS INTO THE PURPOSE

Traditional managers have learnt to survive hierarchy. They focus their energies on managing the boss, rather than performance. Orbit-shifters, on the other hand, don't behave in a subservient or hierarchical manner; they reach out and think and as equals with their bosses and peers. Orbit-shifters don't get preoccupied with managing perception, they enrol their bosses in to the purpose.

While traditional managers have perfected the art of telling their bosses *what they think he wants to hear, orbit-shifters enable their bosses to grasp the way things really are, and are not hesitant to share their viewpoint on what is needed to achieve the purpose. They put the purpose before the position of the person they are talking to.*

Orbit-shifters like Massimo and Sivakumar act equal. As Massimo shares, 'All my board member meetings were peer-peer conversations and not presentations to the boss. *Don't make them happy by telling them what they want to hear, give them the confidence that the idea is worth pursuing.'*

Sivakumar demonstrated this equality mindset most clearly with the board members. It would have been easy to mail his plan to each board member and politely request each for him one to read it; that would have been the right thing to do, what the organization protocol expected. No one would have faulted him, if later, he complained that, *'the board hadn't done its job'*, that in spite of his meeting every member of the board, they hadn't done the needful to read his proposal. What made Sivakumar take that extra step, where he threw caution to the wind and even coaxed and confront the chairman with a statement like, *'I will not make a presentation tomorrow until you read the complete business plan'*? It was his huge belief in the strength of the e-Choupal purpose that gave Sivakumar the courage and the conviction to engage on an equal footing with the board.

As an Innovation Leader, think about this:

Confronted with hierarchy, orbit-shifters don't get daunted with the position, they engage with the person. They don't get into the act of managing perception, they focus on enrolling the stakeholder into the purpose. Sivakumar and Massimo built powerful engagement mechanisms that saw their biggest gatekeepers and the most likely neutralizers of their ideas become their biggest champions.

While Sivakumar and Massimo enrolled their gatekeepers into the most radical, orbit-shifting ideas, the technology group at Microsoft was unable to. They had come up with a game-changing idea but their inability to enrol Bill Gates has left them with only a lasting regret. It is often easy to point towards the stakeholder in hindsight and say, 'He didn't let me do it'. The stakeholder, though, has no crystal ball which lets him see a guaranteed future. His decision-making is based on how well the innovation team paints future scenarios to him.

So how much of this failure is really because of the innovator's genuine incapacity to enrol the stakeholder into the transformative purpose of the orbit-shifting idea?

Where are your comfort zones coming in the way and preventing you from enrolling the toughest of stakeholders? What's your enrolment approach and strategy? Have you fallen into the trap of managing perception rather than managing the purpose?

Rather than Trying to Convince Stakeholders with Data, Connect them with the New Reality

Sivakumar brings alive how a stakeholder like YCD overcame his final doubt when he experienced a snapshot of the new reality in its fullness—when he inaugurated the first e-Chaupal. While YCD believed in the e-Chaupal idea, he doubted that ITC could execute it on its own.

However, this first-hand experience increased his confidence to the point that he decided to raise his and the organization's stake in the e-Chaupal. *He was convinced that rather than partnering with an IT firm, they would go at it by themselves.*

It didn't take a bulletproof case; it took one powerful experience to connect the stakeholder to the power and potential of the new reality.

The New Reality Plays Out

Queen and its producers, on the other hand, followed a very different method of connecting their record company executives to the new reality of 'Bohemian Rhapsody', a song that didn't fit the 'radio play' of 3.5 minutes. By getting RJs to play bits of it directly on the radio, and have it shoot to public notice, with fans clamouring for the song, they gave the record company executives a first-hand experience of how much the public had fallen in love with the song. Getting the record company executives to experience this snapshot of the new reality moved them from doubt to confidence faster than any amount of reasoning, logic or argument could ever have.[3]

Bridge a Divide with a Generative Dialogue

YCD was already positively predisposed towards the e-Chaupal idea. With his first-hand experience, he actually began to see the full power of the idea. This uplifted his engagement further and he now unconditionally backed the idea. He had become a promoter of the idea and not merely a supporter. (He had moved from contributive to generative.)

The record company executives were not anti-Queen, they just didn't believe in the format of the new song 'Bohemian Rhapsody'. This first-hand experience gave them the confidence and moved them from passive to contributive.

In both these cases, one experience of the new reality was enough to transform the stakeholders' engagement. But when the starting point is *deep distrust*, then just one experience of the new reality is not enough. What is needed is a generative dialogue to uncover the deeper stakeholder motivations and forge a new reality.

How do you make representatives across factions with a deep degree of distrust born from years of civil war, even sit down on the same table to co-create the future of the nation?

The dialogue that Adam Kahane facilitated in Guatemala brought alive how deeply entrenched adversaries could bridge the gulf through a generative dialogue, so that they connected with each other at a very personal level. This dialogue broke deep-rooted suspicions and shifted them from trying to convince each other to adopting a shared purpose. It is not as if countries do not attempt consensus either within, or across borders. However, there is often a breakdown of these attempts because the engagement is superficial, with each party sticking to its stance. The difference in Guatemala was that

Adam created the space for vulnerability, for openness and for a sharing of even the most dreadful of occurrences, and making collective meaning of them. It was in the silence of a shared experience, when they heard the story of the discovery of delicate bones of unborn foetuses, that they arrived at a 'moment of truth'. From here, the team moved as one to create a shared vision for the future of Guatemala.[2]

As an Innovation Leader, think about this:

Not loads of data, but one powerful experience of the new reality was critical in uplifting the engagement of stakeholders in the case of e-Chaupal and 'Bohemian Rhapsody'. It took a generative dialogue in Guatemala to get a deeply divided group of stakeholders to build a shared new reality.

Who among your stakeholders need to experience a snapshot of the new reality? And who needs to engage in a generative dialogue to breakthrough to the new reality?

Pre-empt Doubt with Confidence-building Initiatives

Michael Stevens and Carsten Hallund Slot of Arla followed a very different but as effective a strategy to enrol stakeholders into their orbit-shifting idea of putting dairy products into Space. They first went to NASA, co-evolved the outcome with them, established a five-year time frame, signed a contract, and then returned and enrolled the top management.

Once he had got NASA's okay and a sign off, Michael came back and told his boss, one of the executive directors, that they were just going to do it: *You can say yes or no, we're just going to do it and put milk into Space. And by the way, NASA's already agreed too.* At the same time they also showed him that compared to Arla's on-going research and development programme, this project asked for a lower commitment in terms of people and money. They got the director's assent.

What Michael and Carsten understood clearly and empathized with were stakeholder concerns (Arla's directors) that were rooted in business viability, on project certainty, and a reputation built over years. *Rather than react to these concerns as and when they were raised, Michael and Carsten fed into the deeper stakeholder motivations and provided for them pre-emptively.* Business viability is a concern? Ensure that the investment is small enough to not be a pain. This overcame the first predictable doubt. The second predictable doubt was NASA's willingness to partner. Ensuring that NASA was on board even before approaching the stakeholder clipped the inevitable and long back and forth, *what if NASA doesn't agree*, discussions. In addition, *it built stakeholder confidence: 'These guys have done their job; if they can convince NASA, they must have a solid idea'. So the stakeholders gave Project Lacmos the go-ahead.*

The Mico Bosch R&D team had set out on its orbit-shifting challenge: To reinvent the old PF pump—to enable the diesel engine to match the emission standards achieved by modern Common Rail (CR) pumps. But to actually get a go-ahead for this mission, the India team had to enrol Bosch Germany. Rather than trying to convince Bosch, they proactively sought to enrol a customer in Germany, and found success with Deutz. The Deutz group manufactures diesel engines for customers like Volvo and Renault. Deutz had just received an order from Volvo for medium duty trucks. According to Dr Thiemann of Deutz, *they didn't want to make extensive and expensive design modifications to the existing engine that would be required with the new CR systems.* The Bosch team managed to enrol Deutz with the proposition of 'the reinvented PF pump' that would match emission norms and remove the need for CR pumps. Deutz was happy to find a solution that would reduce investments and even agreed to share the developmental costs. Enrolling a client into co-ownership paved the way for the execution of this orbit-shifting innovation.[8]

The Bosch India team got the go-ahead. No one in the head office could have possibly pulled the plug from an orbit-shift project whose development costs were being shared by a customer.

Take Stakeholders from an Unconditional No to a Conditional Yes

Innovators can often come up against decision-makers who might say 'no' to a part or a whole of the big idea. The settler usually tries convincing the stakeholder a few times, but eventually backs off and gives in to the no. He has, in his mind, tried his best and has been rejected. The orbit-shifter on the other hand, recognizes that a no is not unconditional, that behind a seemingly absolute and irrevocable no, is usually a genuine concern or a series of assumptions that is leading the stakeholder to that conclusion. Faced with a no, the orbit-shifter doesn't back off. Instead he/she steps forward to engage with and uncover the underlying concerns, while also enabling the stakeholder to recognize these as concerns, which if not handled, are leading to a no. In other words, it is a conditional no. However, the orbit-shifter reframes it as a conditional yes. Finding a solution for the concern has opened up a path to go from a no to a yes. Post such an engagement, a stakeholder feels more understood and his resonance with the big idea increases.

Enrolling the Regulator

Victoria Hale demonstrated the capacity of an orbit-shifter to enrol, when she engaged with the most difficult of stakeholders—a regulator, the US Internal Revenue Service (IRS)—to obtain non-profit status for OneWorld Health. Most people tread very carefully with regulators, treating them with a great degree of deference for the fear of upsetting them.

The first difficulty OneWorld Health[10] in dealing with the IRS was suspicion. The officials suspected that this was a trick by a 'for-profit pharma company' wanting a tax shelter. *Dr Hale and her legal team were turned down three times, before the non-profit status was granted.* Rather than defer to the regulator and accept their rejection, Dr Hale adopted an approach that was simple and direct: *'You don't have to convince the people who are not going to be convinced, you need to get to the person who you can convince. Focus on people who want to understand and use the questions/*

doubts/disbelief from the ones who don't understand or disagree to sharpen your idea.' Victoria made an effort to understand where the regulator's doubt stemmed from. However, her route to moving them from doubt to confidence was unique.

She genuinely looked at it from their point of view—*if you think about it, people at the IRS are like anyone else, it's hard to suddenly accept that a pharma company can be non-profit and they will be wary.* She kept this in mind throughout her dealings with the IRS.

Once she knew who she needed to talk to, she picked up the phone and dialled. There was no prior email or any formal introductory document. She just called and talked about OneWorld Health and its purpose. Individuals at the other end were polite and heard her out, and then went on to decline, saying they couldn't give a pharma company non-profit status. She'd accept and ask to speak to that person's superior, asking for a twenty-minute call. In a few days, she spoke to the person at the next level, and still got a polite no, *'we are sorry'*. She'd request again to be connected with the next person up the line. Her strong credentials helped move up the chain of hierarchy within the IRS and she utilized them to the maximum. While she had value-adding conversations and she felt they really understood what she wanted to do, they were, nevertheless, firm in their disagreement—that, though it was a very unusual initiative, there was no way in which it could be given a non-profit status. In fact, it was her third conversation with the IRS which finally revealed that the IRS believed that OneWorld Health was simply a tax-avoidance scheme by a big pharma company.

It didn't strike Dr Hale immediately, perhaps because she wasn't expecting it, but after hearing them again and again, she got it. Once she honed in on the real concern, she asked them for options: *What do I now have to do to show you it is genuinely a non-profit? The answer was surprisingly simple, where the IRS responded by saying, 'Show us precedence, show us where a non-profit mirrored a for-profit business and it has worked'.* Now she had a way out, what she had to do was to find the precedence. She had moved the IRS from a flat-out unconditional no, to a conditional yes. As Victoria Hale says, 'It took me five days, and then at dinner, it hit me: NPR and public television. They look an awful lot like for-profit radio and television, but they serve a different audience with programmes that their for-profit counterparts don't provide because they can't profit from them.' Two weeks later, OneWorld Health received the IRS approval, and then set out to tackle its first challenge—black fever.

Orbit-shifters like Victoria Hale show how the power of continued engagement in the face of what seems like firm opposition, helps enrol a stakeholder even as unreachable as a regulator. She didn't fall back when she heard an unconditional no. She engaged deeper to uncover the underlying concern. And once the concern had been identified she moved the conversation into a solution mode, by enquiring what she could do to make them believe that OneWorld Health was non-profit. Now the regulator came forth with a potential solution. The engagement had shifted from participative to generative. The same regulator, who had said no earlier, was now co-evolving the solution with her. The unconditional no had become a conditional yes.

As an Innovation Leader, think about this:

Orbit-shifters don't influence, they enrol stakeholders. The mental model underlying influencing is still convincing—the dominant intent is to move the stakeholder to 'my viewpoint'. Orbit-shifters are fundamentally inclusive in their thinking. They engage with and try to understand the real concern. Genuine enrolment happens when the stakeholder's real concern has been understood and dealt with. This intrinsic inclusiveness is what differentiates enrolment from influencing.

Where in your organization is a new idea stuck at an unconditional no, and you have backed off? How can you re-engage with your stakeholder to convert the unconditional no to a conditional yes.

Enrolling the Team

Rather than resorting to mandates; co-create with the team.

Traditionalists believe in the power of the mandates and they use authority to push their teams to pursue a new orbit-shifting direction that usually the leader himself has thought of. In fact, many intrinsically hierarchical leaders believe that the great management art is in making your team believe that an idea you have thought of is actually theirs. However, orbit-shifters realize that just as kids see through their parents ploys, the team also sees through the leader's camouflage. For orbit-shifters, enrolment is not a game to be played and won, it is a genuine endeavour.

When Laercio Cardoso took over the reins of the hygiene division in Unilever in Indonesia, he did so with a knowledge that he had to turn it around. In the run-up to taking on the job, he had committed to the Asia chairman that he would triple the business results of the division in three years.

And now he found himself with a demoralized team that didn't believe in either the business or in their own capability to turn it around. He felt that he needed first the leadership team, and then the whole division to come together and rally around a big challenge that would inspire and reignite them. He planned an off-site meeting in Bali in May 2005, with the leadership team on the first one-and-a-half days and the entire division on the next one-and-a-half days.

The leadership team gathered around in a meeting room in Bali and began to identify their gravities that were holding them back from winning; whether in the market, or in Unilever. As Laercio says, 'It was a very long day from early morning to late evening. The team reflected about the gravity forces that kept them stuck in passivity and detraction, a painful but liberating exercise…' Once these were identified, the team went on to look for the unifying cause, and here Laercio thought a good way to inspire the team would be by setting the challenge of growing three times in three years. He said it, and said it again. His words hung in the air. The team didn't pick it up or sound excited by it. Their energies were elsewhere. He was sensitive to the moment and stepped back. 'I sensed that they felt dragged, it was important for it to come from them. I told myself "Don't impose. Step back and let them unleash their potential. Release them and they would grow".'

Laercio created space for the team to explore their motivations and needs in the fullest; to allow them to rally around what would inspire them the most. The key was obviously not in numbers; it rested in 'winning respect'. As some team members shared: 'What will move me are not new goals but a new attitude'; 'Empower me and I would be happy to fight'; 'Fight in every way, fight for the market share and for the internal margin, fight for credibility and margin, fight for redemption and market volume'. The sentiment that was re-echoed was 'I want to fight for the team and fight for me'. As they talked and discussed and reiterated this deep need across the room, what they were really seeking as a powerful anchor slowly took shape. And the orbit- shifting spirit was born: Street Fighter—to move out of their comfort zones and win the market street by street; fight for credibility and margin, fight for redemption and volume.

The leadership team was ready to go out there, to be Street Fighter, to win the streets. However, this was just a group of twelve that had been through a collective transformative experience. They now had to infuse the same spirit into the rest of the division, all 120 of them. Again, through a wider dialogue-and-discovery process, the leadership team co-built ownership of the Street Fighter. It didn't come all at once. At the end of the second day, there were heated discussions around dinner tables that continued into the next morning around breakfast tables. Would Street Fighter mean winning at all costs? What about ethics? How fast can we change our mindsets? Will we own and accept it together? How would failure be handled with Street Fighter? How would the rest of the organization react to Street Fighter?

Rather than assuage these doubts with smooth talk and argument; the leadership team listened. They talked about their own fears and doubts as they had gone through a similar journey the previous day. Every single person, every one of the 120, was given an opportunity to express where he connected with Street Fighter and what his concerns were. This collective expression and process of engagement started building up momentum and belief—they could see Street Fighter was not just a glib statement, but something that was beginning to resonate, to create a sense of resolve around the room. And people began looking at what they can do. Because they had opened up, discussed it, immersed themselves in it, seen it from all angles, and all of it collectively, without defensiveness or persuasion, the Street Fighter expanded from being owned by just the leadership team to becoming a way of being for the entire hygiene division. All 120 members committed to being Street Fighters. As Laercio says, *'the Street Fighter challenge conquered the division's heart and became our motto. It unleashed an outstanding energy and a winning spirit. We felt the force and we believed in it!'*

In pursuing the Street Fighter, the team achieved the three-time growth target in just nine months. What had changed irrevocably was individual and team approach to the way in which they dealt with 'business as usual'. The Street Fighter mindset kicked in in every situation. A passive division had become generative. Voluntarism towards team goals, persisting with solutions for difficult problems, converting problems to opportunities, reaching out to find solutions for other departments; all became the new and sustained hygiene way.

For example, a purchase manager requested a brand postponement at the eleventh hour in order to negotiate a more favourable price from a supplier. Not a brand or marketing manager, but a purchase manager working out of his area of influence! A brand manager on the other hand, managed to turn around a to-be released product when its formulation was leaked. The usual time required for a new formulation is three months, but he did it in five days (and nights) in close collaboration with a perfumer! It turned out to be far more successful than the original. The development team's tireless efforts on a Rinso variant (a detergent) faced consistent problems. Whereas earlier they would have quit, this time, they persisted until they found a technical solution.

As each team pressed on with the Street Fighter spirit, they began to infect and enrol divisions beyond their own to also partner and be generative. As Yaqin, the marketing manager for fabric cleaning describes, 'It was about capturing the mind shares of others in the company. Everyone from supply chain, manufacturing, the regional team, and sales had to be told and repeatedly told about our brand, its strategy, and its positioning. We made presentations to sales explaining our perspectives and each time we gained a market share point we celebrated together. Not being the company's "blue-eyed boy" did not deter us like earlier (before the Street Fighter initiative). We spoke more about our brands. It was all about not giving up on ourselves or to the others. With time we realized that the sales folks liked us pushing them.'

As a CEO, think about this:

Laercio could easily have mandated the three-time growth in three years in his position as head of the hygiene division. Instead, he invested three days in co-building an aspiration that resonated with the hygiene division...an aspiration that imposed no hard numbers or success measures as he had originally wanted, but rather a deeper driver that reignited self-belief in the division. So it was not about what they wanted to reach/ do, but a deeper resonance of who they needed to be.

Orbit-shifters recognize a hard truth—you can mandate a person to carry out an activity but you can't mandate ownership. Especially the kind of ownership that will be needed to persevere through the ups and downs of an orbit-shift journey.

Enrolment around a transformation happens only when you anchor it to the team's deepest driver, just as Laercio did. Most leaders, in contrast, equate superficial agreement to ownership. Agreement is NOT ownership. Where are you attempting a transformation? Where are you on Laercio's enrolment scale? Are you attempting superficial agreement or have you uncovered a deep driver that will unleash your team into the orbit-shift?

Carsten did not depend on mandates, instead he built team ownership. As he says, '*You need to give people a vision and a reason*: *Where are we going? Why are we going? What's the opportunity if we go there*?' The first step was the *create history aspiration* where people could see themselves as being part of something great, something immortal. However, inspiration really comes from people seeing their ideas turn into reality. And at Lacmos, (Space food), 'we gave them that opportunity. They can't get that opportunity anywhere else in the company. So they bring in their own ideas. They are already on fire. They see the opportunity and we help them to realize their ideas.'

This drove people, day in and day out, fuelled them to continue without slacking in the face of blocks, obstacles, and slowdowns. Lacmos was much larger than the individual and much larger than the company. If they made it happen, personal and national pride was the reward, much beyond anything all the money in the world could even begin to give them.

As a CEO, think about this:

Laercio and Carsten enrolled their team members to be generative, to not just adopt but build on an orbit-shifting idea. Nothing less than the complete and joint ownership of the best minds is what is needed to bring about a new orbit-shifting reality.

In contrast, quoting Kurt Eichenwald in *The Vanity Fair*, 'Microsoft in their difficult decade, built a culture where Microsoft superstars did everything they could to avoid working alongside other top-notch developers. This behaviour was driven by the fear that cooperating and helping others succeed could hurt their own ranking. Microsoft had adopted a management system called Stack Ranking where every unit was forced to declare a certain percentage of people as top performers, then good, then average, then below average and then poor. Microsoft had built a culture that embedded self-protection, where individual survival overrode the purpose of the project'.

What is your organization's mental model of people and performance assessment? Is it designed to support orbit-maintaining or orbit-shifting? Does it, like the Street Fighter did, influence generative behaviours and outcomes, or does it breed competitiveness and encourage self-protection?

Move the Team from 'Impossible!' to 'How it Can Be Made Possible'

Enrolling the team is not a one-time job to be accomplished at the beginning of the challenge. An orbit-shift journey will be repeatedly confronted with impossibles. Faced with an impossible, even a previously generative team can slip down to a *can't be done* state of mind. They can start reacting passively or even adversarially. Energies begin to fade.

Arla's Carsten Hallund Slot constantly moved the team's state of mind from the realms of impossibility to the beginnings of new possibilities.

A lot of improbables and impossibles had to be cracked just by the nature of the project they were tackling—Space food (creating milk-based food for space). At various points, when Carsten dared his team to do something radical, the first reaction was usually that, 'It's impossible!' Rather than getting into a *can versus can't debate*, which inevitably leads to the yes-no, possible-impossible kind of stances, Carsten focused on moving the dialogue into a generative space. He would initiate the generative dialogue with a frame-shifting question like, *'Let's look at ten years from now for this. Will technology have evolved by then to make it possible?'* Then the answer was usually a yes, and the team members would immediately come up with technologies that could by then make it possible. What he had managed to create was a window of possibility in their minds. Once this window was opened he would then reduce the time frame with the next question: 'We want it in two years, how can you make it happen by then?' People were, by now, far more willing to explore how it could be done and movement was achieved.

Why start with a timeline ten years into the future for a problem that has to be tackled immediately, in the near future? Because people need the space to unlock their minds. Also, there's an emotional block to something immediate. When the immediacy is pushed away, people can think more freely. And then, once the frame has shifted from impossible to possible, even when the time horizon is reduced to the present, the focus shifts to *how to make it possible.* The typical first reaction is usually fear, because people have been asked to go outside their comfort zone. Once the fear is mitigated, the same people come up with ways to make it possible. And by now the energy has positively transformed. They are now engaging with the problem generatively.

Enrolling Partner

Leverage Partners Generatively Rather than Reducing Them to Participative–Supplier Relationships

Executing an orbit-shifting idea often needs expertise that lies outside the organization. To make an orbit-shifting innovation happen, therefore, often needs active collaboration not just across functions within, but also with partners outside.

Increasing acceptance of open innovation has led to an increase in the willingness of organizations to source expertise and ideas from across industries and domains. But most of them do this with the classical outsourcing mindset, whereas the reality is thinking can't be outsourced, only expertise and ideas can be insourced. Truly leveraging open innovation requires generative partnerships, where both sides are willing to step into the unknown to take on a never-done-before out-of-the-box challenge and then co-create solutions.

Most traditional organizations continue to engage with open innovation partners with the same old client-supplier mindset. This leads to efficient participative relationships at best, where the client acts as the order giver and the supplier is comfortable being the order taker. With both sides unwilling to step out of their comfort zones, mature SLAs (service-level agreements) keep the relationship under control.

Organizations seek control; this is the gravity that truly comes in the way of a partnership becoming generative. When an organization in the controlling mindset engages with an open innovation partner, all they expect of the partner is the delivery of a ready-to-use plug-and-play solution.

In the case of an orbit-shifting challenge, it is highly unlikely that a ready-to-use solution exists. So the partner will, in all probability, deliver *work-in-progress solutions*, with still-unresolved questions. When a control-oriented organization gets a work-in-progress answer, it is likely to get impatient.

This control-driven culture has created an ecosystem where the open innovation partners too, are equally uncomfortable working with just an open-ended challenge. They are as comfortable with the supplier mindset and expect detailed briefs, with exact expectations spelt out and no unanswered questions.

Transworld Partnerships Settle at the Lowest Common Denominator

The global IT (Information Technology) industry that opened up in the early 1990s rapidly disrupted all traditional ways of working. It spawned open innovation opportunities—to partner and collaborate across industries, cultures, and even generations, across the world.

Taking advantage of the access provided by the global IT platform, a number of organizations set up transworld partnerships with organizations across countries and cultures. But driving the new platform with the old control-oriented mindset led to the engagement levels in most of these transworld partnerships getting reduced to below even the participative levels.

An Erehwon research across multiple transworld partnerships in organizations like Honeywell, Novell, Philips, Motorola, Hewlett-Packard, Nortel, Silicon Automotive Systems, and Wipro, highlighted how the engagement levels in these partnerships had dipped to participative and even passive levels.

The insights across the companies showed that while each remote site had been set up with the purpose of creating value, it had instead served to create suspicion. When mapped against the generative scale, what stood out was that the degree of mutual suspicion rose when teams went from single to multi-locational across time zones. Plotted against a suspicion index, the mistrust quadrapled in the new work scenario. People were more likely to suspect motives rather than believe the best of the team on the other side. Issues like locational proximity to the team leader, blaming rather than co-owning, believing that the remote locations will steal away jobs dramatically increased suspicion, resulting in adversarial relationships.

On the client side, managers in global sites across Japan, the United

States, and Europe shared some of the complexities of working with partners: the difficulty in transferring knowledge *(how do I communicate fifteen years of experience in one hour, and that too, in writing?)*, hierarchical approaches *(we want them to be partners, but our need for continuous updating is seen as control)* to aligning tasks and people across distances *(derailment can take weeks to discover and we lose precious time in recovery as well)*. On the partner side, the Indian and Singaporean managers and teams had their own set of issues: *'We are supposed to be partners, but treated like suppliers, there is fear and knowledge hoarding on the other side, when things go wrong we are usually blamed first'.*

One of the biggest blocks to building generative relationships with partners is this incapacity of organizations to give up control and truly engage with them like equals—real partners rather than controlling them like mere vendors.

Most organizations continue to find it very difficult to collaborate with external partners to create truly breakthrough innovation, where both have an equal role to play in creating the future. The sad fact is that a number of breakthroughs don't see the light of day because the external collaboration needed to make them happen falls short.

An Orbit-shifting Business Model Founded on Generative Partnerships

Bharti Airtel is among the handful of organizations that have managed to go beyond control orientation and build an orbit-shifting business model that is founded on generative partnerships. Bharti's orbit-shifting business model idea was to convert Capital Expenditure (CAPEX) into Operating Expenditure (OPEX). Execution of this idea didn't need mere suppliers, it needed generative partnerships with organizations like Nokia and Siemens for network equipment. Most important, it needed a generative partnership with IBM who had been chosen to manage the network (the core for a telecom service provider).

Making these partnerships happen was a challenge in itself. When Airtel first talked to potential IT partners about managing the network, they were hesitant, for there was no precedent anywhere else in the world; so the idea stayed on the back-burner till one partner, IBM, was ready. As Anil Nayar, who was on the board of Airtel, says, 'Strategically, IBM had shifted from a box company to a services company. It was very critical for them. Our thought process and vision happened to coincide with theirs.'

This was not an overnight shake of the hands. It was another long six months in the making, with CEOs on either side talking and moving the agenda forward. It didn't matter to IBM that Airtel was small and that IBM was bigger. What mattered was that they were creating history together, and this overarching purpose drove them to create a new working partnership. 'There was a higher sense of purpose, beyond yourself and sometimes beyond the organization, and everyone in the room believes you are doing something *first to the world* and *first to the nation*, and not just being first, but also one that will have great benefit to the people of this country,' Anil says.

And yet, when Airtel went to its board, they were sceptical. A board member shared an experience where something similar had been tried out in Australia and failed. Rather than step back and accept that it could not be done, Airtel stepped forward and spoke to the Australian organization for a first-hand understanding of their failure. As Anil Nayar says, 'We had an experienced board member telling us it wouldn't work, so we had discussions with the Australian CEO: why didn't it work, and the more they said it wouldn't work, the more we were convinced that it would!' Airtel discovered that while the partnership in Australia had been signed on paper, in spirit it was still a control-oriented relationship—where, when anything went right, the kudos would go to the telecom company, but when anything went wrong, it was blamed on IBM. 'The thing was they were holding back control, they wouldn't give everything and the result was that IBM would always feel uncomfortable. They would take all problems to IBM: "You know, you control this and we don't have control over it", when in reality they had all the control. And IBM was saying: "Look here, we are making all the capital investment, we are putting all the manpower, we are giving you a service level agreement, what else would you need?"'

Learning significantly from the Australian experience, Airtel and IBM got into a true spirit of partnership. It was complicated and it took time, but both Airtel and IBM stayed committed to it. 'When you start with the genuine feeling of partnership, the intent is correct. Because, it is easier when you deal with a person-to-person partnership and start with trust. But when you move it to a larger organization, spread over multiple locations, it becomes much more complex. When many more people bring their own different energies to the conversations, it becomes more critical that the people who have conceived it, who are then in charge of the execution, do so with a very open mind and try to build in that element of trust. For example, I remember having a lot of conversations with the head of execution, on our side. And every time, we used to sit on the problems we were facing; "You know," he would say, "this fellow said this, this fellow did this, they don't want to let go, etc." I would say that the "Issue is on both sides. For example on IBM's side also there is this concern, how do we actually work this out." So the issues are on both sides and we need to talk to our own people, the partners also need to talk to their own people. Unless there is clarity at that level, we will never ever be able to have a partnership.' The Airtel attitude of not blaming, but instead addressing issues on both sides, brings alive this *equality with partners in action.*

Their generative partnership was most visible in how they co-evolved the business model. The entire business model was not frozen in the beginning. Recognizing that they were venturing into the unknown, they chose to co-evolve it in the course. It took over three to four years of working together to mature their business model. *In addition, they co-evolved SLAs with the employees. So bottom up, the implementation team was involved in the creation of the partnership.* Even here, the leadership needed to be aware of the controlling behaviour. As Anil says, 'Yes you do, you do involve people. You know, it is interesting when they come up with service-level agreements. Today, if they are delivering at level X, as soon as it goes to IBM, they want 2X. It is about dealing with these demand shifts too and addressing them. But it is also recognizing that we actually need 3X, not just 2X. But there has to be a step-by-step approach in achieving it and we have to do it together, not demand it from IBM.'

Not demanding, but co-creating SLAs is illustrative of the generative partnership that Airtel-IBM had created.

This consistent commitment to partnership and to a shared higher purpose by the Airtel-IBM teams led to the first ever customer support structure being owned by a partner outside the organization in telecom. It took three years of constant work, 'It takes time, it took three years for us and then suddenly it is just business as usual, there was no one point where we stopped, it just became normal. There are no two ways about it, no short cuts. Patience is critical, self-belief is critical.'

The Airtel-IBM generative partnership was most visible in how they co-evolved the business model. They did not start with pre-configured business model, it was not frozen and signed on in the beginning. Recognizing that they were venturing into the unknown, they chose to co-evolve it. As Atul Bindal, the former head of Mobility Airtel shares. 'This co-evolution of the business model was founded on two principles. Instead of input, output became the first unifying principle. Instead of present focussed, being future focussed became the second core principle.' The guiding philosophy that they shared was 'more for more'—the more the business grows the more their mutual returns would be. This central idea steered them through 3–4 years of collaborative effort to mature the business model.

Generative Partnerships to Co-create New Products

Michael da Costa of Food Doctor had taken on an orbit-shifting challenge of 'making the in-between food, the snacks, healthy'. To execute this orbit-shifting idea, Michael has forged a network of *generative partnerships.*

Food Doctor has focused on and built a strong brand, an authority, in the public mindspace. On account of the number of books on nutrition and health produced by Food Doctor, it is seen as an expert in the field. As Vijit

Shekawat, a consultant, says, 'Food Doctor has not spread themselves thin. They concentrated on building their brand through books. The public sees Food Doctor books as authorities on the topic of healthy foods. They get paid for writing books, whereas other companies have to spend hundreds of thousands of pounds on PR.'

To develop and take to market new products and healthy snacks, Food Doctor partners with manufacturers who produce niche health products, have a good relationship with supermarkets, and are seeking a strong brand to extend their business. Food Doctor brings the brand and the marketing expertise, the manufacturers bring the technology and the relationship with supermarkets.

But Food Doctor does not engage with its partners in the usual *vendor like* way. They have built a process of engaging generatively to co-create new products and take them to the market. Cultivating *generative partnerships* is what distinguishes Food Doctor from the other multi-licence models. Phil Whitfield from Humdinger (a partner of Food Doctor) shares this difference between usual partnerships and their relationship with Food Doctor: 'We created a new product in a hundred-year-old brand of one of our large licencees. They took us on board and asked us to manufacture and sell the product and pay a royalty, since they had little knowledge or interest on what the category was about and what was driving it, especially as they juggle so many brands. Most companies do this; they have a *passive relationship. If they want to sit back and take the benefits we have to respect that, because they have built the brand of magnitude.* This is how it works with others.'

The Humdinger relationship with Food Doctor, in contrast, is not passive. It is truly generative. As Phil says, 'Food Doctor is very different. Michael approached me three years ago and said he was interested in being more innovative, more involved. He embraces licencees, adds value to their processes.'

This generative engagement is very visible; Phil Whitfield explains how they worked together to convert buckwheat into a successful health snack. 'It's the way the relationship has evolved and developed. Michael is always looking around for new concepts and ideas, and recently we launched a range of new items that has been truly collaborative. He came across some raw materials that conceptually were good, on the mark. Problem was it tasted like cardboard. In raw form, it is not really edible, unless you grind it. Michael found a company that popped buckwheat in a certain way, where you can actually eat it. It doesn't taste anything—just bland. So it first went from not edible to bland and neutral tasting. We've now taken it and done some really good product development, which is technically quite difficult, because you are now applying flavour but you have to get the right consistency and intensity. And then to mix the blend is also difficult. Not easy!

'So Michael conceptually thought of mixing the grains and found a basic product, and we've taken the basic product into something appetizing and healthy. We've worked together on it: pack size, retail, commercials. And he's now taking it into a section where we aren't going and we're taking it where he isn't; so it's very collaborative.'

What's striking about this relationship is that both partners are mutually creating new value. 'Michael doesn't say this is what we need to do, he is so much more two way, he shares plans for brands fairly quickly, and also embraces our decisions. As the brand owner he is very, very strong, but he doesn't tend to override. This works well because he can focus on brands and we can focus on NPD (New Product Development).'

Phil goes on to explain the complementary purpose that drew Food Doctor and Humdinger together into a generative partnership: 'In 1994–95, there was no such thing as a dry tropical fruits market in the UK. I bought dry mango, pineapple, guava to market as dry fruits. Now it probably occupies a reasonable size of areas of supermarkets, lots of people sell it. Organic fruits were dry and tough, and we also developed a process to put moisture back into the dry fruits to make them soft and ready to eat. So this was a genuine new product and packaging development.' These days, however, it has become an incremental extension of a variety of mixes. 'Now more often than not in our industry, it tends to be different pack size or a different blend of basic components. So you get raisins, apricot, prune mix. That's the product. And then product development becomes raisins, peach, pear mix.' The industry is calling this new product development, which it really isn't.

Food Doctor and Humdinger have gone beyond the incremental range building of the industry, to provide what the consumer is really looking for: healthy and tasty snacks. And they're constantly innovating together in bringing newer products and flavours to market.

Phil adds, 'When we first got involved with Food Doctor, we were looking at different flavours, building flavour profiles. Michael's background before Food Doctor was as a restaurateur and a foodie, so he appreciates the authenticity of flavours. So we developed a lot of flavour profiles that would taste nicer, better. As a result we've been able to make more difficult products, with nutritional elements that are good for you.'

As a CEO, think about this:

Bharti Airtel and the Food Doctor are vivid examples of how generative partnerships brought in a much-needed complementarity to maximize the orbit-shifting idea in execution.

In contrast, some organizations put orbit-shifting ideas on the back-burner saying 'This will take time'; 'we don't have the expertise', while an equal number of other organizations have seen an orbit-shifting idea get reduced to the lowest common denominator as a result of an ineffective partnership.

Where has your organization put an orbit-shifting idea on the back-burner due to partnering obstacles? Or where is your organization faced with an orbit-shifting idea that is stuck in a degenerative partnership?

How can you leverage generative partnerships to not just restart but maximize the orbit-shifting idea?

Enrolling the Frontline

Infusing Passion in the Front-line Implementation Team

While launching the new, most traditional organizations adopt the *hype and launch* model. The front-line sales and service are gathered for a grand launch event, quite like a movie launch. A first-level hype is generated; everyone applauds and leaves with much anticipation.

But we really mistake, as most organizations painfully discover later, the 'hype and rah! rah!' for ownership. When these same people who applauded vociferously at the launch are faced with the first on-ground sales and service barriers/problems, the hype begins to turn to cynicism. 'This doesn't work here', is the starting whisper that grows into a rumble.

While the hype creates much buzz, it doesn't necessarily generate the passion and the ownership needed to implement an orbit-shift. Taking a new orbit-shifting idea to customers means that in the starting days, the number of in-field errors and failures are likely to increase. Surfing through these initial failures and even backlashes, while still continuously learning and retrying, takes a lot of passionate ownership at the front line. Faced with initial failures, most settlers lose energy and become passive or even detractive. *Orbit-shifters go beyond the superficial hype and launch; they treat the execution of the orbit-shift like a movement, where there is as much passion in the people on the ground, implementing the idea as in those who conceived it.* They don't launch with a rah-rah activity, they focus on building ownership.

What does it take for the front-line implementers—those who are far away from the excitement of where the orbit-shift was conceived; those who may have played no part or a very minimal part in its conception or development—*to become generative; to wholeheartedly own it and implement it on the ground without dilution?*

Where are implementers on the generativity index with reference to the new idea? If they are merely participative or passive, chances are the implementation on ground will be diluted. Orbit-shifters succeed in creating generative implementation teams and individuals, those who create an on-ground movement to take the orbit-shifting idea to its full potential.

From Sceptical Customers to Self-appointed Ambassadors

Fabio Rosa had long faced obstacles in on-ground implementation with the government and bureaucracy in Brazil with his 025-norm monophase electricity project. It was shelved even when it brought affordable electricity at 5 percent of the previous costs.

He realized if he had to be successful with his new solar solution project called The Sun Shines for All, he would have to win over deeply sceptical customers. Community after disenfranchised community had become suspicious of city-based messiahs coming with empty promises of light and electricity. As the *Global Envision* article says: 'trust and confidence have to be built for people to adopt solar energy en masse'. In Encruzilhada in the northeast region of Brazil, he first began by forging alliances with a local farmer of repute, to whom he gave the job of development strategy and managing local communications. He then forged a relationship with the mayor. As Rosa says in the article: 'It is important to understand how the municipality and community works and who really has influence.' Rosa also brought in a social psychologist to work as a community motivator. He identified a local electric shop owner as a business partner for installations. *The orbit-shifter in Rosa realized that regardless of how good or elegant his solution was, it would fail if it did not have ownership on ground. He spent as much time, therefore, building a generative implementation team: focusing not only on influencers but also on the psychology of what it takes to motivate groups and communities.* As a result of the careful time and effort invested here, *he had a passionate team of implementers—people who went willingly beyond the script or job description to make the solar home system successful in Encruzilhada. The generative spirit had multiplied beyond Rosa.*

Quoting from the article: 'Initially, when Rosa began marketing the Solar Home System to the villagers in Encruzilhada, the acceptance rate was less than 10 percent. There were many obstacles. People were sceptical. They had been falsely promised electricity many times before. Others had been told by political leaders to "wait for the grids". And many didn't believe that electricity could really come from sunlight.

So Rodrigo Quadros (the first farmer who was Rosa's development manager) and Inez Azevedo (the social psychologist) spent a year in Encruzilhada talking to locals and encouraging them to try it out. "We have to think differently," Quadros told his fellow villagers. "'Your lives will be easier." He reassured them: "It's not dangerous to work with solar energy. It's also very reliable. It doesn't have to be sunny every day. It does work in the winter."

"'I would visit people at night," Quadros recalled, and say, 'Look at your walls. They're completely black from burning kerosene. Look, you've been breathing this smoke. Your children are breathing it.'

"'We needed to build trust and confidence," Inez Azevedo explained. "It takes time to establish credibility. It's all a matter of how you talk to people. You have to ask a lot of questions. It's important to understand why people change or why they don't change. If you understand that, then you can deliver things to people in the way they would like to receive them."

"Most of all, you have to observe and look for local people who can be leaders," she added. "You really have to look for them—not just work with the people who are the first ones to talk. The real doers are not always the ones with charisma or talking ability. But they can listen well and understand—and they have credibility. They really know their own needs and they make decisions quickly. It is fundamental to identify the right people to work with first: it is the key to making things work with communities."

'One such leader is Otila Maria Rosa dos Santos, an elementary school teacher, who lives in a brick house at the end of a red-dirt road 3 km from the electric grid. Dos Santos would have had to pay at least USD 3,000 to have her house hooked up to the grid—a sum greater than her annual income. In a Saturday morning meeting in February 2002, after Rosa presented his products and prices, dos Santos came forward and said to him: "I want it. Can you install it tomorrow?" She says her house is brighter and cleaner than before. After the electricity, she decided to repaint some of the walls. The house no longer smells of kerosene. Next summer, Dos Santos is looking forward to cooler nights, not having to burn lamps inside the house. But the greatest benefit of electricity is the effect on her son. "My son had told me he didn't want to continue living in the dark," Dos Santos told me on a recent visit to Brazil. "He was going to leave home." She added, with a smile: "Now he will stay." I peeked into her son, Emerson's room, and noticed a neat bookshelf with a CD player and a small music collection. "I don't believe I lived my entire life without the grid and now I have electricity," she added. Dos Santos has become a self-appointed ambassador of solar energy, speaking to many locals in her understated but persuasive manner about the benefits of electric lights.'[1]

It took a year to even begin making solar solutions acceptable in Encruzilhada. And it was not Rosa who was at the forefront of the passionate enrolling, but Quadros and Azevedo, and then the inspired locals themselves, like Dos Santos. As they saw the benefits, they became 'self appointed' ambassadors creating waves of believers within the community.

As an Innovation Leader, think about this:

A Quadros moving around the community at night; an Inez taking time to establish credibility; a Dos Santos becoming a self-appointed ambassador.

What Rosa had done was build a passionate set of implementers who owned and propagated his orbit-shifting idea of solar home systems with as much energy and enthusiasm as him, if not more.

How are your orbit-shifting ideas owned and treated by implementation teams? With the passion and generativity of Quadros and Inez, or with indifference and passivity? What will it take for you to build the same passion and ownership in the front liners so that they don't merely champion the idea, but also build idea champions in the local community, like dos Santos?

Building a Generative Implementation Team—the Trichy Police Force

In implementing community policing in Trichy, J.K. Tripathy was faced with a choice: either conceive the entire model and hand-pick the right people for it or first hand-pick the people and build the solution with them. He chose the second. From evolving the model to decision-making, every step was taken in tandem with the implementation team on ground, resulting in a high degree of ownership of the community policing model.

Tripathy's first step was to choose the right people. He screened the 2,600-odd police force and hand-picked 260 constables. These were picked on the basis of internal police CID (Crime Investigation Department) files (those with no corruption, no bad habits, who are polite, and have a track record of effectiveness) and were rigorously screened by Tripathy personally. He met each person a number of times and shortlisted 260 constables who seemed most open to change. This was done in one week. The screening was done for two reasons: one, to select the best constables and the other, to decide which environment he would best fit into. That is, those who were more educated and comparatively gentler would fit into an area where the socio-economic profile was higher. Those who were comparatively 'tougher' would fit into, say, a slum environment. This fitting of the person to the environment was an important part of the selection process. The constables were often chosen because they belonged to a similar environment in which they would work.

Once Tripathy had shortlisted the best people, he created ownership by bringing about an awareness of the non-personality factors that lead to crime. He would ask them to tell him about their early years, and ask them about their childhood friends and what they are doing now. And quite a few were not doing much. So he asked, 'You have come from the same place. Why aren't there more like you there? What opportunities/breaks did you get that they didn't?'

This created a higher awareness that the environment was a major breeding ground for anti-social and criminal activities. It created awareness that people aren't born criminals, nor do they grow up with criminal tendencies. Many often take to crime because it's the easiest way out. When they grow up in severely deprived localities and they see that the rule of law is neither fair nor equal to all, they take to crime as the easiest way to earn a living. Take the crime-conducive environment away, and the vast majority of petty criminals could go straight. If we could improve the environment, we could limit anti-social activity. And hence, Community Policing was a way to enhance this environment. *This joining of dots with the real purpose and benefit of Community Policing—through deep, reflective dialogues—helped increase the engagement levels of the constables with the new idea.*

The next challenge was to build ownership. After Tripathy got the right people in and identified who would go where, he just set to work. Everything was co-evolved with the constables. He suggested the beat system—four people to a beat who wouldn't be moved for at least two years—and asked them how this could be made to work. Whatever suggestions they gave were immediately experimented with. As he says, 'If I had started with a lecture on Community Policing, it would not have penetrated, except at an intellectual level. They began without knowing the principle. They just did it. They learnt on the job, saw results, and came back and asked for more information. When they asked for more information, I got community policing articles translated into Tamil for them. They read the notes and came back saying, *"This is similar, but ours is unique, because we have developed it rather than the bosses".'* That was one factor that created tremendous ownership.

Another factor that led to ownership was ensuring that he involved the constables in decision-making. As he says, 'I ask them, "tell me what problems will we face and how do we go about overcoming them?".' The constables were initially not very aware of different possibilities, so he needed to bring in additional information like government policies and schemes where people have benefitted. From that kind of information, ideas started flowing. And because ideas came from the individuals themselves, it led to tremendous ownership. As Tripathy says, *'It's very easy to issue orders. But that way, I always stay the owner of the issues. And when the next person comes in, he changes things with his own orders. Institutionalization happens when people below take up issues and solve them.'*

Institutionalization happens when people below take up issues, when people below begin to own the initiative, when people below don't wait to be told, but bring alive the innovation with the same passion as the innovator. Tripathy shows how this is a deliberate thought through journey from picking the right people to growing the passion in community policing. From 50 people to 260, from having deep dialogues around crime, its impact and why it happens, to giving them complete independence and respect to do their jobs in the community, to growing them into role-model beat officers to be emulated, to putting their ideas into action first—Tripathy slowly and steadily created a tipping point, where his orbit-shift moved beyond himself as an individual to become an institutionalized way of life. He has been transferred from Trichy, but Community Policing flows in the veins of those he left behind, and they continue to implement it with the same passion they originally started with. The orbit-shift innovation has outlived the orbit-shifter who began it.[9]

Orbit-shifters bring to the fore that succeeding with an orbit-shifting innovation goes far beyond the romance of coming up with a breakthrough idea. It is as much about being able to socialize the innovation. It is as much about taking along stakeholders, enrolling gatekeepers, cross-functional experts, and eventually the implementers. And the key to unlocking stakeholder engagement rests not with the stakeholder's point of view, but with the orbit-shifter himself. It is up to the orbit-shifter to take all the stakeholders on that journey from adversarial to generative. Surely a far more difficult task than arriving at the idea, but truly a satisfying one when stakeholders become as passionate as the orbit-shifter in the journey onward. For then, it means you are never alone.

Overcoming Walls of Doubt: Excite and Enroll Stakeholders

Here are some of the key guiding principles that have enabled orbit-shifters to excite and enroll stakeholders into the orbit-shift: to move them from doubt to confidence in the entire course of an orbit-shifting journey.

Enrolling Gatekeepers

- Don't manage perception, enroll stakeholders into the purpose and the potential of the orbit-shift.
- Act equal, engage with the person, not the position.

- Rather than convincing stakeholder with data, create first hand experiences that connect them with the new reality.
- Proactively lower the threshold of decision making by pre-answering predictable doubts.
- Engage progressively to shift stakeholders from an unconditional NO to a conditional Yes.

Enrolling Implementation Teams

- Co-evolve, Co-own—rather than resortint to mandates, co-create the new reality into a shared dream.
- Infuse passion—go beyond numbers and tasks to create an emotional connect with the new reality
- Enroll into the movement—first to the possibility and then to the doability of the new reality.

Enrolling Peers and Partners

- Bridge the divide—more from an either/or debate to an and dialogue.
- Engage experts in generative partnerships (not as suppliers).

Chapter 7

Navigating the Fog—Overcome Daunting Obstacles

ALL ORBIT-SHIFT STORIES ARE HEROIC, EVEN ROMANTIC, IN HINDSIGHT. They hide the fear, the pain, and the moments of self-doubt when the orbit-shifter was confronted with seemingly insurmountable obstacles. They hide the many, many points when the orbit-shifter was faced with dark nights, when it seemed much easier to give up and return to the comfort of the old orbit.

Orbit-shifters start combating dilution when they enrol stakeholders and prevent the orbit-shifting idea from getting compromised. But enrolment alone is not enough; an orbit-shifting idea will still face many execution hurdles.

Executing an orbit-shifting innovation is a journey filled with tunnels of fog—multiple points where the orbit-shift journey is confronted with fog created by *unforeseen problems*. Faced with fog, orbit-shifters don't give up or give in. It is their capacity to navigate the fog that differentiates an orbit-shifter from a settler.

THE NEXT AND THE NEXT DOOR

In making the LifeStraw happen, the team at Vestergaard Frandsen was repeatedly confronted with fog—the execution obstacles seemed to be never-ending. For a year and a half, the team persisted with research and over 120 prototypes were made, with variations in kinds and quantities of the various chemicals, absorbents, pre-filters, etc. There was a time when the mounting numbers of prototypes seemed daunting, but the organization remained unwavering in its commitment to the research agenda. As Navneet Garg, chief development officer at Vestergaard Frandsen says, 'The question always was, how can we do it; it was not whether we want to do it or not.'

Finally in 2005, five prototypes of LifeStraw were shortlisted and presented to WHO, and Vestergaard Frandsen was given the go-ahead on all of them.

A very excited Torben shares, 'We had cracked two things with one product: access to drinking water and iodine deficiency. Around 200 million children were suffering from iodine deficiency across the globe. The extra dilution of iodine in the water meant that not only would we eradicate harmful germs but we would also solve the problem of deficiency.'

But the time for celebration was short-lived. Their entry into the United States market was stalled when customers there told them that iodine allusion in the product had to be much, much lower. The reasoning behind their demand, as the companies explained, was a case in 1930, where a man had died due to an excess of iodine. And hence for the Vestergaard Frandsen team it was back to the drawing board. They found themselves in yet another tunnel of fog.

For most organizations this could have been the last straw—the point at which they felt they were hitting the wall of diminishing returns, and it was now better to turn back rather than go forward in futility. However, the Vestergaard Frandsen team refused to turn back; they persisted until the prototype had been built into a working model in the United States.

Torben illustrates this state of mind very vividly when he says, 'I constantly felt I would succeed. I felt very clear about the final goal. What unfortunately happens too often is that you feel if you open one door you will find the answer, but when you open that door, you find another ten to twelve doors. But you still feel all the time—this next door you will have the solution. The feeling that you are so close, you can't stop now.'

This is what sets apart orbit-shifters. They don't let these multiple doors stop or block them. They find their way through the fog. They keep opening new doors till they discover light at the end of the tunnel.

As a CEO, think about this:

It is this ability to navigate the fog that separates orbit-shifters from settlers. Settlers usually avoid the fog or at best, try a few times before giving up. Most organization leaders are faced with the same dilemma. 'At what point should we give up? At what point do we cut our losses and say—enough is enough, because we know this innovation is not going to succeed?'

Orbit-shifters are not daunted by fog; they don't give in to obstacles because they are committed to the transformative purpose. It is this commitment that gives them the courage to keep going through the next ten to twelve doors, like Torben. They don't think in terms of cutting losses but they don't aim for perfection either. Rather than cut losses and move away, they find innovative ways to overcome obstacles till they have a solution that will create a progressive and big impact on the purpose, even if it falls short of the starting orbit-shifting challenge.

Where is your organization confronted with fog? When and where have you found yourself in a tunnel of fog, with the orbit-shift journey blocked by an unsolved problem?

When faced with daunting obstacles where have you given up or compromised on the orbit-shifting opportunity? Where has the cutting of losses actually cut you away from achieving what could have been a transformative impact in the market?

Orbit-shifters navigate the fog in execution in three dominant ways:

1. By turning around the never-before-faced problems
2. By attacking the known and persistent problems with a new lens
3. By not letting a new idea enter an old pipe in the last mile

Navigate the Fog: Turn Around the Never-before-faced Problems

Navigating the execution fog is not just about dogged persistence. Overcoming execution obstacles sometimes needs as much innovation as was needed in coming up with the orbit-shifting idea.

Transform a problem into an opportunity—The Columbia *Disaster*

Carsten had enrolled his stakeholders and excited his team with the vision of Space Food. The project was chugging along full steam ahead. And then they were struck with a disaster completely out of their control that had the power to derail the mission, in totality. The space shuttle *Columbia* exploded during re-entry in 2003, and the space shuttle programme ground to a halt. The next launch was uncertain.

From complete certainty, they were suddenly engulfed in a tunnel of fog. Carsten's entire mission road map had been built around integration points in tandem with NASA and an upcoming integration point was due with the next space shuttle launch. Usually, there were anywhere between five to eight planned launches per year. Now there was no information on when the next launch could be, everything was unpredictable. As Carsten says, 'We were looking at it becoming a glorious disaster!' Most settlers would have sought out their superiors for advice or waited for NASA to tell them what to do next. But Carsten energized himself and his team by looking at how they could find the positives in this situation and leverage it to their advantage. He engaged his team members first through one-on-one dialogues and then in a group to explore 'how can we take charge of this moment?' *They reframed the problem into an opportunity.* 'In the past,

NASA has taken about one-and-a-half years to recover and restart. Rather than just a few months we now have one-and-a-half years. What we have been given is an opportunity of stopped time. We can fix the products such that we will be fully ready for the next launch. We can make a stronger case for our products'. The team had found a past reference point that helped to give some anchor to what, until then, seemed to be a completely open timeline. They now had one-and-a-half years as a possible window. Their focus shifted to looking at ways to leverage this time to their advantage, to fix all the outstanding issues in the product. *The problem had now transformed into an opportunity.*

The amazing thing is that they didn't stop here; once their focus had shifted, they transformed it into an even bigger opportunity. For one, NASA had a great many questions and concerns about sending probiotics into Space. What if the bacteria contaminated the space station? How would they contain it? Now, the Lacmos team actually looked for and found another route to send a test sample into Space. A Russian crew was due to leave from Kazakhstan, and the first Lacmos yoghurt sample flew with them on their craft. As Carsten says, 'Yoghurt is a traditional part of the Russian culture, so they didn't have as many problems in accepting it. This became the proven prototype in the real environment and the Johnson Space Centre was convinced *we could send good bacteria on Space missions*, so we bypassed NASA, in a good way. We changed the unfortunate situation to an opportunity.'

It also became an excellent opportunity to build a deep bond of trust with NASA. The ethos of Space and Space travel is one of close camaraderie and fraternal spirit. The team members become closer than family members sharing so much more than they ever would outside. The loss of a Space shuttle is a deeply shattering moment. 'The crisis also built a stronger relationship. Earlier, NASA would ask for a lot of documentation. It would take three months just to document. But after this, and also because we had prove the flight capability of our product on the Russian spacecraft, and had demonstrated success, the levels of trust went up, we were given their trust. No more "Impossible!" or loads of documentation,' says Carsten.

Carsten didn't give in, he didn't compromise. He and his team navigated the fog, they combated dilution, and in fact, they maximized the opportunity from the disaster threat. When the next launch took place exactly one-and-a-half years later, in July 2005, Arla's Space food was ready.

As an Innovation Leader, think about this:

Orbit-shifters don't get daunted by even the densest fog created by an almost insurmountable execution obstacle like the *Columbia* disaster. They find the positive energy to turn around a problem into an opportunity. This capacity to turn around the most unexpected, the toughest obstacles into opportunities not only solves the problem, it can be the single biggest contributor to renewing the team's energy. An orbit-shifter converts a tunnel of fog into a positive rallying point for the team, converting hopelessness to hope.

If Carsten could convert the *Columbia* disaster into an opportunity, what is stopping you? Where is the fog confronting you? What is the most daunting obstacle standing in the way of executing an orbit-shifting idea? How can you move your team to positively navigate the fog—shift from seeing the obstacle as an idea-minimizing threat, to an idea-maximizing opportunity?

Living Up to the Promise of Executing the Impossible: The Qinghai Tibet Railway

When China took on the challenge to build the highest and most difficult railway in the world, the task was made impossible, and not merely by the extreme and difficult environmental conditions that called for extreme solutions in engineering. They were also faced with daunting human limitations in executing the innovative engineering solutions.

The climatic conditions are so harsh on the Qinghai Tibet plateau that just a short visit can make a person sick. The air at an altitude of 4,300 metres contains just 50 percent as much oxygen as it has at sea level. The temperature can drop to as low as -40°C. Hard physical labour in these conditions can easily lead to altitude sickness—mild symptoms of which are headache, nausea, vomiting, and falling blood pressure. Severe altitude sickness can even kill. This posed a humungous execution obstacle.

Executing large-scale engineering projects in inhospitable conditions had caused human deaths in the past. The building of the Hoover Dam in Nevada in the 1930s killed 112 workers, while the building of the Panama Canal cost 30,000 human lives! And the Qinghai Tibet Railway project had 227,000 workers in service. But the Chinese chose to confront and navigate the fog rather than give into it. They were determined to minimize this human impact.

Out of this resolve, innovative solutions for the protection of the workers' lives emerged. The Chinese medical system put in place over 2,000 doctors to monitor the first signs of altitude sickness, for earlier the detection, easier is the cure. Piped oxygen was provided inside the tunnels where its absence would be greater. Shifts were kept as low as four hours to provide time for the worker to rest and recover. Because hospitals are few and far between on the plateau, the Chinese took the hospital to where the workers were. Mobile hospitals were set up to treat patients near the work sites. One solution was the Oxygen Chamber, a fully insulated chamber where up to six patients could be seated and then sealed in an environment with super-enriched oxygen. This oxygen can reverse the effects of altitude sickness. A full 14,000 workers were treated in these mobile hospitals.

The Chinese medical authorities were also concerned about infectious diseases like SARS and plague playing havoc with the workers' health. Special care was taken to monitor hygiene among the workers.

The Chinese claim to have achieved the *3 Zeros* in the six years it took to complete the Qinghai Tibet Railway project: Zero Deaths, Zero SARS and Zero Plague![2]

Having found breakthrough engineering solutions to create the world's highest rail line would have been enough to satisfy most innovators. But the Chinese innovated further to ensure zero loss of life in execution.

They could have easily avoided this fog in execution, shrugged their shoulders with 'in mega projects such as these you have to expect some causalities. We'll be satisfied if we ensure the loss of life doesn't exceed any previous global benchmark for a project of this size'. However, they chose not to compromise, the orbit-shifter in them chose to navigate and not avoid the fog.

Navigating the fog created by new, never-faced-earlier problems and obstacles of the kind Carsten and the Chinese faced is one major execution challenge. *An equally big challenge can be to find new ways to navigate the fog created by the most well-known, in fact, the most persistent problems.*

Navigate the Fog: Attack Known and Persistent Problems with a New Lens

An orbit-shift of an altogether different order occurred when S.R. Rao transformed Surat from a plague-ridden city in the early 1990s into India's second-cleanest city in twenty months. Malaria cases came down from 22,000 in 1994 to 496 in 1997, and doctors' bills reduced by 66 percent. What's more, the change has sustained more than ten years after S.R. Rao was transferred out of Surat.

In executing the orbit-shift, the fog that S.R. Rao had to navigate was not posed by the *new-to-the-world* kind of problems that had confronted the Chinese and Carsten.

S.R. Rao's real orbit-shift was in the way he got an inertia-ridden bureaucracy to break through *paralyzing powerlessness* and take charge of the transformation. It was centred around getting his managers to break through this *mindset of powerlessness* by first radically empowering them and then, more importantly, getting them to *attack persistent problems with a new lens.*

In one instance, Rao was faced with a persistent problem where, within a few hours of the morning clean up, the streets were dirty again. Most citizens just got rid of the house rubbish by dumping it onto the street. The first instinct of the organization was to *penalize citizens in front of whose houses the rubbish was found.* But the city corporators (city councillors, elected representatives of the city) informed Rao and his team that this could not be done. It was against the law. S.R. Rao *motivated his team to not give up, as would usually have been the case, but to reframe the problem. This lead to a solution that was within their power to execute—'we can't penalize, but we can charge an administrative fee'.* They proceeded to impose an administrative fee on all the houses where rubbish was found after the daily clean up. Soon, most people started ensuring that they didn't dump garbage in front of their houses and even started clearing up rubbish dumped by others.

Another fascinating solution emerged when he reframed the ever-persistent problem of dealing with covert pressure from outsiders, like politicians, influential business people, and the media. The reframing of the problem led to a simple but unique solution: to get all his staff to use walkie-talkies for communication, making all official communication publicly audible. He made himself accessible only through his walkie-talkie. Not only public communication, all communication was now official and recorded. Now whenever anyone tried to pressurize him, he turned up the volume of his walkie-talkie so that everyone around him, including the press could hear it. This fear of public exposure dramatically reduced the number of people exerting covert pressure.

These two stories are illustrative of the spirit of navigating the fog in execution—*not settling for less but breaking through helplessness and attacking old, persistent problems with a new lens.* As a result, the organization's administrative, financial, and public health engineering capacity was transformed. Cleaning of garbage went up from 40 percent to 98 percent. The number of people covered by sanitation increased from 63 percent to 97 percent. The net revenue collection also increased by an astonishing 54 percent.[5]

As a CEO, think about this:

Executing the orbit-shift will often need an organization restructuring like the one S.R. Rao did. But a new structure combined with the old mindset usually doesn't work. A new role can be crafted but when executed with the old mindsets (for example helplessness), it will produce little change. It will definitely not produce transformative action. S.R. Rao had to get his people to engage with problems differently. He moved them to 'take charge', to 'reframe persistent problems and attack them with a new lens'.

A number of organization orbit-shift initiatives get lost in the execution fog and get compromised and diluted.

Often, the execution fog in these orbit-shift initiatives is not caused by new-to-the-world problems; the toughest fog is actually caused by recurring, often predictable problems. Faced with persistent execution problems, managers and bureaucrats take refuge in powerlessness—they don't confront and navigate the fog, they simply avoid it. As a result, most actions lose impetus and settle at the lowest common denominator.

Where have you, like a lot of other organizations, attempted to execute an orbit-shift with only an over-simplistic organization restructuring exercise? Making a structural change that sharpens accountability towards executing the new is not enough to navigate the fog in execution. Approaching persistent problems with the old lens, most managers will usually end up avoiding the fog. This will inevitably dilute the orbit-shifting idea.

Where do you need to, quite like S.R. Rao, complement a structural change and provoke your managers to make the mindset shifts needed to navigate the fog in execution, to attack persistent problems with a new lens?

Navigate the Fog: Don't Allow a New Idea to Enter the Old Pipe in the Last Mile

The most threatening fog can often come in the last mile of executing an orbit-shifting innovation. In fact, often the biggest forces of dilution surface in the last mile, when a new idea enters the old pipe.

For most organizations, a mature, proven, well-organized, well-disciplined, and almost-regimented *take-to-market model* is the last mile. It is here that the new idea almost inevitably enters the old pipe.

A team in an automobile company came up with a number of new, radical ways they could convert *the test-driving experience of a new car into an industry-wide differentiator*. But when it entered the old pipe—the sales channel—most of these ideas were either postponed or tried in half-hearted ways and rejected. Even after a few years, their *way of test driving* remained the same, the same as all others in the industry. Their sales people were too caught up narrating the same old sales scripts to customers to have time for any radically new test-drive ideas. A portfolio of *Snow White ideas* was reduced to better pigs in the last mile.

A global organization with a huge business in personal care products wanted to create a new category by launching preventive health care products. Moving beyond the conventional *dandruff removal shampoos* they developed an anti-dandruff shampoo that would prevent dandruff rather than reduce it. But in the last mile, this new idea went into the old pipe. It was launched with the usual go-to-market model: put it on the shelves of stores, backed with a big advertising campaign. It just didn't work. After an extended period of repeated attempts, it was pulled out of the market. On reflection, the team leader later realized, 'We had put a product that needed qualitative engagement with the customer at the sales point, into a channel that was completely transactional. A transactional channel works where the need is well known and well established. But when you are trying to serve a need that is preventive, important but not urgent, it requires a different approach. We have to find a channel that will make the *subtle, visible,* and the *important, urgent.*'

Most organizations mature their sales channel into an efficient pipe and lock it down. New ideas that now enter have to either *fit in* or *die in the last mile*. Now, the idea ends up getting retrofitted to the old pipe, rather than innovating on the old pipe to leverage the new idea.

Navigating the Last Mile Fog

Complementary Innovation: Mass Vaccination Camps

Varaprasad Reddy had put seven years of his life into the making of Shanvac, India's first indigenous hepatitis B vaccine. He thought it would take two years, but the blocks, obstacles, and the sheer challenge of making the vaccine took him another five years. At last his orbit-shifting aspiration was realized. He had a vaccine that he could price at INR 50 per dose as compared to the competitors' price of INR 750 per dose. Surely, as anyone can see, his biggest battle was over, now it was merely a matter of taking the product to market.

And yet for Varaprasad, a challenge of a different order was to come, not a technical or a bureaucratic challenge, but a sales and marketing challenge. He was confronted with the *last mile fog.*

Anticipating Shanvac's release, the competition crashed its vaccine price from INR 750 to INR 520. A major Indian pharma company approached Varaprasad Reddy and offered to take Shanvac to market. They already had a strategy in place—*Shanvac would be strategically priced at INR 519, with a projected sales of INR 5 million in the first, INR 7.5 million in the second, and INR 10 million in the third year.* When Varaprasad asked them the reasoning behind these figures, they said that this was based on their previous experience of *how much a new product could sell.*

Varaprasad's orbit-shifting mission was faced with the old pipe in the last mile. This was a huge dilution threat. He had wanted to price the vaccine at INR 50 to make it accessible to masses of Indians, but this pharma company was suggesting INR 519. After having struggled for seven years to even come up with a vaccine, most traditionalists would have avoided getting into yet another tunnel of fog and compromised; after all, it is better to see your product in the market than not at all. But Varaprasad refused to compromise his orbit-shifting idea. He chose to navigate the fog. He decided to take the vaccine to market by himself.

To meet his dream of making the vaccine affordable to the common man, he now needed a sales and marketing innovation. Varaprasad Reddy realized that the marketing innovation required to make the original Shanvac idea a success could never come from within the old pipe: the existing pharma industry. It was saturated with the gravity of the current way of pricing and selling drugs. Stakeholders were also reluctant to upset the apple cart of the monetary benefits from selling expensive drugs to the public.

So, Varaprasad hired a different order of people, people with pride in India—and with *no sales or marketing know-how*. A doctor offered to train the recruits and the marketing effort was launched. Because of the publicity Shanvac-B received, people had become aware of the dreaded disease, hepatitis B, but the benefit of this publicity went to the existing market leader. The system began to overpower Shanvac. Sales weren't picking up. Varaprasad realized that publicity alone was not enough. The heart of the old pipe was the local doctor who prescribed the vaccine.

While some doctors were collecting huge margins from the competition, others were using Shanvac-B, but charging the patients at the competitor's rates and also telling them that the Shanvac vaccine was not as good. Further, while the vaccine was being put out at INR 50, it was finally hitting retail shelves at INR 180 after the commissions of super-stockists, stockists, retailers and doctors' commissions from the retailers.

So Varaprasad needed to find a way to overcome this last-mile obstacle being posed by the doctor. This triggered the realization that a vaccine didn't really need a prescription. He went to the Indian Medical Association (IMA) with his vaccine. They invited him to give a talk at the association where he received tremendous support. Together they hit on the idea of *direct contact with the masses* and decided to organize mass vaccination camps. Again, there were protests and blocks, this time from the pharma associations and trade unions. But with the help of the IMA, mass vaccination camps were conducted. People began queuing up for shots.[6]

Shantha Biotech ended up selling the vaccine at INR 50 and earned revenues of INR 80 million in the first six months, INR 230 million in the first year, INR 320 million in the second year, and INR 360 million in the third year; far outstripping the prediction of the old pipe—what the Indian pharma company's conventional wisdom had projected.

As a CEO, think about this:

With a series of complementary innovations, Varaprasad navigated the fog in the last mile. He overcame the mindset gravity of the sales force (classic medical representatives) by hiring new people who were impassioned by the purpose. He further overcame the mindset gravity of the intermediary—the doctors—by conceiving mass vaccination camps. And in doing this, he enrolled the Indian Medical Association (IMA) such that they became the co-creators of the mass vaccination camps.

Ask yourself: How do you navigate the last-mile fog?

How often have you seen a new idea being stifled in the last mile?

Reexamine the last time you took an innovation to market, how many complementary innovations were deployed to reshape the last mile?

What has been the real cost avoiding the fog in the last mile?

Complementary Innovation: SMS for Life

The cost of letting a new idea disappear into an old pipe in the last mile is not merely a loss of sales or revenue; it can be loss of lives, millions of lives.

Novartis had orbit-shifted the production and supply of the anti-malaria drug, Coartem, for Africa. But yet, millions of children continued to die of malaria. The real problem, they discovered, was the supply chain in the last mile. And this supply chain was in the domain of the country's administration. Rather than live with the problem, Novartis chose to step forward, fuelled by the transformative purpose of saving lives. They went on to create a complementary innovation SMS for Life, that bridged the last-mile gap.

Quoting from the Harvard Business School case study, *The Coartem Challenge (A)*, 'In November 2005, Novartis CEO Dr. Daniel Vasella sent a note of appreciation to the Novartis Coartem team, writing that, "I would like to congratulate and thank the entire team for an outstanding job, which has helped to ease the suffering of millions of people." By the end of 2005, this team had produced 33 million treatments of the anti-malarial drug Coartem for sale at cost through the World Health Organization (WHO). Their total output was more than 10 percent ahead of the company's earlier projections and many times more than the 100,000 treatments Novartis had delivered in 2002 as per orders placed by the WHO for that year'.[7]

However, while Coartem production was both efficient and sufficient, there was a deeper problem being faced. Anti-malarial drugs were not reaching the end user at the right time.

Quoting from the *SMS for Life (A)* article, 'Every 30 seconds a child dies of malaria. Over 40 percent of the world's children live in countries in which malaria is endemic. Each year, approximately 300 to 500 million malaria infections cause about one million deaths, most of them African children under the age of five. Increasing resistance to antimalarial drugs, coupled with widespread poverty, weak health infrastructure and, in some countries, civil unrest mean that mortality from malaria in Africa continues to rise. The tragedy is that the vast majority of these deaths are preventable. The main reason why malaria is still such a threat, despite the existence of drugs to cure the disease, is a supply chain problem. Supply does not meet the demand where it occurs, and stock-outs of drugs to treat malaria cost lives'.[4]

This was the huge last-mile challenge. What happened was that companies like Novartis were readily rising up to expectations placed on them by raising production—they were putting enough drugs out to market. But unfortunately, the issue was at the other end. In many countries, while the distribution system was up and running, what was often missing was the information. Where were the stock-outs at the local level? What was the projected need for the next week/next month? In the absence of this kind of information, two issues were faced: one, that the drugs did not reach on time; and two, Novartis would get sudden and urgent orders, based on which it had to quickly raise production levels and airlift the medicine to the required destination. Novartis couldn't proactively stock Coartem, because it had promised that the drug would still have a shelf life of at least eighteen out of tweny four months by the time it was delivered.

Faced with this kind of a last-mile challenge, most companies would have shrugged their shoulders, or simply lived with the problem. After all, distribution was not in their hands, but in the hands of the public medical system within that country.

However, Jim Barrington from Novartis intuitively recognized that IT could be leveraged to solve the supply chain problem. In 2008, together with a team from Novartis and their IT partner IBM, along with a group of students hired specially for the job, they crafted a solution that would solve the information gap in the supply chain: SMS for life.

SMS for Life was a complementary innovation, an SMS-driven process to track the stock levels of the malaria drug at key health facilities. At each health facility, the health worker would, once a week, upload the current status of drugs and forecast requirements through a simple SMS. A central data server then collected this information and sent out the report to the central health system for monitoring and for distribution of drugs.

In essence, the complementary innovation of SMS for Life was designed for simplicity of use, on the most basic of mobile phones and with a deep understanding of human motivations as well. A free top-up was made available in order to incentivize positive behaviour from health workers. However, it did not penalize those who didn't do it on time. It only encouraged and created a positive-reinforcement cycle of participation.

SMS for Life was not a solution that Novartis could take on alone—it called for building a consortium of partners. Finding like-minded partners is no easy task, and after many dialogues, many blind corners and disappointments, an inspired group of partners was indeed formed, consisting of Novartis, IBM, and Vodafone, which would, in turn, hire an external software organization, MatsSoft.

Tanzania was chosen as the partner country to prototype SMS for Life and then launch and scale.

The pilots showed a great degree of success, with drastic reduction in stock-outs and high response rates averaging between 93 to 95 percent, with a data accuracy of 94 percent and therefore it was quickly rolled out and scaled across the rest of Tanzania.[1] Quoting from the *SMS for Life (B)* article, 'By November 2011, SMS for Life was deployed in 5,097 health facilities in 131 districts nationwide. The SMS for Life system tracked the five anti-malarial drugs included in the pilot, with the tracking of Rapid Diagnostic Tests (RDTs) and Sulfadoxine-Pyrimethamine (a medicine to prevent malaria in pregnant women) to be added later.'[3]

As of early 2013, SMS for Life is also in the process of scaling to full country implementation in Kenya, Ghana and Cameroon.[3]

As a CEO, think about this:

SMS for Life faced many hurdles. From aspiration to actual realization on the ground took four years. The original ground study in Zambia had come back with a bleak response; partner after partner showed interest and then backed out, money to fund the project was always in question.

Most settlers would back out at the sign of even one of these problems, but orbit-shifters like Jim Barrington and his team in Novartis patiently worked at, resolved through, and just kept moving forward. No obstacle was too big, no fog was too scary to overcome.

How do your complementary innovation obstacles compare with SMS for Life?

If they could work through even the biggest of obstacles, how can you take a leaf out of their book and do the same?

GENERATIVE REVIEWS

The Orbit-Shifter's Tool to Navigate the Fog

Orbit-shifters navigate the fog, they combat dilution in execution by turning around a problem into an opportunity and by attacking persistent problems with a new lens. They prevent a new idea from entering the old pipe in the last mile and getting diluted, by deploying complementary innovation.

What does it take to navigate the fog and to combat dilution by design—to incessantly identify and overcome the potential diluters that threaten to reduce the great to the mediocre?

The biggest contributor, indeed the biggest culprit, to diluting an orbit-shifting innovation is the review mindset. In most organizations, an innovation review is conducted in the same way as a performance review.

An orbit-shifting innovation, reviewed with a performance-review mindset, ends up becoming a *present-and-defend* exercise. The innovation team goes in with the intent of *looking good.* In this state of mind, acceptance of an unsolved problem or an unanswered question equals to admitting incompetence. The focus becomes: *how can I present the data in a manner that I won't look bad.*

The reviewer's intent, on the other hand, is to single-mindedly identify the gaps and then create a deadline pressure to plug them.

As managers across organizations admit:

- *'We propose, God disposes. No discussion.* There is subjective dismissal; ideas are shot down even before they are heard. Mode of engagement is never a dialogue. Always a presentation, followed by 24X7 challenging.'
- 'We propose, present the plan and the idea, and usually wait for the reaction to it. No dialogue, just judgemental reactions. It is difficult to argue. Our culture is to merely take in and listen. You don't argue back.'
- 'The real issue is not the PowerPoint presentations; the real issue is the pre-reads and the controlling environment in a review. The reviewers do a pre-read of the presentation and come to conclusions based on that. I have twenty slides in my presentation; I have never gone beyond the first.'
- 'The attitude is to point out flaws. They focus only on the issues.'
- 'The reviews are gap seeking. What's good is not worth discussing. Let's discuss gaps.'

In this kind of a judgemental environment, why an idea has even been rejected is often not clear. As another person said *'It got challenged. I have no idea of the real intent. It took a full day to understand the gap.'*

Performance reviews are designed to deal with the current orbit, where the outcome is predictable, through years of past experience. The dominant mental model here is *performance equals not failing*. Hence zero error and zero gaps are the prime management focus areas and expectations. Hours and hours of organization time goes into reviews where the management is preoccupied with finding errors and gaps and people are cornered into *protecting and justifying them*.

Executing an orbit-shifting innovation in contrast, is a mission brimming with uncertainty; it is in fact a journey that moves incessantly from one unsolved problem to the next. What is needed in an orbit-shift review is the uncovering and navigation of unsolved problems and unanswered questions.

An orbit-shifting innovation needs a generative review and not a performance review.

In executing an orbit-shifting innovation the team will be confronted with fog, it will be faced with unsolved problems that neither the innovation team nor the reviewing stakeholders have faced or experienced earlier. It cannot be planned and reviewed like any other *project management exercise.* As Anil Nayar observes, reflecting on Airtel's remarkable journey of the business model innovation that made the prepaid mobile card economically viable: 'We would always give timelines to ourselves…by this time we should achieve this. Looking back, I feel it is foolishness. If you try to say we should have achieved this "first-time-in-the-world" exercise in a given time, then we would not have met even one timeline. What is the right answer? There may be many routes, and perhaps we would have achieved a few things faster, but this is in hindsight. Timelines are normally given to projects only—but what is the definition of completion in something like a first-to-world partnering initiative?' This reflection brings alive, very vividly, the unknowns and the uncertainties that dog the footsteps of an *execute-the-orbit-shift* journey.

Navigating through the fog of an orbit-shifting journey

with orbit-maintaining mindsets that underlie project management and performance reviews doesn't combat dilution; it contributes to it.

Driven like a performance review, the innovation review becomes an 'avoid-the-fog' exercise. In an effort to look good, reviewees avoid accepting an unsolved problem. On the other hand, reviewers too, when confronted with the fog of an unsolved problem, don't actively engage with it. They also usually end up avoiding the fog. *An orbit-shifting innovation reviewed with a performance-review mindset will inevitably end up with a deadline to solve the problem, without bringing new insight into what can be done differently to actually solve it .*

Generative reviews don't avoid the fog; they navigate the team through the fog. What certainty-seeking minds see as gaps, the orbit-shifter sees as unsolved problems. What certainty-seeking minds see as errors, the orbit-shifter sees as learning. As Massimo said, 'We shared with our gatekeepers upfront, "we are venturing into the unknown; we will have failures, so stay with us".'

The single-minded purpose of a generative review is not to avoid, but to navigate the fog, to be a catalyst in *progressing the orbit-shifting journey.* The focus here is not as much on ascertaining the current status as it is on uncovering *what it will take to progress to the next threshold and to accelerate that progress.*

In fact the reviewers' most critical contribution to an orbit-shift journey is the ability to *seek out the fog*—to proactively uncover unsolved problems, to *identify potential diluters, and enable the team to overcome them.*

The biggest realization for the reviewer of an orbit shifting innovation project is that he/she is equally in the unknown; he/she doesn't have all the right answers. In a performance review in contrast, the reviewer's mindset is one of *controlling and downloading* because he/she is the *expert* and the *authority. Here is where an orbit-shift review is fundamentally different. There is no expert in the room who has all the right answers.* What the innovation reviewer needs to do is to unblock the team to uncover, confront, and then find new ways to solve the unsolved problems.

Both Carsten of Arla and Anil of Bharti Airtel say that no one knew any better, especially in first-to-world projects such as theirs, so they were far more open to listening and generating ideas. The focus was on progress and not assessing status. According to Anil, 'Yes, the two reviews are quite different because we are looking at things that have not been done before, therefore not in the scheme of normal resolution of problems. So we involved everybody and asked, "What do you think can be done?" And then came up with a bright idea, and it also brought out the creativity of people. The bright ones just loved it, because they were doing something new! And that's also a very, very positive factor in making things happen. But if we were an autocratic organization, where we didn't listen to others, this wouldn't have happened.'

On the other hand, when faced with judgemental reviews, most innovators resort to self-censoring. In preparation for an interrogative review, most teams try to second-guess the reviewer's frame of mind and proactively prepare for it. One team, after having arrived at a portfolio of breakthroughs decided not to share all of them with the stakeholder, but only those ones that they thought would appeal to him. *They were self-censoring.* On discovery of this, the stakeholder asked them to share everything without holding back. He also reflected, 'I find that often when I give a suggestion, it is taken as a decision.' *This mutually defensive approach to reviews holds back both the reviewee and the reviewer from finding solutions to unsolved problems, from genuinely creating positive momentum. This leads to serial dilution.*

Generative Reviews and not Performance Reviews

	Performance Review of an Orbit-Shifting Innovation → (an avoid-the-fog exercise)	Generative Review of an Orbit-Shifting Innovation → (a navigate-the-fog endeavour)
Intent	• Assess the team and the project. • Find and plug gaps.	• Progress the team, enable them to take the next step towards the orbit-shifting challenge.

Reviewer's Approach	Evaluative and Directive: • Identify the gaps. • Seek reason for existence of gaps. • Pressurized gap-plugging plans.	Discovery and Solution Orientation: • Unblock and uncover unsolved problems. • Generative dialogue to find new solution pathways.
Reviewee's Approach	Present and Defend: • Showcase progress. • Present gaps as work in progress. • Don't accept or admit to 'unsolved problems and unanswered questions'.	• Share learnings from the problems solved successfully and surface unsolved problems. • Seek new ways for solution finding.

The innovation team and the reviewing stakeholders are the best minds to progress the innovation. When they rally around and find ways to solve unsolved problems, it accelerates the innovation and the innovators. Traditionalists, on the other hand, seek to minimize problems by identifying gaps to ensure that they do not recur during reviews.

Performance reviews, therefore, move from one gap to the next. In contrast, generative reviews uncover unsolved problems and then co-create solution-finding pathways, following which the innovation team can overcome execution obstacles.

Generating New Solution Pathways: The Four Orbit-shift Gears

Enabling a team to discover a new solution pathway for an unsolved problem is the core purpose of a generative review. Orbit-shifters deploy the *Four Orbit-shift Gears* to enable an innovation team to discover new solution pathways for the unsolved problems. These solution pathways navigate the fog to the point that the light at the end of the tunnel becomes visible.

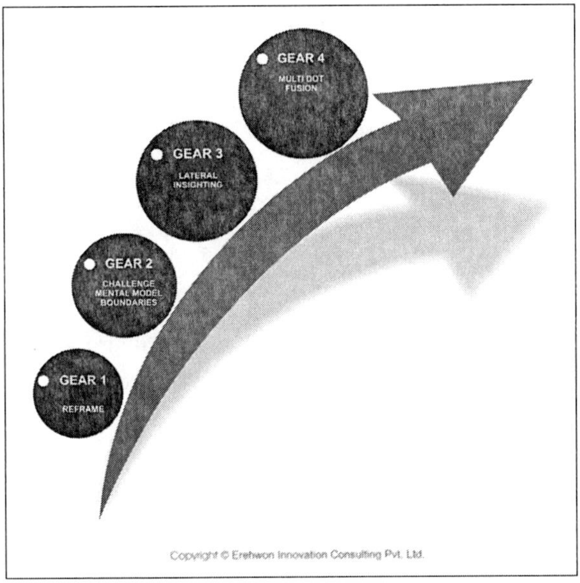

7.1 – The Four Orbit-shift Gears

Deploying the **First Gear**, a generative review evokes a new solution pathway by *reframing* the problem.

A service organization was grappling with a huge attrition problem. With attrition rates exceeding 60 percent, it was bleeding people. When the team working on this issue met for a review, the first question was: 'How do we stop people from leaving?' The immediate response to this question was *'money and position—these are the two key drivers. To retain people we have to give them more money or give them faster ways to climb the hierarchy ladder.'* However, these solutions were no different from anyone else's in the industry. Everyone was doing more of the same, throwing more money and better positions at the talent in the market; these ways had only succeeded in attracting people, but not necessarily in retaining them. The team was facing a blank wall. Until one reviewer reframed the question, and asked, 'While a lot of people are leaving, there is some high-value talent in the 40 percent who are staying. Do we know why they are staying?' Now, with this question he had opened a door in that wall, to explore why people were staying, and to discover an insight into a new career dimension, beyond position and money, that would actually retain people. This was a generative review in action. This reviewer had not been evaluative; he had reframed the problem to create a new solution pathway—*get insights from high-level talent who have stayed to identify other core drivers of retention, beyond money and position.* This new solution pathway gave the team hope; they started co-building in the new direction. It led to a new opportunity.

An R&D team was working on the challenge of *processing ethanol from agri-waste at the lowest cost.* But the project had stalled. On review, one of the unsolved problems that emerged was that *one of the stages of processing 'created microbes as a byproduct' and then these microbes had to be removed.* The cost of removal was proving to be prohibitive. After being stuck for a few months, a reviewer used the generative approach that helped the team reframe the problem and create a new solution pathway. The generative review revealed that the issue was in the way in which the team was framing the problem—how do we remove the microbes. It was now reframed to: *'Why do we need to remove the microbes, what about figuring out a way to live with them, instead?'* A performance-review mindset in contrast, would have merely ended up creating pressure to further reduce the *cost of removing the microbes.* A generative review reframed the problem and carved out a new solution pathway that promised not just cost reduction but cost elimination.

A few months later, repeated attempts at cost reduction had still not yielded results. A generative review now moved the solution finding into the next gear: **Gear Two**. The reviewer provoked the team to challenge their mental model boundaries with the question: *'The way we are currently approaching the challenge of cost reduction is to try to reduce the cost in each stage of an eight-step process. Let's challenge this sacred sequence in itself. Why do we need to do this in eight steps? How can we make this a one- or two-step conversion process?'* This was the Orbit-shift Gear Two in action. It uncovered and challenged the most fundamental mental model that was creating most of the cost problems. It provoked the team to start zero-based and rethink the process into a one- or two-step solution, rather than solving for cost at each stage.

At a watch factory, the reviewer came across a team that had tried multiple ways to tackle an innovation challenge. This team had taken on the challenge of *dramatically reducing the watch assembly time.* The reviewer asked them to describe 'how they had gone about identifying and then solving their unsolved problems'. It soon emerged that the team had consciously applied Gears One and Two. They had made many attempts to reframe and even challenge mental model boundaries, but found no breakthrough. They were now completely stuck: the watch assembly process was virtually the same all across the world. The reviewer provoked the team into deploying the Orbit-shift **Gear Three.** He triggered them to look for new, lateral insight sources, outside the watch industry.

The team explored: 'Who else has a challenge similar to ours, but in a different industry? Where is another industry also managing explosive growth? Whose product is a "lifestyle statement" and also provides a basic functionality like timekeeping in case of a watch? This Gear Three trigger in the generative review culminated with the team identifying Nokia as a lateral insight source.

Emerging from the review, the team set up a visit to the closest Nokia plant. A first-hand experience of the mobile manufacturing process triggered a *process innovation* that led to a breakthrough solution that has the potential of making a 50 percent reduction in watch assembly time.

When even Gear Two—challenging of mental model boundaries—reaches its limits, a generative reviewer triggers Gear Three, *lateral insighting,* to find the solution pathway. And when even this doesn't suffice, **Gear Four** kicks into action, which is *Multi-dot Fusion.*

In a generative review, the business head of an R&D team came across a problem that had remained unsolved for years. First, the business R&D team had attempted a solution on their own, and then even tried to co-create a solution with their corporate R&D team. After multiple attempts over four years, this problem was still unsolved. The business urgency had now become high. The business head needed this idea to get to market soon; the organization couldn't wait much longer. Rather than killing this project, which is what a usual performance review would have done at this stage, a generative review triggered the team into the **Fourth**

Orbit-shift Gear—Multi-dot Fusion. As the R&D head said, 'We have tried everything we know, we have clearly reached a point of diminishing returns. Our lens is saturated; we need a "fresh lens" to attack the problem with. Let's try to get problem solvers from completely different domains to attack this problem'. He had moved the solution trigger into Gear Four to open up a new solution pathway. This problem was then hosted on the InnoCentive Open Innovation network, which has 2,50,000 problem solvers across domains and countries.

In another instance, Roche and its partners had been wrestling with one challenge for fifteen years—*find a means of better measuring the quality and amount of a clinical specimen as it is passed through one of Roche's automated chemistry analysers.* Moving into Gear Four, the challenge was posted on the InnoCentive Network. About a thousand solvers engaged with the challenge in two months; 113 proposals from around the world were submitted. Roche solved a fifteen-year-old challenge in sixty days. Interestingly, the entire history of the R&D efforts on this challenge was also replicated in these sixty days, with all the previous solutions that Roche had attempted also being submitted from all parts of the world!

The driving force in a generative review is to uncover an unsolved problem and then trigger new solution pathways by matching the challenge of the problem with the appropriate Orbit-shift Gear. The more the problem is stuck, the higher the gear needed. Absolutely stuck problems inevitably need the deployment of Orbit-shift Gears three or four to trigger new solution pathways.

In the last decade, organizations have increasingly come to realize that the real difficulty in making an orbit-shifting innovation happen is in the execution. The gravity and the default settings of the current orbit invariably dilute even the most well-crafted innovation agenda. Confronted with tunnels of fog, most organizations get impatient and give up.

Orbit-shifters succeed because they do not settle with the default settings. Instead, they use generative reviews to navigate the fog caused by execution obstacles and combat dilution.

Surfing through the fog and executing an orbit-shift will take as much, if not more, innovation than was needed to come up with the orbit-shift idea. The orbit-shifter will have to find innovative solutions to execution problems all along the execution journey.

As a CEO, think about this:

In a corporate world that separates thinkers and doers, thinkers come with ideas and then the executors (doers) take over. Most strategists get tired and even bored once the big idea has been found, and they leave the job of execution to the foot soldiers.

Does your world suffer from this schism? This divide will be the biggest reason for dilution, because the thinkers who were involved in creating the idea are, in reality, needed even more in the execution stage, to navigate the fog. It is in this phase that the idea will either grow to its maximum or settle at the lowest common denominator.

Orbit-shifting innovation does not need the thinkers to just come up with ideas. It needs passionate entrepreneurs to navigate the fog in execution, and see it through to a glorious new reality.

Chapter 8

In-market Versioning and Fissioning

THE FIRST GO TO MARKET STAGE OF AN ORBIT-SHIFTING IDEA IS NOT THE FIRST STAGE OF MARKET LAUNCH, IT IS THE LAST STAGE OF IDEA DEVELOPMENT.

Orbit-shifters recognize that even after the big idea has successfully reached the stage of having become a working prototype, a larger part of the innovation journey still remains. How can they now make the big idea work in the market, is the dominant question in their mind. *They recognize the reality that they, right now, have only the working prototype of the orbit-shifting idea. It is unfinished. They are yet to discover how to make it work in a live market setting. At this stage, how customers will engage, connect with and adopt the new idea are questions that, at best, are only partially answered.* No matter how well thought out the orbit-shift idea is, there are still a fair amount of unanswered questions. The first in-market experiments will throw up new blind spots and even open up new opportunities.

HOW TO MAKE IT WORK AND NOT 'LET'S SEE IF IT WORKS'

And herein is the key difference between orbit-shifters and settlers. The orbit-shifter sees the 'go-to-market stage' as *not the first stage of market launch but the last stage of proposition development.* He recognizes that the new idea will need to have the space to play out and evolve in the market, and that will in turn impact how it should scale up and grow. Therefore, he is prepared to iterate and grow the idea. The approach is *how to make it work*. The settler, on the other hand, approaches the go-to-market stage as the first stage of launch. Hence, his motive is not to evolve the idea in the market as much as it is to *see if it works*, and if not, then to park it and move on. This *see-if-it-works* testing mindset often results in an orbit-shifting idea being abandoned too early.

This take-to-market gravity stood out in one European organization. An overwhelming majority of managers at the headquarters, and in regions across the world, felt:

- 'The dominant intent of our pilots is to "prove that the idea works" rather than to "discover ways to grow the idea and make it work".'
- The approach to piloting is to design one large, perfect pilot to answer all questions—focusing on getting it right the first time and not on 'designing iterative experiments to learn and grow the idea'.
- 'We do more of demonstration and testing, than discovery.'
- 'Our pilots are more like our presentations—"go/no-go" instead of "build on, maximize". We test to see if it works and not how to make it work. We have lost a lot of potential big ones this way.'
- 'If it doesn't work 100 percent the first time, we get impatient and kill the stuff.'

With such suffocating expectations, it is no wonder then that all innovation in this organization hovers in the incremental zone. It is not that most organizations like this one do not need to do in-market pilots; it is just that they do an in-market pilot of an orbit-shifting idea with business-as-usual tools.

Innovation can't be managed with the tools of business-as-usual operations. If you try to manage the uncertainty inherent in an innovation with the mindsets and tools of operations that are rooted in certainty, it will first throw up blocks, then cause frustration, and finally end up diluting—if not killing—the idea.

Another organization was launching a new product in the market—a healthy snack: They did a classical consumer test and then went ahead with the national launch. *The product was soon hit with all the uncertainties that are likely to be created when an orbit-shifting idea goes into an orbit-maintaining sales channel.* As one manager reflected, 'We weren't clear where the snack should be placed at the point of sale. On the counter? In a dispenser? We tried a lot of sporadic things. But we didn't try out an end-to-end, point-of-sale proposition.' However, having gone national, they were now just fighting to justify the investments. There was no space to even figure out a new solution. What could have been an orbit-shifting idea soon settled at the lowest common denominator, for indifferent customers saw it as more of the same and could not discern its uniqueness.

As a CEO, think about this:

The European organization is preoccupied with designing perfect pilots, where all the variables are tested at once, so that a go no-go decision can be made. On the other hand, the healthy snack was scaled nationally after just a consumer test. The uncertainties faced by the team that launched the new healthy snack are surely not signs of incompetence. They are actually the realities of taking a new product to market. There really are genuinely unanswered questions. These uncertainties need a safe in-market space to build the idea into an in-market success, a safe space to not just play out, but to maximize the in market success of a new idea.

The reality is that, in most organizations, the innovation starts and stops with the discover-and-design stages. The last stage, 'deploy', becomes business as usual.

What this leads to is piloting/testing and in-market impatience. When the idea doesn't fly as expected in the first few months, it becomes a no-go!

Where have you displayed similar in-market impatience with innovations?

An orbit-shifting idea taken to market with a 'testing' mindset is a disaster waiting to happen. After having invested a great deal of energy in creating and developing a powerful orbit-shifting idea, the last stage of taking it to the market can reduce and dilute it.

Orbit-shifters go in with a *how to make it work* and not a *let's see if it works* mindset. They recognize that the first time that an orbit-shifting idea is taken to market, it is unlikely to work; they provide space for in-market evolution. They design for multiple-idea evolutions. Their attitude is to find a way to make it work and they do it through in-market versioning—a conscious process to nurture and evolve the idea into an in-market success model.

From NovoPen® to NovoLet®

One of the big breakthroughs in diabetes care was the NovoPen® from Novo Nordisk in 1985. However, the game changer was the NovoLet® that came to market in 1989. It took four years and two in-market product evolutions (versions) for Novo Nordisk to evolve its biggest breakthrough: from NovoPen® to NovoLet®.

Quoting from Design Management Institute's case study *Novo Nordisk A/S: Designing for Diabetes*: 'In the beginning of the 1980s, research conducted in England demonstrated that diabetes therapy mimicking the body's own mechanisms was more effective than the old method of one injection per day. The healthy pancreas produces insulin "upon demand", when a person eats. If long-acting insulin could be administered once a day ("basal", to maintain a basic level of insulin at all times) and short-acting at mealtimes ("bolus", or several times per day), then an optimal therapy might be reached.'

'The problem was the 'drugstore' that a diabetic had to carry along if he or she were to self-inject several times per day. This involved several disposable syringes, vials of different sorts of insulin, needles, and other paraphernalia.'

As the article goes on to highlight, 'One solution to this problem was the insulin pump, a small Walkman-like device usually placed in the pocket with the needle at the end of a tube taped to the belly. The needle was inserted under the skin much the same way a needle for intravenous medication or feeding is attached to the wrist under hospital conditions. The patient had only to press a button and the insulin shot into his body.'[2]

As is evident from Arne Stjernholm Madsen's research, Novo Nordisk realized that, 'The basic idea of wearing a device, which mimics pancreas, perhaps was good; but the disadvantages socially, personally, hygienically and so forth by wearing a pump weighted against the idea. Also, the first pumps were constructed so that you almost needed to be an engineer to set them; there was no user friendliness. But there was no doubt that the basic idea of delivering small injections of insulin, whenever your body needed it, was right. Simply, let's make something much more accessible, which everybody can use.'[5]

The NovoPen®—First Time In-market

Novo Nordisk introduced the first NovoPen® in 1985. NovoPen® was a reusable insulin pen into which pre-filled cartridges were inserted. The user then dialed a dose by pressing a button at the bottom of the pen. Each 'click' of the pen imparted two units of insulin into the body.[2]

The first, NovoPen® didn't receive much attention within the organization when it was taken to market. It was considered to be *more of a marketing gimmick*. Especially for a company focused on core scientific work, the idea of a device being at the core of diabetic care was looked on sceptically by most. At best, they tolerated it.

As Arne's research highlights: 'Since sections of the top management viewed the idea merely as a "marketing gimmick", some crucial decisions were taken, some of them having long term impact on the subsequent development of the medical device industry.

1) No patents were applied for, leaving it open to competitors to copy the idea (being the first such product, the patent options would have been broad and effective).
2) It was decided to give away most of the pens as free 'samples' instead of selling them.

This made sense for a marketing gimmick: the pens were meant for creating customer loyalty, with the expectation that the patients hereafter would buy the Novo insulin.'[5]

An article titled, *Basal/bolus treatment and NovoPen®*, written by two medical doctors, Ivan Jensen and Birgitte Oxenbøll, cited in the Novo Nordisk's annual report in 1985, states that 'NovoPen® was introduced in the Danish market in May 1985 and by the end of the year, they were already 3,000 patients corresponding to approximately 20 percent of all insulin dependent diabetics in Denmark who used the system on a daily basis. The first clinical trials and the large group of patients who used the NovoPen® daily confirmed that the patients' acceptance of the Basal Bolus treatment had increased by using the NovoPen®.' The NovoPen® made life easier for diabetics and therefore kept getting more popular among patients and doctors. In 1986, it was marketed in more than twenty countries. By 1987, about 1,20,000 diabetics worldwide were using NovoPen® for their insulin treatment.

This success of the NovoPen® moved the organization from doubt to confidence. It was no longer just a marketing gimmick; it had become the future core of diabetes care. This confidence and focus led to the next in-market evolution, NovoPen® II.

NovoPen® II

According to the Design Management Institute's case study *Novo Nordisk A/S: Designing for Diabetes*, in-market observation had shown that the 'key disadvantage of the NovoPen® was the dosage system. The patient clicked a button on the top to measure the insulin—two clicks per depression, which administered two units of insulin (one click for each unit) while injecting it. The problem was that the patient had to count each depression. Further the NovoPen® was also limited to regular (short acting) insulin and was not available for longer-acting suspensions.'

The first product evolution, NovoPen® II, solved some of these problems. The metal in NovoPen® I was replaced by plastic in NovoPen® II, with a new dial-a-dose system. NovoPen® II's most important progress was that a patient could inject a dose from 2 to 36 units of insulin; the original NovoPen® could only give shots of a fixed dose of 2 units of insulin. Further, the NovoPen® II could now be used by a large majority of patients (more than 90 percent) who took long-acting insulin, and it was especially suited for insulin treatment of type II diabetes. It was well received in the market.

By 1988, NovoPen® was being sold in more than 30 countries and the NovoPen® II in more than 20 countries. There were many testimonials from happy users on how NovoPen® had given them flexibility in life, including a story of a young girl who was no longer embarrassed at injecting her insulin.[2,5]

According to the Design Management Institute, 'Novo was still not satisfied with NovoPen® II, however. For one thing, certain patients wished for the dial-a-dose convenience, but preferred the "quality feel" of the heavier metal pen. Others, especially children, wanted the option of administering one unit at a time, rather than two. In the United States, people objected to the stiffness of the locking mechanism, which was too hard to turn, especially for some older people.

'Moreover, Novo Nordisk had distributed thousands of NovoPens in the US gratis, without ensuring that they reach patients whose insulin therapy was appropriate for them, and without proper instruction. 'Doctors passed them out to everyone like candy,' noted Lori Day, manager of marketing research. "That way they lost their perceived value, and we lost credibility with diabetes educators. Now we've learned to say, 'If you have a certain kind of problem, then this product is good'".

As the in-market dynamics revealed, 'more threatening to Novo Nordisk than the dissatisfaction of a few thousand Americans was that competitors were attempting to manufacture cartridges that could fit NovoPen® II. Their success would obviate the key purpose of the pens: to serve as a vehicle for the sale of Novo's insulin. Although the competitors' cartridges had proven ineffective, it was only a matter of time before they could manufacture an essentially identical one.

'More generally, Novo Nordisk was also beginning to face direct competition with its insulin products themselves. Now that the competitors' insulin often matched Novo's in quality, Novo needed to find another way to differentiate itself, rather than to rely on the quality of insulin alone.'[2]

This threat triggered the next in-market evolution challenge: 'To find a way to make a device that was proprietary; that couldn't be copied, and would differentiate Novo from its competitors, assuring future insulin sales'. This led to NovoLet®.

NovoLet®

In 1989 came the second product evolution/version in the form of the NovoLet®. This was now a pre-filled disposable pen which could contain 1.5 ml of insulin and could be used for several days (roughly a week). The NovoLet® was even more user friendly for the consumer—the insulin was prefilled.[2]

As Arne says, 'NovoLet® turned out to be the biggest game changer; it changed the profit model from being based on selling the drug alone to being based on selling an integrated system.

'In the countries where NovoLet® was first introduced (i.e. Denmark, Sweden and the Netherlands), it gained a market share of approximately one third of the total insulin market within two years.

'NovoLet® created a new insulin-delivery category of pre-filled pen systems in 1989. This category of products (including NovoLet® and competitors) in 2004 gained a global market share of 25 percent of the total volume of insulin sold.'[5]

It took Novo Nordisk four years and two in-market product evolutions to develop the NovoPen® into a total in-market success model and to overcome internal scepticism, from being treated as a marketing gimmick to becoming the future of diabetes care. Today, more insulin is sold in pre-filled pen systems than in cartridges for reusable pen systems, thus making pre-filled pen systems (which started with NovoLet® in 1989) the most popular insulin-delivery system.

By the end of this journey, the organization had truly moved its focus from drug development to diabetic care.

As a CEO, think about this:

In the case of Novo Nordisk, it was indeed fortunate that the first market reactions to the Novo Pen® were very positive. A number of organizations, quite like Novo Nordisk, do attempt to evolve a new product into an in-market success. However, their orbit-shifting ideas are not as fortunate as they don't hit a sweet spot in the first in-market stages. The first hint of failure is enough to feed the sceptics. Then, rather then evolve the idea into an in-market success model, the organization just pulls out to 'minimize the losses'.

What does it take to reduce internal scepticism and build in-market acceptance? What has to be done to reduce and minimize this huge element of risk in the take to market stage? What will it take to evolve more orbit-shifting ideas into an in-market success like NovoPen®, for example, and to do it by design? What is needed is a way to build an extraordinary idea into an extraordinary reality.

The first market is not a *test to see if it works* but the final stage of *idea development*. Orbit-shifters use a series of in-market experiments (versions) to evolve the orbit-shifting idea into an in-market success model.

In-market versioning is a way to grow an extraordinary idea into an extraordinary reality.

The In-market Evolution of M-PESA

In March 2007, Safaricom (part of the Vodafone Group), launched M-PESA, an orbit-shifting idea in mobile banking. This idea was to convert the mobile phone into a mobile wallet for millions who were unbanked.

The people in Kenya could now register for free at any of the certified M-PESA agents who sell prepaid airtime cards. These agents were widely available in the neighbourhood stores, gas stations, and supermarkets.

Beyond buying airtime, the people could also now pay cash and buy electronic money. Having bought electronic money, they could now make financial transactions with their phone, transactions like buying additional airtime and even sending money to another person. They could also reconvert the electronic money back into cash with the agent. The agents made a commission for every transaction.[4]

Within the very first month, Safaricom registered over 20,000 M-PESA customers, and as of 2012, M-PESA had 17 million customers.[1]

What did it take to convert an extraordinary idea like M-PESA into an extraordinary in-market success?

M-PESA's original idea in 2005 went through a transformation by the time it was finally launched in the market in 2007. It took more than one-and-a-half years and multiple versions to evolve the final proposition. The key question to ask here is not about how or why M-PESA succeeded; rather, what was the journey that allowed M-PESA to transform the starting proposition to an even bigger in-market success? How did the team keep itself open to these changes? How did they navigate through the dilemmas and uncertainties of evolving a proposition? A large part is because M-PESA approached this with an in-marketing versioning approach and a *how-to-make-it-work* mindset, rather than with a testing approach and *let's-see-if-it-works* mindset.

The Starting Proposition

M-PESA's origin lay in the Millennium Development Goals (MDGs). In 2001, Nick Hughes, from Vodafone, began *exploring how the corporation could contribute to the MDG.* He identified *'financial access in developing economies' as the big market gap that could be filled, not by conventional banks, but by a mobile operators who can adopt mobile technology to deliver financial services in a fast, secure, and low-cost way.*

Nick now set about hunting for an opportunity space where there was already financial activity for the unbanked in existence. Microfinance struck them because it was facilitating entrepreneurial activity by providing easy access to finance for people at the bottom of the pyramid. They co-created the starting proposition with a local microfinance institution (MFI), Fualu Kenya. To quote Susie Lonie who led the on-ground implementation, the intent of the solution was to *'facilitate customers to receive and repay a small loan using his or her handset—as conveniently and easily as buying airtime top-up.'*[3] The focus clearly was on repaying loans. The benefit for the MFI was that it would increase business efficiencies, allowing it to grow its business quickly and to cover more remote locations.

From the proposition to the launch of the first in-market version, the path was fraught with many decisions and obstacles: bringing in servers, finding the right software, customizing for the MFI requirements, making the solution work in Swahili, etc.

The First In-market Version

Eight stores and 500 Faulu customers across three locations became a part of the first in-market version that started on October 11, 2005. According to Susie, 'their incentive was a free phone and a few dollars in their M-PESA accounts'.[3]

The first obstacle they came up against almost immediately was the agent's hesitation to pay out cash to customers when there was a withdrawal. So far, all stores had only been taking money. It took a big leap of faith to be handing out money. Imagine the first time a shop assistant was being shown a text message that asked for cash to be paid out! This was overcome by giving agents separate M-PESA cash floats with repeated assurances from the M-PESA team on the ground and their head offices.

Another obstacle that also cropped up was loss of SIM cards. As Susie says, 'Initially we had problems with clients losing their SIM cards—not the phones, just the SIM cards. How could this be? We learned that perhaps half of our clients already had phones and rather than carry both phones around, they tended to carry the M-PESA SIM in their wallet and swap the SIMs when they wanted to do a transaction. SIM cards are small, easy to drop, and easy to lose when not wrapped in a phone. It also became apparent that if

M-PESA was not readily available on the SIM, the number of spontaneous transactions was going to suffer. After issuing our first dozen replacements it became clear that we needed to fix this and thought of SIMEX cards. SIMEX are SIM cards without associated phone numbers—if you lose your phone but want to keep your number when you get a replacement, the SIM used is a SIMEX with your old number transferred to it. So we ordered some M-PESA SIMEX, transferred the customer numbers to them, and moved their M-PESA accounts to their own phone numbers. The number of lost SIMs dropped to negligible levels, and the number of transactions increased. It seems obvious now, but it was a big step forward for the success of the pilot.'[3]

While there were obstacles and problems to be solved, opportunities to grow the proposition were also clearly emerging. Based on the leading indicators from the market, the in-market proposition evolved. In two months, an additional feature was added. The M-PESA team saw an opportunity to expand business by allowing consumers to buy prepaid airtime with their M-PESA money.

In addition, the M-PESA team began to notice unexpected gains from their customers, in what they called *entrepreneurial behaviour from customers*. They spotted unusual transaction patterns. On-ground research revealed this entrepreneurial customer activity. As Susie Lonie says, 'Aside from the standard loan repayments for which we had designed the system, we observed several other applications:

- People repaying the loans of others in return for services
- Payment for trading between businesses
- Some of the larger businesses using M-PESA as an overnight safe because the banks closed before the agent shops
- People journeying between the pilot areas, depositing cash at one end, and withdrawing it a few hours later at the other
- People sending airtime purchased by M-PESA directly to their relations upcountry as a kind of informal remittance
- People outside the pilot population being sent money for various adhoc reasons; for example, one lady's husband had been robbed, so she sent him M-PESA to pay for his bus fare home

- People repaying loans in return for cash on behalf of a few colleagues who hadn't mastered the use of the phone, or had simply sold it.'

Market Insight from the First Version: Reveals the Bigger Opportunity

By now two things were becoming apparent to M-PESA. On one side, it was clear that they were onto something much bigger than they had visualized at the start. The opportunity was far bigger than *repaying loans on the handset.* On the other, it was also emerging that the service was far more beneficial to the end customers than to Faulu. At one level, Faulu was facing philosophical disconnects with the solution itself, as its microfinance customers stopped attending group meetings, which Faulu felt was core to the microfinance model. In addition, there were also operational difficulties in Internet connections and financial reconciliations.

Post the pilot, in a workshop with the Safaricom commercial team, the M-PESA team crystallized the far bigger and more compelling value proposition as *send money home.*

In Susie's words, 'In Kenya, as in most developing markets, many families have a small number of breadwinners who work away from home in order to provide for the others. Practically every Kenyan I worked with sends money upcountry to some family members. They use various means to do so, ranging from sending heavily disguised parcels by bus or finding someone travelling that way and giving them the cash, both of which are risky in a country where highway robbery is literally a commonplace event, to more formal mechanisms such as Western Union and the like, which are less common as they are very expensive and there are few cash outlets in rural areas.

'The launch service was therefore limited to three features providing the relatively simple functionality, which made the consumer proposition much easier to understand and to use. Users could deposit in or withdraw cash at agent stores; transfer money person-to-person (P2P); and buy prepaid airtime.'[3]

It had taken one year of in-market versioning from October 2005 to October 2006 to evolve the in-market success model. What started out as a dominantly B to B model aimed at facilitating a microfinance institution and its customers to make loan repayments, evolved into a B to C model with the customer proposition to send money home.

The first in-market experiment was called a *pilot*, but the starting intent of the M-PESA team was not evaluative. *They did not set out to assess and evaluate—'let's see if the loan repayment proposition works or not'. They set out to figure out a way to make 'mobile payment' a compelling market proposition.*

Enabling the existing mobile airtime stores to become tellers (like bank tellers) needed a number of operational problems to be solved. As Susie Lonie reflects, 'This experience also has reinforced the insight that there is no substitute for spending a significant amount of time at the start of a project on the ground assessing customer's needs well ahead of designing the functional specification of any technology-based solution. We also learned to keep it simple. When it came to moving from pilot to live system, a significant amount of the complexity in the product was stripped, allowing Safaricom to go to market with a very simple consumer proposition.'[3]

As a CEO, think about this:

What helped M-PESA was that the scale of the first in-market experiments was small enough to allow for quick evolutions in the customer-value proposition and the channel-value proposition. The scale was also just right for the M-PESA team to speedily identify and solve operational problems. What helped was that the core team was in the market personally—the task had not been delegated to the business-as-usual sales and operations teams.

In-market versioning is designed to create a safe space to evolve an orbit-shifting idea into an in-market success model—quite like in the case of M-PESA, the final winning proposition can often be very different from the one at the start. In-market versioning is not just a way to evolve a new idea into an in-market success; it is also a powerful way to de-risk the orbit-shifting idea.

How does your take-to-market model compare with M-PESA? Does your organization's take-to-market model design for ideas to evolve and even transform the way M-PESA did?

The Dynamics of In-market Versioning: *Dainik Bhaskar*

M-PESA vividly illustrates what it takes to grow an orbit-shifting idea into an in-market success model, by design.

The *Dainik Bhaskar* experience goes deeper and brings alive the on the ground dynamics of in-market versioning.

Dainik Bhaskar has built and scaled a dramatic market entry strategy, a strategy that created history in the newspaper industry by making them *leaders from day one, when they launched in a new city.* In Ahmedabad, one of the biggest successes in the history of newspaper launches, the readership/circulation on day one was 0.45 million, far outstripping the market leader at 0.35 million.

Dainik Bhaskar achieved market leadership with an orbit-shifting idea of *co-creating the newspaper with the entire market.* Ahmedabad had 1.2 million households. *Dainik Bhaskar* engaged 1,050 young and passionate college students to contact all 1.2 million households and conduct a survey. Not a sample survey, but a 100 percent market-engagement exercise. They finally managed to actually meet and talk to 0.8 million households. Readers were curious and welcoming. *It was the first time someone was asking them what they wanted to see and read in their newspaper; they were actually being consulted.* However, this mammoth survey was just the end of Round 1. The *Dainik* team used the inputs from the survey to create a mock-up of the paper. The surveyors then went back and met all the 0.8 million households again in Round 2. They showed each customer a mock-up of the upcoming newspaper, pointing out how their inputs had been worked into the design and left them with a coupon and a message: *'If you like the new paper, hand this coupon over to your newspaper vendor, so that he can bring the paper for you on the day of the launch.'* 0.51 million households signed on. This may seem like a tactical activity, but it was a very strategic move. Newspaper vendors who collected the coupons did not need to be convinced of the popularity of a paper that was yet to be launched, the proof was in the coupon. Therefore, they became seamless partners in taking the newspaper to market, rather than just to *wait and watch* until the newspaper succeeds. And hence, what on paper seems like a big survey, in reality was an orbit-shifting marketing strategy. On day one, the paid circulation was 0.452 million.

But this did not happen in one go; this was not the first big idea Dainik had gone in with. This orbit-shifting market entry strategy had evolved through a series of in-market versions.

Newspapers have city-specific launches. *Dainik Bhaskar*'s home city was Bhopal where it owned a Hindi daily. In their first version, they chose to launch in Jaipur, in the neighbouring state of Rajasthan, where the language was the same. It was a new market, but the same language. From here, they went on to more cities in the same state. Their next big move was to enter Chandigarh, where the dominant newspaper was in English—a language familiar, but different. It is here that they matured the survey proposition. From Chandigarh, they continued to grow the idea in another state, Haryana. And only once they had *grown the idea in-market* did they proceed to launch in Ahmedabad in Gujarat, where the market and the language were both completely unfamiliar. And it was a great success. So it was a series of in-market versions that finally led them to the breakthrough take-to-market strategy of 'becoming No. 1 on day one'. Here is how they did it.

To de-risk and maximize a new venture, the first in-market version is in the best conditions—in the most conducive market conditions with the best team conducting it. The challenge is to figure out an in-market success model that will maximize the new idea, given the ideal conditions through multiple in-market experiments and iterations.

In their first market, Jaipur, the ambition was to enter as number two with a print run of 50,000. This was a bold challenge, one that had never been done before, especially in the newspaper industry where newspaper-reading habits are very difficult to change. So the *Dainik* team decided to meet a few readers to find out their habits and how to change them. In the process of these meetings, they came upon an insight—newspaper choice is an intensely personal habit; everybody really decides for himself. Newspaper buying is an independent choice, not dependent on any other factors, and therefore to understand the reading habits of the city it becomes essential that they meet everyone and not just a random sample. They finally ended up meeting a whopping 0.2 million customers.

Though they had set out to only *understand newspaper-reading habits,* in the course of doing so, they *discovered another insight: Every customer meeting was not merely a survey interview, it was an opportunity to build trust. This needed the interaction to be an experience-enhancing contact.* Therefore, what started as routine *survey interviews* transformed into experience-enhancing contacts.

The first in-market version was conducted in Jaipur, with the best team from *Dainik Bhaskar*—the owners themselves. This created the on-the-ground capacity to first conceive of a radical strategy—survey all customers and then transform the survey into a trust-building and experience-enhancing contact. Given the best conditions, they had the authority and the flexibility to make not only incremental changes but to transform the strategy online. This was possible because it was the first city version—in the best conditions. It would never have been possible if the strategy had already been launched nationally—even a small change at that point would have taken a long time.

While building experience-enhancing contacts, there emerged the next—and perhaps the most powerful—insight. 'What about going back to all survey participants for a second contact? This time, show them how the newspaper incorporated their feedback and ask them to sign an advance newspaper subscription. An advance newspaper subscription! This was unheard of, but it succeeded dramatically. This was a breakthrough moment.' Dainik was going to ask customers to pay upfront for a newspaper they hadn't seen. Rather than dismiss this as too radical, the team began working back from here, asking what they would need to do to make this happen.

Again, working back from the challenge, they explored: 'If we do ask the customers to pay up front, what comfort zone do we need to create for the customer?' This threw up two follow-up questions: 'What are the major customer concerns in doing this and how can they be overcome?'

The team realized that there were two major fears that customers have:

- the fear of being taken by surprise and getting something he/she didn't want; and
- the fear of losing money in a bad deal.

To overcome the first fear, the team hit upon the idea of evolving the product with the customer. So they went to each customer and asked questions like: 'What are you not getting in your current newspaper that you would like to get more of?' and 'What would you like your newspaper to do for you?' Then based on the feedback, the survey team went back to all 2,00,000 households to show them what they had created by incorporating the feedback.

A further learning came with the realization that if indeed the key *was to make every contact experience enhancing and trust building, the process could not be outsourced.* They had to lead it themselves. They also realized that it had to be done *by recruiting people locally* from within the market; because they would be intrinsically understood and trusted. This led to another revolutionary move, *to recruit people from within each city to do the customer contacts.* In each new city, they would recruit 500 to 1,200 surveyors for short periods.

So, what started out as a survey became a revolutionary market-entry strategy—a strategy where the newspaper was co-created with the entire market.

How did these orbit-shifting insights arise? Not because the leadership team was sitting in the comfort of some remote office in Bhopal. As the surveyors moved from door to door, *Dainik*'s leadership team was there with them in the field, doing review meetings in the afternoon and evening. So that they got first-hand insight into the real conditions of the market, without a filter, and were able to react immediately to improve/change/moderate an anomaly or an issue and also to pick up a learning and incorporate it quickly across the market.

Deciding on an exclusively recruited workforce was one thing but the next challenge was: *How do we build ownership among this temporary workforce?* To build trust with every contact would need each surveyor to show immense belief and ownership of the purpose: *How do you do this with a temporary workforce and especially a workforce of college students or recent graduates, when even with a regular workforce, this would be a difficult task?*

Dainik tried different ways of building motivation and ownership.

First, they realized that small-town youth had few opportunities and hence *Dainik* made a promise. *Dainik* was new in the city; it would certainly employ locals. The youths who performed well in the survey would have an immediate opportunity of becoming a team lead in the second round and a long-term opportunity of being employed with *Dainik*. The youngsters jumped at a chance to demonstrate their capability and the entire three months of the two survey rounds became an intense and valuable recruitment process, with an opportunity to spot new talent in action on the job.

Second, the training programme they created gave the youth an opportunity to hone their job skills in vital areas, a training that is usually never given in a traditional academic context. So all of them, regardless of whether they were finally absorbed by *Dainik* or not, were learning essential job skills that increased their employability.

In addition, *Dainik* demonstrated a real concern for them. When they discovered, in Ahmedabad, that temperatures were at a peak and a few surveyors were fainting or falling ill, immediate medical treatment was made available. Proactively, energy drinks were handed out every morning as teams began their beat across the city. Moreover, the top leadership team was always on ground with the team, clearly sending out the message, 'We are with you on this'.

Dainik recognized that being on the street, day in and day out, and knocking on doors talking to strangers was not just physically exhausting, but an emotionally draining task as well. Hence they started each morning with a rousing prayer. They would gather all 800–1,200 young surveyors in a large field and begin with 'Hamko mann ki shakti dena' (a prayer song from the Hindi movie *Guddi*, which translated means 'Give us the strength of mind'). The early morning hymn, as it resonated across the ground, created belief and camaraderie. In the evenings, they would close with a review and a refresher of the day. Teams would start and leave energized.

The survey strategy was put into place for the first time in Jaipur. *Dainik Bhaskar* outstripped their starting vision of being number two with 50,000 copies. They ended up launching in Jaipur with 1,72,347 copies. They were not number two, but leaders from day one. The erstwhile leader, *Rajasthan Patrika*, had a circulation of 1,00,000 copies.

Dainik Bhaskar evolved and strengthened this strategy further in four to five markets of Rajasthan, where the language was still Hindi. Having succeeded in these markets, it decided to take the next leap, to enter Chandigarh, where the leading newspaper was in English (*The Tribune*) and not Hindi.

For *Dainik Bhaskar*, Chandigarh brought them out of their comfort zone of Hindi.

Staying true to the purpose, they co-created the paper with the entire market. But here they uncovered an insight that was completely different from the first series of successful entries in Rajasthan.

In Chandigarh, *Dainik* took on a city where English newspapers outsell Hindi ones by a factor of six. It was considered impossible to sell Hindi newspapers in the city.

So they hit the streets again and contacted 2,20,000 households. They found that every household in Chandigarh is comfortable with Hindi and in many cases more comfortable with Hindi than English; they bought English newspapers not because they preferred the language, *but because the quality of the paper was better.*

For thirty years, more English newspapers had sold in Chandigarh than Hindi, and everyone assumed that's the way the market is. In reality, it was the quality of the paper. It was about design. It was about giving the consumers a newspaper they felt good holding.

Once the *Dainik* team realized that design matters, it not only made design the king, it went a step further and incorporated the local Chandigarh dialect into the design. They mixed both Hindi and English in the newspaper, making it a true Chandigarhi newspaper.

In a single stroke, they created an uncontested market space. There were English newspapers competing with each other and Hindi newspapers competing with one another. But there was no Hinglish (Hindi + English) newspaper. It stood alone.

When they launched in Chandigarh, *Dainik* again became leaders on day one. The Hinglish *Dainik* with 69,000 copies at launch replaced the erstwhile leader, the English newspaper *The Tribune* at 50,000 copies. The total readership of Chandigarh was 54 percent before *Dainik*. Today it's 61.4 percent. *Dainik* actually succeeded in expanding the market.

Launching in Ahmedabad was the 'scale conditions version' for *Dainik Bhaskar*. This time they were entering a market where the dominant language was Gujarati, a language completely foreign to them. Succeeding in Ahmedabad meant that they had cracked an in-market success model that was now scalable across the country, with 28 states and 22 official languages.[6]

It took an entrepreneurial, ambitious, and passionate team from *Dainik Bhaskar* and multiple market entries to evolve an orbit-shifting market entry strategy that would make them leaders from day one. Rather than diluting their ambition, they worked out solutions to problems and uncovered new opportunities to lift the orbit-shifting idea to the next level. By the time they launched in Ahmedabad, they were ready with an orbit-shifting strategy that succeeded in spite of the competition knowing what *Dainik* was going to do. The competition could only see the wrappings of the strategy: surveryors covering the entire city. They were unable to see the invisible strengths of this market entry strategy and without understanding the underpinnings of the real intent and process, it was next to impossible to checkmate or combat *Dainik*.

As a CEO, think about this:

Building an orbit-shifting idea into an in-market success didn't merely require problem solving. It required the innovation team to discover and deploy new opportunities to maximize the idea.

The final version of *Dainik Bhaskar*'s city launch strategy was very different from the first version. This was because they spotted and instantly built on opportunities. In comparison, a piloting attitude largely focuses on solving operational problems and is not sensitive to spotting and converting opportunities.

Most large organizations don't have the patience of a *Dainik Bhaskar*, where a gradual build-up was required to evolve an orbit-shifting market penetration strategy.They are actually okay with killing the idea rather than engaging in a gradual build-up.

No wonder they believe in the statement—less than 10 percent innovations succeed. As one organization expressed, 'We randomly try to hit a good idea. So we launch four to five initiatives at the same time, hoping one will click.' In this spray-and-pray mode adopted by most large organizations, this 10 percent strike rate is virtually a self-fulfilling prophecy.

Are you in the gradual evolution or in the spray-and-pray mode?

In-market Versioning and Not Piloting

Orbit-shifters believe that no matter how well thought out the orbit-shifting idea is, there will still be a fair amount of unanswered questions. The first in-market experiments will throw up new blind spots and can even throw up new opportunities that can further evolve and even transform the idea. Going in with a piloting and testing state of mind will clearly not be enough. The classical project management model is also clearly unsuited to a road map riddled with uncertainties.

M-PESA and *Dainik Bhaskar* demonstrate that the most effective way to deal with the uncertainties inherent in taking a new idea to market is to have *an in-market evolution* process: a series of in-market experiments that systematically uncover and resolve the unanswered questions, and also discover opportunities to maximize the market impact. What is needed is *in-market versioning*, with an attitude and approach driven by the *how-to-make-it-work* mindset rather than the piloting approach driven by the *let's-see-if-it-works* mindset.

These orbit-shifters recognize that two key unknowns confronting the orbit-shifting idea are customer engagement and channel engagement. The third unknown that is equally critical is internal—the engagement and ownership of the execution team inside the organization.

Insights from orbit-shifters reveal that to build an orbit-shifting idea into an in-market success model, what is needed is in-market versioning in three stages: best conditions, real conditions, and scalable conditions.

These three stages of in-market versioning are designed to systematically uncover the unanswered questions and evolve solutions for the three key unknowns—customer engagement, channel engagement, and execution team engagement.

In-market Versioning: Best Conditions, Real Conditions, Scale Conditions

The Best Conditions Version:

The first in-market version is conducted under the best/ideal conditions. The market chosen is the one with the most conducive customers and the most ready distribution channel. The focus of

the best conditions version is on customer engagement only. The sole intent is to evolve a *tipping customer value proposition*—a proposition that will engage and enrol the maximum number of customers. The best team from within the organization, the innovation team itself, is directly involved in the execution. This is done to minimize the *controllable variables*. The other two variables, channel engagement and execution team, are ensured to be the *best available* so that *capacity to execute* is not a challenge and the focus can be undivided in evolving the tipping customer value proposition.

As an example, M-PESA's first principle of choice for location was convenience of access. The three locations chosen were the city centre in Nairobi, Mathar—twenty minutes away—and a market town, Thika, about one hour away.

The second principle of choice was, as Susie says, 'Customer groups most likely to understand how to use a cell phone and embrace the service so we could get off to a flying start. Other (less mobile-phone literate) groups were deferred for later.'[3]

Similarly, *Dainik* chose Jaipur, a city in a neighbouring state, and a familiar language—Hindi—for their best conditions version.

At the end of the best conditions version, both M-PESA and *Dainik Bhaskar* had discovered a *tipping customer proposition.*

The Real Conditions Version:

Having worked out a successful customer value proposition in the best conditions version, the innovation moves into the *real conditions version.*

Now the team implementing it is the actual *go-to-market* team and not the best team. Further, the market chosen is not the best but the average/normal market—one where the customer and the channel are both the most natural representatives of the target market. In the real market conditions, the customer engagement proposition is known (though will evolve further). The key unknowns to be solved for are channel and execution team engagement. The real conditions version is focused on *finding ways to engage the team and the channel in making the orbit-shifting idea successful while further evolving the successful customer value proposition*. The team has to be prepared to go through multiple iterations till an in-market success model emerges, a model that crystallizes a successful customer value proposition and the practices needed to engage the channel and the team in executing it effectively.

For *Dainik Bhaskar*, moving beyond Jaipur and launching in the next few markets was the real conditions version. They set out to reach the same level of success as the first market and figure out ways to make the same impact happen with a less familiar channel and a different execution team.

The Scale Conditions Version:

Once the orbit-shifting proposition has achieved the promised impact in real market conditions, it is now ready to be taken into the scale version stage.

The focus of the scale conditions version is to evolve the in-market success model to a level where it can reach the promised impact over a large spectrum of target markets.

Now a market/cluster of markets is chosen where scale variables in customer engagement, channel engagement, and team engagement come into play.

For *Dainik Bhaskar*, the Ahmedabad launch was the first scale conditions version. They had to figure out a way to reach the same level of success but in a market where the language was foreign to them and the culture different from the earlier markets. Their successful market penetration strategy centred on the market survey, which was in turn anchored on *experience-enhancing customer contacts*. These contacts had to be done in the local language by surveyors recruited locally.

Recruiting and training surveryors and then evolving the survey to enable them to succeed in the Ahmedabad market conditions was their scalability challenge. M-PESA, on the other hand, had to deal with a different scale question. As long as it was a small pilot, the Central Bank of Kenya didn't pay much attention. But as it scaled across Kenya, they had to create a new trust company to operate M-PESA. Now they had to work within the banking and regulatory framework and satisfy all requirements of control set by the Central Bank. This called for legal and regulatory elements to be addressed, during scale.

As *Dainik* and M-PESA demonstrate, in scale conditions, variations in customer engagement due to socio-cultural differences and ecosystem variations—as reflected in channel engagement, local recruitment, and even legal imperatives—have to be designed for.

SCALING UP THE ORBIT-SHIFT

Not Cascading, but In-market Fissioning Across Geographies

Having succeeded in one market, traditional organizations like to build the success model into a formula and then cascade it to other geographies. For a traditional manager, once an innovation has succeeded in one market, all that is needed is replication; that is, cascade the success formula to other markets.

This works for incremental ideas, but attempting to simply replicate the success formula in other geographies can run into a major hurdle in case of an orbit-shifting idea.

As a senior manager in one organization explained, 'Standardization across markets just doesn't work. We do a pilot and then do standardization and roll-out. For example, a programme was tested in east Germany but when it was rolled out across all regions in Germany, there was a 50 percent failure.'

Another manager in another organization had a similar experience to share: 'We had introduced a differentiated product, *immunity through tea*. It was a big breakthrough; we had actually put the functionality of immunity into tea! This was the first product of its kind. It made it big in one geographical region, but remained locked to that region. What emerged from consumer research was that it had become premium, and it had acquired an unintended seasonal connection. To make it equally big in other regions, what was needed was a "reworked marketing strategy". Here, replication was just not enough.'

The reality is that even after an idea succeeds in one geography, the orbit-shift journey is not over. Scaling up an orbit-shifting idea to other geographies needs to be done differently.

New market and geographies may even be open to launching the orbit-shifting idea but in making it happen, innovators will always run up against the entrenched beliefs of the current orbit. Once the initial fanfare of the launch is over, and if subsequently, the idea starts to underperform the immediate reactions of people is—'Our market is different, it won't work here. This works for the market where you have tried it first, but not for this market.'

Orbit-shifters recognize that scaling up an orbit-shifting idea is more like building a social movement, where the idea catches fire as it moves across large swatches of community and yet is localized to the flavour of that community. Democracy as it originated in Greece is very different from the democracy of the United States, which is again startlingly different from the dance of democracy in India. Merely trying to replicate the success formula of the first market won't work. An orbit-shifting idea, no matter how successful it was in the previous market, will disrupt the comfort zones of whichever market it enters next. Orbit-shifters genuinely recognize that each market has its own unique configuration and this will need the idea to be adapted to the market rather than blindly replicated.

Scaling Up Across Geographies—Ring Back Tones (RBT)

Ring Back Tones was an orbit-shifting idea that was triggered by the orbit-shifting challenge: ***monetize the non-monetized part of the network.*** A partner of SK Telecom called WiderThan, came up with the idea. Backed by SK Telecom, it succeeded in a big way in Korea.

WiderThan's Asia-Pacific business team, which later set up Access Mobile in 2006, took charge of scaling up RBT into other markets outside Korea.

The first markets WiderThan went to were the Philippines and Indonesia where they were immediately confronted with the first predictable hurdles.

'This is a Korea-specific solution, our market is different.'

'The Korea RBT solution is designed for a CDMA network; prove that it works on GSM and that the network usage will be safe.'

RBT was part of the second generation of Value-Added Services (VAS). The first generation of VAS were downloads like wallpaper, ringtones, games, etc. The user only had to download the appropriate feature on to his individual mobile. So all the network had to do is host these features. The second generation of network features like RBT, however were vastly more complex. They were hosted on the network and not on individual handsets. Whenever a person wanted a RBT to be played during a call, the network became active. It not only dialled in the caller to receiver, it searched the network for the configured RBT and played it back. All of this had to be done with no time lag, as the tune had to play instantly. Hosting RBT therefore involved a significant reconfiguration of the network. Since the network had to be reconfigured, the mobile operators were wary that their sophisticated and sensitive facilities could be affected and that the implementation could go wrong. They wanted complete assurance that first, their core network would not be touched and second, while hosting RBT, the customers using the network for usual call purposes would not be interrupted. The operators in the new geographies wanted to feel safe. And since it was a network feature, they needed assurance from their network partner that RBT would not damage their current network operations.

To move the operators from doubt to confidence, WiderThan adopted the strategy of first enrolling the network partner. They started co-working with Nokia, who was the dominant network provider in the Philippines. Nokia was also interested, as RBT, for them, was a new product and a network feature value-added service. When Nokia, the dominant network provider, began working closely with WiderThan to iron out any network issues, the operator gained assurance and decided to go ahead.

The second hurdle in scaling was that the socio-economics of these markets were configured differently. Korea was largely a postpaid market, while the Philippines and Indonesia were dominantly prepaid markets.

In a postpaid market like Korea, customers visit a phone distributor at regular intervals, either to buy the connection (enrol into the network) or buy/replace new phones. So there is an opportunity to explain how RBT works and to encourage the customer to buy it. A push strategy of incentivizing sales teams was possible, where they found ways to get more customers to sign on to RBT. But in a prepaid market like the Philippines, the organization had no interface with the customer. In addition, unlike in a postpaid market, they did not even know their customer. Prepaid cards are bought at any of the multiple retail stores and need not be coupled with the purchase of a phone either.

Further, the prepaid customers were very price sensitive. So the operator could not push services that encroached on their limited prepaid amounts. As Duoh Leslie Song from Access Mobile, who was in WiderThan APAC Sales until 2006, observes, 'About 90–95 percent of the users in markets like the Philippines are prepaid users who are worried about their balance. Further "vanishing balance" had become an issue. In a number of prepaid markets the customers had not subscribed to certain VAS services but found their balance diminishing without their knowledge.' In order to curb this, the regulator had asked operators to inform customers *twice* when starting a VAS service, especially for subscription services like RBT.

WiderThan worked with the operators to develop a unique go-to-market strategy.

In the Philippines, they introduced a *free trial* period. The customers experienced a musical ring back tone for a trial period of thirty days. After the trial period, they could choose to change the ring back tone to a music/ song of their choice. This led to a 5–10 percent take up rate.

In order to increase take up, WiderThan conducted further in-market iterations to work out ways to segment the user base and customize the trial ring tone.

When RBT was brought to India, Bharti Airtel too, like in the Philippines, first put out RBT for a trial period. But in India the situation was different. For a number of customers, the first time they heard the RBT, it was a distraction. A lot of them started disconnecting when they heard the RBT instead of the usual phone ring. They thought they had accidentally connected to a wrong number. The number of call drops multiplied. So unlike the Philippines, Airtel in India had to, and did, take a different go-to-market route. Bharti Airtel had earlier got India's foremost music director, A.R. Rahman, to create their theme music that was used in all Airtel commercials. They made this Airtel's default theme. When a customer called, he didn't hear the regular *tring, tring*, but Rahman's theme instead. This different but bold move first got callers habituated to hearing a musical ring tone rather than the usual, and then when customers began super imposing their own tune the call-drop rate ceased.

Beyond trials and themes, the next big idea to increase the usage of RBT in prepaid markets was *Star-copy (*–Copy)*, an option for the customer listening to the RBT of the person he/she was calling. If the calling customer liked the RBT, he/she could simply copy it by pressing *star* (*) on his/her phone. *Star-copy (*–Copy)* became a viral marketing *pull strategy*.

RBT also introduced a third player into the ecosystem, the music rights owner. In each market, the tastes of music were different and the approach and attitude of the content providers also varied. In Indonesia for example, the content (music) providers tried to get a large propotion of the revenue. WiderThan got involved in this issue and worked with the operator to find a mutually workable solution.

As WiderThan moved from one market to the next, two primarily different business models evolved:

Buy out: The mobile operator simply buys their solution and WiderThan takes care of the maintenance.

Build-operate-transfer, with joint investment: Joint investment was necessary wherever the client still had some reservations about RBT. As Alex Eunjae Won from Access Mobile, who was in the same work group as Leslie, says, 'We volunteered to invest in the system to create the trust. In some cases, they let us invest and take a revenue share.'

In Indonesia, RBT was bought out by two operators. In the Philippines, it was a joint investment with Smart Communications. If the mobile operators strongly believed in the success of the service they preferred to buy out. When they had doubts, a joint venture was their option. In other cases, operators chose not to invest in hardware. Their preference was not to spend CAPEX for services and hence they preferred joint investment with a revenue share.

For Access Mobile, whose founders are from WiderThan, who were very active in the APAC market back then, the overriding principle was business-model flexibility to facilitate the mobile operators' decision-making in adopting RBT.

Scaling up an orbit-shifting idea needs the mental model of fissioning—where an organization like WiderThan has to be prepared with the product/process and business-model flexibility to adapt to the uniqueness of geographies.

As a CEO, think about this:

RBT had been a phenomenal success in Korea, and yet in scaling it up across Asia, the team faced sceptical stakeholders and regional peculiarities. They now had to innovate on the in-market model in order to scale up effectively across geographies.

Where are your innovations stuck because they have failed to innovate to scale? How can in-market fissioning of the kind used to scale RBT be deployed to unlock the scale potential of your innovations?

Scaling Up as Fissioning: Customize GOLD

New York Life had, over 150 years, cultivated a very successful insurance-selling model—GOLD. The underlying philosophy of this sales model was that each sales manager needed to invest time and energy in recruiting and developing agents. The success of the insurance agency depended totally on the sales manager's capacity to nurture new agents to succeed. The GOLD toolkit provided the sales manager and the agent with micro tools, including scripts for each stage of the recruitment and development process.

When New York Life launched in India, the model was cascaded to the India team. *It was a model that had been built over 150 years and had been amazingly successful in the US. All that was needed was for the India team to implement* and it was assumed success would also naturally follow. But it ran up against a wall.

The local sales managers entered with the mindset that was essentially driven by *'create pressure and results will come'. They didn't believe in nurturing.* In effect, with their pressure-creating beliefs, they continued to *focus on the two most productive agents in their team, monitor them, and ensure their success.* They invested little or no time in developing and nurturing other agents. *In fact, 80 percent of their time went in monitoring and maintaining the successful agents and less than 20 percent in enabling the less successful to become successful. The immediate sales reason was not difficult to understand; it ensured that the sales manager's business target in the short run was met, in spite of the fact that most of his agents did not succeed.*

When the organization audited its sales managers and found these gaps, the first root cause identified was, '*GOLD is okay for the US but not for the Indian market. This market is different.*' This resonated loudly through the ranks of the sales organization. However the success of insurance selling is driven not by products but by agents, the success of the sales organization and therefore the success of most agents was core to organization success. This backlash threatened to derail the core values of the agency model developed by New York Life.

The turnaround started when the organization realized that rather than *cascade and mandate*, it needed to *innovate and customize* the GOLD model for the Indian market. Rather than audit and push GOLD, they decided to build around 'lighthouses'. *Lighthouses were the exceptions in the system, the few who had succeeded in adapting and implementing the principles of GOLD.* Rather than the usual discussions around *what is not working, why it is not working, and how to plug the gap*, they shifted their focus to look for lighthouses. *'Even if there are only 10 percent of the sales managers and agents who are succeeding, let's get insight into "what is making them succeed".'*

They identified exceptionally successful office heads, sales managers, and agents with whom they did an in-depth insight dialogue to understand *what differentiated the 10 percent exceptions from the majority who only average.*

This exercise culminated in the identification of the key mindset shifts needed to accelerate not just the adoption, but the enhancement of GOLD in the India market. Since the process was an intense *bottom-up co-creation*, it led to co-ownership of the *agency strategy* for India. It crystallized in a model they called *Growth Leadership*—a model that could accelerate growth in the India market and be integrated with GOLD principles.

The new model was adopted and activated. However, the next struggle in scaling it up then emerged. In the first phase, only two offices succeeded in executing the new model to success. These two offices had successfully internalized and actioned the growth leadership principles and practices to show dramatic growth.

Once again, the principle adopted was fissioning, and not cascading. Rather than imposing the best practices from these two offices, the organization involved the sales leadership in learning from these two offices and facilitated them in building the model to the next level. The cumulative learning was integrated into the development of new office heads and sales managers.

This entire momentum led to a Max New York Life agents' productivity in the India market becoming three times the industry average. The Indian model went on to become a role model of success for the organization, internationally. This experience has in itself become a lighthouse of how scaling an orbit-shift is not about replicating and cascading but fissioning.

In-market versioning in three stages: best conditions, real conditions, and *scale conditions*, paves the way to navigate the unknown in the last mile and evolve an orbit-shifting idea into an in-market success model. Fissioning is the mental model needed to build in the product, process, and business model flexibility needed to scale up the orbit-shift across geographies.

SECTION 4

LEADING ORBIT-SHIFTING INNOVATION

Chapter 9

Ascending the Orbit-shift Mountain

Making orbit-shifting innovation happen is more like scaling a daunting, unclimbed mountain rather than managing just another tough project.

WHAT MAKES ORBIT-SHIFTERS TAKE ON AND NOT JUST SURVIVE, BUT THRIVE THROUGH THESE AT ONCE AMAZING BUT PAINFUL ORBIT-SHIFT JOURNEYS? Orbit-shifters see the innovation journey as an unclimbed mountain with multiple thresholds. They approach it like an adventure into the unknown, with a sense of both fear and anticipation.

As Todd Skinner, the mountaineer said, *'If you are not afraid, you have probably chosen too easy a mountain. To be worth the expedition it had better be intimidating. If you don't stand at the base uncertain how to reach the summit, then you have wasted the effort to get there. A mountain well within your ability is not only a misspending of resources it is a loss of opportunity across a lifetime of potential achievement.'*[4]

Settlers, on the other hand, see an orbit-shifting innovation journey merely as a process to be followed, another project to be managed. They hope that a mature process will bring certainty to an intrinsically uncertain and unknown terrain. They attempt to fit innovation to the traditional ways of working—'all we need to do is have a chief innovation officer (CIO) and a mature innovation process; this should ensure the success of innovation'.

Settlers fail to take into account the *intrinsic uncertainty* at each stage of an orbit-shifting innovation journey. They fail to recognize that the *capacity to navigate the uncertainty* through the thresholds is the key to success. They don't provide for the intrinsic uncertainty that will fog the path. They also fail to plot for the internal enemy*: the gravity that can reduce the next challenge to the default setting of the old orbit.* In fact, the dominant attitude of settlers is to weed out uncertainty at all stages and demand for a guaranteed route to innovation. Therein lies the paradox—orbit-shifting *innovation has no guarantees, which is why it is an orbit-shift and not business as usual.*

An orbit-shifting innovation journey is not like a process to be achieved stage by stage. It is more of a journey from one energy threshold to the next. A burst of energy needs to be unleashed at each threshold to bear with not just visible organization dynamics, but also with the unanticipated fears, uncertainties, and doubts of all stakeholders, including the innovation team's. It is not only about the task or process; it is as much about the people involved. It takes courage, perseverance, and unwavering belief. *In the end, it is a journey of human endeavour.*

To succeed with orbit-shifting innovation we need to engage with it less like a stage-gate funnelling process and more like scaling a mountain with multiple thresholds. The mountain metaphor is so much more appropriate than a funnel; it brings alive both the challenge and the human endeavour needed to realize the challenge. At each threshold as one climbs the mountain, what is visible is only the scale of the challenge. The satisfaction of the summit is far away and while the heart beats with excitement, it is often silenced by the fear of the unknown. When one threshold is reached, all past successes are brought to naught, for the terrain not only shifts substantively, it also gets more treacherous, difficult, and ambiguous, and the peak is hidden from view. And hence the orbit-shifter, like the mountaineer, has to gear up all over again, both physically and mentally, before he takes on the next threshold. The higher you go, the more difficult it gets. And yet, once you get to the top, to that summit—you have created history.

THE FIVE ORBIT-SHIFT THRESHOLDS— A SNAPSHOT

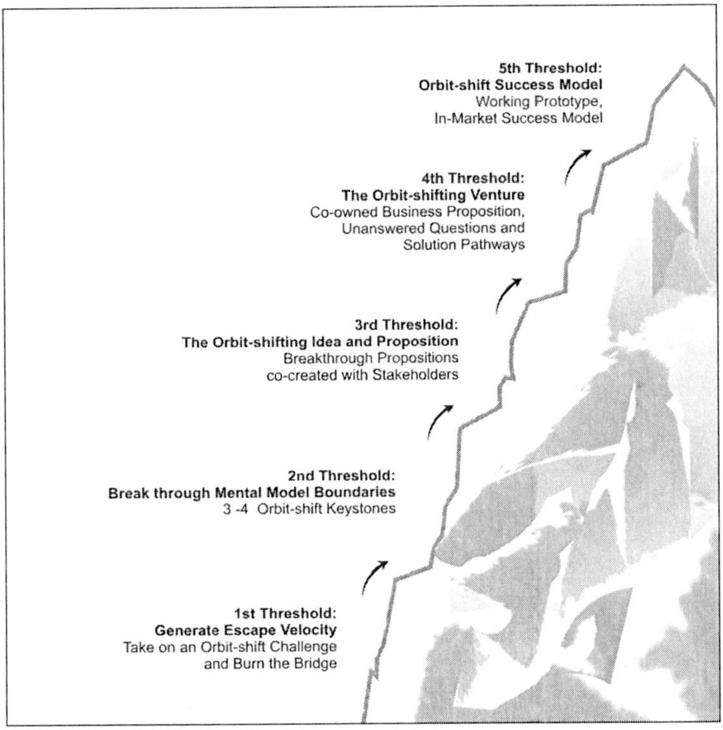

9.1 – The Five Orbit-shift Thresholds

To create and not follow history, to scale the orbit-shift mountain, orbit-shifters need to prepare for and cross five thresholds.

The orbit-shift journey is launched and the **first threshold is scaled**, when orbit-shifters have taken on an *orbit-shifting challenge* and *burnt the bridge*—there is no going back. At the **second threshold**, orbit-shifters focus on *breaking through mental model boundaries* till they have identified the orbit-shift keystones: the key boundaries that, when broken through, can create a disproportionate impact. They cross the **second threshold** when they've broken through mental model boundaries. Post this, they take on an *orbit-shifting Insight Quest* to tackle the **third threshold**. This threshold is crossed when they have discovered orbit-shifting ideas to live up to the challenge. At the **fourth threshold**, the orbit-shifter converts the breakthrough proposition into an orbit-shifting venture, by *co-creating it with the decision and implementation stakeholders*, so that their co-ownership is high. The fourth threshold is crossed when there is a committed road map to develop the idea into a working prototype. **The fifth threshold** is crossed when the orbit-shifting venture is evolved into an *in-market success through live in-market experiments*, with a scaling road map in place.

The Five Thresholds: Integration Points and Not Stage Gates

The Arla Space Food project adopted the NASA model of integration points. Carsten believes that integration points are far better at rallying multiple stakeholders to keep the momentum going. Each integration point has a sharp and overarching purpose, tightly connected to the end outcome, that magnifies the need to come together and energizes the team (both the core and extended team, including stakeholders) to work relentlessly and enthusiastically for the outcome. Silos dissolve, differences disappear, conflicts are resolved, and the purpose becomes the rallying point. Because integration points create a shared urgency around the purpose, they become confluence points where different stakeholders and functional experts come together seamlessly to tackle the next threshold and plot the path forward.

Orbit-shifters recognize that at each of the five thresholds, they will re-encounter gravity that will threaten to dilute the mission and de-energize the team. So they treat each threshold as not just a project milestone, but as an integration point instead. It integrates the people with the purpose and the process. At each integration point, people are re-energized to combat gravity and to plot the navigational path forward in order to cross the next threshold.

A Multinational Company's (MNC) Stage-gate Approach

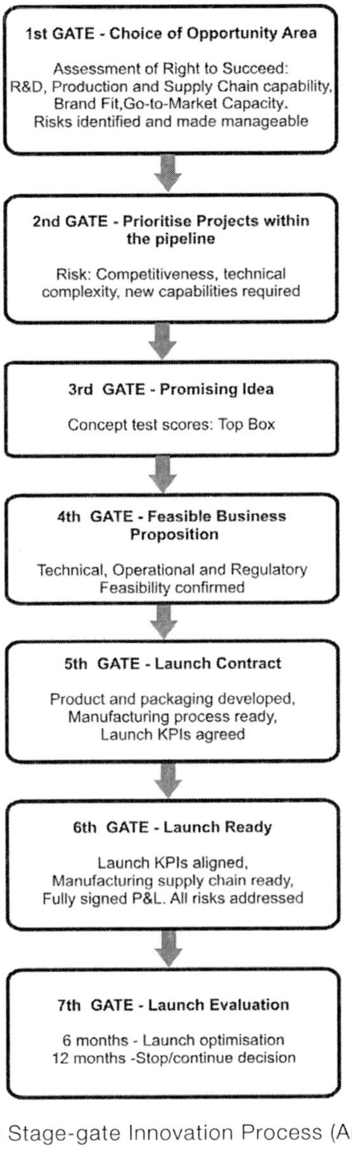

9.2 – The Stage-gate Innovation Process (An MNC)

A multinational, on the other hand, has institutionalized this highly defined and very mature stage-gate innovation process. An innovation is required to pass through seven gates. Each gate is a decision point where the innovation team presents the outcomes for the stakeholders to evaluate. The mental model underlying this stage gate is much like any other classical stage-gate process: **to filter the good from the bad and ensure only the best go through.**

Seven gates, seven decision points to screen out. The biggest assumption underlying such a classical stage-gate process is that there is a wealth of great ideas in the organization, the role of an innovation process is only to filter and screen out the ineffective ones.

The reality for most organizations is that, steeped as they are in four layers of gravity, there is only a wealth of incremental ideas. The emergence and presence of a truly breakthrough idea is a rarity.

Even if there are a few breakthrough ideas in the pipeline, very rarely will they survive the seven gates.

The other unstated mental model underlying a stage-gate process is in the way ideas are screened. Consciously and unconsciously, each gate becomes a fit-in exercise. Only ideas that fit into the organization's capability, capacity, and brand are allowed to go through.

In effect, the current orbit becomes the default setting against which a new idea is assessed. Whatever doesn't fit in is rooted out. A stage gate with such a mental model will screen out an orbit-shift, by design.

By scaling the five thresholds, an orbit-shifting innovation journey flows against the tide of these default settings.

Scaling the Orbit-shift Mountain and the Stage-gate Process: The Difference

Beginning the Ascent—Threshold One: Not Fit In, But Orbit-shift

The very starting point of an orbit-shifting innovation journey is fundamentally different. Settlers start by fitting in the opportunity, orbit-shifters start by taking on an orbit-shifting challenge.

The opportunities that the first two gates allow to pass through are only those that, in effect, fit into the current organization capability. They are rooted in the current orbit. Most settlers succumb to gravity at the very first decision gate. They settle for opportunities that fit the box. Orbit-shifters on the other hand, search for out-of-the-box opportunities by design, and convert them into orbit-shifting challenges. Only then is the first threshold crossed.

This multinational chooses and prioritizes its opportunities at the first gate by evaluating them against a criteria called *right to succeed*. This traditional *right to succeed* mental model screens the new opportunity against the current R&D capability, the current production and supply-chain capability. Further, the right to succeed also examines if there is a strategic fit with the brand image and even further, if there is the go-to-market capacity to pursue this innovation. What this means is that unless the opportunity has a foolproof right to succeed, it won't even get off the ground.

This right-to-succeed criteria are rooted in the past successes of the current orbit. How will a breakthrough idea that transforms the ecosystem, for example, (beyond product, supply chain, R&D, or brand) perform against these criteria? In fact for this MNC, *if there is a red light against more than one right-to-succeed criteria, the answer is a definite and unhesitating: No Go!* Right at the start, the MNC is seeking certainty of the idea's future success.

For an orbit-shifter, it is just the reverse. The first threshold is crossed only when he/she has taken on an orbit-shifting challenge that is beyond the current capability, one that is anchored in uncertainty, in the unknown, and has shown the courage to *burn the bridge*. Now the orbit-shift mission is at the point of irreversibility. To scale and cross this first threshold, the orbit-shifter has to first uncover and then confront the gravity of the current orbit. He/she has to especially challenge the *impossibles* embedded in the current orbit. Challenging the industry, country, and cultural gravity can and will reveal the *next possible*.

Converting the next possible into an orbit-shifting challenge and burning the bridge will require the organization leadership and the innovation team to overcome *personal gravity* too. It will need them to remove escape buttons and take *personal risk*.

Not an elaborate fit-in exercise, but the promise of a transformative impact with the backing of the leadership and a willing innovation team, is all the conviction an orbit-shifter needs to commit to pursuing the orbit-shifting opportunity.

Organizational escape velocity is truly achieved when a 100 percent dedicated team has signed on to the mission, forming an entrepreneurial, extra-constitutional team that will lead the mission end to end, right up until in-market success, and that does not merely hand over at some intermediate stage. It is treated as a mission rather than another business project. *Settlers often under resource the innovation team; they end up putting in part-time, cross-functional teams. The best people are not even involved; they are too busy maintaining the current orbit.*

Gathering Momentum

Threshold Two: Not Ideation, but Breaking Through Mental Model Boundaries and Threshold Three: Not Market Research but Orbit-shifting Insight

For orbit-shifters, scaling the first threshold is like getting to the base camp. It is now that the real challenge begins. The orbit-shift team is set. It is mentally committed to the out-of-the-box challenge ahead, a challenge that can only be achieved with orbit-shifting ideas. Now, mere brainstorming won't be enough; waiting and hoping for the right idea to strike won't help. Orbit-shifters realize that what limits them is not the number of ideas, but that the ideas are all locked into conventional mental models. *No amount of new thinking will allow for breakthroughs if it is rooted in old mental models.* So, orbit-shifters don't start the pursuit of the orbit-shifting challenge by immediately generating ideas. They place the orbit-shifting challenge in front of them and focus on breaking through mental model boundaries.

The second threshold is crossed when the orbit-shifters have identified orbit-shift keystones: the key boundaries that, when breached, have the potential to yield orbit-shifting ideas. In order to convert each keystone into an orbit-shifting idea, what is needed is an orbit-shifting insight, which is the third threshold to be crossed.

The Nintendo team first recognized and broke through the industry mental model boundary of *following technology road maps* to create the next gaming product. They identified *creating a new customer experience rather than following technology road maps,* as the boundary to be breached. Focusing on this keystone and exploring customer experience led to the orbit-shift insight: 'Going beyond the male teenager to involve the entire family in the game.' This led to the orbit-shifting idea: Wii—a family game.[3]

Going forward from an orbit-shift keystone and discovering a Wii-like orbit-shifting idea by design, is not merely an intellectual exercise that can be accomplished through research and ideation. There is the next exciting threshold to cross.

To convert the orbit-shifting keystone into an orbit-shifting idea, the team will need to go out on a quest for insights. This is the third threshold. The orbit-shifting Insight Quest will take them into insight dialogues with a wide spectrum of market and knowledge insight sources: edgy customers and ecosystem players at market and knowledge intersections. Here too, the team confronts the gravity of self-bias. The team members are conscious of not self-projecting their own ideas and biases. They go in to discover new insights, not to validate their hypotheses. Orbit-shifters recognize that getting a new orbit-shifting insight is as much a personal challenge as it is a professional one. Being open to recognizing and re-examining even the most fundamental *personal biases,* will uncover new insight.

During the Insight Quest, orbit-shifters don't jump to collect answers, they look for new questions; insights that open up new frames and new mental models. The team that had taken on the orbit-shifting challenge of creating a new security system started by first identifying a mental model boundary—security meant creating a fortress—to prevent the enemy from entry. What could be a security solution that was not a fortress? Having breached the mental model boundary, they undertook an Insight Quest that engaged in deep insight dialogues with edgy customers, security breakers, educationists, an entomologist, and a doctor. This wide spectrum of insight dialogues joined new dots and created a breakthrough solution insight.

This threshold is crossed when the team discovers fresh insights and builds on them to generate the orbit-shifting ideas that live up to the aspiration of the orbit-shifting challenge.

Discovering an orbit-shifting idea needs the scaling of two major thresholds on the orbit-shift mountain. The MNC's stage-gate process, however, expects the promising idea to be presented in the third gate immediately after the project has been drawn up and assigned in gate two. It grossly underestimates the challenge in coming up with an orbit-shifting idea.

This MNC's assumption, like most organizations, is that coming up with ideas is the easy part; the real challenge is in ensuring only the relevant ones go through. No wonder the stage gate process becomes a pipeline of incremental ideas. When the mental models are not challenged, only ideas within the current mental model thrive.

What an orbit-shifting innovator sees as two powerful and critical thresholds, which require fundamentally different thought and action, are reduced to a mere decision gate by the MNC.

At Higher Altitudes—Threshold Four: Not Evaluate, but Co-Build

The MNC's stage gate process puts the idea through two rounds of evaluation in gates three and four. In the third gate, the idea goes through a concept test with consumers and in the fourth gate, the business proposition is presented to stakeholders for their assessment.

The purpose of the concept test is to take the idea to consumer groups. Only the ideas with top box scores go through. An idea with low scores is a no go. *This is the classical demonstration of an organization using an orbit-maintaining tool to assess an orbit-shifting idea.* The reality is that consumers' ability to react to an orbit-shifting idea is severely limited; not only because it is beyond their current experience zone, but also because it is presented independent of the final context in which they will actually experience the idea. A number of leaders across a variety of organizations have, on reflection, shared a similar irony: *'In hindsight, the ideas that succeeded and those that failed, both had top box scores!' For an orbit-shifter, a concept test is not a judgment gate. It at best, throws up the next set of unanswered questions, like: How can we make this radical idea more comprehensible, more relatable?* The search for these answers will initiate another level of problem solving and possibly even another orbit-shift Insight Quest. But this time to get insights to solve the specific problem.

The fourth gate for this multinational (fig 9.2) is reaching a *feasible business proposition.* Only when the business case is established does the idea go into developing a prototype. Once again the gate focuses on assessing *business feasibility.* It screens for technical, operational, and regulatory feasibility.

Orbit-shifters don't merely convert an orbit-shifting idea into a feasible on-paper business case, they transform it into an orbit-shifting venture.

For an orbit-shift team, the first step in crossing the fourth threshold is accomplished when they have shared and co-evolved the breakthrough proposition with the key decision stakeholders. Successful co-evolution leads to shared conviction and becomes the first anchor in the crossing of this threshold.

A health insurance firm had set up a crack team to reinvigorate growth in a new country market. Their challenge was to come up with new, even radical ways of driving growth. When challenging mental model boundaries, they identified an industry boundary to be *health insurance is a push product. Insurance can only be sold; it is never bought.* The orbit-shift keystone became to *move health insurance from push to pull.* Focussing on this orbit-shift keystone, they struck upon a breakthrough idea: embed health insurance into all health-oriented products that are popular with customers—every such buy contributes to health insurance.

Having come up with a radical idea, they moved forward to co-create it with key decision stakeholders. They invited the most crucial gatekeeper, the actuaries, into the co-creation workshop that included the top leadership. The actuaries could, if they said 'No' to the idea, stall the entire innovation. They were not just implementation partners at a later stage, but crucial decision stakeholders who needed to be co-opted upfront. In the co-creation dialogue, the actuaries got positively involved and started contributing to, and actively co-building, this idea. Significant decision stakeholders who could become strong adversaries at a later stage and even block the idea had now become co-owners.

In the next step to building the orbit-shifting proposition into an orbit-shifting venture, the team then focuses on identifying and enrolling key implementation stakeholders. These are the cross-functional experts and partners (both inside and outside the organization) needed to build the idea into a working solution. *Creating an extended team of cross-functional experts and then enrolling them to a high point of co-ownership is the key to building an orbit-shifting venture. Having come together,* the new, extended team now co-evolves the unanswered questions—both business and technological—and then identifies the solution pathways to take them to the next threshold.

This is the point at which Vodafone, for example, started reaching out to partners and building the on-ground solution for M-PESA. Safaricom would finally be actually running the pilot on ground, so they had to be completely on board. A banking partner was brought to the table to provide conventional banking services. Faulu Kenya became the partner MFI and the platform software to run the entire technology solution was designed by Sagentia, a British company.

What is required of partners? Susie Lonie describes it well: 'As we suspected, the RFP was far from exhaustive; it was important that Sagentia be extremely open-minded and flexible, create a configurable system, and show a strong willingness to get involved in defining the detailed functionality. In fact, Sagentia demonstrated the required skill set and attitude many times during this project.' Such partners are a delight, but they do not happen by accident. The orbit-shifter works hard to draw partners fully in to the mission so that they don't merely respond to briefs but contribute generatively.[1]

And therefore, to cross this threshold, the team needs to re-group and re-engage in a very different manner from what has happened so far. The terrain to scale this threshold is fundamentally different. As the idea moves from being a possibility to a reality, a whole lot of different skills and activities have to be brought in to bear. The orbit-shifter now needs the capacity to enrol decision stakeholders and cross-functional experts, who are the implementation stakeholders. This is essential to combat dilution in converting the orbit-shifting idea into an orbit-shifting reality. Base camp now seems far away; great ground has been covered since. And yet, at this point, the orbit-shifter can't see the mountaintop as yet. He is caught in the middle, too far to go back, and not close enough to the destination yet. At this fragile point, an orbit-shifter successfully gathers all the energies of the new extended team and re-vitalizes them to make the push towards the top of the mountain.

Sivakumar's orbit-shift keystone was: to leverage IT to transform the process of sourcing from farmers. He had converted this keystone to the e-Choupal idea in partnership with TCS (Tata Consultancy Services). From this point onwards, he built e-Choupal into an orbit-shifting venture by co-creating it with his team. They started to identyfy the unanswered questions—Who would own the infrastructure? ITC or another corporation or the farmers themselves? How would they trade? How would they pay? Would it be a one-way or a two-way channel? How would they deal with intermediaries? e-Choupal became an orbit-shift venture called *Project Symphony.* There was total co-ownership of both the purpose and the unanswered questions from the implementation team.[2]

This threshold is crossed when the new extended team has unscrambled the knowns and the unknowns—both business and technical—and has the shared conviction in a road map to find the answers.

Certainty, on the other hand, is what drives decision-making at this stage for the MNC. The business proposition has to have a high certainty of winning; the evaluation of technical and operational feasibility is assessed against the window of current organization capability. The regulator is approached for a yes/no decision. Ambiguity is not tolerated. If there is any sign of unknowns, unanswered questions, and potential difficulties, the innovation stalls at this gate.

Getting Launch Ready Doesn't Need Two Evaluation Gates; It Needs Multiple Generative Reviews

For the MNC, the business proposition has to reach the point of becoming *launch ready* in the next two stages. The key criteria to agree to being launch ready are: the product and packaging are ready; manufacturing and supply chain are ready; the P&L has been signed on, and all launch goals are aligned, with all risks addressed.

Two clinical stage-gate performance reviews as defined in the stage-gate process are just not enough to navigate an orbit-shifting idea from concept to a working prototype.

The reality is that the idea will be confronted with domain gravity at virtually every stage, with experts saying, 'That is impossible, it can't be done'. And that they can only do so much! The Chinese faced it. 'A rail line over permafrost? Impossible!' Queen faced it. 'A song overrunning the usual radio playtime? Won't work. Cannot be released!' Titan faced it at each stage in 'making the slimmest, water-resistant watch'.

Finding solutions to a series of unsolved execution problems that are beyond the current know-how of the domain experts (both technical and business) now becomes the challenge. For M-PESA, getting servers into Kenya was delayed due to incorrect paperwork and customs issues; and once they were in, there was a question of where to host them. In a bank? Would that cause regulatory delay? Where else? Safaricom instead? Further, should agents be given devices with magnetic strip cards or would this become too expensive? Where should they run the prototype and why? And still further, the text messaging needs to be in dual languages: both English and Swahili. Swahili is not as compact as English, how would they get the messages down to 160 characters?[1]

Further ahead, the pursuit of orbit-shifting innovation will inevitably lead to new technologies and new processes. Prototyping them in itself will be a challenge. What will also be needed is the ability and the will to find prototype partners who have the capacity to do rapid prototyping in domains that are beyond the current expertise of the organization.

What is needed at this stage is the willingness to navigate through the fog and not avoid it. Gravity must be combated; else the mission will be diluted. Therefore, stakeholders cannot just conduct two evaluation reviews, they will need to actively engage at multiple points, where unsolved problems creep up or unexpected dilemmas emerge. What is needed are generative reviews that uncover unsolved problems and apply the four Orbit-shifting Gears to find new solution pathways. The stakeholders' role at this threshold of the journey is not merely to review, but to enable progress; to combat dilution and not settle for compromises.

The Summit is Visible

Threshold Five—Not Launch and Optimize, but In-market Versioning

Once the prototype is ready this MNC proposes two market launch and evaluation gates (fig 9.2): six months for launch optimization and twelve months for the final Go/No Go decision. Again, the focus of optimization is on mere tinkering. There is no space for big changes. After a grace period of twelve months, a decision is simply made—let the project live, or die.

This multinational's assumption in gate seven is that the innovative product/solution is ready. Now it is purely a case of launching it in the market, solving operational problems to optimize the process, and then the only question left is does it succeed or not. And therefore, the final decision: Go or No Go!

The mental model of Launch–Optimize–Go/No Go is in itself the biggest gravity that can end up minimizing orbit-shifting ideas.

For orbit-shifters, the first take-to market stage is not a 'launch'; it is, in fact, the last stage of product/solution evolution. Orbit-shifters believe that the final step in crossing the fifth threshold is in-market versioning—to evolve the product/solution into an in-market success model. How the orbit-shift idea will play out against the variables of customer engagement, channel, and implementation-team engagement is unknown. In addition, how the larger ecosystem will respond to the orbit-shift is also unknown; for example, government or regulators. Orbit-shifters believe it is only by experimenting and developing the idea in live market conditions across best conditions, real conditions, and scale conditions, that the orbit-shift will grow to its fullest potential.

They recognize that just optimizing and solving operational problems will not be enough. What is required is not merely to solve operational problems to ensure effective in-market delivery, but also to seek out opportunities that can maximize the in-market impact of the idea. Orbit-shifters are open to revisiting, renewing, and even finding a completely different proposition that has an even bigger impact. *In-market versioning to grow and evolve the orbit-shift is far beyond the test-marketing approach, where the intent is to either accept or reject the product/ solution in-market.*

The Vodafone team didn't merely solve operational problems during the M-PESA pilot, they spotted opportunities and evolved the M-PESA proposition to a point where it transformed from being a business-to-business proposition—repay loans—to become a far, far bigger business-to-consumer proposition—send money home. This is in-market versioning in full flow.[1]

In-market versioning cannot be outsourced or even delegated; the core innovation team has to be present, quite like in the case of Vodafone where Susie Lonie was out in the field herself. And Dainik Bhaskar, *where the key leadership were present on ground to mature the 'co-creation of a newspaper with the readership of the city' model.*

Further, orbit-shifters recognize that the on-ground last-mile teams will have to be excited and enrolled into co-ownership too, so that they don't approach a new idea with the old mindset. They realize that for most regimented last-mile teams, a new idea is not exciting; it is a headache to be avoided and minimized at best. They navigate the last-mile fog by first enrolling and then engaging the last-mile teams *into co-evolving the orbit-shifting idea into an in-market success model.*

The orbit-shifting challenge has turned into an evident reality only when a scalable in-market success model has evolved. The peak is now visible. Orbit-shifters don't even stop here. They go further to identify *scaling challenges.* They realize that merely replicating the success model of the first market can and may work in similar markets, but could dilute in markets that are different.

They identify scaling challenges and evolve market solutions that make the in-market success model adapt to different markets. The Access Mobile team that had abundant business experience in Asian markets with its WiderThan heritage did not replicate the in-market success model of RBT in Korea in other Asian markets. They recognized the market differences and adapted the Korean success model to suit each market.

Now the fifth threshold is crossed and the stage is reached where the orbit-shifting idea can grow beyond the orbit-shifting team.

Finally, rising above the mists, after the long and exhilarating journey, the orbit-shift summit has been reached.

As a CEO, think about this:

Most CEOs have orbit-shifting dreams and aspirations, but they are managed with orbit-maintaining processes, like the stage gate.

Orbit-shifting innovation cannot be managed like a stage-gate process; it is more like entrepreneurially scaling the thresholds of an unclimbed mountain. A stage gate, in contrast, works on the mental model of screening and filtering for certainty in outcomes.

The orbit-shifting journey moves across five thresholds. Each threshold focuses not on screening and decision-making, but on re-energizing and re-engaging, to solve the next set of unsolved problems towards scaling the next threshold.

Orbit-shifting innovation is, by its nature, rooted in the unknown, the uncertain, and the ambiguous—all the innovator has is the orbit-shifting purpose, which is like the pole star and the compass to navigate uncertainty. You cannot have more, as you don't know what to expect. And yet, organization leaders want predictability and a process to manage innovation, a defined road map, not a compass.

The Stage Gate roots out uncertainties; it's no wonder then, that it hasn't succeeded in creating breakthroughs. The stage-gate process promotes incremental innovation, which is good and necessary to maintain the orbit. But it roots out orbit-shifting innovation.

Where is your organization attempting the orbit-shift with orbit-maintaining tools and models like the stage-gate process? What are you doing to transform these models to suit and move the orbit-shift, rather than allowing it to get dragged down by gravity?

Chapter 10

What Differentiates Orbit-shifters?

ORBIT-SHIFTING INNOVATION CANNOT BE MANAGED, IT CAN ONLY BE UNLEASHED. And this is not a one-time effort; rather it will have to be done at each threshold of the orbit-shift mountain. The energy and the focus required to navigate the orbit-shifting journey from one threshold to the next has to be replenished. Resolves have to be re-strengthened and commitments, re-sought. Without this, the default setting of orbit-maintenance is likely to take over and drag down the orbit-shifting journey into just another orbit-maintaining activity.

What gives orbit-shifters the capacity to scale the five thresholds, to confront gravity and new unknowns at every threshold, and restart again and again without feeling de-motivated? And what's more, to not just do it once, but to willingly take on new orbit-shifting challenges again and again?

To start zero-based at every threshold! To do this again and again requires more than tools and process templates. It requires fundamentally different mindsets.

While orbit-shifting innovations like the LifeStraw, prepaid card, Space food, and M-PESA have happened across industries, countries, and cultures, there are six mindsets that are the core drivers that these orbit-shifters share.

ATTITUDE TOWARDS GROWTH: NOT THE SIZE OF THE KINGDOM BUT THE SIZE OF THE CHALLENGE

What really motivates orbit-shifters to take on the unknown, to pursue orbit-shifting challenges, and scale the next orbit-shift mountain? What is their real stake in this? It comes from their deeply held belief that *growth comes from the size of the challenge rather than the size of the kingdom.*

The orbit-shifters' mindset of personal and professional growth is fundamentally different. In their minds, growth comes from handling a bigger, more exciting challenge, and not from the number of people reporting in to them. The *size of the difference* they will make is more inspiring than the *size of the business* they are handling. This motivates orbit-shifters to move out of their comfort zones into the unknown and take on the next big challenge. The journey might be formidable, but the reward of forging a new path that makes a big difference and creates history is inherently satisfying.

Do You Want to Change the World Or...?

John Sculley made this shift from *size of the kingdom* to *size of the challenge*, when Steve Jobs provoked him with, 'Do you want to spend your life selling sugar water or do you want to come with me and change the world?'[18] *Increase in the size of the kingdom* is the conventional manner in which most managers measure career progress. Jobs got Sculley to reframe it to the degree of difference he made on this planet. This one shift inspired Sculley enough to quit his cherished *size of the kingdom* at Pepsi and move into the unknown, to the *degree of difference* role at Apple.

Breakthrough Fears, Hesitation...into Action

Victoria Hale was comfortable being a scientist with Big Pharma and working with the government. The trigger to break out of her comfort zone and follow her orbit-shifting aspiration came when she spoke to a taxi driver.

'It was the year 2000, I was 40 years old, and for a long while I had been thinking about starting another type of pharmaceutical company, one that would target diseases that no one was researching. I was in this taxicab, and I love talking to taxicab drivers. He asked me what I did, and I told him that I was a pharmaceutical scientist in town for a meeting. He roared with laughter, and said something that was extremely painful to hear. He said, "You all have all the money". And that was a turning point for me; it was uncomfortable and true, I really needed to hear that to move into action. I will tell you that it was a profound moment. When he said that, I achieved a moment of clarity. I had to move on my idea. It is the single experience that helped me break through fears, hesitation, etc. and from that moment on, everything felt and still feels effortless.'[27] The difference here, between Victoria Hale and the settlers, is not in the trigger. So many of us have *moment of truth* experiences: a stranger says something in passing, or a child looks us in the eye and utters a few words in candor, or a stop-in-the-tracks kind of life-changing incident occurs. The difference is that Victoria Hale did something about it—chose to let the jolt move her out of her settler state of mind. Most settlers acknowledge the jolt, feel a sense of regret for the way life is, and then return to consolidating the current kingdom. Rather than continue to ascend the conventional ladder of success, Victoria chose to scale an orbit-shift mountain, driven by the passion to make a difference to a vast number of people in developing nations. It was well known that *unique-to-the-third-world* kind of diseases were not being researched or catered to by big pharma companies. She took it upon herself to break from the career-as-usual track and create a new business model that would make a real difference in the world.

Those Lives Had to be Saved...

Jim Barrington at Novartis was inspired to take on the SMS for Life project when he heard Silvio Gabriel describe the problem of stock-out of malarial drugs that kills millions in Africa. 'Each year, approximately 300 to 500 million malaria infections cause about one million deaths, most of them African children under the age of five.' This hit him very hard. The key point is that these deaths were *needless* rather than *inevitable.* At the end of 2008, Jim had burnt the bridge and committed 100 percent of his time and effort to the stock-out problem. Those lives had to be saved.

In alignment with his superiors, he quit his job as CIO to take on the full-time challenge of scaling an orbit-shift mountain, under the aegis of Novartis.

As the IMD's case study *SMS for Life (A)* article describes, 'By January 19, 2009, he was sitting alone in an empty office, with only his computer, a phone and a solitary desk and chair. It was a few days after a US Airways pilot had successfully landed his plane in the Hudson River after birds flew into the engines. Jim described his thoughts at the time:

> "I was tremendously motivated. I was excited. I felt inside that this was a problem I could solve. I thought about the pilot, who did such a fantastic job landing that plane in the Hudson River and I remember him saying afterwards that he felt his whole life, everything he did, all his training, was preparing him for this one moment. I can really relate to that, and I felt that this project was something that would allow me to utilize all the skills, training and experiences I had gained from 40 years in IT. If I could apply all those learnings to solve this one problem, this would be just magic". [11]

Most orbit-shifters like Jim approach the next orbit-shift challenge with a sense of positive anticipation, and not fear.

The Next Mountain

P.N. Vasudevan has, by now, scaled two orbit-shift mountains. His first climb was in Cholamandalam vehicle finance, when he galvanized his team to move out of stagnation into quantum growth. As a result, an organization that had been growing at a mere 3–5 percent grew 75–80 percent, year on year, for the next four years. He got his team to escape the gravity of the current orbit by challenging markets and market share, and *to move them from the game of increasing market share to market creation—'The entire population is our customer'*. He inspired the team to see the orbit-shift possibility and to take on orbit-shifting growth challenges year on year. They began to work challenge back and not yesteryear forward.

After scaling the orbit-shift mountain in Cholamandalam, Vasu moved on to a job with a respectable bank in Mumbai. Within a couple of years, he had to move back to Chennai for family health reasons. As he says, '*Opportunities at my age are few.*' He had been a working professional—an employee—throughout his work life. Yet, he pushed himself to move out of the comfort zone of an employee, to become an entrepreneur, to start a new venture in microfinance. However, *the orbit-shifter in him decided to not start another follower organization, but scale the next orbit-shift mountain—'not yet another MFI, but to create the best MFI in the world'. A firm that would lead the way in creating the next version of microfinance; a firm that would not just remove the bad news that had engulfed the microfinance industry in recent times, but make it the amazing positive that it always promised to be.*

The next three years saw him create the fastest growing MFI in the world, Equitas.[16] *His organization's way of engaging with customers has become the new reference point for the entire industry.* In fact, when his standards of operation were sent to the regulator, they became the reference point for the new norms of the industry.

As he says, 'While pursuing the quantum growth challenge in Cholamandalam gave me enormous professional pride, making a positive difference to thousands of people through microfinance is giving me incredible social pride.' *He exemplifies the orbit-shifter's mindset that personal and professional growth comes from taking on the next big challenge—to make a bigger difference.*

Scaling the next unclimbed mountain is the dominant motivation for orbit-shifters, because it is exciting, challenging, and it means new experiences and new learning. Unlike settlers, it is not the internal credibility—size of office, size of designation, degree of promotion, or exoticness of the transfer location that matters. Orbit-shifters build market and community credibility. For them, life is not a collection of assets or titles. It is a collection of unforgettable moments and of proud *impact legacies.*

ATTITUDE TOWARDS AN ORBIT-SHIFTING CHALLENGE—A DIRECTION AND NOT A DESTINATION

At the beginning of the previous chapter, Todd Skinner aptly described what it takes to scale a mountain. He said, *'If you are not afraid you have probably chosen too easy a mountain. To be worth, the expedition it had better be intimidating. If you don't stand at the base uncertain how to reach the summit, then you have wasted the effort to get there. A mountain well within your ability is not only a mispending of resources; it is also a loss of opportunity across a lifetime of potential achievement'.*[22]

How would a settler, a traditional manager in a traditional organization, have reacted to this idea of an unclimbed mountain? In all probability he would say, *'If you are afraid you have probably chosen an impractical mountain. To be worth the expedition it had better be realistic. If you stand at the base uncertain how to reach the summit, then you are wasting your time. Committing to climb a mountain well within your ability and making it sound like a great achievement is the hallmark of a great manager.'*

This contrast brings alive how orbit-shifters approach an orbit-shifting challenge differently from settlers. For the orbit-shifter, the orbit-shifting challenge is a transformation vehicle and not a performance goal. And hence, the orbit-shifter approaches it like a *direction and not a destination.* They believe that the orbit-shifting challenge is the ultimate peak, and in the pursuit of it, they will get much further than where they are today, even if they never get there. The orbit-shifting challenge is exciting because it provides the trigger and the inspiration to go after the impossible. And what matters is the movement, the progress made with reference to the current orbit, rather than feeling a sense of failure at not having achieved a performance goal. This becomes especially amplified in the last lap of a successful manager's career. Most people, quite like a CEO we have come across recently, do not want a failure in the last lap. This would sully an otherwise successful career. So they focus on legacy protection and not legacy creation.

The excitement of taking on an unknown challenge and making a significant difference in the world, rather that legacy protection, is what drives a person like Jim Barrington to take on an SMS for Life-like mission in the last years of his corporate life. This is what also inspires a person like Fazle Abed from BRAC to give up a safe corporate job in Shell, in the prime of his career in the 1970s and pursue a crazy cause like eliminating poverty in Bangladesh. (Not in a city, or community, or state—but in an entire country!)

It is in this pursuit, with all its obstacles, falls, and uncertainties, that history is created.

Most settlers are so busy *protecting the castles* they've built, that they have lost the courage to abandon them in order to go on and create new structures, new castles, new dreams, and then chase them.

Approaching an orbit-shifting challenge like a direction and not a destination has led orbit-shifters to redefine success and reframe failure.

What triggered Fazle Abed to take on the orbit-shifting challenge of eradicating poverty in Bangladesh? As he says, '*Bangladesh is homogenous and small enough,* (small enough as in when he started in 1972, the population was 75 million people; now it is 150 million), *it is not large like India and I felt that I could actually tackle the question of poverty significantly in a homogenous country which is manageable!*' Imagine thinking that a nation of 75 million is small enough. Today, has Abed achieved his goal? No! But he has created a huge transformative impact with BRAC. The total number of self-employment opportunities created through BRAC: 8.5 million, and the number of people impacted through microfinance: 5 billion in microloans to over 6 million borrowers.[2]

For orbit-shifters like Fazle Hasan Abed, 'success equals the progress made'.

Move Forward or Retreat?

While scaling the orbit-shift mountain, at each threshold, whether a leader moves forward or retreats is entirely driven by the fundamental attitude to success/failure. Mindsets around success and failure are deep-rooted cultural imperatives that most of us take for granted. Risk becomes binary: either you succeed or you fail.

For settlers, failure is not an option, and success is therefore defined as *not failing*. This means the *opt-out* card gets used at the first sign of failure. It is a stigma that cannot be tolerated.

On the other hand, orbit-shifters do not opt out at a failure point; they are constantly looking at the progress made. When the orbit-shift being pursued is so extraordinary, then, as Neil Armstrong said, 'One small step for man' is enough. It is progress made.'

Failure, as Carsten expresses, 'is the one more thing we've learnt to do differently as we navigate the unknown'. There is therefore, a high acceptance of failure as a legitimate part of the orbit-shifting journey, and it is not given any negative stigmatizing attention that paralyses any movement forward.

Scott O'Neill's experience with the Wolbachia bacteria in the eliminate dengue challenge brings alive this approach to success.

Funding is key to pursuing breakthrough research, especially in Scott's type of work. At many points, the funding faltered, or simply didn't come. And yet he didn't give up. The project moved along quite slowly, and it was only the funding from Grand Challenges in Global Health in 2003, from the Bill and Melinda Gates Foundation, that injected a spurt of experimentation and growth.

'Getting a large block of funding allowed us to pull the required team of people together and move forward incredibly quickly. This funding allowed us to intensify our research and the results were exciting. We were able to find a way to successfully introduce *Wolbachia* into the mosquitoes.'

Although the Grand Challenges gave a boost to funding and allowed for progress, it was not enough. Yet that hasn't dismayed or stopped Professor O' Neill. He is now building a consortium of funders. All he sees is progress made so far, and looking ahead, in how to move it forward.[10]

An orbit-shifting project cannot—and should not—even be examined with the same lens as orbit-maintaining. How does one even move bacteria between species? The Wolbachia had to be taken from the fruitfly and inserted into the mosquito by injecting miniature-size eggs with a micro needle. This is fraught with a higher failure rate. As Joe Palca brings alive in his article on the NPR website:

'"It's incredibly frustrating work," O'Neill says. His colleague Tom Walker spends hour after hour, day after day, trying to inject the embryos. Even though he's become an expert at this, Walker can do no more than 500 a day. Then the scientists have to wait a week until the adult mosquitoes emerge to see if any are infected with Wolbachia. Walker says in this latest round of work he's injected 18,000 eggs – with nothing to show for it. "The success rate is very low," says Walker, in something of an understatement.'

The mindset of the orbit-shifter comes through in how Walker talks about the strike rate of the experiment—'the success rate is very low'. He focuses on the progress, whereas a settler would have said, the 'failure rate is very high'. (He focuses on the shortfall!)

Pursuing an 'eliminate dengue' like challenge with a mindset of direction and not a destination, and focusing on success as progress rather than on shortfall, is what keeps orbit-shifters at it for years at end. O'Neill has been pursuing the 'eliminating dengue' challenge, climbing the unclimbed mountain for the last 20 years, and realizes it could be another 20 years before he succeeds.[17]

'You know, I was incredibly persistent in not wanting to give this idea up,' O'Neill said. 'I thought the idea was a good idea, and I don't think you get too many ideas in your life, actually. At least I don't. I'm not smart enough. So I thought this idea was a really good idea.'

Not getting daunted by setbacks and focusing on progress is the spirit that has kept Scott O'Neill going for so many years. This spirit is also shared by the LifeStraw team. As Torben has said, *'There were no setbacks, only tasks.'* When problems are viewed as tasks, the orbit-shifter is more likely to move forward by solving them; but if they are viewed as setbacks, the orbit-shift is likely to get stalled.

Far ahead of where you can otherwise end up being...

The dilemma and the courage needed to pursue orbit-shifting challenges in a hard-nosed business environment comes through vividly from T.K. Kurien's experience.

At the turn of this century, 100-million-dollar deals were an impossible benchmark in the IT industry in India. Wipro's T.K. Kurien, at that time the head of the telecom vertical, aspired for, and insisted that his team must only pursue deals more than 100 million dollars. When they succeeded in making a 70-million-dollar deal a reality, it became the first big deal in the history of IT outsourcing in 2001. This is significant especially because Wipro, until then, thought of 1-million-dollar deals as big. Imagine raising the bar from 1 to 70 in one stroke. So, what brought this about? Kurien had committed to an outlandish goal of 500 million dollars in five years, during the IT boom of the late 1990s. When the bottom fell out of the IT market, he could have revised the goals. He didn't. *Instead, he reworked how people in his division thought of challenges.* He said, 'From now on we will only go after deals that are greater than 100 million dollars, anything below that is unacceptable.' His peers were incredulous and dismissive, until the 70-million-dollar deal came through.' Three years later, Kurien said, 'We did not and may not reach 500 million dollars, but telecom today is at 225 million dollars, which is far ahead of where we would have been (without pursuing this challenge). I believe in aspiring for very high goals, in striving to reach them you get far ahead of where you can otherwise end up being.'

Kurien demonstrated instinctively what orbit-shifters do: that they see the orbit-shifting challenge as a *direction and not a destination*. It becomes a liberator to innovate and create transformative impact, rather than a prison that confines the mind.

Settlers, on the other hand, see the orbit-shifting aspiration as a destination and not a direction; more like a performance goal. They approach an innovation challenge with a *failure is not an option* approach, and end up creating anxiety in the pursuit of the goal. What happens then is that riskier options or the more *far-out* options are left unexplored; leading to missed opportunities. Stakeholders who see the orbit-shifting aspiration as a *destination and not a direction*, in turn, create great pressure on the innovation team. They treat the *innovation review like a performance review*. Rather than, as Kurien said, looking at how much the team has moved/leapt forward, they are constantly looking for gaps and where and why the team has fallen short. This attitude, more often then not, halts the innovation journey at one of the thresholds.

As a CEO, think about this:

This mindset of viewing growth as *moving from one challenge to the next* is what drives orbit-shifters to take on an orbit-shifting challenge, regardless of whether they are in an organization, on entrepreneurs, or social activists.

Settlers, on the other hand, get preoccupied with scaling the organization and the hierarchical ladder. For them, scaling an orbit-shift mountain is both impractical and a highly avoidable personal risk. And hence, when faced with a choice of *taking on an orbit-shifting challenge or accepting a more senior role/title*, they usually choose the latter.

How are you hiring, cultivating, and growing talent in your organization?

As the orbit-shifter T.K. Kurien said to us, 'I tell new people, join me and I promise you unchartered waters, an opportunity to do things you've never done before, unforgettable journeys, and great employability.' This is the kind of thinking that attracts orbit-shifters to an organization. Is this the kind of leader your organization cultivates? What will your people say about you?

Are you seeding and multiplying orbit-shifters? Or has your organization become a breeding ground for settlers?

ATTITUDE TOWARDS GRAVITY—NOT A *DEFENDER* BUT AN *ATTACKER*

The inverted map, which we discovered initially with the teacher from Argentina, also reappeared in Australia, with this statement below it: '*No apologies are called for in presenting the map with the south at the top.*

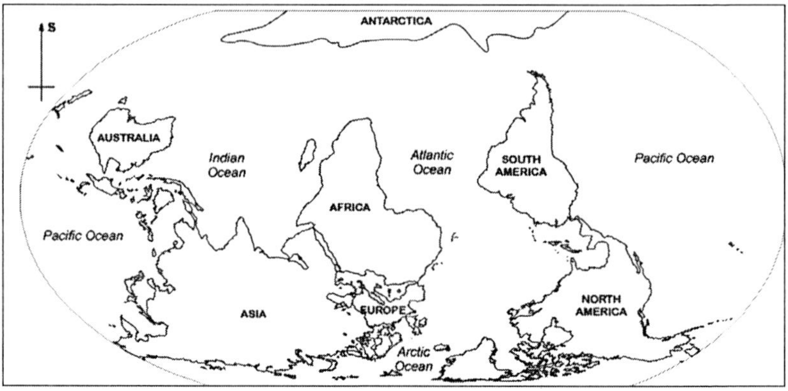

10.1 – The Inverted Map

After hundreds of years of development the southern lands have no reason to be under the northern hemisphere.' This truly manifests the attitude of an attacker and not a defender. Orbit-shifters start by questioning the world order rather than conforming to it; they begin by confronting the gravity rather than living with it.

While ascending the orbit-shift mountain, the innovator will be confronted with gravity at each threshold. He will, repeatedly, need to break through gravity to come through with solutions.

Whether he makes the impossible possible, or whether he succumbs to the impossible is what differentiates the orbit-shifter from the settler.

Attackers look at the current orbit with a sense of positive irreverence rather than with deference. Where others see *how the world is* and accept it, orbit-shifters see *how the world could be* and attempt to transform it.

GE broke through the pivotal gravity of western firms as they adapted to the exploding markets in the East, especially China and India. GE India has now taken on the mandate of becoming *the best Indian company, and not just the best MNC in India,* where it will not replicate the existing technology but focus on new technologies and new products to meet unique Indian needs. As John Flannery, the president and CEO, displaying the mindset of the attacker, said, *'I want GE India to be viewed as one of India's best Indian companies—not one of its best MNCs. One of the really interesting aspects of this opportunity is our potential to impact the lives of the population in India's rural areas. Low cost innovative product breakthroughs are going to bring high quality healthcare at affordable cost to millions of people. How can you be anything but motivated by the prospect of that kind of change?*'[7] His is truly an orbit-shifting vision, putting Indian needs at the centre of his business development rather than extending and customizing existing products from the parent portfolio. Already, products developed in India, like the portable ECG machine—the Mac 400—have shown the potential to create a big blowback impact on the rest of the world. GE is now a shining example of moving from *replication to reverse innovation.*

Dr Zlotkin took on the orbit-shifting challenge to *eliminate childhood malnutrition*. He didn't start like a defender and try to generate ideas to improve upon the existing solutions. He started like an *attacker* and first identified the mental model boundaries that needed to be broken through to discover an orbit-shifting solution.

He recognized that the approach of developed countries, *making available fortified and packaged food products*, could not be replicated in developing countries because this needed an industry transformation. Further, he identified that UNICEF's current solution of providing syrups, tablets, and injections as supplements was not working. These supplements tasted unpleasant and mothers were reluctant to give them to their children. Transporting them was a further challenge.

The attacker in Dr Zlotkin started by breaking through the gravity of the current solutions and framed the challenge as 'create a solution that can be added to food on a daily basis without changing taste or texture. A solution that can be easily pre-measured and easy to transport'. His breaking through the mental model boundaries lead to the orbit-shifting idea—Sprinkles.[21]

In 1989–90, Bosch India had been made the centre of competence for a particular single-cylinder pump used in diesel engines, called the PF pump. For more than a decade this 'centre of competence' only worked at tweaking products developed in Germany and this too after extensive permission seeking. As one of the team members recalls, 'Our bosses used to say don't try to make any major changes or too many changes to the product. After all it's been developed in Germany. We don't have the competence. We are just replicators here.'

However, they were faced with a stark choice when their product became increasingly irrelevant as the new technology—CR systems—took over. Rather than be swept away by superior technology, this team chose to move away from permission seeking. They shifted their approach *from defender to attacker.* They took on the challenge of making the old *diesel engine meet the new Euro 4 norms. They had not been asked by the German headquarters to do so. They broke this self-imposed limitation of the current orbit and set their sights on scaling a truly orbit-shifting mountain and succeeded. They converted a disadvantage into an advantage.*[13]

Zack Snyder adopted this attacker mindset when he took on the challenge to translate the film *300* to the screen at one third the cost of an epic like *Alexander* or *Troy*.[9]

The attacker in Scott Johnson questioned the drug development cycle that had been accepted as given for many many years. Through the Myelin Repair Foundation, he has pioneered an industry breakthrough, that promises to transform the speed with which new drugs are brought to market.[4]

As a CEO, think about this:

The defender mindset is most visible in the boxed-in manner in which organizations identify new opportunities.

In a defender state of mind, organizations get preoccupied with legacy protection—sticking to norms created by past success or those of the parent organization. It is equally visible in how their view of the market is dominated by the industry lens.

Attackers do not conform; they confront gravity. How often

do you engage your organization in attacker conversations that are driven by new legacy creation rather than legacy protection?

ATTITUDE TOWARDS DISCOVERING NEW INSIGHT

Not Validation: Seeking Answers, but Discovery: Seeking Questions to Join New Dots

Orbit-shifters believe that what points the way towards new insight is the discovery mindset, which comes alive in the quest for new questions, rather than a validation mindset, which only searches for answers. The discovery mindset is curious and explorative; looking to join new dots, find new meanings, connect the unconnected. The validation mindset in contrast is self-projective, seeking answers to confirm one's own hypothesis, rejecting anything that doesn't fit in the current perspective.

It is only a new question, in the discovery state of mind, that can create a seismic shift and point towards a new reality. For Sivakumar, it came when YCD asked him, *'How can you leverage IT to improve commodities trading?'* This question prompted Sivakumar to begin joining the dots between the youngest domain, IT, and one of the oldest trades in the world, commodities trading.[15]

This discovery mindset that searches for new questions drives orbit-shifters away from more of the same. They fundamentally become value seekers; they look for value in every experience, in every conversation. *They don't seek prescriptions, they seek possibilities.* They extract value even from the most ordinary conversations. They engage in lateral conversations with a generative and not a critic's mindset. They excel in extracting, identifying, and then transferring the value from every new experience. *They build knowledge bridges, where others see a gulf. This ability to join dots from seemingly unrelated domains leads to the emergence of new perspectives and new ideas.*

Also, if the entire quest is about seeking new questions, then they realize it will not come from engaging with more of the same kind of people. They don't believe that engaging with the same people, in the same environment, in the same way, is likely to produce a new outcome. The usual ways of ideation or brainstorming will lead to some more answers, but the thinking is likely to remain stuck within the same mental model boundary. The available set of answers is very comforting for the settler. But the orbit-shifter steps back to find the right questions, and he realizes if the question is right, the answer will come. And to trigger the questing mind requires new stimuli rather than more of the same.

This search for new stimuli drives orbit-shifters to engage in new/lateral conversations. Each lateral conversation has the power of triggering a new insight, by joining a new dot.

The New Dots that Joined...

In coming up with SLS (Same Language Subtitling), Brij Kothari looked at the same data that everyone else had been looking at for years. Using a fresh lens, he came up with an insightful question, 'Is the world of literacy divided only into literates and illiterates? Could there be a third group?' From this insightful question emerged the *semi-literate group*—partially literate people, who recognize words and alphabets, but are not fluent in stringing them together. His mind then started joining dots: with his own semi-literate experience in Spanish. During a break from dissertation writing in 1996, Brij was watching a Spanish film called *Women on the Verge of a Nervous Breakdown* with friends. They were also trying to improve their Spanish and thought that watching Pedro Almodovar's classic would be a good experience in addition to being a stress buster. The video was subtitled in English, a language that they understood well but that, they realized, was no help in making them understand Spanish. In fact, it made it harder to 'hear' the Spanish dialogue. Brij casually commented: *'If only they would subtitle the Spanish dialogue in Spanish.' Pause. And then, 'What if they simply subtitled Hindi films in Hindi, on TV in India? Maybe India would become literate.'* This new question was the orbit-shifting insight that joined new dots between TV watching and literacy. Brij could not get it out of his mind. Years later, this spark was brought alive in the form of 'Planet Read'. Brij found an amazingly simple meeting point, *between the need of the semi literates and the overwhelming love Indians have for film music.*[8] As Bill Clinton says of Planet Read, 'This is a very interesting thing, it never would have occurred to me. It is amazing how many non literate people *do* watch television.' And, as former President Clinton quotes a Nielsen study on its impact: 'Same Language Subtitling doubles the number of functional readers among primary school children.'[19]

Joining new dots across unconnected domains is what the Microsoft team did as well when they picked out the idea for an e-reader from a sci-fi book, *The Hitchhiker's Guide to the Galaxy.*[3] And it is through this very same capacity that Sonnich Fryland was struck by the idea of NovoPen®, while reading the experience of a young girl in the *Lancet* medical magazine.[20] For orbit-shifters like these, the mind does not rest in silos, it is curiously hunting for opportunities across domains, and this curiosity allows for the penny to drop with the most unexpected of triggers.

Who would think of joining dots between radio astronomy and wireless connectivity for computers? Yet, an esoteric scientist, a radio astronomer, did exactly this when he came up with a solution that is currently being used by over 1 billion people, even if they don't know it. John O'Sullivan, an Australian radio astronomer in the Seventies was interested in finding radio waves from exploding black holes as postulated by Steven Hawking. CSIRO, Australia (Commonwealth Scientific and Industrial Research Organization) was keen to convert scientific thought into commercial applications and in 1992, O'Sullivan leveraged his work in astronomy done two decades earlier—the techniques he and his collaborators had developed to remove distortion in *intergalactic radiation eventually found expression as the technology in wireless LAN.* It became the standard that liberated a computer from the desk and made it possible to surf the Internet anywhere without wires.[12,25,26]

As an Innovation Leader, think about this:

Insight comes to a prepared mind. Orbit-shifters, in the discovery state of mind, go beyond the current domain. They seek diversity of experiences and a wide variety of insight sources.

Are you trapped in finding answers or are you seeking the next question?

How diverse are your insight sources and experiences? How deep is your engagement with them? Are you joining dots in fresh and unconnected ways or merely validating your expert opinion?

Will your stakeholders, like Bill Clinton, a respected thought leader, say of your insight, 'It's interesting, it never would have occurred to me'?

The Insight Quest

An innovation team with the aspiration to create a game changer in the personal care (hair and skin care) industry set out on an Insight Quest in a discovery state of mind. In this search for new questions, they engaged with and joined new dots with new insight sources from within the industry and across other domains, in China, the US, and India.

To provoke their minds to go beyond the usual consumers and join new dots, they got into insight dialogues with people who have lived in extreme conditions, without access to bathrooms, army officers who have served at high altitudes (4,572 metres and above) and adventure experts who went on long treks. They even visited a jail to understand prisoners' personal care regimens. They also immersed themselves in a community that had zealously adopted sustainable living habits.

Their search for new questions did not stop there. They went further and engaged with a domain expert who had studied atmospheric sciences. They also joined dots with an expert in developing medical devices. Further, they explored how a tattoo artist interpreted the world of skin from his domain. Going back in time, they also joined new dots with a doctor of traditional Chinese medicine.

Nothing distinguishes a settler from an orbit-shifter more than their attitude during an Insight Quest like this, that can take 3–4 weeks of immersion in joining new dots.

The settler approaches an Insight Quest like a Herculean task, one that takes away from day to day business (every day that I am out there meeting people is a day away from real business). They are usually taken aback by the amount of time they have to spend, and barter to reduce it: 'Can we do it in three days, instead of four days?' And also barter for the number of dialogues: 'Do we really need to do so many? Why? What is the minimum number of dialogues we need to do to get to the insight?' There is a sense of fatigue when they hit the streets and highways outside their comfort zone of the air-conditioned office—travelling long distances to meet new insight sources. And they heave a sigh of relief when the conversations are done. And if no significant insights come at the end of this, it only justifies their opinion that it is wasted time. After all, they were seeking answers and found none.

Orbit-shifters on the other hand, are always looking for what next and what more. An Insight Quest for them is always exciting, for it is a chance to discover something new that will add and grow their orbit-shift. They are energized and engaged throughout and when they find blocks or hit the wall of diminishing returns they expand the insight spectrum to find the next horizon and a newer insight source. They never look back at how much they've already done or how much time they have already invested; they only look forward with a searchlight switched on to sense the next question and the next new dots to be joined.

ATTITUDE TOWARDS STAKEHOLDERS: NOT CONVINCING BUT TIPPING STAKEHOLDERS INTO CO-OWNERSHIP

Orbit-shifters don't convince, they tip stakeholders into adopting and even co-owning the orbit-shifting idea. They do this by engaging them in tipping conversations and tipping experiences.

Tipping into Co-ownership

When Sivakumar invited Y C Deveshwar to inaugurate the first e-Choupal, it turned into a tipping experience. When YCD saw first-hand the excitement of the villagers, he was moved into co-ownership.[15]

Victoria Hale engaged the regulator in tipping conversations. The real tipping point occurred when she asked 'What do I need to do to show you that I am non-profit?' This question opened up options, in an area where the regulator had until then been closed. The regulator tipped from absolute refusal to the realm of possibility and said, 'Give me a precedent.' This opened up a solution pathway.

Tipping—From Indifference to Initiative

Kiva's orbit-shift journey started when Jessica Jackley and Matt Flannely, went to hear Muhammad Yunus speak on microfinance. They were inspired by Muhammad Yunus's story of the origin of microfinance and Grameen Bank and also wanted to become involved and make a difference to the lives of the people Yunus had spoken of. *This encounter with Yunus tipped Jessica and Matt into action. They asked themselves, 'How can we facilitate loans to rural Africa and other entrepreneurs?'* From this question came Kiva, a breakthrough method of crowd sourcing funding for small entrepreneurs around the world.

The next challenge for Jessica and Matt was how to enrol people to fund entrepreneurs in different parts of the world.

The biggest shift they made was to move lending away from donation and charity, where lenders did not know to whom the money went and how it was used. It became lending to entrepreneurs who needed the money across the world, with expected returns. So from donation and charity, which created inequality between lenders and borrowers, it became lending and financing with repayments, creating an equal business platform. Lending went from being a black box to a white box, when Kiva established a direct connect between individual lenders and borrowers. Being able to connect directly with entrepreneurs became the tipping point that emotionally enrolled funders. What tipped the lender was that he/she was lending to support a human being, in fact enabling a human endeavour to succeed. And it was further de-risked; it was a loan that would be paid back. It was a true win-win.[24]

Tipping into the Purpose: SMS for Life

Jim Barrington had personally connected to the plight of African children stricken by malaria when he had heard Silvio Gabriel speak about the lives lost due to the stock-out of anti-malaria drugs. In 2008, he had an opportunity to rally a larger team of like-minded people when Silvio spoke again at an IMD/Novartis executive development programme. As Cathy Hein, one of the voluteers for the project says, 'A personal belief in the impact we could make as a whole to save lives was more than enough motivation to be persistent in overcoming all hurdles. It was particularly rewarding to know we were contributing to the fight against malaria.'

But it was not enough to rally people within the organization. Once Novartis came up with the orbit-shifting idea—'to create a tracking and reporting system via the mobile phone for stock-outs of Coartem and redistribution of the drug for greater availability'—it had to rally a whole consortium of partners to bring the project to reality. The final solution for Tanzania was built along with IBM, Vodafone, and MatsSoft.

What inspires this large coalition of partners to work together rather seamlessly on a complex project? Jim Barrington comments on their motivations. 'The most important was to establish the emotional connection with what we were trying to achieve. All the people at MatsSoft, Vodafone, and IBM, they knew about malaria, and they are involved in a project that is directly contributing to saving people's lives. That's what drives us and keeps us all together.'

In fact, when this new reality of malaria and the impact of their solution on saving children's lives was shared, it resulted in each organization easing the path to success by letting go of the usual legalese and protection of self-interests. What is usually a careful, slow-moving partnership tied up in contracts, ended up flowing forward with a great degree of alignment. Novartis had succeeded in tipping its partners to co-own the project with as much passion as its own people.

As Jim says, 'The collaboration with them has been absolutely excellent; we managed to establish a team without a need for a contract, without the need for a budget, without any need for a formalized memorandum of understanding or agreements. The goodwill coming from those companies was amazing. And there are external partners that collaborated, for example British Airways gave substantial discount on our air travel, which was a major cost on our project.'[6]

Tip the Heart First; the Mind will Follow

Lt General Ray's principle in tipping the people of Ladakh from suspicion to trust was this: tip the heart first and the mind will follow.

Lt General Ray was confronted with an unsettling question when he took charge of the Indian army in the Ladakh region (a remote region in the Himalayas, bordering Tibet).

In the year 2000, symptoms of a grave problem were visible all around. There was much disillusionment in the local populace. A cold and unfriendly terrain, coupled with apathy from successive governments, had succeeded in alienating the people. The strong presence of the army seemed to reinforce the feeling of threat. And the proximity to Jammu and Kashmir only served to destabilize an already tense atmosphere. As Lt General Ray says, 'There was a lot of talk of azadi (freedom). Communal divisions were openly visible. Buddhist lamas and tourists were shot. Weapons were seized.'

Lt General Ray's challenge was *'to prevent terrorism from coming into*

Ladakh', to ensure that the wave of terrorism sweeping through Jammu and Kashmir did not also engulf Ladakh.

He realized that in order to prevent terrorists from creeping into Ladakh and to bring lasting peace to the region he had to transform the state of mind of the people from 'feeling alienated' *to* 'feeling secure'. And this could only happen through mutual cooperation. Their current sense of insecurity came from terrorism, the forceful attitude of the army and the district administrators. He now had to win over the trust of the people. As he says, 'To build trust, win over the heart first, the mind will follow.' To win over the hearts of the people of Ladakh, he made a conscious attempt to recognize and then proactively address the threats they perceived to their livelihoods. It went beyond the defined role of the Indian army, but it was vital to the purpose of peace.

Operation Sadhbhavana (harmony) that he started went from being a mere public relations exercise to a genuine initiative to connect with and enroll the population.

He set out to win over the trust of the people and to transform the role of the army 'from an agent of war to an instrument of peace'. To do this, he engaged the people and the army in powerful tipping experiences.

Lt General Ray started to recognize the genuine grievances of the locals and taking concrete steps to alleviate them. In TurTok, a cluster of five villages in the Siachen region, the grievances was especially acute. Twenty-two people had been arrested and had been languishing in prison for one year following the Kargil war, as a large cache of arms had been found there. Most of them had large families. Lt General Ray realized that every man in prison meant nine other family members were suffering; their livelihood was directly threatened. He recognized that the army had forcefully occupied a large part of their land, without compensation. The people could no longer farm this land and this forced them further into poverty.

He put into place a three-step initiative to alleviate the pain of TurTok. As a first step, he got the army to vacate the land so the villagers could return it to cultivation. He further ensured that the district authorities updated and re-wrote the land records. Going further, he also took care of the families of the twenty-two prisoners by providing them rations, food, clothing, and kerosene. As a second step, he deployed a vehicle to take the families to the prison to enable the prisoners to meet their family members. As a third step, he influenced the authorities to release the imprisoned men who had never been charged for lack of evidence.

The first three steps tipped the hearts of the TurTok people, and he now went on to win their minds. He then ensured that the twenty-two prisoners were given jobs as porters and carpenters, and grants to start a business when released.

Another tipping initiative was at a girls' school in Padam Valley. Lt General Ray discovered that 220 girls were due to take their class X board exam within a month, and they had no teachers. He persuaded the authorities to postpone the board exam by a month and deployed personnel from the Army Education Corps to take classes. As a result, most of the girls did well in the exam.

In another confidence-building initiative, Lt General Ray ensured that the local population was protected from the pressure of the Bakarwals, sheep grazers who come into the valley from across the mountain passes. As Lt General Ray said, 'The trouble was that they would misbehave with the locals—to the extent of beating them and taking away their sheep. They were also mixed up with militancy. The last time they had come, they stole a horse and raped a girl.'

Recognizing this pain, the general intervened and got the army to *block all passes*. It had a political fallout, with influential people calling for a reopening of the passes, but no amount of political pressure could get the Lt General to change his action. *He was acting for the people.* This action further tipped a number of locals.

All these initiatives inspired confidence. The flow of information from the local population to the army increased; they started to give warnings of terrorist movements, something that had not happened during the Kargil war. Such was their expression of confidence that the local Muslims invited Lt General Ray to address them at the mosque during Friday prayers.[23]

As an Innovation Leader, think about this:

An army and the locals are often at odds; suspicion of authority, draconian practices, heavy-handed policing, and a disruption of life naturally puts them on either side of the fence. Most armies believe, 'this is the way it is—collateral damage'. Or put in superficial measures to win 'hearts and minds'. Lt General Ray actually put the principle into action. Imagine how many families reached a positive tipping poing with Lt General Ray and their confidence in the Indian army surged.

The silo battlefield inside an organization is often as adversarial as the environment Lt General Ray experienced. Functions can evolve into and act like semi independent fiefdoms. Making an organization orbit-shift happen will need these divides to be bridged.

It doesn't take a process, but two to three powerful tipping experiences to transform an intensively adversarial equation into a cooperative one.

What could be your version of Operation Sadhbhavana? What could then be the two to three powerful tipping experiences that can bridge the divide and rally adversarial silos into co-ownership?

The Romance of the Vision versus the Realism in the Execution

What is different about orbit-shifters is that their mental model is one of *romanticism in vision and realism in execution.* Most settlers are the reverse: *They are realistic about the vision and romantic about execution.* When faced with taking on a challenge, the orbit-shifter is romantic about it—he takes on the biggest possible challenge—like eliminating malnutrition, developing a Space food, or becoming number one on day one. Settlers on the other hand, are quite realistic about the vision—*eliminating malnutrition? Stupid and impossible; that cannot be done by individuals, only governments, and certainly not in one lifetime. It is far better to take something more reasonable, more within reach like growing by 10 percent or like expanding a product line—something more practical and into doable, and something respectable, where the world won't laugh at us if it doesn't happen, and we won't lose face.* However, *when it comes to execution, the orbit-shifters turn realistic: They anticipate the uncertainty, the problems/ obstacles that will emerge during the course of the action. They don't see a rosy path ahead. They predict the path will be a tough and difficult one. And hence, when the problems do rise, they are not surprised or let down or disappointed, as they are prepared for them.* They face them head-on, handle them, and move on. Settlers on the other hand, are romantic about the execution: If they have come up with a great new idea, they believe the greatest effort has been done in just coming up with that idea. They now believe that execution should be easy and justified. After all, 'if I've seen the validity of the beauty of the idea, won't the rest of the world?' Or, 'if I've cracked the problem, it's done; there are no further issues that will crop up'. And since they are caught in the clouds of the idea, and are not anticipating problems/issues, they get very disillusioned and demotivated as problems in execution start coming up. Sure enough, each new problem takes a little bit more away from them and they give up. Their romance of execution does them in.

A CEO who successfully transformed an organization was at crossroads when he was originally offered the job. He brings alive the romanticism-realism principle when he reflects, 'I had a great position as chief strategy officer, a plush office, and a cushy job. No one could understand why I would want to give it all up and choose to be CEO of a business that had been in the red for five years, everyone tried to dissuade me.' The settlers could see no romance in the vision, only realism. But this CEO only saw the challenge of turning around the impossible. He knew the execution would be difficult; he was not romantic about it. In fact, he says, 'See these grey hairs on my head. They come from the two years in turning this business around. The story may unfold smoothly and easily, in hindsight, but while living it forward, I had a lot of sleepless nights!'

As a CEO, think about this:

This is what differentiates orbit-shifters. The realism in execution, the realism about the great odds that must be overcome to actually make the innovation come alive in all the authenticity and the grandeur it was originally dreamed up in, without compromise—to bring Snow White alive as Snow White and not as a Pig.

Think about all the orbit-shift mountains you could have climbed or started to climb but gave up.

Where did the romance of execution do you in?

How can you bring back realism into execution and ascend your current orbit-shift mountain?

ATTITUDE TOWARDS EXECUTION OBSTACLES: NOT COMPROMISING, BUT COMBATING DILUTION

Not If Then, but How and How Else?

Orbit-shifters don't start climbing an orbit-shift mountain with an *if-then* state of mind, but a *how and how else* mindset. Faced with an obstacle, their response is never: 'If we can find a solution to the problem, only then will we pursue our challenge'. It is always: 'How can we overcome the obstacle, how and how else can the problem be solved?' Faced with a decision which is outside their sphere of control, the response is never: 'If only we had the authority, we would have done it.' The response is always: 'What can we do that is within our control here? How else can we influence a decision here?' *An 'if-then' ends up compromising the innovation, whereas orbit-shifters combat dilution and move ahead with 'how and how else'.*

As Todd Skinner said, 'You cannot lower the mountain so you must raise yourself. The mountain remains unalterable. You cannot decrease its size or adjust its geology. You can't turn back the storms or add substance to thin air. The only thing malleable in this equation is your resolve. Your perception of the challenge can be shifted from uncertainty to resolution and from apprehension to action. Always adjust the mind to what is possible, do not adjust what is possible to the mind'.[22]

Orbit-shifters recognize that obstacles can come in various forms: in the proposition itself failing in the market, in resistance from stakeholders, in sceptics who *wait and watch* for failure and in the unexpected problems that crop up along the journey of making the orbit-shift a reality. Rather than dilute or give up or say 'it's not my job', they relentlessly ask '*how and how else* can we move towards the top of the mountain?' They convert problems to opportunities and often the original idea grows far bigger than the starting promise.

Orbit-shifters don't compromise; they combat dilution at every step.

Carsten refused to allow dilution to settle in even when confronted with the *Columbia* disaster, which resulted in the Space shuttle programme coming to a halt. A settler might have first felt frustrated, then helpless, and would have finally ended up resigning himself to a wait-and-watch mode. In a wait-and-watch mode, the team could have slipped into an *if then* state of mind: 'If only this hadn't happened...if they don't start in two years then...' In this state the team's energy could have dissipated, and the lost momentum would have made a restart even tougher. Instead, Carsten moved the team into the *how and how else* state of mind and asked first, how the team could adapt to the disaster and even better, how could it be converted into an opportunity. They found the opportunity and managed to send yoghurt into Space on a Russian spacecraft. Now Arla was even better prepared for the next NASA Space shuttle launch.

Not the First but the Best

This *do not compromise, combat dilution* attitude came to the fore in the hunt for the film *Lagaan*'s primary location. In making the iconic film of the last decade, *Lagaan*, the first key decision was the choice of the village location, Champaner, where the story was set and where the unusual cricket match was to be played between the ruling British forces and the villagers, to reverse a proposal for a local tax. The village needed to depict the 1890s' era in true form—no visible communication media, no technology, and no signs whatsoever of modernity. In addition, it had to depict, environmental requirements like parched earth with a lack of rains.

The team stumbled on a perfect location almost immediately: Kanuria village in Kutch. *'I've found the perfect location for Champaner,'* Ashutosh, the director, triumphantly informed Aamir Khan, the star and producer of the film. *'Both Nitin* (the art director) *and I think Kutch is ideal.'* Aamir was concerned that Ashutosh was satisfied so easily, and he pushed them to go out and search more. His *how and how else* state of mind was switched on. He didn't want to live in the hope that Champaner was the best (the *if-then* state). He wanted to be sure that indeed it was. Aamir said, 'Ashutosh, I have nothing against Kutch and it may well turn out to be the perfect location, but do look at other places as well, they may turn out to be more exciting.'

So Ashutosh and Nitin continued the search. Six months later, after having searched through the villages of many parts of rural India, they returned to Kanuria because it was still the best. The difference: they were now certain it was the best, unlike the previous occasion where it was merely the first.[1]

As an Innovation Leader, think about this:

Traditionalists stop with the first seemingly workable solution. Orbit-shifters don't stop at the first; they keep searching till they are sure they have the biggest and the best solution.

How often in the past have you, like Aamir Khan, combated dilution and inspired and pushed your team to go beyond the first working solution to find the bigger and better solution?

Settle for the Same, or Unique Software?

Vodafone had set about the task of creating a *financial access* solution for Kenya, however, they were not sure how they were going to do it. And since they were attempting a first-to-the-world solution without precedence, there were many decision-making points that could have easily lead to compromise. However, at every stage, they combatted dilution. For example, they could very easily have brought in banking software that works for the West, tweaked it a bit and operated it in Kenya. However they chose to build a new solution. As Susie Lonie says,'We had a fair idea of what we wanted the service to do, but we were not sure how to do it. The first big decision was buy or build? If we could buy software off the shelf to meet our needs it would make sense to buy. So we went shopping and found a multitude of financial service platforms with a fairly similar range of functionality. Therein lay the problem: They had all been designed with western banking infrastructure as the point of reference, and then added on other features. It became clear that we would have to make some significant compromises around the functionality and user experience if we bought one of the proprietary products. We reluctantly decided that we would have to bite the bullet and build our own service from scratch.' Reluctant they might have been, but they did not allow this reluctance to dilute the orbit-shifting purpose.[6]

Myths of Bureaucracy

S.R. Rao created escape velocity when he took on the challenge of transforming a plague-ridden city, Surat. He came up with a breakthrough strategy. But to execute the strategy he had to mobilize an army of bureaucrats to move out of their comfort zones.

He realized that no matter how powerful his strategy, it would come to nought if it was executed with the old bureaucratic mindset of trained helplessness. As S.R. Rao says, 'There are five myths under which bureaucrats hide their incompetence:

1. **Existing rules, regulations, hierarchical systems are outmoded.**
2. **We have insufficient finances and therefore cannot implement anything effectively.**
3. **We have insufficient and unskilled manpower.**
4. **Political and administrative interference constantly inhibits our effectiveness.**
5. **There is insufficient delegation of power. Therefore, we have little authority.**

Faced with these five seemingly 'paralyzing limitations', most traditional managers would have immediately taken refuge in the *if-then* mindset: 'If I have authority, then I can do it'; 'If I have the necessary financial and people resources, then I can try it'; 'If you can assure me of no political and administrative interference, then I can give it a good try'. This is the settler attitude that freezes action, leading to dilution.

The orbit-shifter in S.R. Rao emerged when he publicly listed these statements and called them 'myths and not realities'. He was in effect saying, '*You will never hear me excuse inaction on my part by citing one of these reasons.*'

S.R. Rao found 'freedom within the framework'. Where other bureaucrats see themselves as being powerless and helpless, he focused on finding creative ways to leverage what lay within his authority.[14]

As a CEO, think about this:

S.R. Rao recognized and courageously acknowledged the paralysing powerlessness that could block the orbit-shift of Surat. He did not compromise. To execute the orbit-shift, S.R. Rao starting by tackling his own assumption, attacked and broke through deeply entrenched cultural mindsets—mindsets that reduce government and bureaucracy to a paralysing helplessness.

Most organizations, quite like this municipality in Surat, exhibit some level of trained helplessness when it comes to executing an orbit-shift. 'The corporate doesn't allow us'; 'regulation is limiting us'; 'the dealers are too set in their ways; 'the consumers are like this only'.

Can you and your leadership team bust this powerlessness myth the way S.R. Rao did, and actually exhibit freedom within the framework?

Are you compromising or are you combating dilution?

What are you going to do to transform deeply entrenched mindsets that reinforce and even encourage the trained powerlessness that will dilute an orbit-shift?

It is often easy to look up to these orbit-shifting icons in awe and wonder. At their uniqueness and their exceptional impact. Like stars, twinkling, inspirational and yet remote—they can only be messiahs we wait for. It is unimaginable for us to be one of them. However, in all these orbit-shift stories, what has emerged most significantly and powerfully is that orbit-shifters are ordinary people like you and me, but with extraordinary mindsets. If we pass by a Sivakumar or a Victoria Hale or a Scott O'Neil or a Fazle Abed at an airport, it is unlikely we will recognize the orbit-shifter in our midst, they are just one of us. But this gives us hope, for it is someone like us who did it. And surely, if they can do it, so can we.

What starts an orbit-shift journey is a state of positive restlessness, when living with the status quo is simply unacceptable; the scale of the impossible challenge is not frightening; all the orbit-shifter knows is that *it must be done.* Some challenges like M-PESA or the NovoPen® are achieved in a few years. Other orbit-shifters, like Abed, Scott O'Neill, Rosa, and Sivakumar are pursuing their challenges for years—forty years, twenty years, seventeen

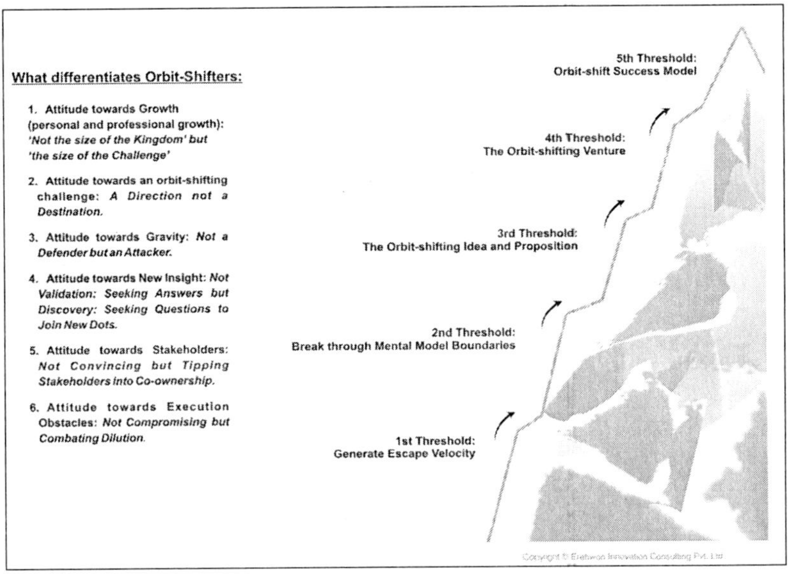

10.2 – Orbit-shifters Create History!

years, or twelve, and still it continues. In fact, Sivakumar is now pursuing e-Choupal 3.0 or the third generation of the e-Choupal idea.

An orbit-shifter is born when the switch flips in an ordinary mind either because of a moment-of-truth experience or because of a mind-jolting insight. Age 25, age 40 or age 60. And there is no going back.

Age, location, authority, and time are not barriers to orbit-shifting innovation. The time has come to stop using these escape buttons and focus on climbing your orbit-shift mountain.

The Food Doctor, headed by Michael da Costa, is now looking to expand from the UK into India.[5] He was *triggered by some of these orbit-shifter mindsets to the extent that it has* transformed his entire approach to the India market. From just partnering with a traditional Indian player or an

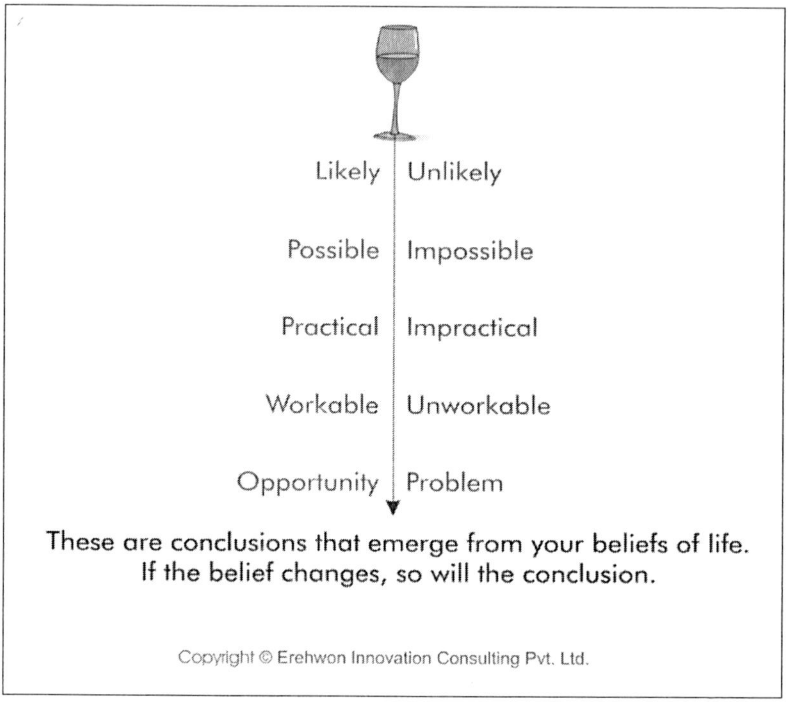

10.3 – Beliefs about Orbits and Orbit-shifting

MNC to launch products in India, Michael has resolved to take on an orbit shifting challenge: *eliminating malnutrition in India.*

Michael is at the start of an orbit-shift journey in India and what plays out in conversation with him is the mindset of an orbit-shifter at the base of the orbit-shift mountain, looking up towards the peak with absolute enthusiasm its uncertainties, ambiguities, and yet ready to scale with all excitement and determination. In July 2012, Michael da Costa first spoke of his orbit-shifting aspiration: 'One of the biggest challenges that India has is the health of the general population. In fact, it is the world's number one in cardiac and diabetic diseases. The massive task at hand right now for us to do is to bring a big health-care business on board to launch The Food Doctor products in India. Essentially, we want to eliminate malnutrition in India.'

Michael realizes that he cannot be romantic about the execution of his orbit-shift, that it will be tough. He sees it as a direction, not a destination: 'Going through a bureaucratic process is going to be quite frustrating and I know it is going to move slowly. I am not underestimating the difficulty or the effort will need. It is going to take time. May take more than three to four years. But to change something fundamental, to bring on a colossal change, it is going to take time and I am in no hurry in doing it. For me, it is more of a cause, rather than a goal.'

Michael has an attacker mindset, where he is not intimidated, but excited to begin this journey. 'It doesn't keep me awake at night, but it does remind how much I need to get done, when I get up in the morning.' And finally, he agrees to be part of this book, as the most public way in which to burn the bridge. 'We would be delighted to be a part of the book; it would be a good way to start. Which means, by the time the book is published, we'll need to get started and we ought to get considerable momentum.'

And so here it is, The Food Doctor is being mentioned in this book, his escape buttons are irrevocably removed, as his challenge and commitment to the cause of eliminating malnutrition in India is out in the open, before every reader. What's exciting about the Food Doctor is that it is an orbit-shift journey in the making. The team stands at the base; looking up with hope and restlessness to the top of the mountain, ready to scale it.

Whether in fiction or reality, the most enduring stories, the ones that excite us the most are the ones of orbit-shifters, where ordinary people achieve the extraordinary. Where they create, rather than follow, history. Where they show us that there are no impossible dreams or problems; only limited dreamers and problem solvers.

So what is your orbit-shifting story going to be?

References

CHAPTER 1

1. Bannister, D. (2012) M-Pesa move into savings and loans underpinned by Temenos. *Banking Technology*, [online] 29 November 2012. Available at: http://www.bankingtech.com/51858/m-pesa-move-into-savings-and-loans-underpinned-by-temenos/ [Accessed: 4 April 2013].
2. Batey, I. (2001) *Asian Branding A Great Way To Fly*. Singapore: Prentice Hall, p.118-119.
3. Bornstein, D. (2007) *How to Change the World: Social Entrepreneurs and the Power of New Ideas*. New York: Oxford University Press, p. 52-76.
4. Bornstein, D. (2003) *Fabio Rosa: Making the Sun Shine For All*. [online] Available at: http://proxied.changemakers.net/journal/03may/bornstein.cfm [Accessed: 4 April 2013].
5. Collins, G. (2011) How over-regulation has stifled the pace of mobile money adoption in Africa. *Memeburn*, [online] 9 June 2011. Available at: http://memeburn.com/2011/09/how-over-regulation-has-stifled-the-pace-of-mobile-money-adoption-in-africa/ [Accessed: 4 April 2013].
6. Enable Network (2012) *Self Help Groups in India: A study on quality and sustainability*. [report] Hyderabad, India: ENABLE , p.5.
7. Globalhealth.mit.edu (2010) *VisionSpring, Vision entrepreneurs – Global health at MIT*. [online] Available at: http://globalhealth.mit.edu/visionspring/ [Accessed: 21 May 2013].

8. Governance Knowledge Centre, Department of Administrative Reforms and Public Grievances, India (n.p.) *Kudumbashree – An Innovative Poverty Reduction Strategy*. [report].
9. Grameen Bank (2006) *Grameen Bank | Bank for the poor – Introduction*. [online] Available at: http://www.grameen-info.org/index.php?option=com_content&task=view&id=16&Itemid=112 [Accessed: 4 April 2013].
10. IBGE, Brazil (2009) *Pesquisa Nacional por Amostra de Domicilos – Sintese de Indicadores 2009*. [report] Brazil: Instittuto Braseleiro de Geografia e Estatistica - IBGE, p.265,266.
11. Kamath, G. (2009) *Tata Chemicals greens the land*. [online] Available at: http://www.tata.com/media/articles/inside.aspx?artid=zN7LvBEzHTY [Accessed: 4 April 2013].
12. Koutonin, M. (2012) Will Nigeria Mobile Money Project beat Kenya M-PESA?. *Silicon Africa*, [online] 4 September 2012. Available at: http://www.siliconafrica.com/will-nigerias-mobile-money-project-beats-kenyas-m-pesa/ [Accessed: 4 April 2013].
13. KPMG (2007) *Mobile payments in Asia Pacific*. [report] Hong Kong: p. 22.
14. Kudumbashree.org (1998) *At A Glance | Kudumbashree*. [online] Available at: http://www.kudumbashree.org/?q=ataglance [Accessed: 4 Apr 2013].
15. Luscombe, B. (2012) Tracking Disease, One Text at a Time. *Time*, [online] 5 August 2012. Available at: http://healthland.time.com/2012/08/15/disease-cant-hide/ [Accessed: 4 April 2013].
16. Man Made Marvels – The World's Highest Railway (2006) [DVD] Discovery Channel, Discovery Communications.
17. Microsoft.com (2008) *Iconic Albuquerque Photo Re-Created*. [online] Available at: http://www.microsoft.com/en-us/news/features/2008/jun08/06-25iconic.aspx [Accessed: 9 May 2013].
18. Munshi, P. (2009) *Making Breakthrough Innovation Happen: How 11 Indians Pulled Off The Impossible*. New Delhi: Harper Collins India, p.116 - 138.
19. Munshi, P. (2009) *Making Breakthrough Innovation Happen: How 11 Indians Pulled Off The Impossible*. New Delhi: Harper Collins India, p.192 - 198.
20. Munshi, P. (2009) *Making Breakthrough Innovation Happen: How 11 Indians Pulled Off The Impossible*. Noida: Harper Collins India, p.34 - 52.
21. Nippon-foundation.or.jp (2012) *Outline of the Nippon Foundation's Traditional Medicine Projects | The Nippon Foundation*. [online] Available

at: http://www.nippon-foundation.or.jp/en/what/projects/traditional_medicine/index.html [Accessed: 3 April 2013].

22. OneWorld Health (n.d.) *About Us.* [online] Available at: http://www.oneworldhealth.org/about-us [Accessed: 9 May 2013].
23. S. Gottlieb, R. (2013) *Liberating Faith: Religious Voices for Justice, Peace, and Ecological Wisdom.* Rowman and Littlefield, p.88.
24. Sadagopan, S. (2009) 400 million phone subscribers by February 2009 and 15.26 million new subscribers in just a single month of January 2009. *Times of India*, 30 March 2009.
25. Smart Communications (2011) *Smart Load – Smart Communications.* [online] Available at: http://www1.smart.com.ph/About/meet/innovations-and-awards/smart-load [Accessed: 4 April 2013].
26. Sood, S. (2013) The Great Indian Healthcare Factories ?II: Aravind Eye Care System-In service for sight. *Express Healthcare*, 7 February 2013.
27. Squad Digital (2012) *Celebrating Five Years of MPesa.* [online] Available at: https://squaddigital.com/beta/safaricom/facebook/saftimelineiframe/pdf/infograph.pdf [Accessed: 4 Apr 2013].
28. Telecom Regulatory Authority of India (TRAI) (2005) *Study Paper on 'Indicators for Telecom Growth'*. [online] Available at: http://www.trai.gov.in/trai/upload/studypapers/2/ir30june.pdf [Accessed: 4 April 2013].
29. Telecom Regulatory Authority of India (TRAI) (2012) *Highlights on Telecom Subscription Data as on 31st August 2012.* [online] Available at: http://www.trai.gov.in/WriteReadData/WhatsNew/Documents/PR-TSD-Aug2012.pdf [Accessed: 4 April 2013].
30. Unknown. (2003) Cellular users talk longer, but average revenue dips. *Hindu – Business Line*, [online] 2 December 2003. Available at: http://www.thehindubusinessline.in/2003/12/03/stories/2003120301730700.htm [Accessed: 9 May 2013].
31. Vestergaard Frandsen (n.d.) *Vestergaard Frandsen: LifeStraw® – Features.* [online] Available at: http://www.vestergaard-frandsen.com/lifestraw/lifestraw/features [Accessed: 4 April 2013].
32. VisionSpring (1996) *VisionSpring At A Glance.* [online] Available at: http://web.archive.org/web/20130203041201/http://www.visionspring.org/about/at-a-glance.php [Accessed: 4 April 2013].
33. World Health Organization (WHO) (2007) *Report of the WHO Interregional Workshop on the Use of Traditional Medicine in Primary Health Care.* [report] Ulaanbaatar, Mongolia: World Health Organization (WHO).

CHAPTER 2

1. Batey, I. (2001) *Asian Branding A Great Way To Fly*. Prentice Hall.
2. Broad, W. (2012) Miles Under the Pacific, a Director Will Take On His Riskiest Project. *The New York Times*, 8 March 2012.
3. Business Week (2006) *The Enemies of Innovation*. [image online] Available at: http://www.businessweek.com/stories/2006-04-23/chart-the-enemies-of-innovation [Accessed: 5 April 2013].
4. Diamond, J. (2005) *Collapse: How Societies Choose to Fail or Survive*. Penguin Books.
5. FNV Mondial (2010) *Let Parents Earn and Children Learn*. [report] Amsterdam: FNV Repro, p.15.
6. India.hivos.org (2012) *Stop Child Labour campaign_Omar's Dream | Hivos India*. [online] Available at: http://india.hivos.org/activity/stop-child-labour-campaignomars-dream [Accessed: 4 April 2013].
7. Iverson, J. (2010) Kiwi Cuvée: The Next Generation of French Wines. *Time*.
8. Jackson, D. (2007) French Wine Exports in Decline. *Creme de la creme*, [online] January 2007. Available at: http://www.oneworldpublications.com/french_wine_exports_decline.html [Accessed: 5 April 2013].
9. Khanna, T. and Song, J., et al. (2011) The Paradox of Samsung's Rise. *Harvard Business Review*.
10. Maltin, L. (1987) *Of Mice and Magic: A History of American Animated Cartoons*. 2nd ed. New American Library, p. 57.
11. Munshi, P. (2009) *Making Breakthrough Innovation Happen: How 11 Indians Pulled Off The Impossible*. Noida: Harper Collins India, p. 17, 28.
12. Munshi, P. (2009) *Making Breakthrough Innovation Happen: How 11 Indians Pulled Off The Impossible*. Noida: Harper Collins India, p.75-97.
13. Munshi, P. (2009) *Making Breakthrough Innovation Happen: How 11 Indians Pulled Off the Impossible*. Noida: Harper Collins India, p. 153-165.
14. Prahalad, C. (2006) *The Fortune At The Bottom Of The Pyramid*. Pearson Prentice Hall.
15. Samsungvillage.com (2011) *From Clamshells to Touchscreens – The Evolution of Our 10-Million Sellers - Samsung Blog - Samsung Village*. [online] Available at: http://www.samsungvillage.com/blog/2011/03/from-clamshells-to-touchscreens-the-evolution-of-our-10-million-sellers.html [Accessed: 5 April 2013].

16. Taber, G. (1976) Modern Living: Judgment of Paris. *Time*.
17. Thomas, B. (1994) *Walt Disney: An American Original*. Disney Editions.
18. Tong-Hyung, K. (2009) Sony Vows Comeback Against Samsung, LG. *The Korea Times*, [online] 7 September 2009. Available at: http://koreatimes.co.kr/www/news/nation/2009/09/123_51434.html [Accessed: 10 May 2013].
19. Walt, V. (2013) MediaPart: Meet the Upstart Journalists shaking up French Politics. *Time*, 5 April 2013.

CHAPTER 3

1. Aiyar, S. (2008) Ratan's Revolution. *India Today*, 11 January 2008.
2. Al-Issawi, T. (2005) Qatar to use robots as camel riders. *USA Today*, [online] 19 April 2005. Available at: http://usatoday30.usatoday.com/tech/news/robotics/2005-04-19-qatar-camalbots_x.htm [Accessed: 21 May 2013].
3. Alternative Perspective (2008) *Alternative Perspective: Making a Difference: ...Not Just a Piece of Cloth*. [online] Available at: http://alternativeperspective.blogspot.in/2008/01/making-difference-not-just-piece-of.html [Accessed: 5 April 2013].
4. Bhushan, R. (1999) Burial Of The Phoenix – The precursor to Gandhi's Sabarmati Ashram lies in utter neglect. *Outlook India*, Iss. 6 December 1999.
5. Bornstein, D. (2007) *How to Change the World: Social Entrepreneurs and the Power of New Ideas*. New York: Oxford University Press, p. 52-55.
6. Boxofficemojo.com (n.d.) *Troy (2004) - Box Office Mojo*. [online] Available at: http://www.boxofficemojo.com/movies/?id=troy.htm [Accessed: 5 April 2013].
7. Boxofficemojo.com (n.d.) *300 (2007) - Box Office Mojo*. [online] Available at: http://www.boxofficemojo.com/movies/?id=300.htm [Accessed: 5 April 2013].
8. Boxofficemojo.com (2007) *Daily Box Office for Tuesday, June 19, 2007 - Box Office Mojo*. [online] Available at: http://boxofficemojo.com/daily/chart/?sortdate=2007-06-19&view=screens&p=.htm [Accessed: 21 May 2013].
9. Boyle, D. (2004) SpaceShipOne wins $10 million X Prize. *Nbcnews.com*, [online] 5 October 2004. Available at: http://www.nbcnews.com/id/6167761/ns/technology_and_science-space/t/spaceshipone-wins-

million-x-prize/#.UV6s9atNtMY [Accessed: 5 April 2013].

10. David, L. (2004) Set to Soar: First X Prize Flight This Week. *Space.com*, [online] 27 September 2004. Available at: http://www.space.com/373-set-soar-prize-flight-week.html [Accessed: 5 April 2013].
11. Eliminate Dengue Program (2012) *Eliminate Dengue – Our Challenge.* [video online] Available at: http://vimeo.com/49661153 [Accessed: 8 April 2013].
12. Fishman, C. Life Saving Textiles (online). Available at: http://www.fastcompany.com/magazine/113/open_31-vestergaardfrandsen.html. [Accessed: 30 August 2013].
13. Freedman, M. (2005) A Fine Mesh (online). Available at: www.forbes.com/global/2005. [Accessed: 30 August 2013].
14. Gatesfoundation.org (n.d.) *Fourteen Grand Challenges in Global Health Announced in $200 Million Initiative - Bill & Melinda Gates Foundation.* [online] Available at: http://www.gatesfoundation.org/Media-Center/Press-Releases/2003/10/14-Grand-Challenges-in-Global-Health [Accessed: 21 May 2013].
15. Grandchallenges.org (2010) *Read the Grand Challenges.* [online] Available at: http://www.grandchallenges.org/Pages/BrowseByGoal.aspx [Accessed: 8 April 2013].
16. Hempel, C. (2012) *Rare Disease Day 2012 – Spread This Call To Action To Make A Difference! | The Addi and Cassi Fund – Niemann Pick Type C.* [online] Available at: http://addiandcassi.com/rare-disease-day-2012-difference/ [Accessed: 21 May 2013].
17. History.nasa.gov (1961) *The Decision to Go to the Moon: President John F. Kennedy's May 25, 1961 Speech before Congress.* [online] Available at: http://history.nasa.gov/moondec.html [Accessed: 5 April 2013].
18. Hughes, N. and Lonie, S. (2007) M-PESA: Mobile Money for the "Unbanked" Turning Cellphones into 24-Hour Tellers in Kenya. *innovations*, 2 (Winter / Spring), p. 63-81. Available at: http://www.mitpressjournals.org/doi/abs/10.1162/itgg.2007.2.1-2.63 [Accessed: 8 April 2013].
19. Jetwings Domestic Magazine. Innovation: Racing with Robots (2013).
20. Jones, B. (2012) Auto Expo2012: Tata Nano is not a flop, just an opportunity wasted: Ratan Tata. *Economic Times*, [online] 6 January 2012. Available at: http://articles.economictimes.indiatimes.com/2012-01-06/news/30597924_1_problematic-supply-tata-nano-ratan-tata [Accessed: 8 April 2013].

21. Khaleej Times (2005) UAE enforces stringent steps to eradicate child jockeys. *Khaleej Times*, [online] 24 May 2005. Available at: http://www.khaleejtimes.com/DisplayArticle.asp?xfile=data/theuae/2005/May/theuae_May691.xml&section=theuae [Accessed: 21 May 2013].
22. Man Made Marvels – The World's Highest Railway (2006) [DVD] Discovery Channel, Discovery Communications.
23. Menshealth.com (n.d.) *300 Workout: The muscle building workout used by the cast of the movie | Men's Health.* [online] Available at: http://www.menshealth.com/fitness/muscle-building-11#ixzz2JZdzkzg6 [Accessed: 5 April 2013].
24. Miller, G. (n.d.) *HowStuffWorks "Introduction to Inside '300'"*. [online] Available at: http://entertainment.howstuffworks.com/inside-300.htm [Accessed: 5 April 2013].
25. Monash.edu.au (2003) *Elliminating dengue - Monash University.* [online] Available at: http://www.monash.edu.au/giving/news/eliminating-dengue.html [Accessed: 8 April 2013].
26. Munshi, P. (2009) *Making Breakthrough Innovation Happen: How 11 Indians Pulled Off The Impossible.* Noida: Harper Collins India, p.16-19.
27. Munshi, P. (2009) *Making Breakthrough Innovation Happen: How 11 Indians Pulled Off the Impossible.* Noida: Harper Collins India, p.99-104.
28. Munshi, P. (2009) *Making Breakthrough Innovation Happen: How 11 Indians Pulled Off The Impossible.* Noida: Harper Collins India, p.172-175.
29. Munshi, P. (2009) *Making Breakthrough Innovation Happen: How 11 Indians Pulled Off The Impossible.* Noida: Harper Collins India, p.32-35.
30. Munshi, P. (2009) *Making Breakthrough Innovation Happen: How 11 Indians Pulled Off The Impossible.* Noida: Harper Collins India, p.158-161.
31. Munshi, P. (2009) *Making Breakthrough Innovation Happen: How 11 Indians Pulled Off The Impossible.* Noida: Harper Collins India, p. 139-151.
32. Myehn Repair Foundation (online). Available at: www.myelinrepair.org. [Accessed: 30 January 2013].
33. Oren, T. and Shahaf, S. (2011) *Global Television Formats: Understanding Television Across Borders.* London: Routledge.
34. Pgscience.com (n.d.) *The "Secret" Behind SK-II - PG Science.* [online] Available at: http://www.pgscience.com/home/news/sake_brewery_skin_care_and_the_secret_behind_sk-ii.html [Accessed: 21 May 2013].
35. Rex, J. (2003) *The Novopen Story.* [report] Novo Nordisk A/S, p. 10-11.

36. Rodriguez, D. and Solomon, D. (2007) Leadership and Innovation in a Networked World. *innovations*, 2 (Summer), p.3-13. Available at: http://www.mitpressjournals.org/doi/abs/10.1162/itgg.2007.2.3.3?journalCode=itgg [Accessed: 8 April 2013].
37. Sensini, P. (2004) Ring Back Tune: A Window into the Personality. *VMA News: Newsletter for the International Association for Enhanced Voice Services*, [online] January 2004. Available at: http://www.thevma.com/Downloads/VMA_News_Jan2004.pdf [Accessed: 5 April 2013].
38. Space.com (1997) *SpaceShipOne Wins $10 Million Ansari X Prize in Historic 2nd Trip to Space.* [online] Available at: http://www.space.com/403-spaceshipone-wins-10-million-ansari-prize-historic-2nd-trip-space.html [Accessed: 8 April 2013].
39 Space.xprize.org (2004) *Ansari X PRIZE | X PRIZE Foundation.* [online] Available at: http://space.xprize.org/ansari-x-prize [Accessed: 5 April 2013].
40. Sridhar, V. and Katakam, A. (2003) The Reliance Splash. *Frontline*, Iss. Volume 20 - Issue 03, February 01-14, 2003.
41. The United Nations Children's Fund (UNICEF) (2006) *Starting Over – Children Return Home from Camel Racing.* [report] The United Nations Children's Fund (UNICEF).
42. Thefooddoctor.com (1999) *About Us | The Food Doctor.* [online] Available at: http://www.thefooddoctor.com/Our-Aim-Aabout/ [Accessed: 5 April 2013].
43. Tozzi, J. (2012) Speeding Up the Discovery of Drugs. *Bloomsberg Businessweek*, [online] 29 November 2012. Available at: http://www.businessweek.com/articles/2012-11-29/speeding-up-the-discovery-of-drugs#r=hpt-lst [Accessed: 5 April 2013].
45. Warrier, S. (2003) An Indian medicine for hepatitis B. *Rediff*, [online] 9 May 2003. Available at: http://www.rediff.com/news/2003/may/09shobha.htm [Accessed: 21 May 2013].
45. Wong, E. (2012) *James Cameron on Chinese Filmmakers, Censorship and Potential Co-Productions.* [online] Available at: http://mediadecoder.blogs.nytimes.com/2012/05/05/james-cameron-on-chinese-filmmakers-censorship-and-potential-co-productions/ [Accessed: 5 April 2013].

CHAPTER 4

1. Aulakh, G. (2012) Airtel, Idea, Vodafone, Tata Teleservices reducing freebies

and talktime to prop up margins. *Economic Times*, [online] 22 November 2012. Available at: http://articles.economictimes.indiatimes.com/2012-11-22/news/35300777_1_special-tariff-vouchers-tata-teleservices-discount-vouchers [Accessed: 15 May 2013].

2. Bajaj, V. (2011) Anant Pai, 81, Is Dead; Comics Told Indian Children Their Country's Stories. *New York Times*, 28 February 2011.
3. BBC (2009) Asian heart disease gene found. *BBC*, [online] 19 January 2009. Available at: http://news.bbc.co.uk/2/hi/health/7833753.stm [Accessed: 15 May 2013].
4. Billboard (2013) *'Harlem Shake': The Making And Monetizing Of The Latest YouTube Dance Craze.* [online] Available at: http://www.billboard.com/biz/articles/news/branding/1539260/harlem-shake-the-making-and-monetizing-of-the-latest-youtube [Accessed: 15 May 2013].
5. Blueoceanstrategy.com (1980) *Novo Nordisk | Blue Ocean Strategy.* [online] Available at: http://www.blueoceanstrategy.com/about/strategic-moves/novo-nordisk/ [Accessed: 9 April 2013].
6. Bornstein, D. (2003) Making the Sun Shine for All. [online] Available at: http://proxied.changemakers.net/journal/03may/bornstein.cfm [Accessed: 15 May 2013].
7. Canadian Community for Dialogue and Deliberation (2002) *Changing the World by Changing How We Talk and Listen.* [online] Available at: http://www.c2d2.ca/sites/default/files/Kahanepercent20onpercent20talkingpercent20andpercent20listening.pdf [Accessed: 15 May 2013].
8. Cunningham, M. (1995) Roy Thomas Baker & Gary Langan: The Making Of Queen's 'Bohemian Rhapsody'. *Sound on Sound*, Iss. October 1995.
9. Daily Mail (1997) *Guinness World Records British Hit Singles – top 100 singles.* [online] Available at: http://www.dailymail.co.uk/tvshowbiz/article-113669/Guinness-World-Records-British-Hit-Singles--100-singles.html [Accessed: 8 April 2013].
10. Delaney, K. (2007) YouTube to Test Software To Ease Licensing Fights. *The Wall Street Journal*, [online] June 12 2007. Available at: http://online.wsj.com/article/SB118161295626932114.html?cb=logged0.18113672314211726 [Accessed: 15 May 2013].
11. Ekal.org (n.d.) *Ekal Vidyalaya Foundation.* [online] Available at: http://www.ekal.org [Accessed: 9 April 2013].
12. Esposito, M. and Kapoor, A., et al. (2013) Enabling healthcare services for

the rural and semi-urban segments in India: when shared value meets the bottom of the pyramid. *Corporate Governance*, 12 (4), p.514-533. Available at: http://dx.doi.org/10.1108/14720701211267847 [Accessed: 15 May 2013].

13. GE Healthcare (n.d.) *GE Mac 400 - Brochure.* [e-book] Freiburg, Germany: GE Healthcare. p.2 . Available through: http://www.mednet-healthcare.net/ http://www.mednet-healthcare.net/Support/downlaods/MAC_400_bro_e.pdf [Accessed: 15 May 2013].
14. Geller, R. (2011) Shake-up time for Japanese seismology. *Nature*, 472 (7344), p. 407-409. Available at: http://www.nature.com/nature/journal/v472/n7344/full/nature10105.html [Accessed: 8 April 2013].
15. Global Alliance of Community Forests (2011) *Nepal's community forest makes it to the top 12 list of BBC World Challenge 2011.* [online] Available at: http://www.gacfonline.com/2011/11/nepalpercentE2percent80percent99s-community-forest-makes-it-to-the-top-12-list-of-bbc-world-challenge-2011/ [Accessed: 15 May 2013].
16. Gracyk, T. (2007). *Listening to popular music, or, How I learned to stop worrying and love Led Zeppelin.* Ann Arbor, University of Michigan Press.
17. Holpuch, A. (2013) Harlem Shake: Baauer cashes in on viral video's massive YouTube success. *Guardian*, [online] 19 February 2013. Available at: http://www.guardian.co.uk/technology/2013/feb/19/harlem-shake-baauer-youtube-success [Accessed: 15 May 2013].
18. IMDb (1983) *Star Wars: Episode VI – Return of the Jedi (1983).* [online] Available at: http://www.imdb.com/title/tt0086190/ [Accessed: 15 May 2013].
19. IMDb (1999) *Star Wars: Episode I – The Phantom Menace (1999).* [online] Available at: http://www.imdb.com/title/tt0120915/ [Accessed: 15 May 2013].
20. Kahane, A (2004). Solving Tough Problems – An Open Way of Talking, Listening and Creating New Realities. Berrett-Kochler Publishers Inc.
21. Kiva (2005) *Kiva | Loans that change lives.* [online] Available at: http://www.kiva.org/gifts/kiva-cards/terms [Accessed: 9 April 2013].
22. Kiva (2005) *Kiva - About Us.* [online] Available at: http://www.kiva.org/about [Accessed: 9 April 2013].
23. KPMG (2007) *Mobile payments in Asia Pacific.* [report] Hong Kong: KPMG, p. 22.
24. Krueger, M. (2011) Four Reasons M-Pesa Succeeded in Kenya. *Mobile Money Exchange*, [blog] 9 May 2011, Available at: http://mobilemoneyexchange.

wordpress.com/2011/05/09/four-reasons-m-pesa-succeeded-in-kenya/ [Accessed: 9 April 2013].

25. Luckerson, V. (2013) How Your Harlem Shake Videos Make Money for the Original Artist. *Time*, [online] 21 February 2013. Available at: http://business.time.com/2013/02/21/how-your-harlem-shake-videos-makes-money-for-the-original-artist/ [Accessed: 15 May 2013].
26. Maher, M. (2013) *Harlem Shake Your Way to a Gangnam Style Pay Day.* [online] Available at: http://globalstrategygroup.com/2013/02/harlem-shake-your-way-to-a-gangnam-style-pay-day/ [Accessed: 15 May 2013].
27. Michael Smith Foundation (2011) *Knowledge Translation Stories #4 - Dr. Stanley Zlotkin.* [video online] Available at: http://www.youtube.com/watch?v=58DR3wp2DYE [Accessed: 9 April 2013].
28. Michigan Ross School of Business (2012) *Business Model Innovation at TutorVista: Personalization and Global Resource Leverage.* [report].
29. Munshi, P. (2009) *Making Breakthrough Innovation Happen: How 11 Indians Pulled Off The Impossible.* Noida: Harper Collins India, p. 81-97.
30. Munshi, P. (2009) *Making Breakthrough Innovation Happen: How 11 Indians Pulled Off The Impossible.* Noida: Harper Collins India, p. 116-138.
31. Nippon Foundation (2012) *Outline of the Nippon Foundation's Traditional Medicine Projects | The Nippon Foundation.* [online] Available at: http://www.nippon-foundation.or.jp/en/what/projects/traditional_medicine/ [Accessed: 15 May 2013].
32. OneworldHealth.org (online). Available at: www.oneworldhealth.org/about-us/ [Accessed on: 30 August 2013].
33. Pasricha, S. and Drakesmith, H., et al. (2013) Control of iron deficiency anemia in low- and middle-income countries. *Blood*, 121 (14), p. 2607-2617.
34. Patients Beyond Borders (1999) *Medical Tourism Statistics & Facts | Patients Beyond Borders.* [online] Available at: http://www.patientsbeyondborders.com/medical-tourism-statistics-facts [Accessed: 9 April 2013].
35. Planetread.org (2007) *Same Language Subtitling (SLS) Project: Some Key Research Findings.* [online] Available at: http://www.planetread.org/pdf/Researchpercent20Summary_SLS.pdf [Accessed: 9 April 2013].
36. Planetread.org (2009) *Clinton Global Initiative: 'Same Language Subtitling' on TV for Mass Literacy in India.* [video online] Available at: http://www.youtube.com/watch?feature=player_embedded&v=juZOlmf9APk#at=11 [Accessed: 15 May 2013].
37. Rex, J. (2003) *The Novopen Story.* [report] Novo Nordisk A/S.

38. Rockhall (n.d.) *Experience The Music: One Hit Wonders and The Songs That Shaped Rock and Roll | The Rock and Roll Hall of Fame and Museum.* [online] Available at: http://rockhall.com/exhibits/one-hit-wonders-songs-that-shaped-rock-and-roll/ [Accessed: 8 April 2013].
39. Rolling Stone (2011) *500 Greatest Songs of all time.* [online] Available at: http://www.rollingstone.com/music/lists/the-500-greatest-songs-of-all-time-20110407/queen-bohemian-rhapsody-20110526 [Accessed: 8 April 2013].
40. Roy, S. (2009) GE Healthcare innovates in India for bottom of the pyramid. *Rediff,* [online] 4 May 2009. Available at: http://www.rediff.com/money/2009/may/04ge-healthcare-innovates-for-bottom-of-the-pyramid.htm [Accessed: 9 April 2013].
41. Sghi.org (n.d.) *Sprinkles Global Health Initiative / About Sprinkles - What are Sprinkles.* [online] Available at: http://www.sghi.org/ [Accessed: 9 April 2013].
42. Sickkids.ca (2009) *Stanley Zlotkin: Micronutrients for children in developing countries.* [online] Available at: http://www.sickkids.ca/Learning/Stories/Knowledge-Translation/stan-zlotkin.html [Accessed: 15 May 2013].
43. Singh, V. (2009) Now, Amar Chitra Katha gets even younger. *Times of India,* 16 October 2009.
44. Smart Communications (2011) *Smart Load – Smart Communications.* [online] Available at: http://www1.smart.com.ph/About/meet/innovations-and-awards/smart-load [Accessed: 15 May 2013].
45. The Information Company (2005) *Erehwon and CII organise first ever global "innovation summit" in India.* [online] Available at: http://www.domain-b.com/industry/associations/cii/20050609_summit.html [Accessed: 9 April 2013].
46. The Kathmandu Post (2013) *One of 12 best innovations – Bardiya keeps unruly rhinos at bay; technique grabs world's attention.* [online] Available at: http://www.ekantipur.com/the-kathmandu-post/2011/09/25/top-story/one-of-12-best-innovations/226681.html [Accessed: 15 May 2013].
47. United Nations Development Programme (2012) *Medicinal plants help reduce human-wildlife conflict | UNDP.* [online] Available at: http://www.undp.org/content/nepal/en/home/presscenter/articles/2012/01/30/medicinal-plants-help-reduce-human-wildlife-conflict/ [Accessed: 15 May 2013].
48. Unesco.org (online). Available at: www.unesco.org/new/en/education/themes/education-building-blocks/literacy. [Accessed on: 18 September 2013]

49. Vestergaard Frandsen (n.d.) *Vestergaard Frandsen: LifeStraw® - Features.* [online] Available at: http://www.vestergaard-frandsen.com/lifestraw/lifestraw/features [Accessed: 15 May 2013].
50. Visionspring.org (n.d.) *VisionSpring » Reaching Our Customers.* [online] Available at: http://visionspring.org/reaching-our-customers/ [Accessed: 15 May 2013].
51. Worldinquiry.case.edu (2006) *VisionSpring: A New Vision at the Bottom of the Economic Pyramid.* [online] Available at: http://worldinquiry.case.edu/bankInnovationView.cfm?idArchive=400 [Accessed: 9 April 2013].
52. YouTube (2011) *Statistics - YouTube.* [online] Available at: https://www.youtube.com/yt/press/statistics.html [Accessed: 15 May 2013].

CHAPTER 5

1. Bishop, T. (2012) Xbox 360 tops Wii and PS3 for 1st time in yearly global sales. *Geek Wire*, [online] 3 February 2012. Available at: http://www.geekwire.com/2012/xbox-360-tops-wii-ps3-1st-time-yearly-global-sales/ [Accessed: 21 May 2013].
2. Biswas, R. (2011) *State wise Mobile Phone users in India Census 2011.* [online] Available at: http://updateox.com/india/state-wise-mobile-phone-users-in-india-census-2011/ [Accessed: 21 May 2013].
3. Eichenwald, K. (2012) Microsoft's Lost Decade. *Vanity Fair*, [online] August 2012. Available at: http://www.vanityfair.com/business/2012/08/microsoft-lost-mojo-steve-ballmer [Accessed: 21 May 2013].
4. Kilind, L. (2006) *The Second Cycle: Winning the War Against Bureaucracy.* Pearson Prentice Hall.
5. Man Made Marvels – The World's Highest Railway (2006) [DVD] Discovery Channel, Discovery Communications.
6. Nintendo (2011) *Iwata Asks.* [online] Available at: http://iwataasks.nintendo.com/interviews/#/wii/wii_console/0/0 [Accessed: 21 May 2013].
7. Nintendo (n.d.) *OFFICIAL: Revolution renamed Nintendo Wii! *UPDATE 12*.* [online] Available at: http://gonintendo.com/?p=2289 [Accessed: 21 May 2013].
8. NintendoProSite (2006) *Nintendo E3 2006 Press Conference.* [video online] Available at: http://www.youtube.com/watch?v=nToFqENmebI [Accessed: 21 May 2013].

9. Rex, J. (2003) *The Novopen Story*. [report] Novo Nordisk A/S.
10. Schiesel, S. (2013) As Gaming Turns Social, Industry Shifts Strategies. *The New York Times*, 28 February 2008.

CHAPTER 6

1. Bornstein, D. (2003) *Fabio Rosa: Making the Sun Shine For All*. [online] Available at: http://proxied.changemakers.net/journal/03may/bornstein.cfm [Accessed: 21 May 2013].
2. Canadian Community for Dialogue and Deliberation (2002) *Changing the World by Changing How We Talk and Listen*. [online] Available at: http://www.c2d2.ca/sites/default/files/Kahanepercent20onpercent20talkingpercent20andpercent20listening.pdf [Accessed: 21 May 2013].
3. Cunningham, M. (1995) Roy Thomas Baker & Gary Langan: The Making Of Queen's 'Bohemian Rhapsody'. *Sound on Sound*, Iss. October 1995.
4. Eichenwald, K. (2012) Microsoft's Lost Decade. *Vanity Fair*, [online] August 2012. Available at: http://www.vanityfair.com/business/2012/08/microsoft-lost-mojo-steve-ballmer [Accessed: 21 May 2013].
5. Lockheed Martin (1943) *Lockheed Martin · Skunk Works®*. [online] Available at: http://www.lockheedmartin.com/us/aeronautics/skunkworks.html [Accessed: 21 May 2013].
6. Munshi, P. (2009) *Making Breakthrough Innovation Happen: How 11 Indians Pulled Off The Impossible*. Noida: Harper Collins India, p.75 - 97.
7. Munshi, P. (2009) *Making Breakthrough Innovation Happen: How 11 Indians Pulled Off The Impossible*. Noida: Harper Collins India, p.152 - 166.
8. Munshi, P. (2009) *Making Breakthrough Innovation Happen: How 11 Indians Pulled Off The Impossible*. Noida: Harper Collins India, p.98 - 110.
9. Munshi, P. (2009) *Making Breakthrough Innovation Happen: How 11 Indians Pulled Off The Impossible*. Noida: Harper Collins India, p.116 - 138.
10. OneWorld Health (n.d.) *About Us*. [online] Available at: http://www.oneworldhealth.org/about-us [Accessed: 21 May 2013].

CHAPTER 7

1. Barrington, J. and Wereko-Brobby, O., et al. (2010) SMS for Life: a pilot project to improve anti-malarial drug supply management in rural Tanzania using

standard technology. *Malaria Journal*, 9:298 Available at: doi:10.1186/1475-2875-9-298 [Accessed: 21 May 2013].

2. Man Made Marvels – The World's Highest Railway (2006) [DVD] China: Discovery Channel, Discovery Communications.
3. Marchand, D. (2012) *SMS for Life (B): Living the Implementation Challenges of a Successful Pilot Project.* [report] Lausanne, Switzerland: IMD (www.imd.org).
4. Moncef, A. and Marchand, D. (2010) *SMS for Life (A): A Public-Private Collaboration to prevent Stock-outs of Life-saving Malaria Drugs in Africa.* [report] Lausanne, Switzerland: IMD (www.imd.org).
5. Munshi, P. (2009) *Making Breakthrough Innovation Happen: How 11 Indians Pulled Off The Impossible.* Noida: Harper Collins India, p. 192-216.
6. Munshi, P. (2009) *Making Breakthrough Innovation Happen: How 11 Indians Pulled Off The Impossible.* Noida: Harper Collins India, p. 172-191.
7. Spar, D. and Delacey, B. (2008) The Coartem Challenge (A). *Harvard Business School*, (November 2008).

CHAPTER 8

1. Bannister, D. (2012) M-Pesa move into savings and loans underpinned by Temenos. *Banking Technology*, [online] 29 November 2012. Available at: http://www.bankingtech.com/51858/m-pesa-move-into-savings-and-loans-underpinned-by-temenos/ [Accessed: 23 May 2013].
2. Freeze, K. (1993) *Novo Nordisk A/S: Designing for Diabetes.* [report] Boston, USA: Design Management Institute.
3. Hughes, N. and Lonie, S. (2007) M-PESA: Mobile Money for the "Unbanked" Turning Cellphones into 24-Hour Tellers in Kenya. *innovations*, 2 (Winter / Spring), p. 63-81. Available at: http://www.mitpressjournals.org/doi/abs/10.1162/itgg.2007.2.1-2.63 [Accessed: 21 May 2013].
4. Lonie, S. (2010) M-PESA: Finding new ways to serve the unbanked in Kenya. *Innovations in rural and agriculture finance*, Available at: http://www.ifpri.org/publication/m-pesa-finding-new-ways-serve-unbanked-kenya [Accessed: 23 May 2013].
5. Madsen, A. (2012) *The evolution of innovation strategy – Studied in the context of medical device activities at the pharmaceutical company Novo Nordisk A/S in the period 1980-2008.* Ph.D. Copenhagen Business School.

6. Munshi, P. (2009) *Making Breakthrough Innovation Happen: How 11 Indians Pulled Off The Impossible.* Noida: Harper Collins India, p. 16-33.

CHAPTER 9

1. Hughes, N. and Lonie, S. (2007) M-PESA: Mobile Money for the "Unbanked" Turning Cellphones into 24-Hour Tellers in Kenya. *innovations*, 2 (Winter / Spring), p. 63-81. Available at: http://www.mitpressjournals.org/doi/abs/10.1162/itgg.2007.2.1-2.63 [Accessed: 21 May 2013].
2. Munshi, P. (2009) *Making Breakthrough Innovation Happen: How 11 Indians Pulled Off The Impossible.* Noida: Harper Collins India, p. 75-97.
3. Nintendo (n.d.) *Iwata Asks.* [online] Available at: http://iwataasks.nintendo.com/interviews/#/wii/wii_console/0/0 [Accessed: 21 May 2013].
4. Skinner, T. (2003) *Beyond the Summit: Setting and Surpassing Extraordinary Business Goals.* Century.

CHAPTER 10

1. Bhatkal, S. (2002) *The Spirit of Lagaan.* Popular Prakashan.
2. BRAC (n.d.) *BRAC – Fact Sheet.* BRAC. Available through: www.brac.net http://www.brac.net/sites/default/files/BRACpercent20Factpercent20Sheet_23Sept10.pdf [Accessed: 21 May 2013].
3. Eichenwald, K. (2012) Microsoft's Lost Decade. *Vanity Fair,* [online] August 2012. Available at: http://www.vanityfair.com/business/2012/08/microsoft-lost-mojo-steve-ballmer [Accessed: 21 May 2013].
4. Fast Company (2010) *The Myelin Repair Foundation Encourages Collaboration for a Cure.* [online] Available at: http://www.fastcompany.com/1693716/myelin-repair-foundation-encourages-collaboration-cure [Accessed: 21 May 2013].
5. FoodDoctor (2013) *The Food Doctor™ The UK's leading nutrition consultancy.* [online] Available at: http://fooddoctor.com/ [Accessed: 21 May 2013].
6. Hughes, N. and Lonie, S. (2007) M-PESA: Mobile Money for the "Unbanked" Turning Cellphones into 24-Hour Tellers in Kenya. *innovations*, 2 (Winter / Spring), p. 63-81.
7. Mahajan-Bansal, N. (2009) "I want GE India to be viewed as one of India's

best Indian companies". *Forbes India*, 16 December 2009.

8. Metro Plus (2011) Same to Same. *The Hindu*, 7 April 2011.
9. Miller, G. (n.d.) *HowStuffWorks "Introduction to Inside '300'"*. [online] Available at: http://www.howstuffworks.com/inside-300.htm [Accessed: 21 May 2013].
10. Monash.edu.au (2003) *Elliminating dengue - Monash University*. [online] Available at: http://www.monash.edu.au/giving/news/eliminating-dengue.html [Accessed: 23 May 2013].
11. Moncef, A. and Marchand, D. (2010) *SMS for Life (A): A Public-Private Collaboration to prevent Stock-outs of Life-saving Malaria Drugs in Africa*. [report] Lausanne, Switzerland: IMD (www.imd.org).
12. Mullin, J. (2012) *How the Aussie government "invented WiFi" and sued its way to $430 million*. [online] Available at: http://arstechnica.com/tech-policy/2012/04/how-the-aussie-government-invented-wifi-and-sued-its-way-to-430-million/ [Accessed: 21 May 2013].
13. Munshi, P. (2009) *Making Breakthrough Innovation Happen: How 11 Indians Pulled Off The Impossible*. Noida: Harper Collins India, p. 98-110.
14. Munshi, P. (2009) *Making Breakthrough Innovation Happen: How 11 Indians Pulled Off The Impossible*. Noida: Harper Collins India, p. 192-216.
15. Munshi, P. (2009) *Making Breakthrough Innovation Happen: How 11 Indians Pulled Off The Impossible*. Noida: Harper Collins India, p. 75-97.
16. Narayanan, V. and Kasturi Rangan, V. (2010) Equitas Microfinance: The Fastest-Growing MFI on the Planet. *Harvard Business School.*
17. Palca, J. (2012) *A Scientist's 20-Year Quest To Defeat Dengue Fever: NPR*. [online] Available at: http://www.npr.org/2012/06/07/154322744/a-scientists-20-year-quest-to-defeat-dengue-fever [Accessed: 21 May 2013].
18. Pbs.org (1996) *Triumph of the Nerds: The Transcripts, Part III*. [online] Available at: http://www.pbs.org/nerds/part3.html [Accessed: 21 May 2013].
19. Planetread.org (2009) *Clinton Global Initiative: 'Same Language Subtitling' on TV for Mass Literacy in India*. [video online] Available at: http://www.youtube.com/watch?feature=player_embedded&v=juZOlmf9APk [Accessed: 21 May 2013].
20. Rex, J. (2003) *The Novopen Story*. [report] Novo Nordisk A/S.
21. Sickkids.ca (2011) *Milestones*. [online] Available at: http://www.sickkids.ca/AboutSickKids/History-and-Milestones/Milestones/index.html [Accessed: 21 May 2013].

22. Skinner, T. (2003) *Beyond the Summit: Setting and Surpassing Extraordinary Business Goals*. Century.
23. Sridhar, L. (2002) Mission: Possible. *India Together*, [online] July 2002. Available at: http://www.indiatogether.org/peace/kashmir/articles/ls0702.htm [Accessed: 21 May 2013].
24. Stanford Graduate School of Business (2013) *Jessica Jackley: A Kiva Cofounder Discusses Stories of Poverty and Entrepreneurship | Stanford Graduate School of Business*. [online] Available at: http://www.gsb.stanford.edu/news/headlines/jessica-jackley-kiva-cofounder-discusses-stories-poverty-entrepreneurship [Accessed: 21 May 2013].
25. Summerfield, M. (2012) *Patentology: The Story Behind CSIRO's Wi-Fi Patent 'Windfall'*. [online] Available at: http://blog.patentology.com.au/2012/04/story-behind-csiros-wi-fi-patent.html [Accessed: 21 May 2013].
26. The Prime Minister's Prizes for Science (2009) *Prime Minister's Prize for Science*. [online] Available at: https://grants.innovation.gov.au/SciencePrize/Pages/Doc.aspx?name=previous_winners/PM2009Sullivan.htm [Accessed: 21 May 2013].
27. usa.ashoka.org (2006). Victoria Hale: an uncommon hero eradicating Black Fever (Video). Available at: usa.ashoka.org/fellow/victoria-hale [Accessed on: 30 August 2013].

Notes

CHAPTER 1

1. Erehwon's case study on LifeStraw, based on insight dialogues with Navneet Garg, Chief Development Officer of Vestergaard Frandsen, and Torben Vestergaard Frandsen, former CEO of Vestergaard Frandsen.
2. Insight dialogue with Fabio Rosa.
3. Insight dialogue with Yuji Mori, President of Vansemberuu Mongolia
4. Erehwon's case study on Kudumbashree, based on facts from Kudumbashree and insight dialogues with their team.
5. Insight dialogue with Alok Adholeya, Director, Biotechnology and Bioresources Division, TERI and N.S. Subrahmanyam, Tata Chemicals.
6. Insight dialogue with Atul Bindal, former President of Bharti Airtel's Mobile Services unit.
7. Insight dialogue with Victoria Hale, founder of OneWorld Health.

CHAPTER 2

1. Insight dialogue with Jacob Kurian, former COO of Tanishq, Titan Industries, from 2000–2003.
2. Insight dialogue with Arne Stjernholm Madsen, former Innovation Management Partner at Novo Nordisk.
3. Insight dialogue with Shanta Sinha, founder of MV Foundation, and Venkat Reddy, National Convener of MV Foundation.

4. Insight dialogue with Ravish Kumar.

CHAPTER 3

1. Insight dialogue with Peter Mukerjea, former CEO of Star TV.
2. Insight dialogue with Michael da Costa, MD of the Food Doctor.
3. Insight dialogue with Atul Bindal, former President of Bharti Airtel's Mobile Services unit.
4. Erehwon's case study on Arla Foods, based on insight dialogues with Carsten Hallund Slot, previously Head of Innovation Portfolio at Arla Foods.
5. Insight Dialogue with Laercio Cardoso, former VP of Marketing, Unilever Indonesia.
6. Erehwon's case study on Lifestraw, based on insight dialogues with Navneet Garg, Chief Development Officer of Vestergaard Frandsen, and Torben Vestergaard Frandsen, former CEO of Vestergaard Frandsen.
7. Erehwon case study on Wipro GCC, based on insight dialogues with G.K. Prasanna, Senior Vice President, Technology at Wipro Technologies.
8. Live dialogue with the Tata Nano team during the First India Innovation Summit, by CII, partnered by Erehwon.
9. Insight dialogue with Miriam Chandy Menacherry, documentary film maker (Robot Jockeys)
10. Insight dialogues with the Tata Power team.
11. Live dialogue with the Tata Nano team, during the First India Innovation Summit, by CII, partnered by Erehwon.

CHAPTER 4

1. Live dialogue with James Sutherland at the First India Innovation Summit in 2005, convened by CII, Bangalore.
2. Insight dialogue with Victoria Hale, founder of OneWorld Health.
3. Erehwon's case study on GE MAC 400 based on insight dialogues with the respective teams.
4. Erehwon's case study on Vision Spring based on insight dialogues with the team.
5. Erehwon's case study on PlanetRead, based on insight dialogues with Brij Kothari.

6. The Clocks Example taken from Mukul Sharma's Column "Mindsport" in *Times of India*.
7. Insight dialogues with J.K. Tripathy.
8. Insight dialogues with the team at Tutor Vista.

CHAPTER 5

1. Erehwon's Caste Study on Tanishq based on Insight dialogues with Jacob Kurian, former COO of Tanishq, Titan Industries, from 2000–2003.
2. Insight dialogue with Atul Bindal, former President of Bharti Airtel's Mobile Services unit.
3. Insight dialogue with Girish Wagh, Vice President and Head Small Cars Division, Tata Motors.

CHAPTER 6

1. Insight dialogue with Carsten Hallund Slot, previously Head of Innovation Portfolio at Arla Foods.
2. Insight dialogue with Laercio Cardoso, former VP of Marketing, Unilever Indonesia.
3. Insight dialogue with Victoria Hale, founder of OneWorld Health.
4. Insight dialogue with Michael da Costa, MD of the Food Doctor.
5. Insight dialogue with Phil Whitfield, MD of Humdinger Foods.
6. Insight dialogue with Anil Nayar, former President of Bharti Airtel.
7. Insight dialogue with Dr. Jorg Thiemann of Deutz.
8. Erehwon's case study on Titan Edge.
9. Erehwon's 'Transworld Collaboration' research paper presented at the HRD Asia 2000 Conference, Singapore.
10. Insight Dialogue with Atul Bindal, former president of Bhartel's mobile services unit.
11. Insight dialogue with Massimo Pozzetti, Global Brand Development Director, Unilever, UK.

CHAPTER 7

1. Insight dialogue with Carsten Hallund Slot, previously Head of Innovation Portfolio at Arla Foods.
2. Erehwon's case study on LifeStraw, based on insight dialogues with Navneet Garg, Chief Development Officer of Vestergaard Frandsen, and Torben Vestergaard Frandsen, former CEO of Vestergaard Frandsen.
3. Insight dialogue with Anil Nayar, former President of Bharti Airtel

CHAPTER 8

1. Insight dialogue with Arne Stjernholm Madsen, former Innovation Management Partner at Novo Nordisk.
2. Insight dialogue with Alex Eunjae Won, CMO of Access Mobile, and Duoh Leslie Song, Director of Access Mobile.

CHAPTER 9

1. Insight dialogue with Carsten Hallund Slot, previously Head of Innovation Portfolio at Arla Foods.
2. Insight dialogue with Alex Eunjae Won, CMO of Access Mobile, and Duoh Leslie Song, Director of Access Mobile.

CHAPTER 10

1. Insight dialogue with Victoria Hale, founder of OneWorld Health.
2. Insight dialogue with P.N. Vasudevan, CEO of Equitas.
3. Insight dialogue with Carsten Hallund Slot, previously Head of Innovation Portfolio at Arla Foods.
4. Insight dialogue with Michael da Costa, MD of the Food Doctor
5. Insight dialogue with Fazle Abed, Founder Chairman of BRAC.
6. Insight dialogue with Lt. General Arjun Ray (Retired).
7. Insight dialogue with T.K. Kurien, Head Telecom Vertical, Wipro (2001), now CEO Wipro Technologies.
8. Erehwon's case study on PlanetRead, based on insight dialogues with Brij Kothari.

Acknowledgements

A book of this nature, 20 years in the making, cannot be anything but a collaborative experience.

We want to first and foremost thank our partners in Erehwon, Prabha Parthasarathy and Ranjan Malik, for their insights into Orbit-shifting Innovation. Ours is a collective journey in working with organizations and in attempting to navigate through the dilemmas of Orbit-shifting Innovation. This book is, therefore, our shared outcome with both of them.

In writing the book itself, we had great support from Bindu Chandana and Pavithra Solai Jawahar. Both of them have unfailingly anchored the secondary research, identified unique orbit-shifters from across the world and have undertaken the fact checks and references. They have also helped with the proof reading of the manuscript; a painful and exacting task. Rohit Choudhary and Ashrafi Dhunjeebhoy have pitched in enthusiastically at key points when we most needed them.

We also thank Chhavi Goyal, Kamini Kinger, Neeru Marya, Porus Munshi, and Madhujith Venkatkrishna. At various stages, they have identified orbit-shifters, conducted firsthand insight dialogues and written out case studies that are now central to the book. Manu Vats, Bhawani Singh Shekhawat and Gokul Ranganathan, we thank you for bringing new orbit-shift examples that have been included in the book.

We thank Atul Bindal and Vijit Singh for always taking the time and effort to connect us to orbit-shifters, whenever we reached out to them.

Pushpa Krishna has patiently and efficiently supported us in the manuscript production through its many versions. Rajesh Shivanna and Mubeena have helped design the visuals and the layout of the book.

This book came to be published due to the untiring effort of our agent and close friend Priya Doraswamy.

Our families are at the heart of this effort, bracing and sustaining us constantly through weekends and long absences as we worked upon draft after draft of the manuscript.

Rajiv's wife Sandhya, and daughters Vijayta and Damini have been his unfailing anchor through the ups and down of this journey called Erehwon.

Devika's family, her mother Jaji, father CM Devaiah and sister Dena have been her source of perennial strength.

And finally, to all the orbit-shifters in the book:

First, the clients with whom who we have worked in the course of all these years in leveraging Orbit-shifting Innovation. In climbing many innovation mountains with them, we made new discoveries, forged new paths and overcame innumerable obstacles.

Joining them are the orbit-shifters who shared their stories with us. Staying patient through countless insight dialogues, repeated questions, and 'aha' moments as new dots were joined.

You are the real heroes in this story.